THE COMPLETE GUIDE TO SIMULATIONS AND SERIOUS GAMES

About Pfeiffer

Pfeiffer serves the professional development and hands-on resource needs of training and human resource practitioners and gives them products to do their jobs better. We deliver proven ideas and solutions from experts in HR development and HR management, and we offer effective and customizable tools to improve workplace performance. From novice to seasoned professional, Pfeiffer is the source you can trust to make yourself and your organization more successful.

Essential Knowledge   Pfeiffer produces insightful, practical, and comprehensive materials on topics that matter the most to training and HR professionals. Our Essential Knowledge resources translate the expertise of seasoned professionals into practical, how-to guidance on critical workplace issues and problems. These resources are supported by case studies, worksheets, and job aids and are frequently supplemented with CD-ROMs, websites, and other means of making the content easier to read, understand, and use.

Essential Tools   Pfeiffer's Essential Tools resources save time and expense by offering proven, ready-to-use materials—including exercises, activities, games, instruments, and assessments—for use during a training or-team-learning event. These resources are frequently offered in looseleaf or CD-ROM format to facilitate copying and customization of the material.

Pfeiffer also recognizes the remarkable power of new technologies in expanding the reach and effectiveness of training. While e-hype has often created whizbang solutions in search of a problem, we are dedicated to bringing convenience and enhancements to proven training solutions. All our e-tools comply with rigorous functionality standards. The most appropriate technology wrapped around essential content yields the perfect solution for today's on-the-go trainers and human resource professionals.

Essential resources for training and HR professionals

THE COMPLETE GUIDE TO SIMULATIONS AND SERIOUS GAMES

How the Most Valuable Content Will Be Created in the Age Beyond Gutenberg to Google

Clark Aldrich

Pfeiffer

A Wiley Imprint
www.pfeiffer.com

Published by Pfeiffer
A Wiley Imprint
989 Market Street, San Francisco, CA 94103-1741—www.pfeiffer.com

For additional copies/bulk purchases of this book in the U.S. please contact 800-274-4434.

Pfeiffer books and products are available through most bookstores. To contact Pfeiffer directly call our Customer Care Department within the U.S. at 800-274-4434, outside the U.S. at 317-572-3985, fax 317-572-4002, or visit www.pfeiffer.com.

Pfeiffer also publishes its books in a variety of electronic formats. Some content that appears in print may not be available in electronic books.

Library of Congress Cataloging-in-Publication Data

Aldrich, Clark.
    The complete guide to simulations and serious games: how the most valuable content will be created in the age beyond Gutenberg to Google / Clark Aldrich.
        p.   cm.
    Includes bibliographical references and index.
    ISBN 978-0-470-46273-7
        1. Simulated environment (Teaching method)   2. Electronic games.   I. Title.
    LB1029.S5A43 2009
    371.39'7—dc22

                                                                            2009025589

Acquiring Editor: Matthew Davis
Director of Development: Kathleen Dolan Davies
Marketing Manager: Brian Grimm

Production Coordinator: Seth Miller
Manufacturing Supervisor: Becky Morgan
Editorial Assistant: Lindsay Morton

Printed in the United States of America
FIRST EDITION
HB Printing
10 9 8 7 6 5 4 3 2 1

To my family

Special Thanks

This book would not have been possible without Drew Davidson, Denis Saulnier, Scott Perrin, Chester Cooke, Mark Biscoe, and The Chewonki Foundation

CONTENTS

PART FOUR: BUILDING INTERACTIVE ENVIRONMENTS   241

FOREWORD

By Jeff Sandefer

Don't let the title *The Complete Guide to Simulations and Serious Games* fool you. Yes, this is an encyclopedic overview of the simulations and serious gaming world, a complete lexicon for those who want to build the next generation of simulations for advanced learning. But it's far more important than a comprehensive "how to" book about simulations.

Clark Aldrich makes his call to action clear. *The Complete Guide to Simulations and Serious Games* is "nothing less than a manifesto intended to overthrow the intellectual legacy of civilization to date." Aldrich is signaling the end of the age of Gutenberg, a time of great learning, no doubt, but of linear learning—learning "how to know" rather than "how to do" or "how to be" in a complex, interactive world.

Why should you care? If you are an education reformer, Aldrich's revolution could transform the way we learn. If you are a CEO, this is the way the next generation will want to be addressed. And if you are an entrepreneur, the intersection of serious games and simulations may signal one of the greatest investment opportunities in a generation.

For far too long there's been a divide between the gaming community and educators. The gamers have dismissed educational simulations as boring and irrelevant; the educators have dismissed gaming as trivial. Both have a point, but in their squabbling over turf, both have missed how serious games and engaging simulations can change the world of education.

Aldrich takes direct aim at why the K–12 and higher education systems are failing, myopically trapped in a nineteenth-century world of "learning by knowing" in a twenty-first-century world that requires the judgment and skills of "learning by doing" and the individualized attention to "learning by being."

If this doesn't strike a nerve—if you are satisfied with the antiquated assembly-line process that passes for education in the United States—then you really need to read this book. Particularly if you are a parent.

So why listen to Clark Aldrich? Because he is the Tiger Woods and Michael Jordan of the serious gaming and simulation world, all rolled into one. He's one of the few people who not only see the big picture of how simulations and gaming will transform education and can walk you step-by-step through what does and does not work in simulation design, but he also can create leading-edge games and write first-rate code.

Not many people in any industry can see where future trends are leading and get the details right. In *The Complete Guide to Simulations and Serious Games*, Aldrich moves from genres—the ways you classify games—through the elements that separate the great simulations from those that don't work. He explains why the "big skills"—those that really count, like leadership, negotiation, and stewardship—and the "middle skills" like directing people, probing, and procurement cannot be learned from a book or lecture, but only through simulations, or through the much more difficult school of hard knocks in real life.

Then, having clearly established why linear content (meaning books) is the "white bread" of learning, and why the academic intelligentsia have failed us, Aldrich shows how formal learning programs, properly understood, can use simulations and serious games to create real learning, and how formal learning programs in the hands of educrats or corporate learning officers can destroy them.

So why am I so sure that Aldrich is right that today's "classrooms, curricula, term papers, corporate training programs, business plans, and linear analysis should be banished to the intellectual slums and backwaters"? Because I have seen the future firsthand, or at least a glimpse of it.

As a pilot, I've experienced how the most sophisticated flight simulators instill the skills, judgment, and coolness under pressure needed to safely land a crippled Airbus on the Hudson River.

As a parent, I've watched my six-, seven-, and twelve-year-old children have fun playing Zoo Tycoon and Sim City, while absorbing sophisticated business pattern recognition skills that took me years to learn at Harvard Business School.

Finally, as an education reformer at the award-winning Acton School of Business, I've spent over a million dollars of my own money designing six interactive Sims on customer acquisition, production processes, pricing, working capital, and bootstrapping. Our games aren't perfect, but they are engaging enough that my children want to play them, and challenging enough that an Acton, Harvard, or Stanford MBA cannot master them.

Yes, I've seen firsthand how much more powerful—and engaging—serious games and simulations can be than books and lectures. By the end of this book, I'm confident you'll not only have a glimpse of the future too, but even better, a blueprint for how you can get started creating that future.

About the Foreword Author

Jeff Sandefer runs an energy investment firm, Sandefer Capital Partners, that holds over a $1 billion in assets. For the last sixteen years, he has also taught entrepreneurship at the graduate level. Four years ago Sandefer and a band of successful entrepreneurs left a nationally recognized program they had built at the University of Texas to start the Acton School of Business. For two consecutive years, Acton was rated among the top MBA programs in the country by the *Princeton Review*, which called its students the "most competitive" MBAs in America and rated the faculty in the top three in the nation. While at the University of Texas, Sandefer was voted by the students as UT's Outstanding Teacher five separate times and was named by *Business Week* as one of the top entrepreneurship professors in the United States. He has served for over a decade on Harvard University's visiting committee and as chair of the university's academic research committee. He is a director of *National Review* magazine, formerly served as chairman of the Acton Institute of Religion and Liberty, and was a member of Texas Governor Rick Perry's 21st Century Commission on Higher Education.

PREFACE: THE ELEMENTS
OF INTERACTIVITY

This book, with its definitions of the structures of simulations and serious games, presents itself as a helpful guide for Sim authors and sponsors who wish to better ply their craft in both stand-alone environments and in virtual worlds. I hope, incidentally, that it is.

But underneath that pleasant veneer, this book is a challenge to everyone in all of the educational and knowledge industries, from instructors to publishers to business analysts. Identifying successful design patterns from computer games, academic study, business analysis, and military and corporate learning programs, this book is nothing less than a manifesto intended to cast off the intellectual chains of civilization to date.

These elements of interactivity challenge all the traditional linear content models, putting a new focus on actions, systems, and results. The book recommends augmenting or even replacing the traditional passive presentation of content with an active "learning by doing" approach. Having said that, here are some caveats.

This book is not complete. I have attempted to include enough terms in each of the various categories not to exhaust a topic but to define it. But many individual entries refer to subject areas whose full treatment would fill entire books.

Second, as any good Sim designer would hope, this book is as nonlinear as a book can be. It is organized as a virtual world might be, meticulously, logically, but not assuming any prescribed path. You can go through it from beginning to end, but you can also bounce around. When you get sick of a section, skip to the next. Or dig into a term and its context that interests you, following the references to related topics. Or go to the index at the back. You can scan or dig in, zoom out or zoom in. I have tried to create the best of both worlds, but some people, when reading this, will be frustrated by the lack of traditional structure. This book is about learning by practicing, which will involve reexamining the same content, often from different perspectives, not just learning by seeing how much ground is covered. You might return to the same entry several times, each time seeing more in the same words. In this regard, using this book is similar in part to the user experience in a simulation. This book will reward your effort, not displace it. Your role is participant, not audience.

Finally, this book deals with concepts and constructs, not programming. This is because many different technologies are available, and while the constructs are universal, the implementation changes dramatically from one toolset to another. People might use this approach in video editing, Adobe Flash, a PlayStation 3 game, a research paper, an iPhone app, or an island in Second Life. The technical techniques are different, and fast moving. The philosophy is the same, and I suspect timeless.

INTRODUCTION

Capturing the Wisdom That Has Fallen Through the Cracks of Gutenberg and Google

Imagine you and I are by the pool at a nice hotel in Lyon, France. We are negotiating some business deal, perhaps the creation of a new company or a piece of intellectual property.

Now imagine that a twenty-five-year veteran of hospitality management walked by. What would she see? Maybe that our coffee is old, and that the table's umbrella should be positioned to block the sun. She might notice the water in the pool is a little green, suggesting not enough chlorine. She might wonder, because we are people of business, how to pitch the new virtual conference service. She might note that we need new towels.

In contrast, what if an expert in negotiation saw us? He might read my body language as tense, yours as relaxed. He might notice that we are on the verge of coming to agreement, and we are both committed to success.

How about a nutritionist? He might look with disgust at the white bread in our rolls, and the processed sugars in our jams. He might approve of your orange juice, but not my Coke, and then look for any pallor in our faces. He might look around for the buffet table and evaluate the contents. Or maybe even look for a snack machine, and see whether there are any peanuts or other protein sources.

How about a lawyer? She might look at the documents on the table. She might try to find a nondisclosure agreement. She might be curious to see exactly what notes I am taking. How binding is what we are saying? Are we each revealing too much at this stage of the conversation?

The big point here: People at the top of their game see things when they encounter a situation that others do not.

For example:

- What did George Washington see as he walked through colonial Boston that was different from what the majority saw?
- What did Louisa May Alcott see when her house was filled with people?
- What did President Jimmy Carter see when he looked at a map of the world in 1978? Or Jack Welch in 2001? Or Barack Obama in 2009?

These are all issues of situational awareness. Let me define the term formally:

Situational awareness: The ability to filter out certain details and highlight and extrapolate others, to better understand and control the outcome. Different people with different domain expertise bring different situational awareness to the same situation.

Seeing the world as experts do is the hallmark of any domain expertise, and makes problems and appropriate actions more obvious. Given that, how is situational awareness developed in an individual? How is multiple situational awareness developed and then balanced?

In most formal learning programs to date, using classrooms and traditional media such as books and movies, situational awareness has not been rigorously developed in students. This is for two pretty big reasons. First, it has not been documented and analyzed from the point of view of many experts, including historical leaders and contemporary experts, in any meaningful way. Second, and almost inevitably given the first reason, few environments have been designed to help students and other interested parties learn the skills.

The Most Important Skills

Situational awareness is a good example of content that has fallen through the cracks of linear structures. Other major instances include awareness of patterns, use of actions, and many other types of knowledge. But there are even simpler and broader examples to understand how big our blind spots really are.

Let me ask you, what are the most important skills a person can have, across professions or ages and even in technical fields such as engineering or medicine? Many people would at least consider that the list of "big skills" would include leadership, project management, stewardship, relationship management, innovation, security, and many others. But your own list may be better.

Now, how many of these are taught in schools or corporations? Almost none. How many are taught in a way that actually works? Absolutely none.

Why is it that we as a civilization have failed to record from experts and then rigorously develop in others the most valued skills? The reasons for this stem from what can only be called a technological fluke.

The Campfire and the Veld

Let me back up a bit. Imagine the time in our pre-Paleolithic history (in a time before consistent writing) when formal learning consisted of two balanced parts:

During the day, people with skills would show others how to *do* something. "Grab the spear here," the teacher might say, taking the hands of the apprentice and putting them in the right spots. "Go over there in that veld where you won't hurt anybody and throw your spear at trees until you can hit the smallest tree every time."

At night, people around the campfire might tell of great adventures, including myths and legends. People would share rules, and help their community expand their thinking. The audience would learn to *know* something. The best storytellers would gain bigger audiences and develop their own craft of narrative and suspense.

Then came the technology of writing. And suddenly the balance shifted. Written work scaled well, where the work of one village could impact villages all around it. Communities were able to build on the "open source" written work of the past. The discipline of drama evolved geometrically.

Meanwhile, practicing in the veld didn't change much. It was still a one-to-one activity.

Since the introduction of the technology of writing, many subsequent discoveries have further augmented the learning-to-know skills. Paintings, theaters, printing presses and books, photographs, schools, universities, sound recordings, movies, scanners, and Google all gave our culture mastery of linear content, enabling great artists and building an exquisite vocabulary around plot devices, antagonists, suspense, and the hero's journey, just to name a few. We can watch a Spielberg movie, a piece of campfire-style intellectual property that is the recipient of cumulatively trillions of dollars of investment and R&D, and evaluate it at a level of cultural sophistication that would awe citizens from a even a hundred years ago.

And yet, in the learning-to-do area, most of us are little better than our hunter-gatherer ancestors. For teaching the simplest skills, we mirror our ancestors ("put your hands here"), and for the more complicated skills, we don't have a clue. Ask a top business school professor to develop leadership (or any of the big skills) in a student and she will go into campfire mode with PowerPoint slides of grids and graphs, case studies, and so-called inspirational stories.

The advent of flight simulators and computer games, however, has finally introduced technology and examples of media around learning to do that can scale. Today, a robust if nascent set of veld tools is receiving a significant intellectual investment. Today's authors, often in the form of game and simulation designers, are creating virtual velds where participants can repeatedly practice skills, instead of just hearing about them.

And, correspondingly, an entirely new language is being developed. Gamers now effortlessly talk about *simulation content*, such as mapping actions to interfaces, and the attributes of units on maps, as well as broader Sim elements such as end-of-level bosses and what constitutes good or bad level design.

During the next twenty years, the veld technologies (the learning-to-do skills built through games and simulations) will successfully challenge the campfire institutions of universities, movies, and books not only for the discretionary time of the community (which we have already seen), but for help in improving people's quality of life.

Glimpses of the latter are already available through both serious games such as Carmen Sandiego, The Oregon Trail, Age of Empires, America's

Army, and Brain Age, and educational simulations such as flight simulators, Full Spectrum Warrior, and Virtual Leader. Will Wright, the creator of SimCity, The Sims, and Spore, is the first Shakespeare or Beethoven of this medium.

In other words, people will engage Sims not to play a superhero but to actually become more like one. And the balance between learning to do and learning to know may finally be restored.

How to Use This Book

This book is for anyone who creates or manages content. It begins with pure simulation content models—how to record and model knowledge beyond the linear. If you are in the business of research, including researching business, this is what you should focus on. It goes on to discuss how to build interactive environments to turn that pure simulation model into experiences to be engaged. It is a good opportunity for game designers, a challenge and framework for corporate, academic, and military educational designers, and a glimpse into the all-too-possible future for traditional media publishers, analysts, and researchers. The Appendix discusses several successful simulation projects, including metrics.

This book defines key terms and concepts necessary for Sim design. At its heart, it is essentially a glossary, although broken up into topic chapters to provide enough connecting tissue to make it easy to read. Each chapter has an introductory section that introduces the concepts and highlights some key terms. The chapter then contains *entries*. Each entry is a definition, usually one or two paragraphs, and includes references to other entries or even complete topics. There are also conclusions and author's notes spread out, with a bit more context and notes from the field.

The narrative underlying and connecting the topic chapters is as follows:

First, traditional linear content—books, movies, and lectures—while leveraging brilliant technologies and capturing brilliant thoughts, has been limited in capturing and sharing the world. Linear media focus on the passive content of learning-to-know, rather than the active content of learning-to-do.

For example, linear content cannot develop in people big skills (also called "21st century skills," "soft skills" or "thinking skills") such as leadership or stewardship, nor capture the intellectual property needed for dynamic planning and execution, nor create an accurate representation of time and place. This is why most research that has been created to drive intelligent actions does not do so.

Second, the creation of any research-based intellectual property, be it academic or corporate, should focus on simulation elements, including actions, system content, and desired results, not just linear content.

Third, those simulation elements can further be processed for education and entertainment to make them "practiceable" (through the addition of game elements and pedagogical elements and being shaped into tasks and levels). Given that, just as books have styles such as paragraphs, appendixes, bullet points, and bold fonts, so to do Sims have styles that are just as critical, well-defined, and meaningful, such as sandbox levels and balanced scorecards.

Finally, to simplify the task, just as books come in genres such as dictionaries and mystery novels, so too do Sims come in genres such as first-person shooter and branching stories, and matching up the right Sim to the right task is just as important as selecting the right book genre.

The Babel Problem—"Serious Games" or "Educational Simulations"

As noted, the focus of this book is to present common definitions of concepts and terms that apply to Sims. The lack of common terms is a huge problem, and it has substantially hindered the development of the simulation space. Sponsors, developers, and students have not been able to communicate intelligently.

Perhaps the most salient example of this is the total lack of a universal name for the space (as in, "For our next program, we will use a___ approach," or "I am going to a conference to learn more about___ ").

Here are the top ten candidates:

10. *Virtual experiences.* Pros: Captures the essence of the value proposition. Cons: Overlaps with "social networking."

 9. *Games.* Pros: Unambiguous and unapologetic; all smart animals from cats to otters to African Grays see play as a way of learning core skills. *Computer games* (a subsection of all games) are a $10 billion industry, therefore computer games should be in classrooms (something other people say even more convincingly than I do). Cons: People play lots of games anyway—what is the value of forcing them to play more? Besides, the term is too diverse; would you want your doctor to have learned from a game?

 8. *Simulations.* Pros: Scientific, accurate, really serious-sounding. Cons: Includes many approaches that are not instructional (weather simulations) or engaging; implies 100 percent predictive accuracy.

 7. *Social impact games.* Pros: Conveys the nobleness of the cause. Differentiates from the default notion of games as not having a (or having a negative) social impact. Cons: Still emphasizes the tricky word *games*, and doesn't fit in

corporate or military cultures. In any case, has any social impact game actually had a social impact?

6. *Practiceware.* Pros: Emphasizes the core of practicing to learn skills. Recalls physical models such as batting cages and driving ranges. Cons: It's a frankenword; besides, it doesn't include a lot of puzzles and awareness-raising activities. It sounds vocational.

5. *Game-based learning* or *digital game-based learning.* Pros: Spells everything out— game *and* learning—any questions? Cons: Sounds dated and academic.

Serious games? In eLearning Guild's 2008–2009 landmark survey of corporate, military, and academic practitioners, most suggested not using the "serious games" name.

		Keep it - The term "Serious Game" is just fine	Ditch it - go with "immersive learning" and it will be easier to sell	Ditch it and use my suggestion
Women	20 to 44	19.43%	72.44%	8.13%
	45 and older	14.73%	75.89%	9.38%
	Total	17.36%	73.96%	8.68%
Men	20 to 44	16.73%	68.77%	14.50%
	45 and older	15.92%	65.17%	18.91%
	Total	16.38%	67.23%	16.38%
Grand Total		16.89%	70.73%	12.38%
		0 500	0 500	0 500

Source: The eLearning Guild Research. © The eLearning Guild. All rights reserved.

4. *Immersive learning simulations.* Pros: Hits all the key points. Cons: Doesn't roll off the tongue. Name sounds a bit redundant (wouldn't any two of the three words work just as well?), and besides, it sounds expensive. (And does "immersive" equal "3-D"?)

3. *Educational simulations.* Pros: Sponsors like it. Cons: Sounds hard and perhaps too rigorous for casual students.

2. *Serious games.* Pros: Nicely ironic; students like it; press loves it—*loves it* (I mean *New York Times* and "serious games" should get a room); researchers use it as a way to get foundation grants; it's the most popular handle. Cons: Sponsors hate it, and instructors from academics, corporate, and military hate it. It emphasizes the most controversial part of the experience—the fun part (that is, the game elements), and it often describes content that is too conceptual (you would never call a flight simulator a "serious game").

Most examples of serious games are neither very serious nor very good games. For better and worse, the term is the successor to *edutainment*.

1. *Sims*. Pros: Attractive to both students and sponsors; it captures the essence, and it's fun. Cons: Also includes computer games in general, as well as one very famous franchise.

Some of the other names include *action learning simulations, performance simulations, interactive strategies*, and *activities-based training*.

Overlap with Virtual Worlds?

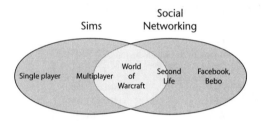

And then there is the question of whether to include virtual worlds or not. Most people lump Second Life and World of Warcraft into this area on their own. But it's not that simple. Virtual worlds can be a platform for Sims, much as Flash or commercial game engines can. If used for that purpose, they both increase the speed of development and shape the content of the product. But accessing a virtual world does not give one a Sim for free.

A New Science

One reason for the lack of common terminology is that Sims represent a rethinking of content itself: they cast traditional content from Gutenberg to Google as a tiny subsection of all possible captured knowledge. To embrace simulations ultimately means ushering in a new era of history and awareness—and accepting some major limitations in what we know and what we have studied. As a result, each current term focuses on one small part of the total shift.

Seeing the world (and modeling it and presenting it) through the approximation of a simulation rather than a book will require new tools and even a new syntax and corresponding style guide, but will mint a new generation of scholars—and a new generation of leaders.

PART ONE

GENRES

Savior or Saboteur for Literacy 2.0?

It doesn't matter whether the class is on history or math or project management. What students learn in any classroom is how to be a student in a classroom.

Throughout this book I will help you dive into the smallest constructs of content—the punctuation and grammar of Sims. And while business analysts and researchers would do well to skip to Part Two, on simulation elements, for everyone else, it may be useful to start with a consideration of the largest established prepacked structures of content, and that is genres.

Across all media, most content settles into genres. Television genres include situation comedies, news programs, reality TV, and sports. Music genres include rock and roll, classical, opera, hip hop, and rap.

And genres matter tremendously. Mystery books follow different frameworks from cookbooks. Even *comic book* is a meta-genre, with overlapping sub-genres that include supers, supernatural, children's cartoons, social dynamics of high school, and the more adult-oriented graphic novels. Stabbing title characters works in some of these sub-genres but not in others.

Each genre has its common set of styles, including rules and expectations. In television, it might be a laugh track, establishing shot, or happy ending. If someone said that the television network ABC is premiering a show on the issue of dating, one might reasonably wonder, is it a reality show or a documentary or a sitcom or a drama? Typically, industry awards are given either to finely honed examples of established genres or examples of new genres altogether (once the new genres are done being mocked, as dramedy or reality shows were).

Sim Genres

Sims also come in genres, including in the meta-genres of educational simulation, computer games, and serious games. The genre shapes much of the interface, user interaction, goals, visual style, and other mechanisms. And while genres are never static, they provide an established framework that does three things: it eases use for the participant, guides the developers, and provides an evolution path for the industry.

For example:

- Educational simulations include branching stories, interactive spreadsheets, virtual labs, and practiceware.
- Computer games have dozens of established genres, including first-person shooters, real-time strategy games, racing games, sports games, and tycoon games. These game genres been evolved from their rough origins to the well-polished examples we see today through the work of many designers over many iterations from many different companies.
- Traditional educational experiences also come in genres, including lectures and labs.
- Other relevant media genres include blogs or the broader term, Web pages.

And genres have to be chosen carefully. Some educational genres are much better for stand-alone programs, while other genres are better for proctored classroom environments.

Author's note: When creators adhere to a genre, they have some clue what the "feel" is going to be like. Movie directors, for example, have decades of shots, from "title credits" to "zoom out from good guy and reveal bad guy coming out of the shadows with nasty weapon" from which to draw when telling a suspenseful story. Further, if a movie studio risks $100 million on a new release, its bean-counters understandably want the safety of an established genre, like action-adventure, and even the inclusion of an established scene, like the main character's beau taking a shower.

In a Sim, a team that adheres to a genre can use established control structures. Its designers even have a sense of timing for a level or action sequence. In brainstorming sessions, they can say, "This is going to be a first-person shooter, but give the players the ability to build their own weapons." Or, "This is going to be like Civilization, but on the moon." Further, toolkits and prepackaged content are available by genre, greatly reducing cost and time to develop, while increasing profitability.

In contrast, when a team creates a new genre, it has no clue what it is going to look or feel like. Its members have no sense of whether it will be fun or not. They can't even play it until they are 90 percent through development.

Genres, for serious game and educational simulation designers, are safety nets and traps. They make things easier, but they restrict the possible range of accomplishments.

Original Learning-to-Do Genres

Before I get to the Sims, here's a brief look at traditional learning-to-do genres. For starters, here are definitions for two key terms:

Experience

1. A Sim, microcosm, or open-ended real-life event engaged in by one or more participants. Any experience can be supported by pedagogical elements.
2. The learning take-away in a participant from been repeatedly exposed to #1.

Experiences enable emergent learning.

Real

Being from the physical world of atoms, as opposed to the *virtual* world of bits. For example, *real* person, *real* world, or *real* money. Often the opposite of *virtual*. The real world can also be described condescendingly. Traditional mail is "snail mail," traditional magazines may be "dead tree publications," and the real world itself may be called the "meat" world.

But the transitions between the real world and a virtual world, real experience and virtual experience, are fuzzy, and getting fuzzier:

- Real employees can work virtually but do real work.
- Virtual money can be converted to real money, as in Second Life and massively multiplayer online role-playing games (MMORPGs).
- A premise of all educational simulations is that *virtual experiences* can provide real experience.
- When is experience in a virtual world translatable to the real world, such as with leadership skills? How about with jacking a car?
- Should any real-world laws impact a virtual world? What about regulating stealing, verbal abuse, vandalism, or protection of intellectual property?

Real can also distinguish something from a fictional story world.

With these distinctions in mind, here are some classic learning-to-do genres.

Practice Environment

The genre of practice environments includes things like backboards, driving ranges, and batting cages that are built and accessed to allow participants to repeatedly practice a focused set of actions. Participants thus get immediate, short-term feedback, with the learning goal of applying skills to a more complex and dynamic environment.

Practice environments can be informal. For example, some people practice speeches in front of the mirror. New automobile drivers might do laps around their neighborhoods. Basketball players spend hours (days, years) shooting hoops.

Practice environments have fewer consequences, more feedback, and are more repeatable than a microcosm, and have much less pedagogy and coaching than a training level. Practice environments require intrinsic motivation and enable emergent learning.

While the systems aspect of a practice environment may be abstract (hitting a baseball in a batting cage involves less variables than from hitting the same baseball in the ninth inning of a close game), the actions and interfaces themselves must not be.

Practice environments can greatly decrease the time to achieving mastery level, and they are necessary even for the acquisition of procedural knowledge. Practice environments can reduce the chances of choking under pressure.

One traditional practice environment is a role-play.

A second learning-to-do genre is microcosm.

Microcosm

Microcosms are real environments and experiences that serve as a case study, analogy, or training ground for a larger, more important, and less controllable environment, and as a result, they provide some of the best learning out there. For example:

- A lemonade stand can be a microcosm for any business.
- Speaking Chinese in a chat room or parts of Second Life can be a microcosm for speaking Chinese while in China.
- Growing a garden or raising chickens can be a microcosm designed to develop stewardship.
- Social networking can be a microcosm for working in a community.
- Running a business unit can be a microcosm for being CEO.

Microcosm. This small house has most of the properties of a larger house.

Real-world microcosms can potentially have as much pedagogy and coaching and even structure (in the form of tasks and levels) as an educational simulation, and while more expensive and impossible to fully scale, are also less contrived. As with a Sim, a microcosm encourages emergent learning. Unlike a Sim, however, a real-world microcosm can take a long time to play out. It can also be unfair, risky, and susceptible to noise—that is, subject to distraction outside the control of either the participants or the sponsors—leading to very different results for different participants.

Still, it turns out that identifying microcosms is often necessary in designing a simulation interface. For example, a meeting can present a microcosm for all leadership situations.

Achieving mastery level, including with big skills, almost always requires success in a real microcosm.

Here is an example of a microcosm from a class on negotiating by the Center for Army Leadership's class called: Influencing Others: Building Commitment Through Effective Influence, as quoted in the program's *Instructor Manual:*

Homework Assignment—Applying Influencing Skills to Everyday Negotiations

Your assignment is to conduct a negotiation with someone in your everyday life, using one or more of the tactics described in your reading assignment. This means your first task is to reread the recent excerpts that have been provided to you. Then identify an everyday negotiation situation. Be sure that what you are negotiating for is actually negotiable. Also, you should negotiate over something that is "real world," meaningful, and the outcome of which has actual consequences of some importance. To give you some ideas over what to negotiate, ask yourself the following questions:

- Am I contemplating a major purchase (car, appliance) whereby it would be legitimate for me to visit a dealership and do some preliminary negotiation to determine the type of deal I might expect to receive?
- Is there any activity or behavior I would want those senior or peer to me in the workplace to change or adapt to?
- Is there any behavior my spouse/significant other/children would want me to start/stop/do differently (and that I am willing to negotiate over)?
- Is there some future event (vacation location, visit with in-laws) over which I and others have differing views and that is subject to negotiation?

There are a couple of caveats to this assignment:

- Do not try to influence a gas station attendant to give you a free tank of gas when he would be breaking the law to comply (something that is non-negotiable with the other party).
- Negotiate for something that is real to you. Don't string a salesperson (or your spouse) along on something you don't intend to do.
- Do no harm.

Other than these guiding principles, use your common sense and creativity to determine what you are negotiating for and with whom.

Other microcosm assignments in different classes could include:

- Raise $100 for a cause or candidate.
- Make $100 by reselling items on eBay.
- Sell ten books by going door to door.
- Sell five hundred sheets of paper with some type of writing for at least 25 cents each.

Author's note: In most academic situations, the analysis and write-up of a microcosm gets more emphasis than the success of the experience. If a student grew a garden and then wrote a paper on it, the academic philosophy would suggest grading the paper heavily, as opposed to grading the garden.

- Win five sports games.
- Find the cheapest online price for a buffalo.

Is there a more scalable, more fair, more practiceable, less expensive way of learning to do?

1

SIMS

The New Media of "Learning to Do," Not Just "Learning to Know"

Sims are a broad genre of experiences, including computer games for entertainment and immersive learning simulations for formal learning programs.

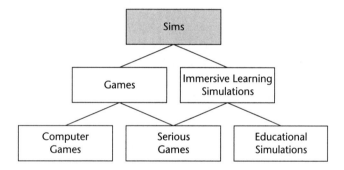

Sims use simulation elements to capture and model experiences, including

- Actions, reflected in the interface
- How the actions then impact relevant systems
- How those systems produce feedback and outcomes, including desired results

The simulation elements are then used with game elements to make the Sim engaging and pedagogical elements (including scaffolding and coaching) to make it effective. The elements are also organized into tasks and levels to create incrementally challenging practice environments, leveraging linear content for motivation and context.

To further expand on the discussion, Sims, when virtual, differ from real microcosms, role-playing, and labs in that they more efficiently leverage economies of scale and pedagogy. Sims can be multiplayer. Sims may use any of the following elements as a platform, support them, or be supported by them:

- Massively multiplayer environments
- Real-world environments
- Informal learning
- Social networking environments

A Spectrum of Scale

The scale of the Sim also shapes the genre. For example, a Sim may be a huge, complex game or a tiny mobile game.

Complex Game

A type of computer game that represents investments of time and resources to create on par with those that are commercially viable today, between $5 million and $20 million if developed in the United States (contrast with costs for educational simulation).

A complex game typically has advanced graphics, campaign or single and multiplayer options, complex systems, and compelling and well-honed gameplay.

Author's note: While the difference in budgets between computer games and immersive learning simulations is pretty high, the actual difference in resources required is probably 100 times greater. This is because a commercial computer game is almost always a new example of a genre that has had hundreds of previous iterations before it. And each one of these iterations has experimented with new ideas while refining old techniques, including interface, display, and goals structures.

For example, when you play a first-person shooter released last month, you are accessing intellectual property that has been constantly refined since well before Castle Wolfenstein 3-D in the form of both design and supporting tools. If one had to truly build a similar first-person shooter from scratch today, it would probably cost about $1 billion.

The time spent in Sim is between fifteen and fifty hours. Typically, inevitably, a player learns high-level skills, such as personal responsibility for results and problem solving.

Most first-person shooters are examples of complex games. In contrast, most educational simulation genres like interactive spreadsheets or branching stories are not. For educational simulation genres, practiceware comes closest to sharing the attributes of a complex game.

Mobile Game

A mini game, frame game, or other game designed for cell phones or smart phones (such as an iPhone) and other highly portable devices. Typically, the genre of mobile games does not include hand-held game consoles.

Conclusion

These definitions are ostensibly obvious. But about three or four times a year, I have a conversation where a sponsor says something like, "I want you to build me a Sim that is as robust and addictive as World of Warcraft or the newest SimCity game, but that can be playable over a browser and that costs about 100K."

2

IMMERSIVE LEARNING SIMULATION

Because You Can't Learn to Ride a Bicycle from a Book

Immersive learning simulations are a broad genre of Sims used in formal learning programs, encompassing educational simulations and serious games.

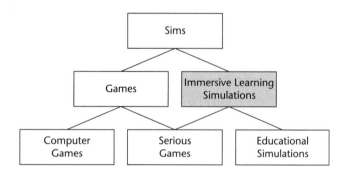

Immersive learning simulations include a variety of genres:

- Branching story
- Frame game
- Interactive spreadsheet
- Mini game
- Practiceware
- Virtual experience space
- Game show (arguably)
- Real-time strategy game
- Tycoon game

Educational Simulations

Educational simulations are a broad genre of immersive learning simulations focused on increasing participants' mastery level in the real world. They are how you want your pilot or doctor to learn.

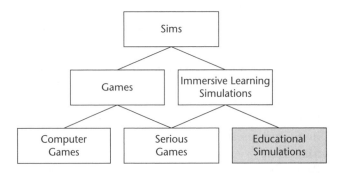

Educational simulations differ from computer games in that they

- Do not have a program goal of necessarily being fun for participants (although they do engender a level of engagement).

- Are part of a formal learning program and are built primarily to nurture specific learning goals in participants (called students or *learners*, and every once in a while *players*), while adhering to program goals to achieve desired results. As a result, they are often chosen or paid for indirectly by program sponsors, not the participants themselves.
- Often are supported by real coaches or facilitators.
- Tend to have lower production values than full complex games.
- Focus on replay using different approaches.
- May be uniquely critical tools for developing middle skills and big skills.

Yet as with all Sims, educational simulations

- Require participants to develop real skills, and do so through emergent learning.
- Can be single player, multiplayer, or massively multiplayer.
- Are first described in design documents, then programmed, debugged, and distributed.
- Can be complex or mini.

Educational simulations include many genres. I'll start with the branching story genre, and spend a little more time with it than with subsequent genres.

Branching Stories

Branching stories are an educational simulation genre in which students make a series of decisions through a series of multiple choices to progress through an event (or story) that develops in different ways according to the choices each student makes.

Specifically, students start with a briefing. They then advance to a first multiple-choice decision point, or branch. Based on the decision or action they make (such as "I'll take the red pill" or "I'll take the blue pill," or "I'll take the road more traveled" instead of "I'll take the road less traveled"), they see a scene that provides some feedback, advances the story, and then sets up another decision; students continue making decisions, traversing some of the available branches, until they either win or lose—that is, reach either a successful or unsuccessful final state. Students then get some type of after action review.

The branching story's basic input, a multiple-choice interface, typically focuses on the actions of the player's character, which often involve choosing specific statements to direct other people.

A branching story structure. A branching story contains many different developments and outcomes, leveraging a state-based system.

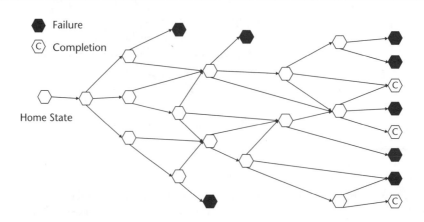

First-person example branching story from Performance Development Group.

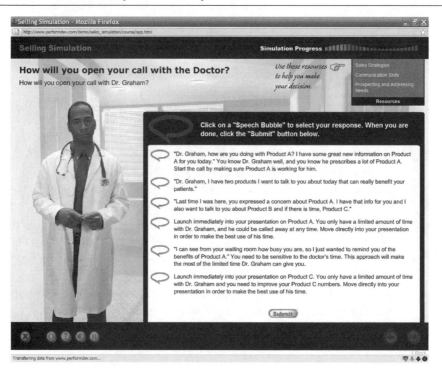

The simplicity of the interface is both branching stories' greatest strength and their greatest weakness. Their ease of use, ease of deployment, use of discrete decisions, and dynamic visual content style make them highly appropriate for reluctant learners. However, some critics call them all trigger and no complex system. Many high-potential or highly creative individuals eschew their simple, all-or-nothing interface.

Companies like WILL Interactive have advanced the genre to handle more moral and complex situations, making a few branching stories also appropriate for high-potential employees and business school students.

Third-person example from WILL Interactive.

Source: Courtesy of WILL interactive, Inc.

Branching stories can be presented in text, full-motion video, or pictures with or without sound, and with enough budget can take on an almost cinematic quality. Any high production values becomes a game element, adding appeal and overlapping with advanced graphics.

Branching stories can be designed to be gone through by a student multiple times. When this is the case, the program might use *breadcrumbs*—on-screen clues—to show what decisions the player made last time.

A Brief History. The early paper examples of branching stories might be best epitomized by the choose-your-own-adventure books, where readers would go through a page or two of story, be given a few options, and based on their choice, skip to a different page in the book.

With the early emergence of the surprisingly Frisbee-like videodiscs, branching stories as an educational genre were born. The genre evolved from there in several directions. Videodiscs were directly replaced with CD-ROMs and then DVDs and Blu-Rays. Some vendors, such as Ninth House, initially used streaming Web video instead. Other vendors, such as Skillsoft, took out videos and replaced them with pictures as a way to facilitate Web deployment, decrease cost, and increase access.

Recent branching stories have often replaced the video characters with computer-generated characters, first to replace the real actors, but then to create much more fluid and dynamically generated characters.

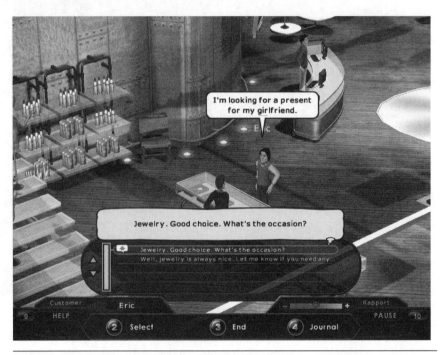

Source: Courtesy of Minerva Software and Blueline Simulations.

Practical Use. Technology poses no barriers to creating content in branches, rather than just linearly. Papers and PowerPoint presentations can be designed to take users where they want to go. Many authoring environments have built-in templates around this approach. Creating branching stories is, in fact, a first crack at dismantling the monopoly of linear content. Branching stories are also called virtual role-play, interpersonal simulation, open-ended story, or story-based soft skills training.

> *Author's note:* As with all Sims, watching someone else go through a branching story is fairly uninteresting. But when you are in the hot seat making the decisions yourself, the experience is quite vivid. So play one before you judge it.

Interactive Spreadsheets

Interactive spreadsheets are a wonkariffic educational simulation genre in which students typically try to impact three or four critical *metrics* (primary variables) indirectly by allocating finite resources (money, time, good will, swag) among competing categories over a series of turns or intervals. (Admittedly, the marketing for these types of Sims makes them sound sexier, screaming "You can be in charge of running an entire country, company, or campaign. Every decision is yours to make! Will you fold under the pressure or become the next Laird of all you can see?")

Students get feedback on their decisions through graphs and charts. The entire Sim might continue for anywhere from three to twenty intervals. For example, the head of a nonprofit organization might try to optimize the variables of funding and community impact by allocating each week's working time among these categories:

- Fundraising
- Creating new services
- Doing menial tasks
- Doing paperwork
- Evaluating existing services
- Sleeping
- Spending time with family
- Spending time with classmates who have more money than you do

This genre of Sim is often done in a multiplayer or team-based environment, with significant competition between learners, and often with a coach or facilitator. Interactive spreadsheets are often the cornerstones of multi-day programs intended to align a fractured department or organization by building shared knowledge and understanding.

Forio Business Simulations interactive spreadsheet.

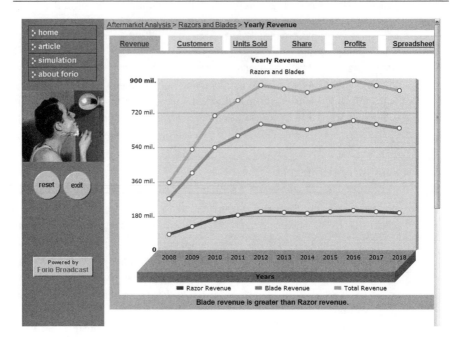

Interactive spreadsheets typically focus on business school issues such as policy, supply chain management, product life cycle, accounting, and general cross-functional business acumen, which are their historical roots. Despite the genre name, spreadsheets are not a realistic platform for deploying these models, although they may be used in the design document. The genre's subtlety, unpredictability, and variability make it appropriate for training b-school students and high-potential supervisors up to and including direct reports to the CEO. Interactive spreadsheets require—and provide a pure introduction to—systems.

Some interactive spreadsheets also use *cut scenes*—a type of linear, story-based video content described in Chapter Nineteen—to set up a scenario and provide feedback, as well as provide a welcome break from numbers and charts.

Interactive spreadsheets are also called *business acumen simulations* or *systems dynamic simulations*. They have influenced (and some would say they have been replaced by) tycoon games.

A more complicated interactive spreadsheet example on global warming.

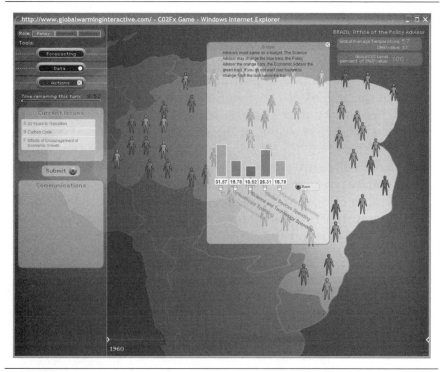

Source: Reprinted with permission of Michael Hillinger.

Interactive Diagrams

Interactive diagrams are an educational simulation genre in which the entire screen display becomes a living," organic visual diagram of key concepts, relationships, and patterns.

Interactive diagrams are often used in school programs to show, for example, food webs or how Washington, D.C., works. Students can increase the number of wolves or sheep (in the first example) and lobbyists or interns (in the second) and see what impact that has on the whole system.

The content is heavily layered. Arrows and graphs typically pepper the display. Control buttons and throttles present options to players. Interactive diagrams themselves then become a model and pedagogy to apply to real-life situations. Usually without trying to achieve any victory conditions, students begin to understand at a gut level what a piece of data means and how it relates to other data. The interface is simple and immediate, even if the relationships are complex.

Virtual Products

Virtual products are an educational simulation genre in which a collection of simulation elements creates a high-fidelity virtual model of a real-world item. Participants can play around with these items or test hypotheses regarding their behavior.

Virtual product. The buttons on the full example match up perfectly to the actions of a real-world watch. The button at 2 o'clock changes the state (which the participant can see visualized in the chart to the right of the watch). The button at 4 o'clock has different functionality depending on what state the watch is in. But in all cases, when the participant presses the button is critical (such as to stop the stopwatch or change the date), and even the length of time the participant holds down the button matters (for instance, holding down the button when in stopwatch mode resets the stopwatch). This is a very simple example; many virtual products are much more complex.

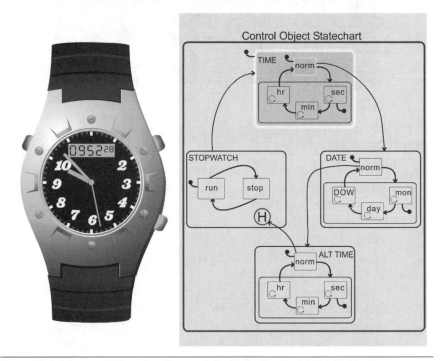

Source: Flashsim.com and Kaye, Jonathan, and David Castillo. *Flash MX for Interactive Simulation.* Delmar Learning, 2002.

Virtual products have many advantages over their real-world counterparts, including ease of transportation and in fact ubiquitous availability, freedom from physical limits such as cool-down times and little pieces that break, and annotations as to internal workings.

As with interactive diagrams, virtual products have neither tasks nor levels. Participants require intrinsic motivation or they won't bother with them. Virtual products, however, are often the basis for subsequent virtual labs.

Virtual Labs

Virtual labs are the educational simulation genre where participants engage a virtual product in an experience structured by tasks and goals to learn about using some real-world item to solve problems or complete products (rather than just to explore what it does).

For example, a student may have to repair a Geiger counter or composter using diagnostic tools and some spare parts in three minutes or less to pass. Or the requirement may be to create a chemical compound. In more complex virtual labs, with each subsequent level, a student may receive less and less helpful information, such as no longer having access to an x-ray view, or may have to face more complicated situations.

Virtual labs are often used for formal learning experiences that result in certification, and are successful in the learning goal of application of new content.

Practiceware

Practiceware is the educational simulation genre that encourages participants to repeat actions in high-fidelity real-time (often 3-D) situations until the skills become natural in the real-world counterpart.

The first practiceware genre was the flight simulator, used for training pilots. Today, practiceware has been developed for a variety of big skills. It's the way to get results if you really need them, or even just want them.

Pieces of Practiceware. The practiceware interface constantly presents participants with five to twenty different actions, aligned with real-world options. Many of them require mastery of split-second timing (when to do an action) and magnitude (how hard to do an action).

Role of Practiceware. Practiceware is used for learning goals that include implicit knowledge and can be a significant piece of a mastery-level program.

Practiceware has at least some of the production attributes of a complex game. Its typically high development cost makes it more efficient for most implementing organizations to buy off-the-shelf or configurable products rather than build it from scratch or even have it customized by the vendor.

Author's note: In most practical simulation design situations, the term *practice-ware* is useful to acknowledge what the sponsor of a simulation really wants but can afford neither the money or time to build. For example, the simulation designer may say, "What you are describing is practiceware, which is very similar to a computer game in terms of scope. But you may not know that many computer games have budgets of tens of millions of dollars and take three years, while your budget is two beaver pelts and your project has to be done by Thursday." Still, more powerful authoring tools are making practiceware more possible more often.

Virtual Experience Spaces

Virtual experience spaces are the educational simulation genre where students, in a role-play, practice some real-world skill, such as consulting or creation of intellectual property, or even disaster recovery using Web-based materials as props.

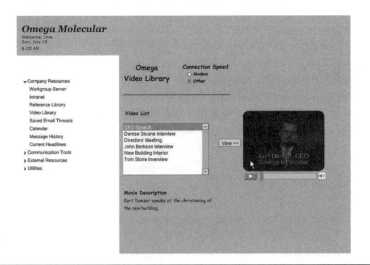

Source: Courtesy of David Fisher, Ph.D.

To best understand virtual experience spaces, step back and consider a bit of simulation history. Twenty years ago, in traditional extended role-plays, students might be given the mission (often in teams, sometimes competing) to reengineer a work process, create a new advertising campaign, or make some important and defendable choices, to develop both big skills such as project management and middle skills such as sourcing.

To do this, students often explored some created experience space as critical input and context to their assignment. This space was defined though prop documents (such as fake annual reports) and other items (business cards or mugs of a fictitious company) handed out over the course of the role-play. Typically the instructor managing the experience played a central role such as the CEO.

Now, with the genre of virtual experience spaces, using relatively common-place Web technology, instructors can create scalable fictitious situations using large linked, state-based multimedia repositories for students to explore. The elements can include e-mails, video interviews with the CEO or other clips, and PowerPoint presentations, all accessed through a common portal (or portals if there are multiple teams).

Here's the key: only certain links in the repository are available at the start of the role-play. As it proceeds, new links open up based on different types of triggers, typically time and contacts.

At intervals, the instructor (or the simulation on its own) opens up links that create the effect, for the students, of time passing. This could simply represent the start of a new week or, more dramatically, the occurrence of an external event such as a hostile takeover or the death of a senior executive (which may change the mission). Again, new video clips and e-mails would become available to the role-players. Of course, time can also cut off certain links, making them no longer accessible.

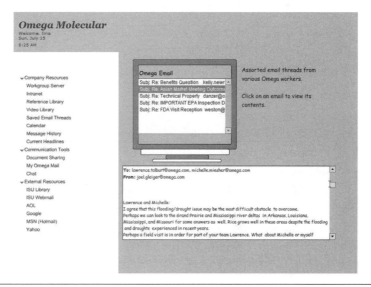

Source: Courtesy of David Fisher, Ph.D.

Contacts are the other core trigger to open up links to elements. After reading an e-mail, a player in the role-play might want to ask a follow-up question of the fictional character, and would "e-mail" the character. Then either an automated system or the instructor would "reply" to that e-mail, opening up a link that would result in a new e-mail appearing in the participant's in-box.

During the beta rollouts of virtual experience spaces, the instructor has to be "live," carefully monitoring the queries of the students and creating new information that will then be refined and added to the canned experience in the next iteration.

By accessing this type of space, consultants can learn enough to create recommendations, projects, and plans, even introducing fictitious characters to each other. The resulting products can then be evaluated by real humans for all sorts of projects—evacuation plans, new Web sites, IT infrastructure, strategic plans.

Serious Games

Serious games make up the other broad genre under immersive learning simulations. They increase awareness of real-world topics and can be used both for entertainment and in learning programs—essentially, if you think about it, they're how *you* want to learn.

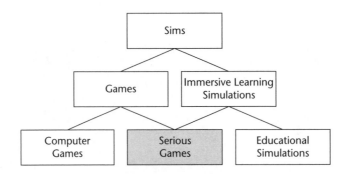

Serious games draw from both computer game and educational simulation genres. Some would say that a goal of serious games is stealth learning: students learning transferable content without realizing it. Serious games (and often enough all Sims) might be most commonly characterized and dogged by frame games and modified—*modded*—traditional computer games. (For more on modding, see "Community-Created Content" in Chapter Twenty.) But they can and should be much more.

Serious Games use Game Elements to Engage the User

Compared to educational simulations, serious games tend to be more fun—they're more engaging, but they have lower fidelity and greater abstraction, and they're less transferable to the real world (see Chapter Sixteen). They tend to have an interface optimized for quick engagement.

Compared to computer games, serious games have specific learning goals and desired results, and often lower production values than a full complex game.

Frame Games

No one wants to take a test, but everyone wants to be in a game show. So—with the goal of "making learning fun"—program directors often have students engage familiar games and puzzles such as Wheel of Fortune, solitaire, or memory, with important pieces of awareness or task-based content replacing trivia or icons. For example, the player might have to answer a question correctly to draw the next card in a solitaire game.

While making heavy use of game elements, and more diagnostic than instructional, game-based models work well to support compliance programs and in other situations where broad audiences need to cover some basic information.

Frame games are also known as *exogenous games*.

Frame game. Familiar game structures can present traditional educational content.

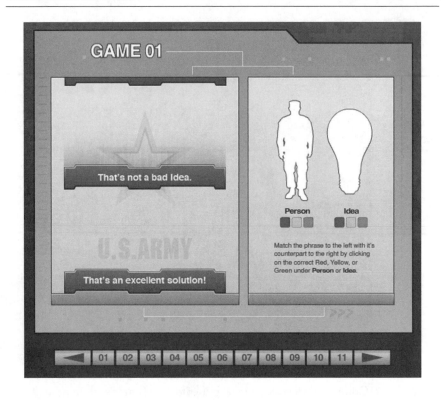

Mini Games—Best of Both Worlds?

Source: Screenshot courtesy of Persuasive Games LLC.

Mini games are small, easy-to-access Sims. Mini games are often "one-note" in terms of gameplay. They're built to be addictive and often focus on simple actions and abstracted systems.

Mini games can be used for editorial, explanation, marketing, and messaging, or even commerce (where players will play a few free levels, and then buy the full game). Mini games can sometimes provide an awareness of some more complicated issue, such as fit (think Tetris).

Mini games are often created in Adobe Flash, resulting in generally a lower cost than other genres of Sims. The visual style of mini games is closer to comic book art or illustration than to photography.

Mini games are also called casual games, or micro-games, and include puzzle games. While some think of mini games as the opposite of complex games and practiceware, I prefer to think of them as just bite-sized versions.

The First Examples

To summarize, one might be able to best differentiate between educational simulations and serious games by their original examples.

The best example of an educational simulation, and also its earliest success and justification, is the flight simulator for training pilots. Flight simulators have many of the attributes respected and desired in educational simulations today. They are first-person (what you see in the simulation is what you would see in real life), they relate directly to the needed skills, and their value is self-evident (in this case, they keep both pilot and plane from crashing, which would result in killing hundreds of people and costing millions of dollars, and just making a big ol' mess). Flight simulators impressively deal with simple actions like turning a flap or adjusting a throttle, as well as nuanced actions such as using the throttle, but these actions are also interfaces into complicated, dynamic, and intertwined systems like wind shear and flying with broken equipment. And these actions and systems are all coordinated toward the straightforward goal of landing a plane safely, and ideally at the right airport. The hope and promise of the educational simulation movement is that this model can be used for more academic and higher-level skills such as "understanding the decisions of a historical leader" or even "applying leadership."

In contrast, the prototypical *serious game* is Will Wright's brilliant SimCity. In SimCity, players are highly entertained while designing and nurturing the cities they have evolved. It was designed to be (and published as) a game, and yet it has found its way into many academic curricula. It is simple to use, originally even presenting a model train interface, but the systems it presents

Simulations and serious games can be in any medium. Here, serious games meet social networking in "IndustryMasters for Facebook".

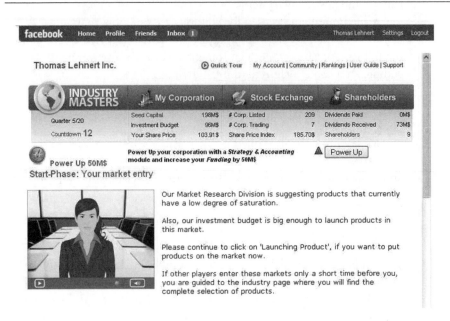

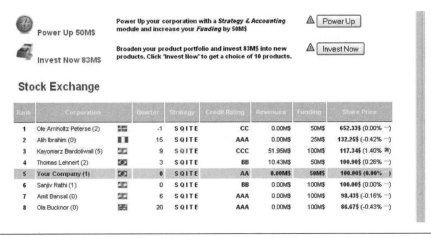

Source: (c) 2009 Tycoon Systems Inc.

are complicated and interesting. Players become proud of their cities in a way that few are proud of homework assignments. They even view their cities as an extension of their own views and priorities. Players also gain at least some insight into urban planning. However, the underlying mechanics are highly inaccurate for a real city. Still, the hope and promise of this serious games approach is that many more examples will emerge that are likewise addictive and educational.

3

COMPUTER GAMES

So this is what teenage boys are doing instead of watching television? Seems like a lateral move.

Computer games are a broad genre of Sim built for entertainment. Sometimes computer games and serious games (covered in the last chapter) together comprise the broad genre of Sims called games.

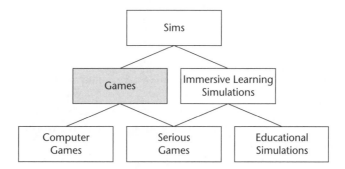

And zooming in a bit further gets me to computer game genres.

Computer Game Genres

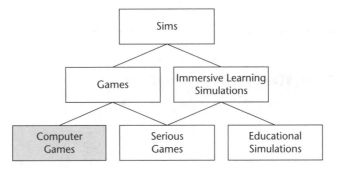

Computer games include the genres of

- First-person shooters
- Real-time strategy games
- Racing games
- Tycoon games
- Game shows
- Squad shooters

Computer games bring together simulation elements with significant game elements and more subtle pedagogical elements.

Computer games differ from educational simulations, and to a lesser degree from all immersive learning simulations, in that they

- Are optimized or used for engagement of participants called *players* and *gamers*
- Tend toward high-conflict situations
- Tend to be highly abstract situations, especially at the interface level

Having said that, despite the work that goes into making a game fun, for at least 99 percent of the population, playing your favorite game would be a tedious and painful chore.

These computer games are also called *video games.*

First-Person Shooter

The first-person shooter (FPS) is the mainstay of the computer game world, a computer game genre in which the player sees the world through the eyes of an on-screen counterpart, usually down the barrel of a weapon. The player is a fantasy hero (or *anti*-hero).

First-person shooter. In Halo: Combat Evolved, players battle mercenary mutants, and aliens on a distant ringworld.

Source: Microsoft product screen shot reprinted with permission from Microsoft Corporation.

FPS Interface. The interface is built around movement and aiming. The point of view is first-person, augmented with a heads-up display (HUD).

FPS Systems. The player traverses a 3-D map in real time, trying to reach key locations and solving simple puzzles while shooting (winning conflict by clicking quickly and accurately) and being shot at by avatars controlled by the game's artificial intelligence (AI). The player's primary attributes in the game include health and armor, location on map, amount of supplies, and perhaps capability.

Author's note: The genre is mature. It has evolved dramatically, and now consists of numerous complex games. As the title implies, like branching stories, it is first person. Unlike branching stories, it allows you to move around physically, which is satisfying. The physics, interface, graphics, level design, and puzzles are all much more refined than even ten years ago. Innovative games have added sneaking around, decisions about which weapons to bring, even what skills to upgrade. When one adds up all the developer time spent on creating and improving the FPS genre over the years, it probably adds up to about $1 billion of research and development. Few other computer applications have been the recipient of such vast resources. The result is that most FPS games are very accessible.

On the other hand, FPS games are optimized around fun, not learning. The underlying framework is not very interesting. Very few real activities of the last few centuries line up with the systems and interface modeled in these games (traversing mazes; finding, picking up, and delivering things; killing things). In fact I would suggest that FPS games are a red herring when it comes to educational simulations. Expecting them to provide a model for education is like asking a brilliant surgeon to prepare your tax returns.

To me, what are more interesting are Sims like Full Spectrum Warrior that superficially look like FPS games but have completely different interfaces and strategies, so they nurture the development of different situational awareness and scrambling techniques. But of course such games represent a new genre that is necessarily much more raw, less refined by several orders of magnitude, than FPS.

Sports games, such as golf, can also look superficially like FPS games, but again have completely different systems and interfaces and are correspondingly more raw as well (somewhere between FPS games and Full Spectrum Warrior).

Real-Time Strategy Games

Real-time strategy (RTS) games are the original "serious games." In this computer game genre, players manage and transform limited territory and units on maps into large and diverse territory and units, to succeed in conflict against competitors trying to do the same, in a real-time environment.

The available actions include gathering resources, building and upgrading units and structures, some logistics, and directing units in combat.

Basic RTS strategies include *tech up* (researching technology more quickly than anyone else), *tank rush* (building a large single-unit army), and resource *domination* (being very effective at gathering resources and keeping opponents from doing the same).

Real-time strategy game. A screen shot from Age of Empires.

Source: Microsoft product screen shot reprinted with permission from Microsoft Corporation.

> I believe real-time strategy games (along with SimCity) make the most compelling case for serious games to date, combining engagement, long-term strategy, interesting systems, and potentially educational backdrops.

Racing Games

Racing games form a computer game genre in which the core gameplay is some type of chase.

The player is often in a vehicle and traversing a map (sometimes with properties of a maze). Key attributes typically involve movement.

In career mode or other campaign structures, players might make decisions around investments from winning races to buy or upgrade their cars. The computer AI might cheat by using *rubber banding*—defining what its units do as tied to whatever the player units do. (For more on rubber banding, see Chapter Sixteen.)

Racing game. In the Midtown Madness Series (from Microsoft), players race in both formal and pick-up races across real world cities.

Source: Microsoft product screen shot reprinted with permission from Microsoft Corporation.

The point of view can be any or all of the following: first-person, third-person, overhead, isometric, and cinematic view and often includes radar and other heads-up display elements. (See "Point of View" in Chapter Nineteen.)

Author's note: One of the most interesting parts of racing games is their seamless integration of first-person and strategic map perspectives. Players must constantly make decisions using both views. Compare this to the first-person-only perspective of branching stories and the strategy-only perspective of interactive spreadsheets to realize what an impressive trick that is, and how much this double view should be the default model for almost all serious games and simulations.

Tycoon Games

In Theme Hospital, players manage medical facilities and staff.

Tycoon games are what schools would teach if influenced more by Will Wright than Noah Webster. Age of Empires, The Movies, Zoo Tycoon, Railroad Tycoon, and Roller Coaster Tycoon are other examples of tycoon games.

A tycoon game is a computer game (and often serious game) genre where players have the goal of creating a thriving ecosystem by managing and transforming small and unstable territory, structures, and units on a map into large, diverse, and stable ones, in a real-time environment.

Player actions include

- Building and upgrading units and structures (often to minimize movement and cost of travel)
- Creating paths
- Filling roles
- Refining old processes, and researching and implementing new processes

- Gathering, extracting, consuming, and allocating balanced resources
- Managing profitability
- Directing people
- Handling alerts

Map locations tend to have different values, and some are of high value. But there may also be global conditions or capability limits.

Typically, the units themselves perform necessary activities. Some units may be a form of constituent, either political, employee, or consumer. *Tycoon games* also feature AI or real competitors.

The level design tends to be variations of a back-loaded sandbox mode (where players start off with only a few resources and try to invest and otherwise build them up in an environment with few structured goals or time limits), and players may strive for awards. (For more on this point, see the discussion of sandbox levels under "Campaign" in Chapter Eighteen.) Failure in tycoon games tends to involve stagnation rather than death.

The display in tycoon games tends to use an overhead or isometric view. These games also often use mixed scales and radars to ease navigation.

Tycoon games tend to focus on developing big skills including applying economic, value, and governing models, nurturing and stewardship, probing, project management, and negotiation, as well as middle skills including long-term planning, budgeting, ownership, estimating cost, and estimating benefit.

They are sometimes referred to as *builder games.*

Game Shows

Game shows are a computer game genre where players, called *contestants*, answer trivia questions and apply basic strategy to compete against other contestants or a timer (or both) to win prizes.

Game shows provide templates for frame games. While seldom really complex, a game show can be either a mini game or something more elaborate.

Squad Shooters

Squad shooters are a computer game genre where players manage a small team (two to six units), each with different strengths, in enemy territory on the game map. Squad shooters are often thought of as an evolution of real-time strategy, without the resource collecting and unit and structure building, and more of an opportunity for both story development and realizing each unit as a character that uniquely fits into a team.

Squad shooters may have a load-out screen after any briefing and before the core gameplay where the player might have to choose which four characters from a stable of five or more to bring on a given mission, matching skill sets with the task and with each other.

Squad shooters emphasize probing, directing people, conflict, aligning strategies and tactics, decision making, and dead reckoning.

Games Appreciation 101

It is tempting to look at one's favorite computer game genres (such as first-person shooter) and themes (such as film noire) to gain insight into serious games and simulations. Rather, I would do exactly the opposite. Try playing a computer game with a theme and story world that you really don't like at all. Further, try to find a game that presents the first generation of a new (and often failed) genre—that is, an interface and level design scheme completely foreign to you. So if you hate *Star Trek*, play Star Trek: Bridge Commander. If you have never played The Sims, play it now. This will often be closer to the student experience.

4

TRADITIONAL EDUCATION

Sims and computer games are often looked at in contrast to traditional education. Ultimately, Sims will need to build on and be part of traditional education to be successful.

Educational Genres, Environments, Activities, and Media

Education also involves a number of activities, environments, and media that can be viewed as genres. Here are some examples:

- Classrooms
- Case study
- Role-playing
- Lab work
- Books
- Web pages
- Workbooks

Classrooms

A classroom is an open-minded environment in which students are gathered at the same time and location, typically to hear a presentation of prepared material or lecture by an instructor, coach, or expert. Classrooms can be augmented with a lab, and can build community if students interact with one another.

Also called *on ground* or *face-to-face (F2F)* environments.

Classrooms can be replicated on the computer, so the work proceeds in much the same fashion without actual F2F presence. Virtual classroom tools provide an infrastructure for *synchronous* (same time, different location) courses integrating voices, slides, application sharing, and control tools. Experienced instructors will use light class games to get students used to using the various interfaces and other features of the tool. For example, they may instruct all students to talk to other students to learn three things about them via text chat, or to draw a self-portrait on the screen using the whiteboard markup tool.

Case Study

A case study is a sequential, detailed description of real events (or at least a story world) that has some instructional value, either as being cautionary, typical, or inspirational. Case studies may or may not include how the event was eventually resolved. Some case studies are aggregations of several real events, not just one.

Case studies can be used as a type of simulation activity, where participants are briefed on the first part of a situation in detail via a case study, and are then asked to make a big choice (a single, complex action), in the form of "what would you do if you were in this situation?" Typically there are a range of "right" answers, and the exercise activity focuses on how well students argue their decisions, as judged by the instructor and perhaps other participants.

In other situations, case studies are media that set up the activity of an after action review. Participants experience a complete common situation and then sit back and evaluate and analyze the actions taken by the story characters, perhaps also exploring what they would have done differently.

Case studies can also be included and discussed in a program's background material.

Role-Playing

Role-playing is the educational simulation genre activity where students practice some real-world skills by interacting with other real people, including other students and instructors or actors, with everyone assuming specific roles and characters.

Some role-plays are short, about ten minutes, while others may span out across days, or even run part time for months, or, in an academic setting, an entire semester.

Role-plays are a well-understood genre of simulation and highly regarded by formal learning professionals. Their interface, for example, is nearly perfect. They greatly support the learning goals of application of new content and mastery level and reduce the risk of choking under pressure, making them far and away the instructors' favorite Sim.

However, they have several drawbacks:

- They tend to be "one-shot," and do not allow participants to repeatedly practice a set of skills as they could with a backboard or a batting cage.

- They are expensive and do not benefit from any economies of scale. At one extreme, it might take five or six instructors to support just one end-learner, such as in a commercial airplane simulator or a senior manager role-play.
- Access to role-play opportunities tends to be very limited.
- They have fidelity issues, in that actors and players may take the simulation more seriously at the beginning of the day and less so as the day wears on. Further, when students play all roles, few play the so-called target of influence accurately.
- The pedagogy and coaching, including after action reviews, tend to be subjective and inconsistent.
- Often, only one or two people are role-playing, while the rest of a class is watching.

Even though ease of deployment is an issue, however, most instructors are more likely to support role-plays over other types of Sims.

While vendors of branching stories are quick to call the experiences they offer "virtual role-plays," their multiple-choice interface precludes the interpersonal fidelity necessary for a legitimate claim to the description. Massively Multiplayer Online Environments (MMOs) have a stronger claim, for better or worse, on replicating role-plays.

Role-plays are typically used to train people-facing jobs (including sales) and any role that may have to deal with an emergency.

Lab Work

Educational laboratories can be regarded as the genre activity of using a place to accomplish a stated goal by demonstrating a working knowledge, gained through repeatedly practicing and observing, of what actions are available, how the actions impact the relevant systems (possibly including units, maps, and processes), and, then how those systems produce results.

Labs should have some, but not complete, fidelity to the real-world situation, as their main purpose is helping students realize that theory isn't as useful as theorists hope. Labs can have both pedagogy and coaching and structure (in the form of tasks and levels).

Related topics: See Chapter Twenty-Two, especially the "Mastery Level" section.

Books

Books are the traditional collections of linear content designed for self-paced consumption by broad audiences.

Books are media optimized to capture and share three types of content: inner monologues (such as fiction), processes and time lines (such as cookbooks or history overviews), and random access entries (such as dictionaries and photographs). Books are often chunked into chapters, and dense or tangential material is included in the back in appendix chapters (see Chapter 15 on Linear Content).

Books typically raise awareness.

Author's note: Books may just be white bread for the mind. Now, I freely acknowledge that white bread is wonderful. Our parents and their parents swore by it as key to our diet. It is part of our culture, depicted in oil paintings and discussed in epic poetry. Preparing bread is a cultural milestone from our own Paleolithic history. Just mentioning a great baguette, brioche, or even peasant bread makes my mouth water.

And yet we are learning that it is not the perfect food. The process of preparing white flour can remove much of what was good in it. The result is something that tricks the body into thinking it is getting nourishment, while spiking and upsetting parts of its internal chemical balance.

White bread is still a fabulous treat, and it fits nicely into a healthy diet. But to go overboard with it results in bloat rather than health.

That brings me back to books. We are very proud of books. Many people have a religious zeal about them, especially those old enough to remember when books were scarce, or with strong connections to people who did. We all have books that transformed our view of the world and influenced our moral and career decisions. There is no better way of transferring someone else's internal monologue than a good book. They teach us empathy and respect. We can also get facts, allowing us to make more informed decisions.

Books are also a great example of mature technology. They are cheap to produce, easy to store, and require no energy or other supporting infrastructure. The only access barrier is literacy. Libraries are filled with them.

And yet, as I try to take what I have read and apply it to real situations in an attempt to get a desired result, I have a sort of Atkins "aha!" I become increasingly aware of what books don't contain, such as a focus on actions, and the impact of rigorous systems including the emergent actions of units, as much as what they do contain. I love the buzz of a good book, like a good vacation, but hate the transition back to the real world—and I find that the more people I talk to about this, the more I meet who are discovering the same response.

Consider the pairing of frustration and resolution (a topic addressed in detail in Part Five). Frustration and resolution are at the heart of, well, probably everything to do with life and growth.

But look at frustration and resolution in passive stories and at frustration and resolution in simulations; you can see why stories might be making us feel smarter by tricking us, rather than actually increasing our capacity.

In creating a passive story, it is fairly easy to set up a good frustration-resolution pairing.

- Shark attacks swimmer.
- Physically attractive ex-girlfriend or ex-boyfriend re-emerges after ten years with a dark secret.
- For a better life and to avoid a major problem follow these instructions . . .

In all stories, whether in a novel, a movie, or the evening news, we just have to sit back and consume more, and we will get the resolution. We can be members of an audience. It feels so satisfying, for a few moments. But we are instantly hungry again, and the right masters of the medium will once again tantalize us with another frustration-resolution pairing (or have three or four recursive pairings going on at once, so while we are told the resolution of a more specific pairing, we still have the bigger one to resolve).

In an educational simulation, much like a computer game, and of course in learning to ride a bike, swim, speak a foreign language, close a big deal, make a customer happy, or build something, the frustration-resolution pair can not be closed by passively consuming more. The frustration can only (and not even all of the time) be resolved by actively doing something.

Passive stories are thought to be crowning achievements of our civilization: the concept drives books, movies, magazines, and most of our school system. We all have intense, positive relationships with at least a few examples of each.

But like white bread and refined sugar, books may be a form of addiction, actually reducing the ability to act, not increasing it. And maybe, just maybe, the proper role of knowledge creators is to help people overcome this addiction, not to enable it.

Web Pages

The Web offers a media genre combining easy-to-access text and pictures—and increasingly sound and video—laid out into discrete packages (or elements), and linked to other Web pages.

Web pages can be dynamically generated, and can include posts, such as in blogs or chat rooms, that are at the center of most social networking models.

The interface of Web pages is turn-based rather than real-time, and seldom lines up with real-world actions, minimizing the genre's effectiveness at meeting the learning goal of application of new content (that is, learning to do). The Web page has nevertheless become the default media genre of much of e-learning's first generation of content.

Workbooks

A workbook is typically a paper document that students engage sequentially. It can include tips, information, walk-throughs, illustrations, exercises, and tests and quizzes.

Workbooks are media that can accompany an educational simulation. Or, workbooks can be the primary content, and when formatted for online use are called asynchronous e-learning courses.

A typical structure for an online workbook that may also track the students' progress looks like this:

- Introduction, including importance of material, greater context of course, and learning objectives (this may include a canned lecture)
- Outline of material to be covered
- Any conventions used in the course, such as navigation, bread crumbs (annotations of prior actions or choices), or naming
- Lessons, typically three to five, each with introduction, content (including some interactivity, and hands-on if possible), and "knowledge checks"
- Final test
- Where to go for more help, references, or additional courses
- Evaluation of the course and queries re how to make it better (optional)

Traditional e-learning workbooks are often called, derisively, "page turners."

PART TWO

SIMULATION ELEMENTS—ACTIONS AND RESULTS

Framing the Missing Essence of Research and Analysis

Simulation elements capture and model some part of reality, and the role of someone in it. While they are the core of any Sim, they also are what is missing from most business analysis.

Specifically, simulation elements are content that describe:

- What actions are available
- How the actions influence relevant systems
- How those systems produce feedback and results

The following chapters explore each of these areas.

Often, the value of content comes from the interaction of all three layers. For example, if a riptide is pulling a swimmer out into the ocean, the *action* is swimming and the *desired result* is getting to shore. But because of the *system* of ocean currents, the best action to get the result is not naively swimming toward the shore (against the riptide). The swimmer instead needs to move at a right angle to the riptide first, and then swim to shore. Likewise, a salesperson is not going to make a sale by approaching a prospective customer, waving the product about, and saying, "Buy this thing right now."

Further, when used in a Sim, any simulation elements are typically measured in part by their fidelity to the real world, but in some way are incomplete or abstracted from it. They are driven by learning goals or research questions.

Sweet Spots of Simulations

Emerging from the model of actions, systems, and results, four major knowledge constructs are as natural to simulations as internal monologues and time lines are to books. The first is the situational awareness that I have discussed in the Introduction, and the others are conceptual dead reckoning, understanding of actions, and awareness of patterns over time.

Dead Reckoning

When hiking, it's easy to get lost. So it is pleasant when someone pulls out the map, takes out the compass, does some internal calculations, points, and says, "That's the way." It's especially pleasant when, having hiked along winding trails, everyone is at the new site before nightfall.

Dead reckoning is navigation by first deciding on a destination, and then creating a vector based on understanding of the difference between the current and destination locations, and then making a series of movements based on reconciling the vector on a map against real options and obstacles, like paths or walls. It is often contrasted with navigation based on milestones. The term comes from aviation, animal research, and orienteering.

This process, conceptually, is identical to those used by most people when attempting to navigate challenging and unknown situations. Consider political leaders trying to figure differing governing models for a new nation, scientists wrestling with different combinations of chemicals and therapy to reduce the impact of Parkinson's disease, or thought leaders considering differing drama genres for conveying a complex idea.

They first create a conceptual (and imperfect) map. Once the map is roughed out, leaders commit to a destination. They then create a vector based on understanding of current and destination locations, and finally make a series of short-term decisions based on reconciling the vector against real options available to them.

To understand and learn from these people, it is critical to understand the conceptual maps that the leaders saw and their strategy for identifying and working toward their destination.

Understanding of Actions

What do leaders view as viable things to do? Here are some situations to consider for the potential actions:

- Before and during the battles of America's Revolutionary War, what were the ten or fifteen options that General George Washington repeatedly considered? What sequence did he use each time, and with what relative intensity?
- Every week, what group of discretionary actions did Joseph Stalin consider while in power? Of those choices each time, which did he take? How did those actions (both considered and taken) shift over his years in power?
- What options did the Ottoman Empire have to deal with its neighbors?

This content identifies the activities that can be infinitely and repeatedly combined to create often wildly divergent outcomes. They are bundles of discrete action, timing, and magnitude that are a natural concept to us when understanding how to operate a machine like a car, use a typewriter, or even perform with a piano, but must be used as well for modeling and presenting the options of people in business and other higher-level situations.

Awareness of Patterns

What are the three or four factors that a leader most cares about? What impacts these variables and the underlying systems, and how do they play out?

For example:

- What were Albert Einstein's highest priorities during any given year? How were those measured, and what changed them? How were his activities divided between them?
- How about the Marquis de Lafayette?
- Or the government of Saigon from 1954 to 1975?

Ironically, sometimes a drop in one factor results in the increase of another. For a leader, a foreign attack (decrease in national security) can boost domestic popularity. Or a population explosion can lead the same species to starvation and population decimation. Crises of faith can lead to new approaches to solving problems. First understanding and then taking advantage of these patterns defines most of history's successes, political and intellectual.

Part Two address the action and results parts of a simulation model in more detail. Part Three will then examine the creation of systems.

5

BASIC ACTIONS

Actions are what a person in an experience actually does at the most tactical, or basic, level—be it "pat Lee on the back" in one scale or "buy small company" in another. The granularity and scope of the simulation also determines the granularity of the actions modelled and presented. For a country president, an action might be "send an assertive letter to another country's leader." But if the simulation is about the staff writer drafting the letter for the president, an action might be "recall a shared positive experience to start off the letter."

Some actions are only available in certain contexts, and others are done over and over again in cyclical patterns.

Contextual Actions

Many actions become available based on context, such as where on a map (or other system) one is. Physically, you can't open a door unless you are next to it. You can't shake a hand unless you are next to the person whose hand you wish to shake. You can't do certain scientific experiments unless you are near the right equipment. And many contexts in conceptual maps have to be earned.

Maps that provide the context for actions can also be conceptual. That is, if you're working within an organizational map, you can't promote an employee unless you are at the right organization level. From a business process map, you can't sell to retail customers unless you have a store or Web site. From a political capital map, you can't get your boss to endorse a radical idea without past successes to build trust.

Cyclical Actions

Other actions are *cyclical*, as with tennis or negotiation or writing. The same finite set of actions is available throughout an experience, like notes of music or words in a sentence, and the actions typically have two analog components, timing and magnitude.

For example, in driving a car, it is not enough to "turn right"; the steering wheel must turn the right amount and at the right time. Further, drivers will have to "turn right" not once a trip, or ten times, but an almost indefinite amount of times. Likewise, in managing a project, it is not enough to increase the budget, but to increase the budget the right amount, and at the right time. In eating well, it is not enough to eat protein. It has to be the right amount and at the right time.

Cyclical actions are effective in contexts of each other and only in sequences. The collection of actions is ultimately as logical and fluid as the collection of words in a sentence, or notes of music and it needs as much practice to master.

Cyclical actions themselves tend to be recursive; larger actions are made up of smaller actions. Further, actions in combination enable middle skills (discussed in the next chapter), which then enable big skills. Actions may get you close to a long-range goal via conceptual dead reckoning. Certain hardwired successful combinations of actions are called *combo moves*.

Actions and Basic Inputs

The educational challenge of actions is building a new awareness of students' real-world options. Conquering the actions challenge sometimes means seeing things at a higher level. (For example, "When I think I am helping someone, I am really just enabling her.") Sometimes it means not allowing students to do things the way they have in the past to break bad habits.

Meanwhile, presenting to students so many options in an interface, often dozens at any given time, is unnerving at first—for the students. Nonetheless, the wide range of choices (often built up through subsequent levels) is necessary if students are to personalize the experience and own the outcome.

The challenge of actions is also the challenge of applying what one learned outside of the simulation, in the real world. Most traditional courses or research leave the task of applying the material for the students to figure out on their own after the course, which means that most do not do it, and therefore much learning is wasted. By forcing practice in applying the material to the front of the program, a Sim paves the way for the material's productive use after the program.

In a simulation, actions are accomplished by pressing buttons, moving sliders, entering numbers, clicking on a text window or icon, moving a joystick, or making other basic inputs. Future Sims may also increasingly use voice recognition and full body movement.

In Operating Under the Influenza – a game for business continuity planning in the event of a pandemic flu, players spend points on specific available options.

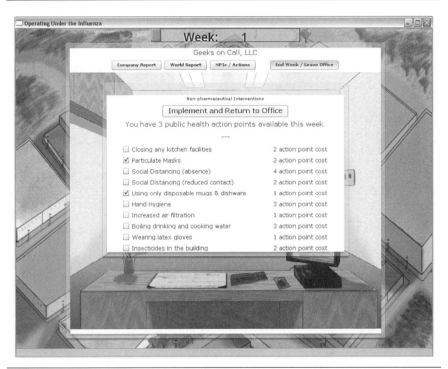

Source: Developed by NJ Dept. of Health and Human Services in partnership with Rutgers University and Raritan Valley Community College

Actions in a Sim can be abstracted all of the way into simple multiple-choice selections. But real-world actions are better represented by collections of options. The presentation and availability of actions through basic inputs greatly influences the look and functionality of the simulation display.

The sidebar illustrates the process of developing a cyclical interface.

The Creation of a Leadership Interface

To create a simulation called Virtual Leader, SimuLearn first mapped out the most common generic actions considered and used by a leader. They are summarized on this table:

Table of possible leadership cyclical actions.

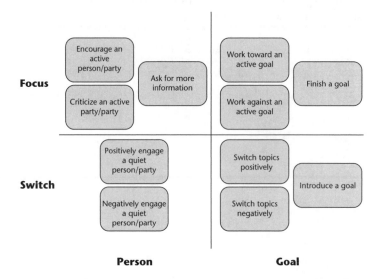

And as with most cyclical actions, all of these have timing and magnitude components and can be infinitely combined (if not equally successfully). For example, in a meeting, consider how you might introduce an idea with different magnitudes:

- Introducing an idea with force establishes it as your idea. You attach some of your credibility to it. You get credit if it is agreed to, and later if it works. If you are the CEO in some conditions, the senior team falls into place in support of it, and alternatives are never discussed.
- But if you introduce the same idea softly, you can separate it from you. People will debate it on its own, consider alternatives, and possibly even build up some momentum against it. If it succeeds, no one even remembers how the idea came up. But it also may succeed exactly because the participants have come to think of it as their idea.

Both approaches to idea introduction are valid, but they impact the leadership system differently.

This table was used to create the leadership simulation interface.

The following sections describe some other actions (and their corresponding interface) from different Sims. My goal here is not to be complete, but to advance your understanding by showing how some designers solved some problems.

An interface designed to present possible leadership actions. The interface to SimuLearn's Virtual Leader presents one-click, real-time access to a variety of different actions, including "bring in quiet person" or "switch ideas," each with an associated magnitude

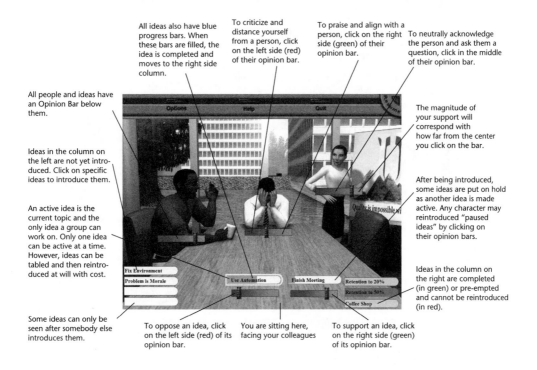

All ideas also have blue progress bars. When these bars are filled, the idea is completed and moves to the right side column.

To criticize and distance yourself from a person, click on the left side (red) of their opinion bar.

To praise and align with a person, click on the right side (green) of their opinion bar.

To neutrally acknowledge the person and ask them a question, click in the middle of their opinion bar.

All people and ideas have an Opinion Bar below them.

The magnitude of your support will correspond with how far from the center you click on the bar.

Ideas in the column on the left are not yet intro-duced. Click on specific ideas to introduce them.

After being introduced, some ideas are put on hold as another idea is made active. Any character may reintroduced "paused ideas" by clicking on their opinion bars.

An active idea is the current topic and the only idea a group can work on. Only one idea can be active at a time. However, ideas can be tabled and then reintro-duced at will with cost.

Ideas in the column on the right are completed (in green) or pre-empted and cannot be reintroduced (in red).

Some ideas can only be seen after somebody else introduces them.

To oppose an idea, click on the left side (red) of its opinion bar.

You are sitting here, facing your colleagues

To support an idea, click on the right side (green) of its opinion bar.

Assigning Roles

In Lionhead's The Movies, players must complete the activity of assigning (hopefully the right) characters to critical roles in a movie production before moving to the activity of rehearsals, then the activity of shooting the movie. Players make each selection by dragging the character's icon into the chosen box.

Raising Awareness in Voters

In the Dean for America game, players must complete different simple activities to raise awareness in voters, including handing out pamphlets, going door to door, and waving signs. In this example, as a microcosm, they have to move to a position with the most people and display their signs. These actions were chosen by the mini-game designer for their correlation with real-world activities.

The activity of assigning roles.

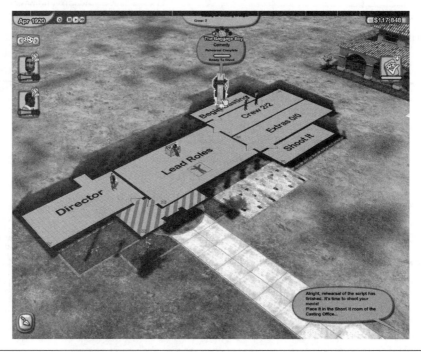

Source: Microsoft product screen shot reprinted with permission from Microsoft Corporation.

The activity of raising awareness in voters.

Source: Screen shot courtesy of Persuasive Games LLC.

Orchestrating and Optimizing

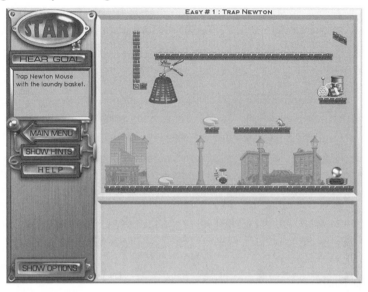

In Return of the Incredible Machine: Contraptions, players must place unique objects to direct the predictable, on-screen movement of a few objects toward a preset goal.

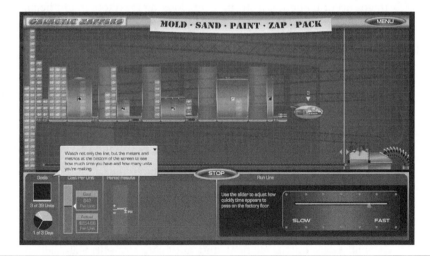

Source: Acton Foundation for Entrepreneurial Excellence.

In this Acton Business School simulation, players must successfully build an assembly line to maximize profits, focusing on throughput, quality, and appropriateness to the task.

Traditional Sim Actions

Games and simulations generally include some or all of the following actions:

Move

To move something is to change its location. Most first-person Sims have common and consistent controls for moving the player's avatar. In a third-person Sim, the move commands can also change the position of the camera.

Use

Using something means engaging with an on-screen object, often for a single task. For example, a player may "use" a door to open it, "use" a light to turn it on, or "use" a found scrap of paper to pick it up, read it, and store it.

Pick Up Tools

"Pick up tools" is the generic term for selecting and keeping items for productive use. When inventory is limited, this might include balancing between need and space. Even if space is not limited, units might only take what they need or might need. If there is a strong need, looking for a tool might become a priority.

Select

To select something is to identify an item or group of items for subsequent action. For example, a witness may *select* a probable assailant from a lineup. A president may *select* a country to invade. A consumer may *select* a box of cereal to buy. An investor may *select* a stock to tag and watch.

At an interface (basic input) level, a game can offer different ways of selecting elements:

- Click: Left-click or right-click with a mouse or other device.
- Click and select all: Click on one item to automatically select all items that meet the same attribute.
- Fill: Click on an element and automatically select all elements that both meet a similar attribute and are tangential.
- Draw: Drag a pointer around a map to identify a location by putting a closed shape around it.
- Lasso: Draw a closed shape, and then identify only certain elements inside it.

Graphic elements that are selected are often highlighted. For more on Sim actions, see Chapter Twenty-One.

Switch Lenses

A participant who switches lenses is choosing to see the same experience differently, including through a new situational awareness. "Lens" can refer to an actual vision aid or to other aspects of perceiving the game.

Switching lenses can involve

- Looking through a different filter or point of view
- Tracking events with time slowed down or sped up
- Zooming in or zooming out
- Seeing or tracking different units
- Tracking different variables

The new point of view can make the participant aware of new aspects of the map. In the real world, for example, a dog's lens—its sense of smell—reveals animal tracks that humans can perceive only in newly fallen snow.

A new lens can become available as the result of discovering a new process, or by using different sensors. In a multiplayer Sim, different people can have access to different lenses.

Related topic: "Situational Awareness," in Chapter Nineteen.

Automate

Automating something means having the AI, reflexes, or a simple set of rules take control of a unit or an activity for the player. This can help the player avoid micromanagement or stop attending to a boring and repetitive task.

Automating a unit in a Sim usually produces actions that are about 70 percent efficient, so a good player is not motivated to automate to gain a competitive advantage.

In some Sims, as participants advance to higher organizational or game levels, they find that tasks that had to be done manually at lower levels are automated. This frees up their attention for new, higher-level tasks.

Also called *autopilot*.

Whiff

To whiff is to fail utterly. A whiff occurs when a participant puts all available energy toward an action, only to miss or otherwise have no effect. The term comes from basketball or golf, when a player swings at but completely misses the ball.

Questions for Researching Actions

It is common for researchers to build up complicated and accurate data models of systems and relationships, without ever thinking about the choices and decisions that people have to make as they work through those systems. Here are some thought-starters:

- What does a company's top salesperson do when talking to a prospective client?
- What did your CEO or president do at 10:15 today? Why?
- How does a top researcher begin the process of collaborating on a new idea? What are possible options, and how is the right approach selected?
- What are the fifteen things you did today around food? How did the actions change from meal to meal? And why?
- What patterns of actions did a historical leader choose? What were other options, and why were they rejected?

Here are some of the questions to ask when researching actions:

- What does an expert actually do all day? What are the individual activities?
- What is the collection of options that experts are constantly evaluating? Why do they do one rather than another?
- How do experts know whether they have done an activity too soft or too hard?

A List of Actions

How would you create an interface design for the following:

allocate	call	convince
analyze	call for help	court
argue	calm	cover your back
ask	change reporting	create
assemble	structure	create contract
assign	clean up	create wedge
beg	comfort others	cut corners
believe	comfort self	cut someone out of the
borrow	conclude	loop
build	confess	decrease pain
buy	connect	describe

destroy	misdirect	show interest
disarm	not believe	show up
draw	order	sign up for
eat well	order someone to do	slow down
exaggerate	something	speak
excite	organize	steal
exercise	outsource	stop activity
expend effort	pair up	submit to peer pressure
find	pay less	suppress noise
find someone or something	pay more	swap
flex power	place sensors	take apart
flirt	play death match	take someone off duty
follow practices	play hardball	take shortcut
get an audience	play king of the hill	thread needle
get credit	point	threaten
get revenge	present	trade
give	probe	travel
go it alone	put out fires	turn on alarm
hire	quit	turn off alarm
hurry up	race	use
identify	remove contagion	use a friend
increase pain	rent	wait
inquire	repair	walk
insert wedge	run	watch
introduce	sacrifice	work overtime
lie	sanction	write
listen	scapegoat	write up
mail	scare	
make noise	schedule	
make oneself more	select	
attractive	set priorities	

Some actions impact activities and process, and some actions impact big and middle skills. Some actions impact both simultaneously.

The Hardest Action for a Serious Game Player—Doing Nothing

Getting the hang of thinking in terms of actions can require a shift in mind-set. Many games are *twitch games*—the ones where you act or you die. In games like Tetris, for example, it's necessary to manipulate falling objects quickly, and even

Actions impact both processes and big skills, sometimes simultaneously.

a moment's hesitation at the later levels spells Game Over. The timer is a great game element, adding excitement to otherwise dull activities (both in Sims and in real life).

So it is understandably difficult for players of simulations, and for simulation designers themselves, to embrace the action of "doing nothing." Staring at a screen with things moving around on it seems to cry out for action if action is possible.

Yet doing nothing at the right time is critical to the successful execution of many big skills, like project management and stewardship, so a successful Sim has to be able to develop this aspect of the skills.

Some "do nothing" moments can be a matter of timing. It is the length of the pause that can separate good from great. Or even failure from success.

Think of a great pianist playing Mozart. The nuanced timing is critical, even if the sequence and broad timing are predetermined.

Think of being in a position of high authority, such as a CEO. Do you give your opinion on a new concept before others have weighed in on it? Or think of driving a car. Do you turn the wheel right now just because you can?

And then there are the issues of doing nothing at all. Do you intervene when your top salesperson is flirting with another employee? Do you introduce your great new idea when the team is excited and working hard on their good-enough plan? Do you as an instructor intervene and "give help" to a student who is challenged by a hard simulation?

Now, building the interface to support "doing nothing" can also be tricky.

Branching stories always focus on the next action. Do you want to do a, b, or c? Now one of those choices of action can be "do nothing." But that may make as much sense to the participants as shutting down Microsoft Windows by clicking on "start."

The easiest thing, in a real-time interface, is just let the player actually do nothing. But does a player even appreciate that doing nothing is actually a successful action? Do you need to visualize the value of doing nothing? Do you have a recharging energy bar or a growing city? Some games accomplish this through the concept of earning interest. If you don't spend money that you could spend, you have 20 percent more in the bank the next turn (a fact that may be described each turn).

Linear content is biased toward action. In stories, heroes do great things. Articles about successful scientists or CEOs are sequences of the right steps. Adjectives like *bold* or *skilled* appear a lot.

But to make the transition to learning by doing, it is necessary to embrace the concept of "doing nothing," and both look for it in the experts whose skills form the basis for instruction and develop it in the participants as consciously as any other action.

6

MIDDLE SKILLS

Design Patterns for More Complicated Actions

Some actions in a Sim are more complicated than just *move* or *use*. These actions or combinations of actions are *middle skills*, which are the layer between actions and big skills such as gathering evidence, directing people, or budgeting.

Middle skills can be combined with either big skills or actions, and have these properties:

- Middle skills require finesse and calibration.
- Middle skills are easy to describe (that is, simply raising awareness of them is easy) but challenging to apply appropriately.
- Middle skills often require *indirect* influence of the on-screen units, something that works well for simulations.

Quite a few middle skills are used in different forms across multiple examples and genres of educational simulation, just as weapons, vehicles, and exploding barrels have proliferated in more traditional computer games. Having said that, future computer games designers would do well to include many of these middle skills themselves, as they add some substance and meaning to connect more traditional game activities.

Most middle skills are necessary for most big skills.

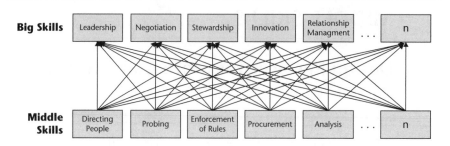

Types of Middle Skills

To some degree, the middle skills discussed in this chapter represent generalization of concepts across many different categories, professions, even industries. The formulation of a middle skill is akin, somewhat, to the ways that words evolve. For example, the word *router* came out of railroad jargon, and now is used more often to describe a part of a computer network. For each of these examples, imagine how to execute them using the basic actions and basic inputs from the last chapter. Later, think how to combine them to execute big skills.

Alignment of Strategies and Tactics

Strategic and tactical alignment is the basic meta-strategy of following up long-term strategic decisions by making short-term decisions and actions to take advantage of the enabled condition.

For example, if an organization hires a great researcher it should be sure to assign that person some important accounts and set up a compensation plan to provide that person great equipment, top notch facilities, and a supportive staff.

Success in any open-ended campaign requires aligning strategies and tactics.

Analysis

Analysis is the middle skill of using broad labels and major themes (and possibly detailed citations) to identify what happened and why in:

Source: Jay Cross, Internet Time Group.

- Behaviors of individuals (as seen in a Sim or captured in a case study)
- Prepared artifacts (such as a book)
- Communities (such as historical events)
- Use of tools and technology

Some analysis strives to have predictive qualities. Analysis may include dragging items into taxonomies, Venn diagrams, or time lines.

Analysis requires awareness and can lead to understanding complex systems.

Some media pretend to do analysis while really interested in reinforcing assumptions. Analysis is the favorite skill of most schools.

Bubble World Calibration

A bubble world is an environment that provides rich feedback and context and that has a deep set of consistent rules, but is nonetheless primarily self-referential and has poor fidelity with the real world or a larger context.

Examples of bubble worlds:

- Schools (with the exception of some labs)
- Math (discussed in more detail in "Sims and the Nature of Math," in Chapter Seventeen)
- Single-player computer games and campaigns
- Monopolies
- Charity foundations
- Gated communities
- Start-up companies before customers
- Ecosystems with few predators
- Certain books
- Sports
- Badly designed immersive learning simulations
- Story worlds
- Games
- The office of the president of the United States

Bubble worlds are almost inevitably the result of sophisticated containment patterns. For example, Australia's ecosystem has oceans to protect it, and the White House has surface-to-air missiles.

Creating a temporary bubble world is a critical part of nurturing and stewardship. For example, a wounded soldier may spend time in a hospital. A new company may get venture capital or state funding. Existing in a bubble world can also help members think strategically, away from the tactical concerns of day-to-day life.

Sometimes a leader might create a smaller bubble world (such as a skunk works) to protect innovative employees from a larger bubble world (a corporation); the smaller bubble world may actually be more aligned with the world outside the corporation or with certain customers. Likewise, in a negotiation, a break may be called to create an opportunity for both parties to meet one-on-one in an unofficial venue (like a bathroom or outside).

However, over time, if in a bubble world for too long, community members often develop superstitions, groupthink, and counterproductive rituals.

Weaning someone from a bubble world is a critical skill, and often requires some form of practice environment and microcosm.

Changing Level of Alignment

Changing alignment level is the middle skill of influencing or creating positive or negative associations between factions, people, or ideas.

Politicians set up activities like PR operations and perform actions like "shake hands" or "appear in news clips" to seek to form alignment with groups of people. Corporations try to create alignment between consumers and their products, often through branding. Universities cite great thinkers.

Creating productive alignment is often called "winning hearts and minds" in a war.

Conflict

Conflict is the middle skill of using techniques to reduce others' capabilities, processes, or value when two or more participants or teams compete for the same zero-sum resource. Many people assume competition in a game, and realize only afterward that a better solution is cooperation.

Containment

Containment is the middle skill of creating and setting up the appropriate walls, barriers, or membranes, as well as doors, to restrict access to a valued area.

Conflict. Reducing the capability of others takes many shapes.

Containment. How many containment zones can you find in this picture?

For example, airport security creates zones of various safety levels, each accepting only people with certain attributes. Correspondingly, cells and bodies have walls to keep out viruses and the wrong chemicals. Clubs, chat rooms, and other communities allow participation by some people, including members, guests, and workers, and not others.

Some units are designed specifically for breaking walls. Different security strategies include various levels of walls and other forms of protection. Some walls have back doors that circumvent traditional security measures.

Other examples of containment:

- A key activity of law enforcement is to contain a crime scene to avoid contamination.
- Networks should have firewalls.
- Enterprise information, from research to salaries to short lists for promotions, is shared only selectively.
- Apartments have walls, doors, windows, locks, and possibly alarm or alert systems.
- Some managers contain employees, either by protecting employees from politics and bureaucracy, or by keeping the employees from making mistakes.
- Skunk works protect their working employees from traditional processes.
- New projects are tested in contained pilots that allow easy measurement and, when involving technology, reduce risks of causing network failure.
- Privacy is a measure of the containment people put around themselves.
- On a conceptual market map, organizations want to contain access of competitors to their most profitable areas.

Creation and Implementation of New Actions or Processes

This is the middle skill of putting together new ways of accomplishing activities and delivering value.

New actions require long-term planning to predict, and the ability to mutate to create. In some cases, the new process has to be contained.

Deception

Deception is the middle skill of making, often at a cost, a part of a community believe that some action, system, goal, or result is different from what it really is.

Deception is often done through communication.

- For example, one might amplify or damp information. The George W. Bush White House tried, mostly successfully, to keep photographs of soldiers' coffins out of the press, to defer the costs of the war, and to avoid discussing war budgets or other costs.
- One might outright lie. Apple's Steve Jobs famously said, "People don't want to watch video on their iPod" at the same time Apple was developing a video iPod. George W. Bush said that Defense Secretary Rumsfeld would "remain with him until the end of his presidency" at the same time he was planning Rumsfeld's replacement.
- President Bill Clinton said, "I did not have a sexual relationship with that woman," which is a true (if still deliberately and highly misleading) statement if sexual relationship is defined very specifically, and an outright lie if sexual relationship is defined more broadly.

One can also deceive through actions, referred to as *feints*.

- In basketball, an offensive player may give a head fake, looking and even beginning to move one way to encourage the defensive player to commit to the wrong direction, before moving in the opposite direction.
- A Wall Street firm may buy a bit more of a stock it already owns in bulk to set off a rally, and then sell a lot at the new, higher price.
- A general may send a small group of soldiers to attack in one place, hoping to draw the other army's defenders to that place, weakening the defenses when the larger army attacks in a different place.

If a deception is found out by the community, it costs alignment.

Estimating Benefits

Estimating benefits is a matter of determining within a range of error of typically 15 percent what benefits will come from a plan—without concrete knowledge on which to base the estimate.

Estimating Costs

As with benefits, estimating costs involves looking at a plan and being able to determine how much it is going to cost, typically within a similar margin.

Expulsion

Expulsion is getting rid of an unwanted unit.
Also known as *firing, termination*.

Extraction

In a systems model, extraction means removing something nonrenewable, often of value, from a system.

Resources such as copper, aluminum, coal, and oil can be extracted from high-value locations, reducing the locations' value. *Extracting* value is often confused with *creating* value, but is nonsustainable.

Tetris ® and © 1985 – 2009 Tetris Holding, LLC, used with permission.

Fit

Fit is the middle skill of bringing together different building blocks with minimal gaps, overlaps, or waste; making or finding a shape that fits into another shape.

Leaders throughout history, or people looking for a spouse, or engineers, or project managers, or IT people, spend a lot of time searching for a good fit. Fit requires balanced inputs.

Fit can be mechanical:

- Parts of a car should fit together tightly enough so that there is not ever a rattle. Replacing any one piece, or even augmenting an entire function, requires the right fit.
- Puzzle pieces or elements from the game Tetris fit together seamlessly.
- Elements of an ecosystem fit with each other.
- Fit is essential to smooth business processes. Every time a truck leaves half-full or a document sits on a desk for days waiting for a signature, it is a sign of bad fit.
- Chemical components fit together to make complex molecules such as DNA.
- One type of fit is the way ornaments hang on a Christmas tree, an open-ended fit. (Much software is written to provide a Christmas tree style back-bone, with new code riding on top using something called an API as the hook. Operating systems work this way.)
- If you fit the wood together too tightly in building a fire, there is no room for air, and the fire dies.

And most confusing, fit can be a social matter:

- The right team, the right divisions of a company, the right communities, all have great fit. The pieces interlock, and it is hard to know where one ends and the other begins.
- When hiring a new person, we often look for compatibility with the old team.
- Marriages form interesting patterns of fit, from bad boys and teachers (think George W. Bush and Laura Bush) to geeks and babes.
- Sometimes an organization's leadership fits like a good marriage—for instance, a dynamic CEO with a budget-crunching no-ego number two.
- The way an individual fits into a group can vary. Actor Alan Arkin spent time in the comedy troupe Second City and said the best part of the experience was learning to know his place on the stage—leading man, comedy relief, foil, love interest—as it changed from one skit to the next.

- There are even deliberately discordant fits, as when a supervisor, agent, or director might shake up a group by adding a new member to a stale group, be it a work group or artist.
- There are "natural fits." People hire people like them, people marry people like their parents. Some natural fits have negative consequences, such as the enabler and the addict.
- Salespeople have to adjust their behavior to create an initial fit with potential customers and then find the fit between potential customer and offerings.
- Children need parents. When they don't have father or mother figures, they often look for that kind of fit in others.
- Political speeches and comedy have to fit with the audience, and the tighter the fit, the better.

Challenges around fit include finding pieces, assigning roles, knowing what the hole looks like, when to go for perfection rather than settle for good enough, and when to assign multiple roles.

Gathering Evidence

Gathering evidence is the middle skill of sifting through 90 percent extraneous information and communication, 3 percent misinformation, and 5 percent disinformation, to find the 2 percent relevant information. (Yes, I made up these numbers—but they feel like they often come close to reality.)

In a Sim, a participant can gather evidence by clicking through media links, making multiple-choice inquiry decisions or budgeting zero-sum resources (including time), and observing the results.

Gathering evidence is facilitated by a working hypothesis, although that hypothesis can be modified or outright discredited.

Gathering evidence is part of due diligence and researching.

Long-Term Planning

Long-term planning involves creating assumptions about the future, understanding the present, and creating a plan or path to be best positioned when the future arrives.

Long-term planning often focuses on best-case, worst-case, and probable outcomes.

Maintenance

Maintenance is the middle skill of putting resources toward keeping existing units functioning at acceptable levels.

Maintenance requires some type of resource, such as time or parts, and therefore has to be budgeted, which contributes to a thing's total cost of ownership. Without maintenance, some things break or overheat. It may be a strategy to save money by deferring maintenance. Typically, deferred items cost more to fix than if they had been properly maintained.

Maintenance in Sims

In The Sims, items such as dishwashers need maintenance or they break, possibly causing damage. In Sid Meier's Civilization series, vehicles have an automatic maintenance cost, limiting the total number of vehicles a player can have. In SimCity, mayors control the road maintenance budget. When it is too low, the roads develop potholes.

New processes may reduce the need for maintenance.

Introducing New Processes

In models of work, this is the skill of making available and using a new, higher-value process for an individual or organization.

New processes typically are the result of technology or insight and allow a person or organization to better meet traditional desires or to begin to meet emerging desires. This could include the creation of an aqueducts system, commuter airplane service, self-service at gas stations using credit cards, or the integration of males and females in a single college campus, then dorm building, then dorm floor, then bathroom.

Discover. An organization might specifically invest energy to try to be the first to discover and then implement new processes, or it might evolve out of a functioning ecosystem. Of course, an organization might wait for everyone else to do something first before waddling over and adopting the new process.

In a serious game, new processes might be made available as an award.

Implement. When, how, if, and where to implement a new process is a matter of balance. New processes, such as e-commerce, might augment existing processes, replace some part of an existing process, or require a complete redesign. Each requires leadership to implement and is a form of innovation.

There is a window between when a process is new and when it becomes a global condition or capability.

Two Steps Forward. Technology is, at best, two steps forward and one step back. The science of genetically modifying vegetables is certainly a new process. But when it is aimed at achieving the wrong desired results, such as increasing the distance that a tomato can be shipped, rather than increased growing conditions or creating something more nutritious, the results are more cul de sac than progress.

Calibrating Ownership

"People only support what they create."

—Meg Weatley, LtF Conference 4/22/98

Calibrating the control, responsibility, or the right to derive value is a middle skill in its own right.

Ownership, in life and in a Sim, can take on many forms. Just to rattle off a few examples:

- Ownership of an object (depicted in a Sim as an item in an inventory)
- Ownership of some popcorn (to consume)

Ownership and development. In the Roller Coaster Tycoon game series, participants can develop land only if they own it. Here, a fence shows the border between the amusement park and the forest.

- Ownership of budgeting (one could decide when to drain the accumulator)
- Ownership of a cell phone
- Ownership of an award
- Ownership of a company
- Ownership of territory (depicted in a Sim by borders and shading of maps)
- Ownership of property (one could develop, live, limit access, leverage any home court advantage in a competition, resources to manage, or focus on extraction)
- Ownership of regions (such as coverage of oil multinationals as an analyst, or selling to the Rocky Mountain states, where one might have to battle encroachments)
- Ownership of ideas (if you think of a great idea of a new business while an employee, who owns that idea?)
- Ownership of your dreams (you can decide when to amplify)
- Ownership of responsibility (in a Sim through level design and list of tasks)
- Ownership of profit and loss (or other balanced scorecard metrics)

- Ownership of pets (nurturing and stewardship)
- Ownership of client relationship (the sole right to negotiate)
- Ownership of a team or community (using leadership)
- Ownership of processes (one constantly shifts allocation)
- Ownership of employees (do you care enough to develop them through formal learning programs?)
- Ownership of your own time

Ownership is a typical middle skill; it requires firmness and finesse.

- If you interact with a community and you have too much ownership, you lose support and buy-in. But if you have too little ownership, you lose control and accountability.
- Every start-up company asks equity holders the same question—would you rather own a lot of something small, or a little of something big?
- Anything you own also takes care, housing, and maintenance. Will Wright, when creating The Sims, had one theme that the more you bought and owned, the more time you had to spend taking care of it, fixing it, and cleaning it.
- The notion of both increasing and decreasing ownership is critical in all big skills.
- Ownership is easy to describe and challenging to apply appropriately.
- Ownership can also be depicted graphically with, for example, a color border, even if real life isn't so clean.

Ownership can be taken, bought, awarded, earned, a gift, a right, a blessing or a curse.

Prioritizing

Prioritizing involves changing the order (or weighting) in which a list of activities will be accomplished or otherwise funded. Typically, the top three priorities receive most of any available assets.

Priorities can be set for items or activities that are important or urgent, or that need the most time to come to fruition, or that are dependencies of other activities.

Lists of activities tend to be dynamic, with current activities removed when completed or no longer necessary, and new activities appearing that may themselves be prioritized at the top or bottom of the list. Learning what activities are available may require probing.

Prioritize. In Star Trek: Bridge Commander, the captain prioritizes repairs to the ship in combat by clicking (upper left of the screen) on the most important sections from a dynamic list. Only three areas can be repaired at any given time. Clicking on an item in the top three puts it at the bottom of the list.

STAR TREK and related marks are trademarks of CBS Studios Inc.

Different people may disagree with the priorities. Accomplishing some priorities, such as hiring a new engineer or building a new structure, may cause a subsequent draw on resources.

The act of prioritizing may be a de facto selection of most important activities. If one has ten things to do, but only time to do five, prioritizing eliminates five activities.

Changing the priorities of desired results can subsequently change the priority of activities. For example, a scientist who prioritizes fame over performing repeatable experiments will then emphasize different activities. There is the old joke about the top three priorities for choosing real estate are location, location, and location.

Basic Inputs for Prioritizing

Prioritizing can be done in a Sim by dragging icons, clicking on buttons or icons in a corresponding order, or filling in or selecting numbers. AI characters may change their own priorities, which then changes their perceived topography.

Related topics: "Allocation Triangle" in Chapter Nineteen and "Weighting" in Chapter Twelve.

Probing

In this WILL Interactive simulation, participants take the role of a doctor trying to identify a patient ailment through uncovering key information using both interview questions and diagnostic tools.

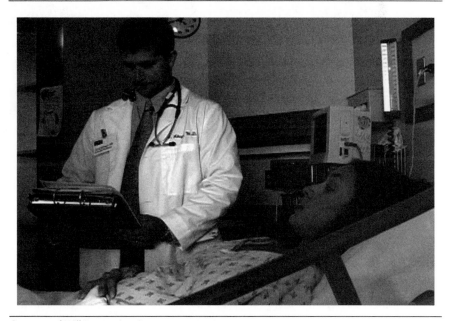

Courtesy of Will Interactive, Inc.

Probing is the middle skill of using resources to try to reveal obstructed spots of a physical or conceptual map, often trying to find locations of high value.

The action of probing might also take time and have only a probability of success. One classic board game of probing is Battleship.

One of Acton Business School's Sims has an unrevealed market map of the relative profitability and demand for each of two dozen products.

Source: Acton Foundation for Entrepreneurial Excellence.

Players probe this map indirectly by discussing needs with individual prospective customers (at a cost of time). They then commit to a single product, and success depends on how well the player has understood the until-then invisible map.

On many maps, it is easier to probe closer locations than more distant ones, and under certain conditions, such as day as opposed to night. Further, probing in someone else's territory can have negative repercussions.

In a military or police investigation, someone being probed is called "a person of interest." The act of probing can imply that a person is unsure. For example, if a lawyer is probing a witness, the opposing lawyer might assume that there is no hard evidence.

Also called *scouting*, *diagnosis*, or *reconnaissance*.

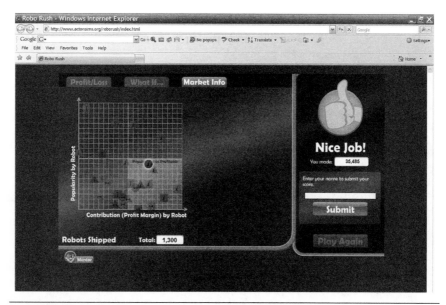

Source: Acton Foundation for Entrepreneurial Excellence.

Author's note: Probing could be used as a major activity in every Sim. There are very few actions that a player should take without looking into the situation. Further, in almost every situation, the more one knows, the better one acts. The problem is that probing is often boring from a game-play perspective. The question of Sim design then becomes, should there always be a probing component, or can we just present "free" access to information and abstract out the probing process? Or can we present a few options and have the player make a single strategic decision on how to allocate probing resources?

Procurement

Procurement is the middle skill of bringing in needed resources. It includes the following elements:

- Substitution
- Shopping

- Creating competition between vendors
- Sourcing, contracting, and outsourcing
- Cost reduction
- Shifting ownership
- Budgeting

Research

In City Interactive's Beauty Factory, players formulate new products and test them.

Research is the middle skill of probing to fill in the unknowns—the fog of war on the knowledge and conceptual map—looking for locations of high value, often at a cost.

Research can include gathering evidence and performing analysis.

Scheduling

Scheduling is the middle skill of planning start and finish dates for involved people and relevant activities.

It includes the following elements:

- Negotiation
- Fit
- Sourcing, contracting, and outsourcing
- Ownership
- Long-term planning
- Budgeting

Selective Enforcement or Breaking of Rules

Deciding when and how to enforce rules is a middle skill in itself.

While hard rules always have to be followed (gravity comes to mind) there are also soft rules, such as the ones that address speeding, or copyright protection, or ethics, or sexual harassment.

The challenges can be many:

- If you work on anything, you have to constantly decide when to break these rules, and what to do to prevent getting caught. This might be loosely akin to so-called first-person sneakers like Thief, when players work hard to not get caught breaking in or out of a guarded building. Most heroes break rules.
- If you are a manager or a teammate, however, then perhaps the challenge will be when to interrupt a well-running process in order to enforce rules, including ethics and sexual harassment. This is never easy. It also might mean setting up containment around rule-breakers.

For individuals or managers, following rules, including procedures, can also lead to a lack of creativity and ownership for results.

There are also meta-rules. Part of the challenge is when to actually challenge the rules.

- This might be challenging the balanced scorecard, primary variables, or score against which you are evaluated.
- This might be destabilizing an entire industry, rendering old metrics obsolete (or at least trying to).
- This might be realizing there are better predictors of success than what is tracked by the current HUD.

Adaptation requires breaking some rules.

Sourcing, Contracting, and Outsourcing

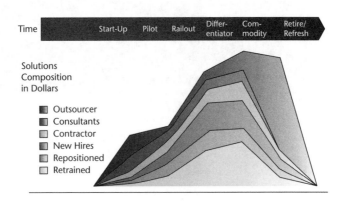

This is a middle skill to produce the right portfolio of skills over the life of the project, balancing cost, skill level, ownership, and flexibility. The following categories can be drawn upon:

- Outsourcers
- Consultants
- Contractors
- New hires
- Repositioned employees
- Retrained employees

Finding the Skills for New Projects

New projects and new processes often require skills that do not exist within the existing employee pool, creating a gap that needs to be filled across the project's life.

Some organizations have outsourced everything, a strategy that gave them the immediate ability to compete, but ultimately was too expensive and rigid. Other companies have tried to develop the capacity from within, only to find that it took too long and the window of opportunity passed.

Many leading organizations take a hybrid path. They have begun with bringing in outside experts in different capacities and jump-started the process. While the project was being designed, they also began a parallel track of building an internal capacity, through formal learning program, augmented by hiring and shadowing. At some inflection point, the primary responsibility could be shifted from external to internal. Finally, near the end of the life of the project, an enterprise once again flips, but time pushing the effort out to low-cost contractors.

Negative Middle Skills

There are also some negative middle skills. While any of the skills already discussed can be misused, the overtly negative ones are explicit easy traps, seen in the real world. They can be presented as choices to any Sim player, just as they would appear to people in the real world.

Churning

Churning involves the emergent system pattern of quickly getting and getting rid of a number of things. Churning often gives the illusion of progress.

Some examples:

- Having an employee quit an unpleasant job, hiring a new person, and leaving conditions untouched, so the newcomer soon quits as well.
- Cleaning out a basement every May, only to fill it up the rest of the year.

Some people can churn for a legitimate profit. Other profits come in a bit more immorally. During the initial savings and loan deregulation, pairs of unsavory individuals would sell the same house back and forth, artificially increasing its sale price and therefore book value each time, jacking it high enough to use as collateral on risky loans.

Kick-the-Can

"Kick-the-can" is the pattern of taking an existing problem and, through actions or refusal to act, forcing it to be resolved at a later time instead of immediately.

Oftentimes, kicking the can makes the problem worse or reduces a unit's ability to deal with it. Creating a multiplayer immersive learning simulation often enables the designers to kick the can of learning goals and objectives to the coach or students.

Microcalibrating

Microcalibrating is the pattern of doing something over and over again making only tiny changes, in the hope of getting significantly different results. Without an intervention, if most players are asked to play a Sim ten times, all of the subsequent plays are microcalibrations of the play before. It often requires a complete failure before a participant will begin the true innovation process.

Naive Commanding

Naive commanding is the pattern of ignoring any invisible system and forcing or repeating a simple action in the hope of getting a simple result. The head of a research university may, frustrated with the lack of patents, order all scientists to work harder and stay later until they meet some artificial goal.

The Critical Role of Middle Skills

Middle skills may be the most important scaffolding in this entire book. While basic actions like sliding a mouse may seem too simple to be interesting, and big skills like stewardship may seem too complex to be accessible, middle skills connect easily to both, and therefore create a pathway between them.

Middle skills are also critical life skills. This chapter, expanded, could be its own stand-alone self-help book or management book. It is hard to imagine a good life without these skills.

Finally, middle skills have fallen through the cracks of most books and most classes. It is hard to find research that would support the rigorous creation of a simulation using them. It is hard to learn about or compare techniques regarding them. Only by listing them and thinking about them can we start the process of appreciating and using them more explicitly.

7

DESIRED RESULTS

Desired results are what a participant or team is trying to accomplish in an experience through using actions (including middle skills and big skills). They are a subsection of all results and outcomes, including positive, negative, trade-offs, and even unintended consequences. Any kind of feedback, in fact, is a type of result. In the real world, achieving a desired result may be done without thinking as part of a normal day, or it can be a stretch goal. Some results are all or nothing, but most are nuanced. Regardless, results require their own dedicated set of descriptors for Sim design and for life.

Defining Results

Desired results can be made up of smaller tasks and objectives, and such a result can be a recursive element of a larger mission. In fact, *results* themselves are often actions that are then plugged back into a larger system, such as in a feedback loop or chain reaction. Accomplishing an objective, for example, may be a key input into getting a promotion or grant.

The desired result can also be called *the object* (as in "What is the object of chess?") or can be called the victory conditions.

A flaw of traditional business analysis, for example, is the tendency to describe "good results" or "bad results" generically. Instead, analysis needs to begin with a description of how success should be measured, even characterized.

Questions to ask of a subject-matter expert when developing a list of desired results:

- What does victory look like? What is the nature of victory?
- What are the trade-offs in victory?
- What are analog components? What are the thresholds?

The following sections include examples and attributes of results outside of the traditional formal learning program desired results of score grade and certification/graduation.

The Mission

The mission is a desired result that is explicitly defined, and for which failure is not an option. Typically, although trade-offs can be made within a mission, there are no substitutes for completing the mission, which often requires at least some conceptual dead reckoning. For related topics, see Chapter Fourteen.

Balanced Scorecard

A balanced scorecard is based on a philosophy of metrics that maintains that no single metric is valuable on its own or safe to optimize in isolation. In addition, the management of any complex system, process, or set of activities should require the creation and monitoring of specialized metrics (see "Primary Variables" in Chapter Twelve), both financial and nonfinancial, aligned with specific strategies, not simply the use of generic metrics.

While all scorecards are different, themes tend to appear. For evaluating leadership, as an example, the four categories are usually variations of these:

- Character and results: We do what we say we are going to do, and we don't cheat along the way.
- Team: We really like working together; we are freed to focus on our own areas of strength and have our backs covered in our areas of weakness.
- Solution sales: We work hard, creatively building on what we have, to meet the needs of the customer, constituent, or sponsor better than any competitor, and get rewarded for it.
- Reinvention: We will be different and better tomorrow than we are today, in part because the world will be different.

Balanced scorecards can align communities with goals and are usually associated with Robert Kaplan and David Norton. During the Walmart "made in China" spike, cost was seen by many as the single most important attribute in a purchasing decision. Then other attributes such as quality, sustainability, and safety became actively valued as well.

Multiple Victory Conditions

There can be different possible types of victory. In the real world, some people may want a large house or a building named after them in a university. Others may value a close and supportive family. Some may want to leave an intellectual legacy, or to be famous. The business best-seller *The Discipline of Market Leaders* by Michael Treacy and Fred Wiersema argues that organizations should choose just one of three different victory conditions to be pursued, because each requires different approaches. Zoomed in, some people may want to just make it through a cocktail party sober, while others may want to network show off their spouse, while still others may want to gossip.

A Sim, just as an organization or individual, need not have a single victory condition. Instead, a level design can allow any player to be successful by achieving one of typically four or five different outcomes.

In some strategy games, including the Civilization computer series, each player has the option of winning by military, political, building, or other universal approaches. In some cases, multiple winners are possible; many or even all of the players can win together.

In some Sims, certain victory conditions are universal, while others might be available only to some players. For example, in the Steve Jackson card game Illuminati, people play different factions that are trying to rule the world.

There are universal victory conditions that can be achieved by any faction, such as taking over a large chunk of the world or eliminating all other players. But there are also faction-specific victory conditions, such as one group stockpiling a huge amount of money, or another group controlling most of the world's computers. In some situations, a player might achieve an exotic victory condition without the other participants even being aware the player was close.

Hidden Victory Conditions

Hidden victory conditions are not known at the beginning of a situation, but emerge through some other type of success, and often supersede the original stated victory condition. For example, by showing kindness to a researcher while working on one product, a person may earn trust and loyalty that results in an entirely new and more powerful product being created.

Creating Value

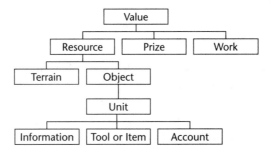

Value is the goal of the use of a system. Value can be a new structure, unit, process, or item. It can be an abstract award, or something that brings one closer to finishing a task or mission, or one or more criteria in a balanced scorecard. It can be work, including the completion of an activity or process.

It can also be a capability, such as a learning goal.

Financial Matters

Both in Sims and in the real world, many desired results focus on money. What follows are some variations.

Funding

Funding involves covering the costs for delivering a value or securing equity. Some would say that funding is the ultimate program goal, and a critical part of applying any economic, value, and governing models.

Profitability

Profitability is a program goal or desired result of having resources left over after costs are subtracted from revenue. Profitability can increase dramatically when an effort taps into economies of scale.

As a program goal, formal learning programs themselves can be profitable if they bring in more than they cost to deliver, and as a desired result, if they can lead to more profitable behavior of participants in an enterprise, such as if researchers were better at getting grants.

The metric of profitability is more important than the metric of revenue for a group, but potentially less important than finding the right long-term economic, value, and governing models.

Return on Investment

Return on investment (ROI)—again, whether in a Sim or outside it—is a desired result of providing positive monetized measurable results (the return) as a percentage of the cost of a program (the investment), minus 100 percent. For example, if a program cost $200,000 to create and deploy, and delivered $260,000 of measurable value, the ROI (return on investment) is 30 percent, figured out as follows: $260,000/200,000 = 130\%; 130\% - 100\% = 30\%$.

The idea is to normalize and compare different investments. If an organization can spend $1,000,000, should it spend it on new hardware, advertising, research and development, or formal learning programs? Ultimately, ownership of stock in a company results in an unpredictable but hopefully positive and better-than-market ROI.

Despite the seeming precision of the ROI metric, it is fraught with vagueness. For example, should the cost of participant time be calculated? This is easy to measure but harder to swallow if one is paying hospital employees to stay past their shift to take a HIPAA compliance program. But how about salaried workers, where the work just piles up for them to do on their own time later on?

Author's note: ROI is often positioned as the highest-order goal of formal learning programs. But ROI is fundamentally an infrastructure and tactical measurement. Telephones themselves don't have an ROI, but switching long-distance carriers does. The location of the corporate headquarters doesn't have an ROI, but the location of a warehouse does. Buying a car doesn't have an ROI (especially a really nice one), but keeping it serviced does. Hiring a new CFO or HR executive doesn't have an ROI, but hiring another call center employee does. The concept of ROI has come out of the manufacturing world. And as with anything constantly changing, you can only measure the success of programs by looking backward. That is, you can only figure out the ROI after the training has happened (and by the way, it doubles the cost of the program just to try).

Defining Common Types of Results in a Sim

Desired results in a Sim (or a level of Sim) are apt to include one or more of these events:

- Completing or managing a process
- Defeating a competitor
- Developing a functioning ecosystem or reengineering a set of processes
- Discovering and implementing a new process
- Arriving at (or holding) a location on a map, including a conceptual map
- Creating an outcome that is measured against a balanced scorecard
- Applying big skills or developing them either in individuals or in organizations

Achieving any game element (see Chapter Sixteen) can also be a desired result. Desired results can involve finishing a level of a Sim or an entire Sim.

In the context of serious games or educational simulation, desired results are not just internal (what the player wants to accomplish in the simulated environment) but external (what the sponsor of the Sim wants to accomplish by having people use the Sim). These can overlap. For example, successfully negotiating (a big skill) with avatars in a Sim might be the desired internal result of a certain educational simulation, and the successful application of negotiating in the real world is the (external) learning goal of the formal learning program that includes it.

Now, most people are comfortable using actions toward accomplishing results in the real world. What they don't realize is that actions don't directly deliver results. Instead, multiple invisible systems get in the way. . . .

PART THREE

SIMULATION ELEMENTS OF SYSTEMS

Connecting Actions and Results

The use of any unknown system is indistinguishable from mysticism.

—With Apologies to Arthur C. Clarke

We all play variations on this type of scenario: What if someone from two hundred years ago watched us live today? What if an ancestor watched us, say, wash dishes? The steps we took, from scraping off the remaining food, to loading up the dishwasher, to putting some form of soap in a small box, to running the disposal, to pressing some buttons and turning a knob, to walking away for an hour, would seem like we were performing mystical incantations.

More specifically, some steps would make sense, some would seem random, and some steps would actually appear to the opposite of what we should be doing. Nonetheless we are completely confident with what we're doing: we understand the system.

Here are other examples of successful uses of systems:

- A couple falls in love with a house on the market. But when the salesperson enters the room, they act bored.
- A project manager, with a deadline fast approaching, fires two programmers.
- A health-conscious actress, a week before a big scene, injects a neurotoxin into her face.
- An environmentalist forester cuts down a third of the trees in a grove.

- A dieter eats a large breakfast.
- A doctor deliberately exposes a patient to a small quantity of a fatal virus.

The Invisible Layer

Systems are the often invisible layer between what we do (action) and what we get (results).

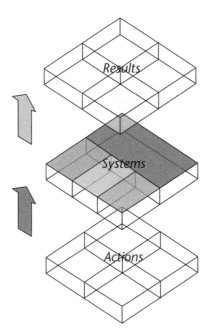

Thus some people are continually surprised by unintended consequences. They don't notice, for example, that naively optimizing just one part of a complex system may have no positive impact on the entire system, and possibly a negative impact.

Meanwhile, other people perform concise actions and get remarkable results. These are the people who understand and can use the invisible systems. "Going to where the puck will be, not to where it is now" requires a working knowledge of the system.

These examples of lables of hidden systems are "the glass ceiling" or "the invisible hand of the market."

Simple and Complex

Most hidden but sometimes not, our world is filled with systems as complex as the universe or simpler than a light switch. And even complicated systems are made up of simpler systems, equations, variables, relationships, processes, units, and actions.

People traditionally learn more from the underlying systems content and interface in an educational simulation than from the story or wrapper. This is also called the "Killing Kings" paradox, as people who play chess don't learn how to kill kings, but they do learn some high-level strategy. Playing a violent computer game does not teach transferable killing skills, but more likely some underlying systems and relationships. The corollary is also true. Most students learn more in classrooms about how to game courses for credit (which over the years they master at multiple levels) than about the actual subject matter.

Complex system. A system that is made up of multiple components, such as equations, units and maps, processes, or other smaller systems. Complex systems often produce counterintuitive results when naively acted upon.

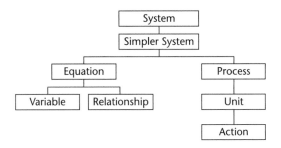

The Seven Models in a Sim

There are seven different techniques for building out educational systems in Sims. All of them are compatible with one another, overlapping, scalable, and recursive. Each will be explained in more detail in subsequent chapters.

Units on Maps as System

Some systems are best captured by the activities of units on maps. Vehicles drive on roads. Armies invade countries. Viruses spread from person to person, or computer to computer. Companies exist in markets. Roller Coaster Tycoon (discussed in "Presenting Choices to Users" in Chapter Fourteen) is one example. Navigation often requires dead reckoning.

Artificial Intelligence as System

Directing or competing against AI characters can represent compelling and repeatably engaging systems.

State-Based System

Some systems are best modeled through an abstracted "units on maps" technique of state-based systems. Most light switches have two states, on and off. Almost all board games from chess to Risk use this as one type of system.

Pure Mathematical System

Some systems are purely mathematical. That is, their primary variables are impacted by aggregations of secondary variables, as defined by equations and relationships. This is the primary model for the Sim genre of interactive spreadsheets.

Work Process as System

One type of system is a work process (or even a time line). Just knowing who gets what business form can spell the difference between success and failure for an activity.

Middle and Big Skills as System

Some systems are middle skills as discussed in Chapter Six, combined with and into the big skills discussed in Chapter Fourteen. In particular, the "Leadership" section of Chapter Fourteen is a useful example.

Community as System

Perhaps the least predictable system is a real community, such as organized by a social networking model. Here are two examples: if other people use less fuel, my cost of fuel goes down; if other people do not watch a television show I like, the show goes away.

What do CIOs want of their HR's IT representative?

Global Performance Management

Develop new competencies

Succession planning

Plan for future IT talent requirements

Recruit targeted or critical talent

Retain strategic talent

Rigorously track talent, including high potentials

Broad focus — Narrow focus

Time to fill position — Diversity

Discretionary training filled

Create skills model and identify broad gaps

Develop internal talent through training and rotational assignments

Engagement

Building and broadcasting career paths and career options

Onboard new employees — Internal filling of position

Broad retention

Create a culture of joint career management

Identify, propagate, and drive corporate HR best practices

Manage a unified and productive global culture

Cheerleader

Training for compliance

Performance review

Performance rating distribution

Job descriptions

Broad training

Headcount

Payroll

Broad recruiting

Benefits

Job posting

HR help desk

Traditional HR Responsibilities

Get out of low-value commodity services

Where possible, teach the person to fish

Sourcing

Establish and manage global sites and centers

Evaluating the quality of outsourcers' work

Balance use of a different sources for the development of specific applications

Creating a network of diverse talent sourcing (such as different outsourcers, contractors)

Managing the contracts with outsourcers

Create contracts

Bring legal perspective

CIO Inner Circle

Represent people issues

Participate with inner circle

Receiving daily CIO phone calls

Mentor or coach the senior team

Participating in non HR strategy

Attend meetings — Speak IT

Re-engineering the HR capacity to better meet IT needs:

Align IT budget and business priorities:

Help IT know the business

Develop business skills in IT

Help IT integrate with business, and represent IT to the business

Lowering cost for legacy IT services

Consolidate and improve application

Identifying and deploying standard global processes

Communicating new or evolving IT strategies and processes to business groups:

Brainstorming and problem solving on business issues around external customers

Change management

Business Facing

Proactive solutions and enabling transformation

A Business Analysis Example of Actions, Systems, and Results

The chart on the previous page is an analysis using the model of actions, systems, and desired results.

The topic is, "What do CIOs want of their HR's IT representative?"

From a traditional analysis perspective, this issue has five broad themes:

- Global performance management
- Support sourcing
- Serve in the CIO's inner circle to advise on all IT issues
- Increase the degree that IT is business facing
- Reduce or eliminate traditional low-value IT responsibilities

The chart maps specific contextual actions (in a Roman font) and short-term results (in italics). In other words, it tells the reader of the research what to do, as well as what to look for as tangential signs of success.

For example, an action in Global Performance Management is "Plan for future IT talent requirements," and a related result metric is "Time to fill position." Likewise, an action within CIO Inner Circle is "Mentor or coach the senior team" and a related result metric is "Receive daily CIO phone calls."

The invisible system is the position on the chart, in terms of distance from the lower-left corner. An IT representative cannot even try to do the higher-value actions in the periphery of the chart before completing the actions and getting the results nearer the lower left corner. The IT representative cannot "participate in the CIO's inner circle" without first being able to "talk IT," and cannot "maintain succession planning" without being good at both "predicting future skills" and "recruiting and retaining strategic talent."

8

MAPS

The Context for Life

Maps populated by units (described in Chapter Nine) are a basic tool for both modeling and presenting a dynamic system. Their importance, complexity, subtlety, and multiplicity of purpose mean that, to use maps well, one has to start by understanding some almost philosophical points about them.

Maps represent abstractions. In the real world, a long drive is easier with a road map than with an aerial photograph.

In simulations, maps are also the complete context of life. Computer-defined units have to exist on maps and be optimized for their environment (just as humans, with our optical bias for yellow-blue light as an example, are optimized for Earth). And one's location on a map determines a great deal, from birth country to airport gate.

Games have almost always used maps as context. From chess to Monopoly to Defender to The Sims to World of Warcraft, the concept of a map focuses the activities. (Card games are an interesting exception, by the way.)

Further, maps are often how levels are defined in computer games. In this role, they often contain mazes, opponents, and hundreds of triggers.

The Nature of Structuring Maps

While simple maps are easy enough to build and use, maps in Sims are more often complex. They can be complex to build, and they can be complex for a player to navigate. Below are two examples: one rigorous and the other subjective.

Layers

Maps have properties. They come in layers. Layers for a geography-based map may include

- Global condition or capability
- Climate

- Territories
- Units
- Structures
- Topology
- Infrastructure
- Resources

Strategy

Maps also shape strategy. Players strive for control, management, growth, personalization, and optimization of their part of the map. Likewise they focus on probes, incursions, take-overs, and surgical strikes in other parts, based on their vulnerabilities, relative value, or openness.

The Canadian Standards Association's Response Ready. Response Ready gave students the ability to identify potential hazards and, for each, associate emergency response procedures. In the mini-game, participants are given a broad panorama of a city scene. Their goal is to identify places on that map that are at high risk. They assign to these areas both a probability of problem and severity of problem if it does occur, which in turn unlocks a set of procedures specific to that risk.

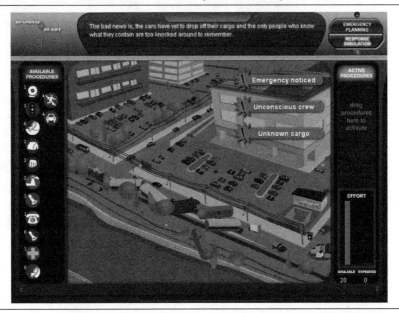

Source: Reproduced with the permission of the Canadian Standards Association and the DISTIL Interactive LTD. From "Response Ready,", which is copyrighted by CSA, 5090 Spectrum Way, Suite 100, Mississauga, ON, L4W 5N6, and DISTIL Interactive LTD., 16 Fitzgerald Road, Unit 200, Ottawa, Ontario, K2H 8R6, Canada. While use of this material has been authorized, CSA & DISTIL shall not be responsible for the manner in which the information is presented, nor any interpretations thereof.

Players have to allocate resources strategically across a map (given where my strengths are, and where I want to go, and my tolerance for risk of failure, where is the next best move?). There might even be places that are easy to move into, or well-defended places that are very hard to move into.

Different Types of Maps

Maps in a Sim can also range from representing highly concrete environments to highly abstract. Here are the two extremes.

Geography-Based Maps

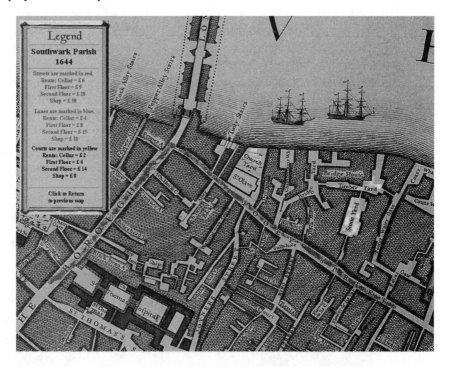

Geography-based maps are virtual-world maps that share major elements with real-world maps. Creating this type of map is critical for educational Sims such as flight simulators and military simulations, serious games such as the history example in the illustration, and realistic computer games.

Geography-based maps need to balance fidelity and abstraction. They can also be drawn at different scales. A realistic model of Yale-New Haven Hospital, for example, could provide the location, including doors and walls, for participants to apply containment strategies and direct people, perhaps to manage a contagion like bird flu, for real training of doctors and staff.

Corporations may use geography-based maps to do cost-benefit analysis around where to build a manufacturing plant to dispense products with a minimum cost of travel.

Geography-based maps can help players develop a sense of dead reckoning.

Conceptual Maps

Maps can be conceptual as well as physical. A conceptual map is a chart of ideas—a collection of elements—with the relative distance between any two elements corresponding to their similarity. In educational simulations, the quality of the conceptual map may well determine whether the Sim will live or die.

Conceptual maps can be process, organizational, and market maps. But the same map attributes exist as with physical maps. People engaged on such maps try to contain secrets or market positions just as much as they would try to contain water and crime scenes and private property in the real world.

It is against these maps that true leaders engage in conceptual dead reckoning.

Conceptual map. Different genres of simulations are plotted along the two continua of process versus dynamic and instructor-supported versus stand-alone.

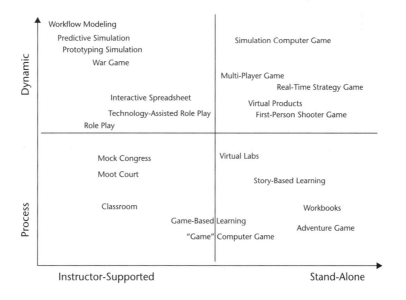

Any collection of ideas can be charted. Conceptual maps, complete with large dark spots labeled "unknown," could include any of the following:

- Differing governing models for a new nation
- Process maps
- Organizational charts
- Different combinations of chemicals and therapy that may cure Parkinson's disease
- A collection of symptoms in a patient
- Market maps, with containment strategies around highly profitable "sweet spots"
- Differing communication genres for conveying a complex idea

While some conceptual maps are created simply by identifying adjacent elements, grid-style conceptual maps can also plot elements against two identified analog attributes that serve as the axes.

Gartner's "magic quadrants," market maps, or Zachman structures are examples of conceptual map genres. A person or organization can occupy a specific location or a broader region or territory on such a map.

The term can be synonymous with "mental map." Related concepts: "Taxonomies" and "Venn Diagram" in Chapter Seventeen.

Specific Map Elements and Related Terms

The following concepts all make a difference in the creation and description of maps for both SIMS and traditional analysis. They are presented in no particular order, as they come together in an almost endless variety of ways.

Arena

An arena is a map on which teams or individuals engage in direct, typically zero-sum competition as their core gameplay. Arenas don't need corresponding setup stories and are often used for dynamically created quick battles, providing instant action with human and AI-controlled players.

Arenas can be tied together in campaigns. Also called *playing fields* or *battlegrounds*.

Attractor

Something that influences resources or units to move toward a certain map area or unit is called an *attractor*.

Arenas take on many forms.

Convention centers can attract people to a real world location.

For example, an engineer might put in a magnet to attract metal filings, a city might put in a convention center to attract business travelers, a manager might hand out stock options to attract more alignment between workers and shareholders, or a nonprofit organization might put up posters to attract people to its bake sale.

Or a town might offer tax breaks to a company, a new salesperson might work on commission only, and a teacher might have to join an organization that has a great reputation for rigor. Choosing the right economic and value models can also make something or someone more attractive.

Just because something attracts, that does not mean resources or units will complete the journey. For example, gravity attracts a flying airplane, but other forces keep it in the air. An advertisement for McDonald's might make someone want to eat a hamburger, but if a Burger King is closer, that might be the destination.

Attractor is the opposite of *repellant*.

Door

A door is a construct that selectively shifts between being a path and a wall.

Doors can be literal, as in the preceding picture, or figurative or conceptual, as with access to a powerful politician, higher education, or a reliable supply of clean water.

Characters or other units might need to have certain items or allegiances, to pay tolls, or to have certain levels of attributes (college degree, employment) to pass through a door. Doors can also block a link.

Placing doors is part of any containment strategy, and doors can provide access to communities, even clubs.

Glass can be thought of as a door, as it lets in light but blocks heat and air. In a greenhouse situation, light passes through glass, converts to heat when it hits an object, and the heat is trapped by the glass.

Wall

A wall is a construct intended to prevent movement or access. Players and biology create walls to keep out enemy units.

Walls, like doors, can be attributes of a structure. Walls are necessary for containment. A teenager's fear of the ocean or lack of knowledge of how to drive a car could each be presented as walls.

Walls can be absolute or porous. They can be designed to let certain types of units pass, while stopping others. Cells, for example, have semipermeable membranes. They can also be destructible.

Building walls is a common action of a player in a real-time strategy (RTS) game.

Contrast walls with paths.

Author's note: Prisons can exist without walls. Picture an ant trapped on a basketball.

Firewall

A firewall is reinforced, special-purpose door (or wall, depending on its current state).

Firewalls can be set at different levels of protection. Building codes require fireproof doors or walls in key locations to contain real fires. Meanwhile, most intranets (internal or private networks using Internet technology) have software- and hardware-based firewalls to isolate them from the Internet and prevent unauthorized access or tampering. These firewalls allow some traffic.

Firewalls, both real and virtual, can sometimes be circumvented by a back door.

For firewalls to be effective, they must be part of a larger containment strategy.

Ecosystem

An ecosystem is a map with a relatively stable group of different types of interconnected and interdependent units.

An ecosystem can be a pond, a partnership including shared business processes between a town government and several private companies, a president's group of senior advisers, Peter the Great's Russia, the manufacturing plant of a large automobile company, or hardware and software developers.

Ecosystems have many attributes:

- Typically, healthy ecosystems produce minimal waste, and they build up some type of value, such as energy, over time. (*Gross primary productivity* is the rate at which a natural ecosystem builds chemical energy.)
- Units within ecosystems complete a variety of activities, in part based on their mental state.
- Different groups, sometimes called species, compete for the same resources within the ecosystem (so-called interspecific competition), sometimes causing conflict.
- Multiple balancing loops are always in play in an ecosystem.
- An entire ecosystem can be viewed as a single unit. All of Earth's natural ecosystems together compose something called the *biosphere.*
- Units often mutate and adapt in the ecosystem, and the entire ecosystem is in constant calibration.
- A diversity of species often allows the entire ecosystem to better adapt.
- Many units in an ecosystem have a symbiotic relationship with each other.
- Ecosystems can be destroyed slowly (referred to as being *degraded*), or quickly by destruction or elimination of critical input energies or the map itself.
- Ecosystems often have indicator species, the reduction of which suggests long-term problems with health of the system. The indicator species might be frogs in a marsh—or creative people in a research department.
- Natural ecosystems provide processes such as purification of water and air, moderation of climate, and breaking down of wastes.

The ownership of an ecosystem is almost always indirect.

Balancing Loop

A balancing loop is a system with a goal of equilibrium.

Here are some simple examples of balancing loops:

- A thermostat-controlled heater has the goal of keeping a room at a constant temperature (sensor, heater).
- Demand for a product amplifies the price; amplifying the price of a product damps its demand (price/demand curve).
- More snakes increase the hawk population, and then more hawks decrease the snake population (hawks convert snake flesh into hawk flesh).

Balancing loops may require some level of critical mass, and also may have significant delays and may overshoot in their attempts to balance.

If one part of a balancing loop fails, the other parts often experience wild fluctuations. For example, if several competing companies merge and form a monopoly, the price of the service and profit of the institutions may increase dramatically, but customer loyalty is reduced. Then, if another competitor or substitute is attracted to the market, the price of the service and profit of the former monopoly crashes as unhappy customers quickly defect. Similarly, if wolves and other predators of deer are removed from a system, the deer population increases. The deer then consume all the available food, after which most of the population starve. Or a general insecticide is used on a lawn to kill ticks, but also kills creatures that eat ticks. The lawn is free from ticks (and tick enemies) for a year. But the ticks return to the lawn faster than the enemies, so the next year, the tick population explodes. Related concept: "Critical Mass" in Chapter Nine.

A balancing loop is the opposite of a chain reaction.

Author's note: Between 1998 and 2005, there was a successful neo-conservative movement in U.S. politics, positioning certain philosophies and solutions. Starting around 2002, a counter-movement developed, including in movies, as a refutation.

Global Condition or Capability

A global condition—the 2008 financial crisis, for example—is something that impacts every location on a map. In Sims, global conditions are triggered, last for a duration, and may then recede. Sometimes local events, such as nationalism in a country, can cause a global chain reaction.

Here is a typical example. With the global condition of the advent of internal combustion engines (arguably a new process), the attribute of presence of

oil on a piece of property significantly increases the property's attractiveness. In an earlier era, the presence of oil would have been a liability.

Likewise, the value of a location on a conceptual map of consumer electronics changes with the global condition of the lowering of the cost of computer chips or flat panel displays.

Also known, in culture, as *zeitgeist*.

Pandemic

A pandemic is a contagion that is spread by and affects units, and that grows in a chain reaction to impact large regions on a map. Pandemics can behave as a single unit, including the ability to move, consume, reproduce, and adapt.

The fourteenth-century bubonic plague outbreak across Europe is one example of a pandemic. Arguably, the spread of McDonald's or Starbucks can also be regarded as pandemics. The impact of a pandemic can resemble a global condition or capability.

Fog of War

Source: Sid Meier's Civilization IV Screenshots Courtesy of Firaxis Games and Take-Two Interactive Software, Inc.

The "fog of war" is named for the phenomenon that happens in a battlefield, or any unexplored or shifting terrain where participants do not know what is going on beyond their sight, but still have to make decisions and take actions that both impact and are impacted by the obstructed areas. It can just as easily be encountered on a conceptual map, such as cures for cancer, as on a literal map.

For example, a couple's parents might push hard for them to have a child, not knowing that they have been trying and can't. Likewise, when accepting a new job (or new employee), one never really knows what one is getting.

Often on a Sim map, as in this example from Civilization IV, a fog of war is represented by a blackness over unexplored terrain and a graying out of terrain that has been explored but is currently out of visual contact.

Certain objects, such as doors or other containment, can block sight. Unknown territory increases cost of travel. Understanding the impact of the unknown is also one challenge of dead reckoning.

In the military, unless a unit can actually see an enemy unit, the exact locations (and more important, intentions) are never 100 percent certain.

Related topics: "Probing" in Chapter Six, "Partial View" in Chapter Nineteen, and "Noise" in Chapter Seventeen.

Home

Home is the place where the player has the most information and options, and is briefed before missions. The player might also be safe there.

High Value

Places on a map (including a conceptual map) that are worth more relative to other places on a map. This could be because of its attributes, location, resources, information, climates, utility, or aesthetic appeal.

Proximity can also add value, as when a transport hub makes a location especially convenient. (For a real-world example, printing giant RR Donnelly built a new facility next to the Reno Stead Airport runway to save on cost of travel.) Adjacent paths or roads can also add value.

In traditional military situations, high value might mean greater height or control of a bottleneck. In corporations, high value might mean a market sweet spot of high profits or high control of standards. Socially, a club can be the spot of highest social value. High value can also refer to the defensibility of location.

Many containment strategies are built around high-value areas. Value can change quickly with changes in global conditions or capability.

Increase Surface Area

Increasing the surface area means growing the perimeter without changing the volume, or growing the perimeter at a ratio faster than the volume.

For example, a research organization might decide to increase the surface area between two internal groups, say such as the lawyers and the scientists, or between the internal organization and external customers or suppliers.

Many containment strategies seek to minimize the surface area between secure and insecure zones.

Market Map

A market map of the U.S. corporate e-learning space in 2001.

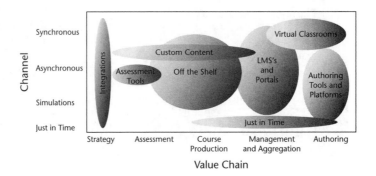

Source: Microsoft product screen shots reprinted with permission from Microsoft Corporation.

A market map is a conceptual map showing vendor capabilities with proximities corresponding to likely expansions.

Maze

A maze is a map where the goal is to travel to the right location (or locations), or get an item (like a key) to the right location, sometimes even requiring the player to learn what the right location is in the process.

Mazes are used extensively in many computer game genres, including first-person shooters and mini games.

Path

Source: Microsoft product screen shots reprinted with permission from Microsoft Corporation.

Paths are links that connect or direct people, processes, work units, or even information and alignments on a map. Essentially, creating the right paths is what great leaders do.

Paths can

- Be bidirectional or one-way (or asynchronous)
- Represent a no, low, or high cost of travel
- Be expensive to build, or cheap, or free
- Connect the right things or connect the wrong things
- Provide access
- Wear down with use (as roads do), or strengthen with use (as with neural paths)

A good example of paths are capillaries, the tiny blood vessels that get nutrients and oxygen to tissues.

Participants create paths on maps, especially in tycoon games, typically by dragging (one of the mouse inputs discussed in Chapter Twenty-One), to connect processes and places.

Leaders spend much of their time strategizing around paths. They phrase the questions in terms like these:

- How do I create better communication between different departments? How do I get different groups to know what other groups are doing?
- How do I build a relationship between users and designers?
- How do I get better access to another group's technology or markets?
- How do I take advantage of the high values of different locations, such as the design skills of Italy, the tech savvy of San Francisco, and the cheap labor of China?
- How do I build alignment with trustees?
- Are the current organizational lines right, or should I reorganize (destroy old paths and create new ones)?

A few real-world examples: Every canal and channel ever dug provides a path from somewhere to somewhere. And paths need not be physical: Xerox's PARC research center has a permanent video link to its sister research organization in France, connecting two well-traveled hallways.

Paths can charge for access, such toll roads. A path is the opposite of a wall. Also called roads.

Resources

In a work process, resources are inputs, somehow limited, that are consumed for maintenance, growth, or production. So the real question is, Who needs what?

Examples of resources (and their uses):

- Grassland (to support cows)
- Goodwill (to get access to top people)
- Money (to buy food)
- Labor (to produce cheap goods)
- Oxygen (to support the heart)
- Electricity (to run a building)
- Ideas (to support a lab)
- Building space (to expand facilities)
- Bandwidth (to keep media flowing)
- Computer memory (to run advanced programs)
- Legal advice (to battle lawsuits)
- Food and water (to sustain life)
- Information (for a news story)
- Access (to let cows graze)
- Units or actuators (to do work)
- Structures (to house workers)

For success in certain situations, resources need to be budgeted and allocated well. Resources can be produced, gathered, transported, refined, consumed, and bought or traded.

Resources may be finite or infinite. Where resources are infinite, they may still require other finite resources to enable them. A farm might be able to produce crops infinitely, but need water, sun, compost, and time.

Some resources can be infinite as long as some portion, called the principle, is left intact. The codfish, for example, could have been considered infinite in the ocean off Massachusetts three hundred years ago, but because it was overfished, today it is commercially extinct. Grass, likewise, can be overgrazed.

When time is the primary enabler or barrier, the resource is considered renewable or regenerative. Water in a bucket or well might be thought of as renewable with rain.

Increases in cost of a resource may reduce consumption or drive a search for and use of substitutes.

Increases in productivity can reduce the need for resources or result in greater output. Temporary delays in getting resources can delay production or shrink infrastructure. Permanent limits on the availability of a resource, when there is no substitute, can limit the growth of a system. Other features of resources:

- The consumption of a resource can produce waste.
- Budgets should track resources, and the better budgets cover more types of resources (tracking ideas and not just dollars, for example).
- The notion of limited resources drives competition.
- Access to resources, as in a corporation, may require approval and security clearances.

Any map location can have resources that provide value to the player. Often, these resources can be tapped if a player meets one or more of the following conditions:

- Has the location in owned territory
- Has access to it from units
- Builds a road or path to it
- Builds a structure on it

Resources might be everlasting, seasonal, regenerative, or consumable.
Related topics: "Real-Time Strategy" in Chapter Three and "Inventory" Chapter Nine.

Source

A source is a place or unit that produces some resource or waste that affects the game. A source may need to consume other resources.

Strength of Position

The strength of a position on a map is an index of how easy or hard it would be to displace the current owner.

Table

A table is a column- and row-based matrix (a simple form of a map, but don't tell that to the people who are building them) that shows how various elements relate to one another. Tables of numbers are used when equations are not accurate enough. For example, if a company was building a simulator of driving a car, its designers might use a "close enough" mathematical equation to describe the car's breaking ability at different speeds, or they might use a high-fidelity table to precisely describe breaking at very specific predefined intervals.

Tables, to be effective, require rigorous data, such as gathered from wind tunnels or mounted speed sensors.

Territory

Territory is the part of a map, including conceptual map, owned by a player.

Related topic: "Calibrating Ownership" in Chapter Six.

Topography

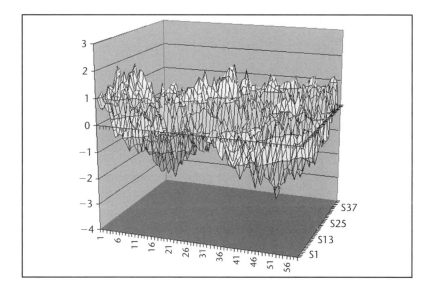

A view of a map that focuses on one or two attributes illustrates the topography—the detailed arrangement—of those attributes.

A typical (and literal) attribute for a map topography is height, and different altitudes may be displayed with different associated colors. But the attributes, depending on the filter, can just as easily be oil deposits, ease of defense, or amount of sun exposure.

Topographies can also be aggregated, addressing questions such as, "Of every room in my house, what is the current attractiveness of each?"

This topography also changes, depending on whether I am thinking about eating, working, or sleeping (or other activities). Topographies also change with the presence of structures and units.

Author's note: Most military units value "high ground," both because it provides a great view and because it is easier to do work, such as attack or defend, from that position. Similarly, social relationships also have high grounds, where certain situations and actions give one party an advantaged place from which to do work.

Value of Proximity

Proximity value refers to a condition by which some value increases the closer together two resources are and decreases the further apart the resources are. Examples:

- Volunteer organizations can serve a community better the closer they are located to it.
- Voltage drops the further a house is from the transformer or power station.
- Political power increases the closer one gets to the top of an organization.
- Sound gets less powerful as it moves from the source, using an equation called inverse square.
- A retailer can add another store more efficiently if it is close to an existing warehouse.
- Teams of people can bond more naturally if they are co-located.

Related topic: "Cost of Travel" in Chapter Nine.

Random Map

A random map defines an unpredictable game space that still follows enough rules to make it playable. To meet a participant's request for a random map, a Sim might use a prepared map stored in a large database, or it might dynamically create one. Participants might be given the ability to influence some aspects of the map, including difficulty adjustment or the number of occurrences of certain features.

Random maps, especially arena-style, support instant action and open-ended campaigns.

Some Sims randomize the unexplored sections of a map every time the software reloads, minimizing the cheat of saving (that is, bookmarking) one's place.

Random map. In the dictator Sim Tropico, players can define attributes to a random map generator.

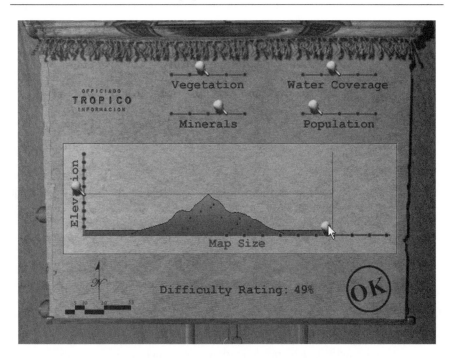

Triggers

Finally, a trigger is something in a system that reacts to a specific condition and brings about some discrete and significant change, or at least presentation of information. Triggers are best understood by their role on traditional maps, but they can also exist in completely abstract systems, including mathematical systems.

Any definition of a trigger needs at least two sections: first, the condition that sets the trigger off (including the necessary sensor), and second, the consequences (often multiple consequences) that occur when the trigger is set off.

From a design perspective, triggers are the reverse of primary variables (discussed later, in Chapter Twelve). While primary variables tick up or tick down, always ready to be calibrated, triggers are typically all-or-nothing: they are the built-in answer to the question, What changes everything?

For example, in a game world, your character, after losing health (a primary variable), might die (a trigger). In the real world, after working hard to improve organizational productivity (a primary variable), you might get a promotion (a trigger). After working hard to figure out a solution with a prospective client (a primary variable), you might get the contract (a trigger). After building support for your bill in the legislature (a primary variable), you might get a favorable vote (a trigger). Of course there are failure triggers as well: losing a big client or having a factory break down reflect changes in variables such as customer satisfaction and plant maintenance.

When studying what a subject matter expert knows and does, the question is, What are events that, if they happen, are (at least temporarily) irreversible and change the dynamics of the situation?

Author's note: A person pulls a trigger of a shotgun and kills a quail. One can only imagine how hard it would have been to kill that quail without a shotgun. Likewise, the notion of a trigger in practice boils down to "what is the least amount of work I can do to have the biggest possible reaction?" I throw a rock and a window shatters. I swipe a credit card and walk away with six new shirts and a great pair of shoes. I buy a stock and lose a lot of money.

Map-Based Triggers

Many types of triggers are strewn across maps in games of all sorts. These maps may be activated by predefined activities such as when a player (or other unit) moves on, moves off, moves through, or uses an item. On the screen, the results of setting off a trigger may be to

- Play video, quote, or animation
- Get bonus supplies
- Clear fog of war
- Finish the level with a win or lose
- Change the player location
- Change the current goal
- Change an attribute such as health
- Show tip and highlight object

Metrics-Based Triggers

Sometimes the system in which triggers are set is more theoretical, although they may have the same result in the Sim as the map-based triggers. Accomplishing any task, objective, goal, or mission is typically a trigger.

Table-Based Triggers. A table-based trigger is a special type of trigger that is activated by the behavior of two or more tracked variables, including (possibly) the position of character and time.

Table-based triggers are used extensively in interactive spreadsheets and other pure-math-based systems to deliver in-game tips and directions (for example, if market share drops for more than three consecutive terms in the first half of the Sim, play full-motion video of supervisor highlighting the problem and suggesting solutions).

Systems That Act as Triggers. Finally, there are organic systems that have many of the properties of set triggers. Feedback loops (where the rich get richer) and chain reactions represent trigger-like behavior, even if no predefined triggers are at play.

Related concepts: "In-Game Tips and Directions" in Chapter Seventeen, and "Autosave Trigger" in Chapter Eighteen.

9

UNITS

How CEOs, Presidents, and Hostile Aliens View Life on Earth

For creating many types of systems, creating units is critical. Units are self-contained, distinguishable, discrete objects. Units exist in a context, typically on a straightforward map (described in Chapter Eight) or in higher-levels maps such as work process (Chapter Thirteen) and with other units. They can move, often along paths. They have attributes, and sometimes momentum.

When on a map, their geographical position matters. They can probe, and might have some advantage if close to resources, such as water or the CEO. They also have size.

Some can be bought, built, placed, and upgraded. They can be destroyed (when their health is gone) or shut down.

More complex units play a role in any ecosystem. These are automatons optimized for environments. They have sensors, creating internal views. They may reproduce—even mutate, as one type of adaptation. They may catch and spread contagion, such as ethics or the flu. And they can both be physical as well as conceptual.

Unit. Workers in the computer game Tropico perform necessary activities, such as moving raw materials to factories and finished goods from factories to the docks. They require food and shelter, and they have the built-in ability to vote for or against the player in every election.

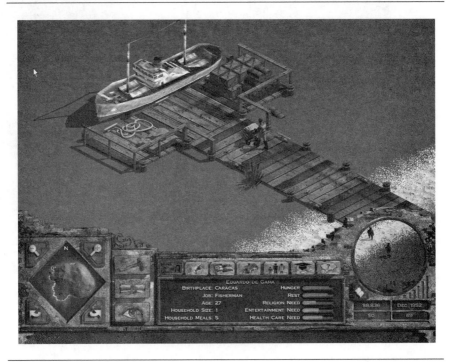

Source: Tropico by Take2 Interactive Software.

Properties of Units

Units turn one resource into another. They might turn money into customer satisfaction. They might turn research into finished products. They might turn time into information. They might consume a constant stream of resources (fixed costs), a variable stream, or both. They may have an organization level, and may work in roles and in formations. Emergent behavior occurs when enough units act simultaneously.

Units can represent a complex system by themselves. They may recursively be made up of smaller units. They may have goals. They may have items, even an inventory. They may communicate with other units, beginning by handshaking.

Skins and meshes can differentiate units. Very distinctive units might have character.

Memes are ideas that have many of the property of units. Vehicles can be considered units. Structures can be considered larger units that are unable to move.

Units, especially with robust artificial intelligence (AI), can also be called agents. They may run scripts, even have situational awareness, conceptual dead reckoning, and intuition. They can even be players themselves.

Token is another name for a unit, especially one that is on a state-based map, or one that, when possessed, can provide access. For example, a coin is a token that can provide access to food in a vending machine.

Attributes and Stats

Attributes are descriptions of the way a unit or map location interacts with its environment, including with other units, maps, and systems. Attributes also answer the questions. How do units or locations differ from other units or locations, and how does one unit or location differ from an earlier or later version of itself, including amounts of energy?

Attributes. Attributes of a draft horse, considered as transportation in the computer game Railroad Tycoon.

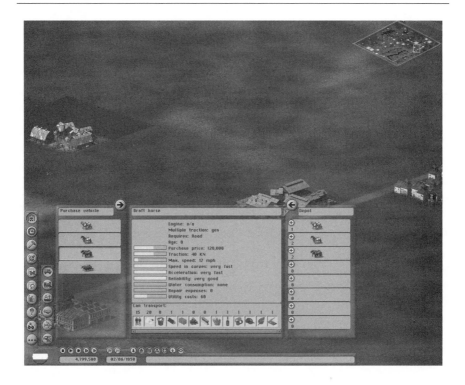

Attributes show variation in units. In Railroad Tycoon, for example, vehicle units have fifteen attributes, including cost, road requirements, acceleration, maximum speed, speed in curves, carrying capacity, and traction.

Different units in different Sims need different attributes. For example, "freshness" or "flammability" might be relevant for some and irrelevant for others. Map squares can also have attributes.

Some attributes get stronger when used, such as a character's skill in negotiating, and others are weakened by use, such as a piece of rope or car brake-pads. Attributes are almost always analog, that is, subject to continual adjustment by very small increments, rather than on-or-off qualities.

One type of attribute is the way others interact with a unit. For example, the attribute of a toaster might include the animation of a character putting bread in it, pushing down the plunger, and then coming for the toast when it is done.

Attributes for people-units in leadership simulation might include any or all of these qualities:

- Curiosity
- Ambition
- Selflessness
- Feeling of having been heard
- Age and gender
- Argumentativeness
- Network of friends and allies (some times referred to as "relationship with others" whether inside or outside the group)
- Salary
- Position of authority
- Speed
- Capacity to learn
- Energy
- Charisma
- Networking ability

- Intelligence
- Tendency toward deference
- Willingness to trust
- Job satisfaction
- Resilience to change
- Tolerance of risk
- Competency in soft and hard skills
- Tendency toward brown-nosing
- Empathy
- Conviction
- Hypocrisy
- Competitiveness
- Openness to people and ideas
- Tendency to act as leader (or follower)
- Preferred leadership style when leading others
- Preferred leadership style when being led

Attributes are almost always *capped*—that is, restricted to a limited range of values. When randomly generated, attributes often follow bell curves.

Also called *stats*.

Author's note: Attributes can change on the same item. Most books that are studied in school literature programs are valued as weighty, rich with historical references, elite, and conveying large themes. But when they were written, most of the time, they were valued as being witty, scandalous, popular, and risqué. The most revered books are those that can survive the transformation from being read to being studied.

Energy

A catch-all for any resource the player values, has in limited amounts, and must both nurture and spend wisely. A player might use up energy in a variety of actions. For example:

- Turning on an electrical device such as a flashlight (energy equals battery)

- Sprinting (energy equals stamina)
- Preparing a cost-benefit analysis for a meeting (energy equals attention span)
- Dieting (energy equals willpower)
- Directing a group (energy equals their regard)
- Accelerating production (energy equals dollars and overtime)
- Swimming under water (energy equals oxygen)
- Getting projects started (energy equals political capital)
- Driving a vehicle (energy equals fuel)
- Getting hurt (energy equals health, or perhaps armor)

Energy can spontaneously recharge, or it can require stations or power-ups on a map to recharge, be generated or collected through structures, or can never recharge. A player might have three or four types of energy in a Sim.

In some Sims, energy might have to be allocated among three competing categories, or budgeted among even more.

Energy level is often an attribute. Running out of energy might prohibit an activity, have a negative impact on other attributes, or result in the end of that level.

Energy is usually displayed in some type of heads-up display (HUD). Deciding when to use up energy is a critical gameplay element.

Balanced Inputs

Multiple types of inputs that are required for a system to operate.

For example, traditional combustion engines need air, fuel, and a spark to operate, and no one can compensate for a lack of spark with extra fuel. Both in Sims and in real life, however, substitutions can sometimes be found for a given input, such as wind for oil.

Health

Health is the generic term for a type of energy that is essential to a unit's survival. When it runs out, the unit dies.

It can be physical health, political relevance, financial health, even organizational tolerance (when it is gone, a unit is fired or expelled).

Size

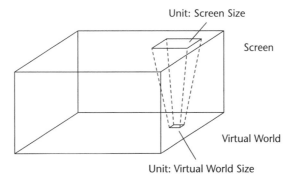

Unit: Screen Size

Screen

Virtual World

Unit: Virtual World Size

Size is the amount of a map that a unit occupies.

Physically, increased size can prohibit movement (as when a unit is blocked by a narrow door), but it can also enable movement (as when one unit can step over a crack that another would fall into). Size can affect other attributes, such as resources needed to consume to survive or move (see "Cost of Travel" later in this chapter).

Conceptually, *size* can refer to the number of members and the unit's influence on others. The "size" of Albert Einstein or William Shakespeare is enormous.

Size can finally refer to the amount of the display's real estate a unit occupies, independently of the size in the virtual world (see "Mixed Scales" in Chapter Seventeen).

Death

The end of the presence of a character on a map or story with the elimination of health.

Death of a mentor, including a parent, is part of the hero's journey. Death of a hero is most often a form of failure. Sometimes, when a character dies, items the character had in inventory become available to other players or units.

Accumulator Storage Capacity

An accumulator is a repository where stocks of a resource can increase or decrease.

A good accumulator can lessen the need for good pipes. Water pressure needed to flush a toilet can be generated from the built-in water tank, even if it is then refilled slowly. A large warehouse can provide a steady stream of inventory, even if the transportation from the source is inconsistent.

Within a simulation, the ability to accumulate can be part of a unit (as in the attribute of health), an external structure (like a water tower), or an abstraction (such as a bank account). It can also include softer areas like goodwill between characters, attractiveness of a company, the appeal of an idea, or the amount of research a new idea attracts requires to complete.

When stock or inventory represents what would be physical quantities in the real world, it may have to be transported by units in a Sim, or transported automatically, and there may be a cost of travel. Meanwhile the "destruction" of the accumulator (such as the cancellation of a research project) may result in the destruction of all the stock it contains, the freeing up of that stock for other players or units to possess, or the shifting of the stock automatically to other accumulators.

Accumulation isn't always good. Pollution accumulates in the atmosphere and animals. Dislike can accumulate in a new employee. Salinization is the accumulation of sufficient quantities of salt in soil such that plants can no longer live.

Also called a *reservoir.*

Capacitance is the ability of an accumulator to smooth out bumps. Specifically, capacitance gives the ability to draw from an accumulator to maintain a steady output when inputs are interrupted or reduced, or to capture the excess when a surplus appears.

The shock absorbers in cars, for example, extend to fill ruts and compress to absorb bumps.

Special Unit

A type of unit, with enhancements (either exaggerated attributes or entirely new available actions), only accessible to one side (or faction), and only when they meet certain conditions.

For example, in the Civilization series, the "England" side or player can create powerful "Redcoat" Units, stronger and more accurate than other players' comparable units, after discovering the technology of rifling.

Special units are a characteristic feature of real-time strategy games, although they can be used wherever units are used.

Character

A unit or avatar with distinctiveness, depth, unique competencies, or attractiveness, often with some scripted part in the game, and with which the player has some emotional interest or connection. Characters can invoke endearment, humor, or competition.

Characters are described through looks, animation, dialogue, story, strategies, and tactics and abilities. One character, for example, might speak in colloquialisms, another in formal English.

Characters might have important roles to play in any story, including hero's journey archetypes such as mentor or villain, and themselves have backstories. Some characters have unique AI routines that prioritize certain behaviors. Finally, characters can die.

Other uses of characters:

- An end-of-level boss might have a strong character.
- Any hero is almost always a character.
- Players should align toward some characters and away from other characters.

Also called *personality*.

The best characters are often not those that align completely with positive stereotypes but rather those that challenge them, earning respect over time.

Organization Level

In a hierarchically structured organization, units have an attribute that specifies how many levels between that unit and both the top and bottom of the tree.

Typically, the higher the organization level, the more ownership the unit has, including span of control and budget, the more information is available, and the more high-value the location is.

A chain of command dictates that when a person who is organizationally the "parent" of another gives an order, that order must be followed.

Also known as *pay-grade*.

The concept also applies in the real world. See "Student Promotion" in Chapter Twenty-Nine.

Signature

A signature is a unit's unique or telltale identifier, used for confirmation of identity.

For people, signatures can include retina and DNA information, as well as their handwritten signatures. Some people's style or standard operating procedures are their signatures. Most fuels, including residue from discharged weapons, have identifying signatures. Many computer viruses have signatures that antivirus programs use to identify, isolate, and erase them.

Signatures can be forged, or they can also reveal the real identity of something fraudulent. A signature can also be a form of key and can provide access to contained areas.

Masking

Masking is a localized technique used to keep something from undergoing a process or scrutiny through which every surrounding thing is going.

Some examples: Two bank robbers may mask their weapons by putting them in duffel bags, then put on masks to hide their identities while committing a robbery, and then mask their scent by running through a stream.

The most stealthy masks may not appear to be masks, such as with camouflage, where the covering of information with noise or decoys blends into the environment rather than standing out, as a way to avoid detection.

Meanwhile, a silkscreen artist may mask a part of a shirt to keep it from getting painted.

Probing may detect and possibly even enable a participant to see through a mask.

Also called *cloaking*.

Goals

Goals are desired results—what a unit seeks to accomplish. Every mission has at least one desired result. Simple units may have simple goals, but AI driven units may have goals as complex as a human player.

- Goals might take a few or many activities, steps, or sub-goals to complete (see process map).
- Goals might require a direct path or an indirect one (calling for dead reckoning or conceptual dead reckoning).
- Goals often require the balancing of processes and big skills.
- Goals may be evaluated against multiple criteria (such as the primary variables discussed in Chapter Twelve or balanced scorecards in Chapter Seven) or just one (see "All-or-Nothing" in Chapter Twelve).
- Goals might be tactical or strategic.
- Goals may be enabled by a Sim level (see "Award" in Chapter Sixteen), required by a level (see "End of Level" in Chapter Eighteen), or self-imposed.
- Different goals may be prioritized differently, requiring different behaviors (see "AI States" in Chapter Ten).
- The completion of goals can attest to the mastery of a learning goal, or it can aid in the mastery.
- Participant goals and Sim goals may not be aligned, at least not initially.

Goals may be necessary for games. Games environments without goals but with feedback (such as SimCity and The Sims) are considered toys.

Upgrade

Upgrading involves spending some value to increase the ability of units, including items and structures.

Upgrades often increase key attributes (either targeted or global), or enable a unit to be replaced by a better or more specialized unit. In a marketplace, announcing upgraded items reduces the value of non-upgraded ones.

Upgrades should be made in a way to align strategies and tactics.

Enhancement

Enhancement is the substituting of some attribute, building block unit, or other ability to perform an action with a more powerful version.

Characters can be enhanced in many ways, in both cyberpunk stories and real life (including through natural mutations). For example:

- Eyes can be enhanced with an augmented view (including binoculars and HUDs).
- Cars can enhance movement.
- Forklifts can enhance strength.
- Enhanced reflexes (or Red Bull) can make the world seem as if it has slowed down, and can even make some responses automatic.

Environments can be enhanced, such as through phones, clocks, moving sidewalks, and elevators. Another way to experience enhancements, albeit conditionally and temporarily, is in a virtual world, such as a first-person shooter.

Developing skills is a form of enhancement, and in the real world can be done primarily through a backboard, batting cage, or other practice environment. Pedagogy and coaching either serve as a form of enhancement or can lead to enhancement.

In many science fiction stories, and throughout human history, enhancements often bring about long-term problems. Slaves and serfs rebel against masters; performance or mood enhancing drugs have unwanted side-effects, including addictions and dependencies.

Also called *augmentation*.

Affiliation

Affiliation refers to people's associations or connectedness with broader categories, institutions, or stereotypes. Affiliations can affect a person's appearance, behavior, context, and mission.

People choose some of their affiliations, through professions, marriage status, books, and music. Some affiliations are earned, such as being a Navy SEAL or a CEO of a large company, a club member, or an Ivy League graduate. Some people have default affiliations put upon them, often by where they live or grew up, access to financial resources, or gender. Some affiliations, such as felon, are often unwanted.

Affiliations may be private or public, amplified or damped. A public affiliation may be broadcast through clothes, vocabulary, even bumper stickers or phone answering machine messages. People may likewise try to lose regional accents or, in contrast, practice using more stylized words affiliated with a certain profession of perceived education level. At the beginning of the relationship, people benefit through the affiliation. Into the relationship, the members increasingly define and impact that with which they are affiliated.

Regeneration

Regeneration is a system property of being able to gain what has been lost. Regeneration can happen to map or character attributes such as energy (including health) or other resources.

Regeneration can happen in a variety of ways:

- Spontaneously (such as healing)
- At or near a map or unit location (such as a hospital)
- As a unique or special ability (such as a doctor)
- Through spending a power-up (such as a bandage)

Some regeneration is an attribute of a healthy ecosystem.

Something that regenerates is also called *renewable*. Opposite of attrition or degradation.

Handshaking

Handshaking is the process of trying to establish a successful communication process and language between two or more units, or the signal that such a protocol has been established.

Mutate

To mutate is to unpredictably change, add, or subtract some attribute or building block of a unit or activity of a process.

Managers and leaders can take actions to amplify or damp mutations. For example, the Quality movement, including Six Sigma, focuses on eliminating mutations. Hiring creative people increases mutations.

When appropriate controls are not in place, work processes mutate and propagate, often evolving into behavior that does not support the originally intended desired results as reflected in balanced scorecards.

On the other hand, mutations can lead to improvements in processes or products. When mutations spread, reproduce, or propagate, they can lead to a chain reaction in an ecosystem. The propagation of mutations is necessary for evolution.

Related topic: "Noise" in Chapter Seventeen.

Reproduce

Reproduction is the ability for a unit or attribute to create other copies of itself, perhaps perfect, or perhaps in some way mutated (through random changes) or adapted (through breeding or the introduction of new processes).

Units can reproduce themselves, but also have the attribute of catching, hosting, and spreading contagions. As a result, ideas can spread in the form of memes.

Reproduction can theoretically create a chain reaction, potentially leading to a population explosion, but is often balanced in an ecosystem.

Managing reproduction often means setting up regions of containment (see Chapter Six).

Rock, Paper, Scissors

The term refers to a modeling framework where only unit type a can beat b, b can beat c, and c can beat a. The framework is based on the children's game of the same name, where paper can wrap rock, defeating it, while rock can break scissors, and scissors can cut paper.

Variations also can suggest that only a can help b, or a has a huge advantage of b.

A rock, paper, scissors framework defeats a playoff tree model of figuring out who the best player is. Many real-time strategy games use a rock, paper, scissors model for units engaged in conflict, especially to defeat a tank rush strategy.

Also called *triangularity.*

Author's note: I developed a new variation of Rock, Paper, Scissors. It is called Punditry. Here's how it works: Players, in a conversation, can either express sincerity, outrage, or sarcasm.

In this game:

- Outrage beats Sincerity by drowning it out with simplistic, self-evident statements.
- Sarcasm beats Outrage by mocking the bombasticness and pointing out obvious flaws if one bothers to take the thinking just one step further.
- Sincerity beats Sarcasm by making the sarcastic person feel silly and superficial.

Thus Rush Limbaugh beats David Gergen, Jon Stewart beats Rush Limbaugh, and David Gergen beats Jon Stewart.

Memes

Memes are ideas that have similar characteristics to units, including ability to reproduce, transform other things, and mutate. Memes are associated with

Richard Dawkins. For example, in the eighteenth century, the seemingly insane meme of democracy and self-rule spread through Europe and then various colonies, mutating from theory to governing principles, culminating in quite a few revolutions. Today, we are developing a meme of serious games and simulations; it may change how education is created, or it may die out.

Items (The Stuff of Life)

An item is something that grants the holding unit or character some ability, often at a cost.

For example, holding a key (or other token) might grant access to a door, but might take up room in a finite inventory.

Towing a cart behind a vehicle might increase carrying capacity at the expense of top speed, maneuverability, and gas mileage.

Some items can be taken apart (into building-block units) and fitted into other items. Some items can be rare, exotic, and powerful enough to be an enabler of a hero's journey. And some items are just there to be collected. Often finding items in a map is a Sim or game task.

Items can be limited by inventory. Items can be modified, and be of different quality. Items have their own attributes, and some need energy to perform.

Sometimes, certain skill levels are necessary to either use an item or use an item effectively. Items can be bought or traded.

Inventory

From Deus Ex, players must evaluate what objects to bring, limited by size and shape.

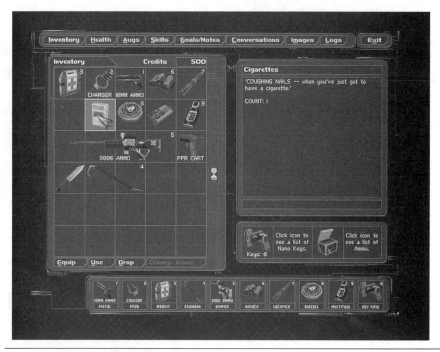

Source: Deus Ex by Eidos Interactive.

Inventory is an accumulator for items in possession of a resource, structure, unit, or character.

First-Person Scale. At a personal scale, an inventory is what a character is carrying. In a Sim, it can either be infinite (determined by what a character has found so far), or finite.

Finite inventories can be limited by an absolute number (say, a character can have seven items), or by carrying capacity (some items are larger or heavier than others, therefore taking up more of the available inventory space).

Where inventories are finite, choosing what to bring and what to leave becomes strategic.

Some Sims have "load out" preliminary levels, where players can plan and assemble appropriate inventories to bring.

Structure Scale. At more of a tycoon scale, inventories refer to what inputs or outputs a structure or process accumulates.

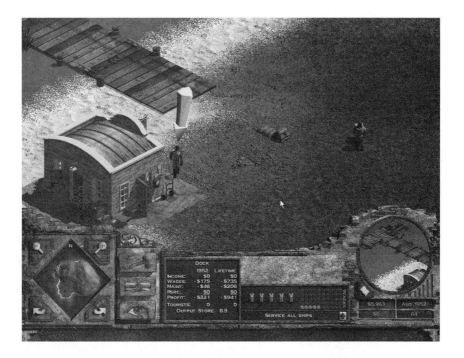

To take the game of Tropico for an example, if an island-state is exporting furniture, it has to cut down trees, then bring the cut trees to the lumber mill, then bring the lumber to the furniture factory, and then bring the furniture to the dock and load it onto the ship. At each point in the process, too much inventory (either inputs waiting to be processed or output stores of finished goods waiting to be picked up) leads to cash flow issues, while too little inventory can result in having factory workers sitting around doing nothing.

Just-in-time inventory is a manufacturing strategy of keeping minimal stocks of raw materials, parts, and finished goods.

Exotic

An exotic unit is something that is very rare, and has greater value than more common units. Gaining possession of an exotic unit can be a type of award.

Loss

A loss means no longer having something of value (including a character, item, high-value map location, or ecosystem) that was once possessed or to which one had access.

Loss can be the cost of getting something needed (as when food is consumed) or wanted. Alternatively, it can be an unlucky result of a risky situation, such as gambling, conflict, a chase, or life itself. It can also be feedback for doing something wrong or less good than a competitor.

Related topics: "Collecting" (Chapter Sixteen); "Death" (earlier in this chapter).

Overheat

In Halo, some weapons overheat if used too much in a short period of time.

Source: Microsoft product screen shot reprinted with permission from Microsoft Corporation.

Something that overheats temporarily becomes either increasingly inefficient or completely disabled when used too intensely over a short period of time.

An engine can overheat, as can an economy. Researchers can need a rest after being pushed too hard. Factories, when producing at 100 percent productivity, defer maintenance and vacations, which can cause an eventual complete stop. A person can sprint for a while, but then often needs a complete rest (as opposed to walking or loping, which might be possible to keep up for longer and thus reach the destination in less overall elapsed time).

A pedagogical meter might visualize when something is getting close to overheating. The threat of overheating causes a participant to act more carefully.

Upgrades may be used to reduce the impact of or allow greater use before overheating. Overheating is more extreme but also less permanent than having something weaken by using (discussed later in this chapter).

See also "Budgeting," in Chapter Fourteen and "Throttle," in Chapter Twenty-One.

Overload

To overload something is to break it (permanently or temporarily) by giving it too much of an otherwise expected, typical, even desired input.

The computer world is subject to "denial of service" attacks, where many coordinated computers send communication to a single site in order to overwhelm and shut the site down.

Overloads can cause and occur in chain reactions (discussed later in this chapter).

Substitute

A substitute is a resource that can be used instead of another resource, often at a different cost or usage ratio.

For example, fish can replace beef as a protein source. People might drink bottled water instead of bottled soft drinks. An automatic teller machine can replace fifteen tellers, but there is an investment up-front that eventually results in lower operating costs.

Building Block Unit

Building blocks are the reusable smaller units that make up larger and more complicated units. For example, amino acids are the building blocks of proteins. The power of political parties is made up of constituents. Cars have thousands of parts.

Building blocks can often be assembled differently to form different things. The same ingredients can be prepared differently to create different meals.

Similarly, a more complicated unit can have parts switched out to increase or change functionality. For example, a computer system can get a new monitor; an outfit can be dressed up or dressed down with the right accessory.

Both are efficient ways of adapting.

Creative destruction is the process whereby certain configurations of units dissolve and new, better-adapted configurations, made up of different subsets of building block units, replace them.

Strengthen by Using

In a systems model, "strengthen by using" refers to a relationship that gets stronger when invoked, or a process that grows more productive when used.

For example, the connections between brain neurons strengthen when used, creating habits and implicit knowledge. Middle skills and big skills are strengthened by use in an individual, sometimes mandating practice for originally learning skills and then maintaining infrequently used skills.

In the computer game series The Sims and Grand Theft Auto, players' characters improve their skills with specific items and actions the more they use them. Some alliances are strengthened when not only used but challenged and tested.

A strengthen-by-using attribute can also decay when not used.

Some things get more refined when used, but not necessarily better. Consider the useless so-called inspiration stories that are the primary output of industry gurus.

Weaken by Using

In a systems model, "weaken by using" refers to a relationship that grows less strong when invoked, or a process that grows less productive when used.

For example, a piece of rope might fray a little bit each time it is used, eventually breaking. Deceptions might seem credible in the short term (especially when amplified by multiple sources), but eventually lose their effectiveness in the long term.

Movement (The Life of Stuff)

Source: Far Cry.

Movement is the broad attribute of a unit that allows it to change locations on a map. In a simulation, moving elements requires significant programming, almost amounting to AI.

For example, living things move toward sources of health: plants toward sunlight and associate professors toward recognition and grants. All maps have one or more layers of topography including ease of travel and value.

Specific movement attributes:

- Cost of travel
- Speed (a critical function of any chase, as well as most processes and activities)
- Accessibility of terrain and location (including the ability to go through certain doors)
- Noise of travel
- Range
- Carrying capacity and inventory

Understanding movement can provide other information. Planets or suns may move toward an otherwise invisible black hole, revealing its location. Sound travels more slowly than light, so the delay between the sight of a ball being hit by a bat and the sound in a ballpark can tell a viewer how cheap the seats are in a given area.

Presenting the concept of movement, often called *agility*, is critical for the creation of a practice environment to support big skills.

In Sims as in real life, movement enables an organization to probe an unknown situation and then mobilize resources to take advantage of an opportunity or resolve a problem once identified:

- Communication is the attempt at movement of information and ideas.
- Conflict management requires that people move their opinions and sometimes their alignment.
- Moving people and ideas around is critical to finding a better fit.
- Preventing some movement is the role of containment.

Directing people includes telling them to move their locations, what they are doing, and even what they are prioritizing and thinking. Budgeting and allocating involves moving resources, something often easier to do in theory than in practice. The phrases "we don't do that" and "that's not my problem" are indicative, rightly or wrongly, of lack of ability or incentive to move.

Some items are optimized to be moved, with features such as lightweight, hardy, concentrated, or even digital. This can be a problem when, say, vegetables are bred or genetically modified to survive two-thousand-mile trips without bruising. The modification may appear to have value, even if it leaves the product with less intrinsic worth—being less nutritious or harder to grow.

Cost of Travel

In models of work, the amount of resources required to go from one map location to another is referred to as the "cost of travel." This can be a tactical issue, such as fuel for a car. But for some organizations and events, managing the cost of travel can mean the difference between success and failure, as with a resort monorail, or logistics for an army.

When the map is conceptual, the travel might be conceptual as well:

- What is the cost for a new country to learn about democracy, to create the infrastructure around democracy, or to build a functioning democracy?
- Or what is the cost for Microsoft to learn about MP3 players, or what is the cost of Microsoft to build a competency in producing MP3 players, or what is the cost for Microsoft to build a profitable business in MP3 players?

The cost of travel might also be indirect, such as noise or pollution to a local environment.

Friction

Friction is the additional cost to a system for movement in a given environment.

Some friction, as movement gains complexity or energy, increases proportionally (viscous friction from the physical world), while other types remain constant (coulomb friction from the physical world).

Some examples of friction:

- Some argue that there is a "natural rate of unemployment" that is the friction of an economic system.
- Waiting in airports is a friction of air travel.
- Larger companies have friction in the form of coordinating staff meetings and overhead of management salaries.
- Some taxes are proportional friction on an economy, while others are constant.

Some friction is beneficial. Car brakes use friction to slow the vehicle. Raising interest rates can slow an overheating economy, lowering the chances of inflation.

Momentum

Momentum refers to the tendency of ideas or units to continue to do (or expand doing) what they have been doing.

Cars have momentum when moving on a map, and taking advantage of momentum is a key to achieving desired results in a racing game. But ideas (memes) and work processes have momentum of their own.

Momentum can take the shape of a chain reaction when growing or a balancing loop when continuing. Momentum can be stopped at the turning point of a pendulum or cycle, or at an inflection point.

Also called *inertia*.

Formation

Formation is an action to either create or order a diversity of units into a preestablished distribution, often with different capabilities, to meet requirements or goals, such as players in a sports game or staff in a restaurant.

Leaders often have to both design and switch formations, taking into account fit and necessary activities.

Teleport

To teleport is to instantly go from one part of the map to another without occupying the spaces in between. Communication can, practically, teleport, whereas

atoms cannot. Thus in the real world, memes can propagate globally and reproduce almost instantly, causing global buzz, and in MMOs such as Second Life,
avatars can teleport as well. Teleporting in a Sim corresponds to a low cost of
travel.

Ergodic

An *ergodic* unit is one that has the same probability of being in any space on a
map. Or Alternatively, it visits every space before starting over.

Emergence

Emergence occurs in a system in which the behavior of a large number of units
or equations creates a new behavior, different from what is evident in each piece.

An ant may not be very smart, but ant colonies are brilliant. It is hard, for
example, to understand things like these:

- *Die Hard* from studying the string of bits that comprise the DVD
- The human brain from studying the behavior of neurons
- Traffic patterns from understanding the interactions of molecules

Structure

In Tropico, structures serve transformative functions, require staffing and sometimes electricity, and have inventory and budgets.

Any of a variety of stationary units can be referred to as structures. They have a subset of descriptors that seem more appropriate for them, but anything here could describe a mobile unit as well.

Attributes

As with units, structures have attributes. They have or require inputs such as energy. Structures themselves may have inventory. Structures might have various functions, making it necessary for the participant to allocate resources among them. Structures may take resources or time to build or acquire. Structures might be accumulators and dispensers.

Building and placing the right structure is necessary to creating a healthy ecosystem. Participants might have to pick a structure from different options, often through a menu interface, and then place it in the right location.

Dispenser

A type of structure that provides discrete units.

Barns dispense milk and meat, colleges dispense graduates, factories dispense durable goods, and some people dispense bad advice.

Structure (as Process)

In a SIM, a structure can be a microcosm or abstraction of a more complicated action, activity, or process. Building an immigration office, for example, might institute an immigration policy and be a location for the participant to go to change immigration policies.

The availability of a new process for a player to select might manifest itself as a new structure. For example, the widespread use of the Internet might make Internet cafés available. Some structures serve as power-ups.

Valve

In a system, a valve is an automatic process for releasing damaging pressure or disrupting a reinforcing or feedback loop before it reaches critical mass.

Valves can be mechanical. A valve can release water pressure from a pipe.

But they can also be political, or social. One type of political valve might be process in the court system for deporting unhappy citizens. Or a social valve might be taking a team to a night out every Thursday to release stress. Or a complaint box to focus discontent.

Some people who want to trigger change may try to destroy valves.

Valves can be set at different levels and can be established at different costs. There is a constant debate whether doing some mild bad activity (watching boxing, smoking a little) is helpful, serving as a valve, or hurtful, creating a strengthen-by-using situation for something intrinsically negative.

Location, Location, Location

The location of structure often matters. Locations farther away from a political capital might have more corruption or less respect for centralized priorities. Some structures attract and others repel.

Corporate headquarters. EDS built its monumental corporate headquarters to project strength and stability (and as a place for employees to park all their GM cars).

Different locations are of higher value to different types of structures.

In a Sim, if not in real life, a police station might reduce crime within a 20-mile radius. Structures may be placed to minimize time and cost of travel. On the other hand, supermarkets place the attractive milk section in the back corner of the store to maximize the number of shelves that customers will walk by.

Some structures can only be built in some locations. One has to build a harbor on the border between land and sea. A mine, built to extract resources, must be built in a place with natural resources.

Structures Within Structures

In Theme Hospital, the entire map is a structure, in which the participants place rooms (that is, smaller structures) with specific functionality in the hospital. Structures may have doors.

Structures as Level Design

In a first-person shooter that takes place inside various levels, the structures are the level-defining maze.

Structures Within Structures

Source: Theme Hospital

Structures as Backdrop

Structures can also be used as sets or backdrops. In any type of cut scene, the exterior of a structure might also be used for an establishing shot.

Related topics: "Mixed Scales" (Chapter Seventeen), "Process Map" (Chapter Thirteen), "Radar or Mini-Map" (Chapter Nineteen), "Real-Time Strategy Games" (Chapter Three), and "Path" (Chapter Eight).

Events in Sims

When capturing what domain experts know and do for a simulation, one has to interview them or watch for high-level patterns. What are the patterns that they see play out time and time again, and what are the variations of those patterns?

Some patterns are basic and universal, like bell curves. Then there are higher-level patterns, like people hiring other people who are similar to them, or the fact that new technology is almost always overhyped.

Systems theorists have a library of patterns like "success to the successful," "the tragedy of the commons," and "escalation." From a Sim perspective, however, patterns are a might tricky. There is always the hope that they emerge organically from a portfolio of well-designed rules. More often, they have to be wired into the units and maps. It is easiest to hardwire them into level design. But that can make a Sim feel forced and artificial.

Here are some examples:

Chain Reaction

A chain reaction begins with an event that triggers a dispersed series of similar events, which may yet again trigger even more events. Chain reactions can spread geometrically, potentially causing a large, sudden, and unexpected impact to a global condition.

For example, one bank failing just prior to the Great Depression set off failures at many other banks. One currency can quickly devalue, setting off a chain reaction of similar devaluations. Atomic bombs are the result of chain reactions, with energy being released from a few atoms releasing the energy in their neighbors. A single match can burn down a forest.

Chain reactions require units with the following characteristics: stored energy; triggers (which might include a delay); and communication and transport ability (called a communication wave, shock wave, or vector).

Where there is no release of stored energy, chain reactions diminish over time, such as with a wave in a pool.

Some organizations go through chain reactions of key people leaving. Others get multiple bumps up or down in stock price. Reorganizations can cascade, as can new leadership and direction. Interest hikes, lowering or raising prices, spreading rumors, and viruses have chain reactions all their own.

Word of mouth about how good or bad a product is can spread, as they say, like wildfire; when positive, it is called *buzz*.

Buzz. Positive, all-or-nothing spontaneous advocacy that propagates in a chain reaction. Buzz can be helped along by a "tell a friend" button on a Web site.

Catch and Spread Contagion. Units sometimes have the ability to be carriers for some spreadable attribute, which often has a positive or negative long-term impact on the unit or the greater system. These contagions can include new ideas, traditions, diseases, rumors, religion, or desire for representative government.

Contagions can change the output of a process as a way of spreading. For example, factory employees in a capitalist enterprise might use their workplace's facilities to produce Marxist literature. Likewise, viruses might subvert a host body process to produce more viruses.

Critical Mass

The critical mass is the volume of units necessary for a system to either be self-sufficient or generate a chain reaction.

At some critical mass of . . .

- Customers: Businesses like Google and Netflix and TiVo become profitable (budget in the black) and stable.
- Buzz and support: Political candidates become viable.
- Research produced: Universities can then attract top-tier researchers.
- Energy produced: Uranium, plutonium, or even hydrogen can go nuclear.

Critical mass can be triggered by moment-by-moment activities or longer-term accumulation.

Related topic: "Balancing Loop" in Chapter Eight.

Cluster

A cluster is a region or location that has deep and growing knowledge and expertise around a specific area.

According the Council on Competitiveness, these are some U.S.-based clusters:

- Atlanta-Columbus, Georgia (focus on financial services, information technology and transportation logistics clusters)
- Pittsburgh, Pennsylvania (focus on biotechnology and pharmaceutical, information technology, and production technology clusters)
- Research Triangle, North Carolina (focus on biotechnology and pharmaceutical; chemical, textile, and plastics; and communications equipment clusters)
- San Diego, California (focus on biotechnology and pharmaceutical and communications clusters)
- Wichita, Kansas (focus on aerospace vehicles and defense and plastics clusters)

With the growth of outsourcing and offshoring, global clusters include

- India: Programming, help desk, research
- Poland: Back office support
- Singapore: Networking, data centers

Due to the high value of clusters, organizations often want to link to them, and in some cases build structures to stabilize any relationship.

The cluster concept was successfully rebranded and relaunched by Michael Porter.

Also called *regional core competencies*.

Doom Loop

A doom loop is a system where each piece functions according to specifications and in a way that seemingly adds value, but when taken as a whole results in an outcome at odds with expectations.

For example:

Company needs to boost profit

Company has a sale on its core product

Customers buy more product on sale

Company ends sale

Customers don't buy product at original price

Company profits drop

Go back to top

Equilibrium (Stalemate)

Equilibrium is a situation of aligned inputs and outputs, often arrived at via calibration.

Here are some examples:

Zero population growth occurs when the number of births plus migrants in is the same as the number of deaths plus migrants out.

A rock flies through space. It gets caught in the gravitational pull of a planet. As it gets closer to the planet, the rock speeds up. As it speeds up, it goes faster. As it goes faster, it increases in altitude. Finally, at the right height, the rock achieves a stable orbit.

Two countries engage in war. They reach a point, eventually, where neither side can make any significant long-term gains as long as the other is there, nor can they pull out because they will lose significant ground when they do. This type of unhappy equilibrium is referred to as a *stalemate*.

A speaker is in a room full of people. He tells a joke. People laugh. The speaker and the audience both relax a bit. The speaker is more lucid. He goes out on more intellectual limbs, telling some ad hoc stories. The audience nods more, and smiles. He is "on." About a third of the way into the presentation, the speaker is as good as he will be that day, and the audience is as supportive as they will be. They have hit equilibrium.

A woman is hired. She starts her job slowly, and the organization gives her a mentor. She understands the role and does a better job. She is given more work to do, as well as a raise. Other people now come to her. When her boss retires, she takes her place. She grows her group's responsibilities. The challenges grow now, and she works hard to keep up. She thinks she is going to get another promotion, but she does not. She begins to stop working on weekends. Her department shrinks a bit, but not too much. And now she has found her organizational equilibrium.

10

ARTIFICIAL INTELLIGENCE PLAYER-AGENT

More Patient Than Real People

As games become better at adapting to the talent and skill Levels of their players, more video games will be decoding the players as much as players are decoding the games.

—"PLAYING WITH OUR HEADS, WHY VIDEO GAMES ARE MAKING OUR KIDS SMARTER—AND MORE OBEDIENT," BY CHRIS SUELLENTROP, *WILSON QUARTERLY*, JANUARY/FEBRUARY 2007.

Artificial intelligence (AI) players and agents are special types of units (broadly described in Chapter Nine) that have a high level of intelligent system-aware and adaptive behavior.

In some cases, an artificial intelligence simply creates more interesting and accurate models. In other cases, an AI player or agent can be a full character in a story or even a player (such as an ally or competitor) in a single-player environment in a role that can be eventually taken over by a real human in a multi-player environment.

This latter role is especially important in the evolution of all educational simulations. AI players provide at least three significant advantages over real players; they don't get bored with the human using the program, they are consistent enough, and they are always available.

As a result, the final criterion is that AI characters can serve as backboards to enable players to repeatedly practice actions and appropriately calibrate their actions against the response. And ideally, these avatars need to be consistent, and they often have some degree of visualizable inner workings.

Author's note: I sometimes prefer to discuss the concept of Artificial Personality rather than Artificial Intelligence with a client or in a design document, because it has less of the burden of AI. The three key attributes of an artificial personality are

- Computationally lightweight (runs in Flash), and more often a form of fuzzy logic
- Provide behavior models that are instructional to engage, aligned with the learning goals
- Are dynamic enough to respond to a student in an open-ended way; to accomplish this, and also allow for a programmer or level designer often has to identify to create (at least) three or four distinctive attributes to shape the behavior (a good physical analogy would be how shifting just five variables can change the behavior of a vehicle from dynamically handling like a sports car to handling like a garbage truck)

An AI can also be called a *virtual player* or *computer-controlled player*.

The How

AI players might use a combination of: AI states to capture and quantify different moods, fuzzy logic, scripts and rules, adapting, and mirroring.

Here are some core concepts in more detail.

Sensors

Sensors are tools that allow units to update their knowledge about their world. They can also be detectors of information for heads-up displays or other

The specific AI state can change what the unit sees or prioritizes. In this screen shot from Terminator 2, the point of view is that of a cyborg in the state of "vehicle acquisition" and therefore dedicating sensors and processing power to finding something with a close match. The heads-up display is highlighting a possible match for the cyborg.

Source: Still from TERMINATOR 2: JUDGMENT DAY used courtesy of StudioCanal.

decision support. After all, whether you're human or a game feature, what you do is shaped by what you detect and highlight.

Sensors can be tuned—for example, to identify map landmarks like paths or walls, or to react to other units or to higher-level world features, like things that can make units happy, or even text phrases. Sensors often can filter out irrelevant information and noise.

Sensors might also see through any fog of war, with more powerful sensors seeing farther than weaker ones.

Situational awareness requires sensors. Meanwhile, powerful sensors can take significant burdens off of any artificial intelligence (AI).

In the real world, for example, automated pavers have six sensors: four to measure the thickness of the poured pavement, and two to steer. In our own lives, part of the role of emotions is to put urgency onto our own sensory inputs, around both food and loved ones.

Sensors are also called *detectors* or *receptors*. Compare with "Triggers" (discussed in Chapter Eight).

AI States

A *state* is a mental condition or frame that changes what a unit or AI-controlled player sees, what it thinks, and how it behaves. (The screenshot from Terminator 2 illustrates one possible state.) A unit can have a collection of distinct mental states, of which just one is typically invoked at a given time.

Even living creatures can have states. For example, a dog might walk out of the house in a "relaxed" state. A squirrel appears, and the dog gets excited, changes into a "chase" state, and runs toward the squirrel. But before reaching the squirrel, the dog notices a stranger walking down the driveway and promptly shifts to a "protect" state.

States, and switches between states, can have voice and graphic cues.

Related concept: "Fuzzy Logic" (discussed later in this chapter). AI states are often determined by a unit's role or goals.

Script

A script sets triggered, predictable actions for a predictable situation. There are many types of scripts:

- *Map script:* A place in a level or map where a specific event is launched, such as the appearance of a character or the playing out of a scene. This is handled by a level editor. Map scripts often compensate for bad AI. Also called a level script.
- *Unit script:* Sequences of actions that are designed to be effective, given a role and situation. In a Sim, these should look and feel spontaneous. Viruses also follow hostile scripts to take advantage of security holes. Also called an AI script, this type of script can reset an AI state.
- *Psychological script:* A familiar and commonplace sequence of events that real people repeatedly do in real situations, governed by a knowledge of the context.
- *Procedural script:* Another term for "procedural knowledge," discussed in Chapter Twenty-Two.
- *Dialogue script:* What an actor reads, or what certain workers, such as call center reps or hotel staff, follow in dealing with the public.

Fuzzy Logic

Fuzzy logic is a type of artificial intelligence (AI) that considers multiple analog inputs and then outputs a response (such as an action) that might have both analog and discrete attributes, or either type alone.

Fuzzy logic can create more realistic and subtle behavior in avatars, and introduces the notion of partial truths. Fuzzy logic can also create behavior that seems random (that is, unpredictable) but is still consistent with higher patterns.

Internal View

The internal view is a unit's information about its world, perhaps including location and characteristics of map features and other units. Sensors may change some part or all of a unit's internal view.

Internal views have ranges—a portion of a map that their view includes. Certain items, such as research reports or binoculars, may increase the range or depth of an internal view.

Intuition

Intuition is the ability to predict how things will be based on how things are now, or better understand how things currently are based on earlier observations.

Intuition is often based on understanding of hidden systems.

Making an AI Better Than the AI

AI players, also called 'bots, are ultimately not as clever or interesting as real players. Most designers will therefore build layers of support around the AIs to make them more integral.

Cheating for Gameplay

The best AIs are given the same action options as the player. They also both simulate real, imperfect behavior and recognize and adapt to strategies of competitors.

More often, for better and worse, AIs are designed to cheat to make a Sim or game more compelling. They take advantage of techniques such as rubber banding (described in Chapter Sixteen), building free units, and accessing detailed knowledge of the player's actions.

Turning an AI into a Character

AIs might be coupled with level-based triggers and linear scripts to flesh out a character. For example, a Sim might show a cut scene of a main character to set up an interactive level. Then the Sim transitions to an interactive component with the same character, who is now AI driven. Finally, when the player either completes or fails a task, the Sim once again shows the same character in a scripted segment that provides results and closure.

Other Uses of AIs

The term *AI* is broader than defined here. AIs might control other systems in a Sim. Often simpler AIs are used to control all Sim units, including those engaged in specialized activities.

Meanwhile the term *AI* can also apply to other constructs:

- *Expert system:* A system used to solve a task that provides judgment or other help that takes the place of or augments an experienced professional. A doctor may use an expert system to suggest what might be wrong with a patient.
- *Model of human brain:* A computational model that strives to both use the same techniques as a human brain and provide similar output. For example, using an artificial stroke on a neural network may not destroy any data, but simply make it take longer for the program to access it.
- *Adaptive problem solving:* An algorithm that has a goal, sensors, and parameters, but otherwise may grow and evolve in response to an unpredictable environment.

The Success of Serious Games

Most people blur the line between single- and multiplayer Sims. But when they do differentiate, they express a greater excitement and even predilection for the multiplayer type.

This preference for multiplayer Sims has several sources:

- Multiplayer environments have been hugely successful, including entertainment successes like World of Warcraft and social successes like Second Life.
- Multiplayer environments feel real, rich in interface, and dynamic.
- Multiplayer environments are, in theory, reusable. They represent capability and process, not just content.

But multiplayer Sims still have huge limitations. In most current educational simulations and serious games (unlike MMORPGs), multiplayer activities share more characteristics of a classroom role-play.

- Everyone is on his or her best behavior.
- People are reluctant to try risky new strategies.
- The logistics of setting up the scenario are expensive and brittle.

- People can go through a scenario once or twice, but then the players get bored.
- There is little consistency. Some people take them seriously, some do not. Friday afternoon role-plays are different from the ones run Monday at 10 A.M.
- There is little ability for rigorous after action reviews (also called debriefings; discussed in Chapter Eighteen).
- They allow people to play out existing techniques and strategies, neither learning new ones nor rigorously practicing old ones.

Now admittedly, the live role-plays are often the best part of any classroom experience. They are staggeringly better than the lecture that surrounds them.

The correct model in a perfect world, however, is to first role-play in a single-player Sim for exposure and practice, and only then role-play in a multiplayer environment for engaging in increasingly complex and open-ended behavior. (This is the same model as computer games, by the way. In almost all cases, people practice in a game or even genre first by themselves, and then join teams.) I could even argue that in a perfect, perfect world, another live role-play might fit before the single-player role-play to add motivation, but again, logistics makes it tough.

I can understand why outsiders have jumped on the "multiplayer first" bandwagon, but what is alarming is how many insiders have fanned this flame. I cynically think it is because single-player requires much more work on the part of the developer. Just to name four elements, single-player Sims need artificial intelligence, interface, story, and level design. Each is hard to create (believe me, I know). By pushing multiplayer first, designers can meet the perceived needs of the sponsor and align with the global buzz. When it fails, they can just blame the deployment, and hope the industry has moved on to a new hot topic.

11

STATE-BASED SYSTEMS AND MODELS

A Shortcut to Simulations

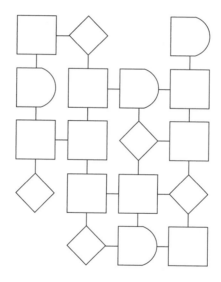

Of all systems, state-based are perhaps the easiest to program, describe, and understand. State-based systems are a special case of map, with discrete elements (or nodes) that are organized (and traversed) through selective linking.

A traditional light bulb is a state-based model with just two states. This simple on-off relationship is called *binary* (or *digital, or all-or-nothing, and an example of discrete*).

Some state-based systems are open-ended. For example, imagine entering a museum. You can start by going to the dinosaur room. Then, you can explore the exhibit on Eskimos. Later, you can visit the room with information about whales. If you want, you can return to the dinosaur exhibit.

Some state-based systems have gates (or doors). To extend the museum analogy, you might encounter a guard who will only let you through a certain door if you have a pass (in Sim terms, a token). Therefore, you will have to walk to the lobby where you can buy the pass before you can get into the room.

Other state-based systems can be organized into a hierarchy, with parents and children (terms borrowed from database design; discussed later in this chapter).

Some hierarchical structures are further organized into branching trees. Here, imagine a very busy museum exhibit, where everyone enters through one door. Then, as you go through, you have choices as to what rooms to enter, making trade-offs between which rooms to see, never able to backtrack. Perhaps a better analogy is dialing a phone number, where every digit is a decision that gets you eventually to a unique location.

This is the structure for the educational simulation genre of *branching story*. Further, state-based models smaller components, such as AI states, maps or tech trees.

Some state-based systems have logic associated with them, including process maps, with not only branches but conditional links. State-based systems can also be used as a framework for more complicated algorithms, such as with AI states.

Computational Theory Models

State-based systems are derived from computational theory models (and are called *finite-state machines* or *finite automata*). They are made up of the following:

Element

Elements are discrete locations, processes, artifacts, equipment, or people that, with links, are the building blocks of state-based systems and models. Elements might include documents or video clips and cut scenes, graphics, processes, and interfaces or decision points or crossroads.

Elements are accessed via an entrance link and left via an exit link. If a participant is in an element, it is called the *current* element.

Link

A link is a connection from one element to another, or from a place in one element to a different place in the same element. Networks enable communication between (that is, link together) users and equipment, allowing a user to send an electronic document to a printer, for example. Some links are one way (or asynchronous). In a virtual environment, a participant might create a link between two elements by dragging one on top of another.

A link can be a specific term for an address to some electronic media, such as a Web page. "Giving someone a link" is a convenient way of giving someone access to a large amount of information.

Hyperlinks are a special type of link that connects electronic media and is activated by the user mouse-clicking on the hyperlink. Hyperlinks are prevalent in the Web, and are often properties of text, where they are indicted by an underline and a highlight color, and graphics. Text with significant links is called *hypertext*.

If a link has already been traversed by a user, it may change colors or leave some other form of bread crumb. Some links are conditional, and therefore may be available.

A participant's location can be described by the current link.

Also called an *edge*.

Conditional Link. A conditional link is available only if stated conditions are met, including time and possible possession of token. If the conditions are not met, the link is unavailable. Unavailable links may be grayed out, or not displayed at all.

Links becoming available can be as a result of or give the sensation of time passing or other progress or accomplishments made.

Available Link. A conditional link becomes available when the conditions are met.

In Bullfrog's Theme Hospital, a virtual coach alerts the player when links to information become available.

When links go from being unavailable to available, the new choice is often highlighted via a flashing inbox or icon, or noted by the virtual coach, mentor, or guide.

Some links may only be available one time, and once traversed, become unavailable.

Current Link. The current link is the one that the player or process is traversing at a given moment.

Current Element. The current element is the one where the player or process is at the moment in question.

Dead Link. A dead link is one that is supposed to take the user or process to a new element, but does not. Dead links are identified and fixed as part of the debugging process.

Elements connected by Links are the structure of most game boards.

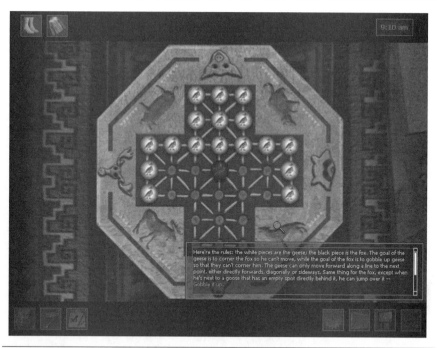

Source: Her interactive – Nancy Drew ® The White Wolf of Icicle Creek.

Active Link. An active link is one that succeeds in taking the user or process to a new element. The term can be used to describe a hotspot in a display, or when debugging (where it is the opposite of dead link).

Branch. A branch is a place, element, state, or decision with at least two different exit links.

The visibility and usability of exit links can depend on user decision, system variables, token possessed (such as a key to "unlock" a door), attributes, or probability.

Multiple-choice questions present common branching basic inputs.

See "Branching Story" in Chapter Two.

Entrance Link. An entrance link is one through which a process enters an element. An entrance link might play media, such as a cut scene, or in some way change an attribute or variable.

Exit Link. An exit link is one through which a process or participant moves away from an element. An exit link might play some media, such as a cut scene, or in some way change an attribute or variable.

Certain exit links might be conditional. If two or more exit links are available, the element serves as a branch. Available exit links might be highlighted.

Hierarchy or Tree

A hierarchy is an organizational structure in which each element has one and only one element, called the parent, above it (except the highest element), but no limit to the number of elements, called the children, below it, including zero.

Hierarchical structures visually form a tree.

Child. In a hierarchical tree, any elements that are directly below another element (the parent). Typically, each child can have only one parent.

Parent. In a hierarchical tree, elements that are directly above one or more elements (called children).

Also called *owner.*

Binary

A simple system that has only two states, on and off, is referred to as *binary.* Traditional light switches and forks in the road are binary.

See *all-or-nothing.* Opposite of "Analog" (discussed in Chapter Twelve).

Knowledge Asset

Knowledge assets consist of any recorded content or element that has value to an organization for operational or strategic purposes. They can be as simple as phone numbers or as detailed as descriptions of procedures in an instruction manual.

Memory Element. In a Sim, a memory element is a knowledge asset that, once found and experienced, is always accessible, often stored and automatically organized in an auto-journal.

For example, in Sid Meier's Alpha Centauri, once a player either discovers a technology or new process or finds contact information for another leader, that information can never be taken away, traded away, or otherwise lost. It can, however, be shared.

In a multiplayer Sim, different players might find different memory elements. In some Sim genres, such as virtual experience spaces, memory elements must be found and then reordered and selectively combined to create final reports or presentations.

12

PURE MATHEMATICAL SYSTEM

The Real Stuff

Some systems are purely mathematical. For example, a system's primary variables may move according to changes in aggregations of secondary variables, as defined by equations and relationships. This is the principal model for the Sim genre of interactive spreadsheets, but a necessary piece of most Sims.

Lines and Relationships

Nineteenth-century mathematicians discovered to their discomfort that as the conceptual machinery of mathematics became more precise, it became more difficult.

—David Berlinski, *The Advent of the Algorithm*

I suspect that Berlinski's observation will turn out to apply equally well to the serious games industry.

One precision tool likely to show this behavior is *relationships*. At the base of any good domain expertise pyramid is a whole mess of relationships between two or more variables. What is the relationship between compensation and performance? When a criminal successfully steals money, what impact does that have on the subsequent crime rate?

Here are some of my favorite generic shapes of relationships.

- The linear relationship
- The bell curve
- The S-curve
- The asymptotic relationship
- The price/demand relationship

Or visually:

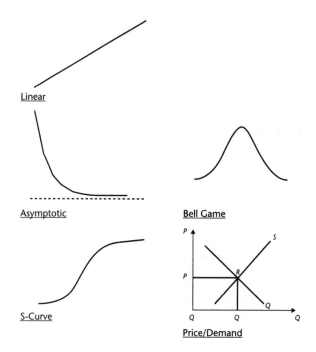

Linear

Asymptotic

Bell Game

S-Curve

Price/Demand

Sim designers must be as comfortable with using these relationships to characterize knowledge as authors of reports currently are with bullets, headings, and fonts. This process requires aggregating a lot of little equations, each embarrassingly trivial in themselves, but powerful and even surprising in their totality.

Taxes are a great example of different types of relationships: sales taxes are a fixed percentage of the cost of an item, whereas a progressive income tax means that the proportion of income one has to pay increases as income bracket rises.

Here are examples and attributes of lines and relationships.

Primary Variables

Primary variables are the measurable criteria participants need to optimize for success. For example, a walk in the woods might have these primary variables: Here are examples and attributes of lines and relationships.

- Fun
- Low cost
- Safety
- Exercise

Primary variables. In Virtual Leader, participants have a final score, made up of averaging two primary variables—leadership process and business results—each of which is an average of three secondary variables.

Leadership Score

The Power, Tension and Idea charts are qualitative metrics/feedback that give you an assessment of how well you prepared and positioned your team to have a successful outcome. The Business Results metrics/feedback are communicated through the Storyline Continuation dialogue determined exclusively by the ideas that were passed. This screen offers a quantitative assessment of the performance of your organization over the next business quarter in the areas of Financial Performance, Customer Satisfaction and Employee Morale.

Leadership		88 %
Power	72 %	
Tension	92 %	
Ideas	100%	
Business Results		93 %
Financial Performance	95 %	
Customer Satisfaction	95 %	
Employee Morale	90 %	
Total		90 %

Simul earn   Use the arrow keys on your keyboard to move between screens
Press the SPACE BAR to exit to the Main Menu

Screen 1 of 11

In a Sim, the collection of primary variables should be designed so that effective play will optimize them all in the long term, even though they sometimes conflict with each other in the short term. Further, primary variables are often influenced indirectly, that is, by actions that shift the values of secondary or tertiary variables. In the case of the walk in the woods, for example, buying good boots might increase safety but add cost.

The concept of primary variables is often framed by a balanced scorecard in the consulting world and built into system dynamics in the type of simulations called interactive spreadsheets.

Sometimes, the primary variables are balanced inputs. This means that all are necessary for success, and an abundance of one cannot compensate for a lack of another.

Secondary Variables

Secondary roads feed into primary roads (highways), providing a good visualization of the relationship between primary and secondary variables.

Secondary variables, unsurprisingly, are the parts of the system with direct impact on the primary variables.

If a primary variable is health of an economy, for example, a secondary variable might be average labor productivity (the output per employed worker).

Often, a single action may have an impact on two or more secondary variables. For example, amplifying the productivity of a town by providing electricity might also produce pollution that damps a different secondary variable, the cleanliness of air, which in turn damps a second primary variable, the health of the citizens.

Equation

An equation is a consistent mathematical action that creates (or defines) an output from an input, or a mathematical statement declaring that what is on one side of an equal sign (=) is the same as what is on the other side of the equal sign. Related terms:

Input. Inputs are what goes into a system (where the system includes units, maps, and processes).

Output. Outputs are what comes out of a system (where the system includes units, maps, and processes).

Variable. A variable is a placeholder in an equation for one of any of a range of numbers.

Variables often have constraints, such as limits on how high or how low they can go.

Variables can also have granularity. If the constraint on a variable is "dates of Mondays in June 2009," the value of the variable could only be 8, 15, 22, or 27.

In an equation, there are independent variables and dependent variables. In the equation y = x/2, x is the independent variable and y is the dependent variable.

Variables can impact each other (called causality). For example, a rising cost of inputs can lead to rising cost of output. Variables can also move at the same time without one being impacted by the other (see "Correlation," later in this chapter).

If a variable is tied to one number, it is called a *constant.*

Related topic: "Attributes" in Chapter Nine.

All-or-Nothing

A state that is either on or off, with nothing in between, is referred to as *all-or-nothing.* One is, as the saying goes, either pregnant or not. Some view social standards like loyalty, religious views, or moral codes as all-or-nothing issues.

An all-or-nothing algorithm is a mechanism that translates analog signals into a single digital signal. A restaurant-goer might have only a slight preference for the beef brisket over the pulled pork, but commits to a single option when the waiter comes. National political elections are dramatic examples of all-or-nothing results. They turn a few percentage points' difference in constituent opinion into entirely different administrations.

Chain reactions, such as rumors or fires or neuron signals, typically spread (or, more technically, *propagate*) in a series of all-or-nothing reactions.

Automated coaching systems and triggers (including those that might launch alerts) tend to use all-or-nothing algorithms to give advice, turning complex and subtle input into absolute comments and observations.

A hero's journey is often all-or-nothing. Also called *binary*. Opposite of *analog* (discussed later in this chapter).

Edge Enhancement

Edge enhancement is a process in both human eyes and Xerox machines to make edges more dramatic for the sake of clarity.

Technically, edge enhancement exaggerates the difference between two states or takes an analog signal and makes it increasingly all-or-nothing. Many digital scanners include edge enhancement algorithms, especially useful when digitizing text to make the output crisp and clear, while ruining photographs.

Politicians often employ some form of edge enhancement in their rhetoric to draw and exaggerate distinctions between themselves and their opponents, however slight they might really be. Membership in a club or social clique can often serve as an edge enhancement socially. Some "no-tolerance" policies, whether religious, cultural, or institutional, serve as social edge enhancement, pushing people who straddle boundaries into either being better or being worse, labeled "good" or labeled "bad." Individuals can also "fall from grace" or "be reformed," quickly moving from one group to the other.

Correlation

A correlation is a relationship between two or more variables or occurrences that are connected.

Correlation does not prove causation, however. For example, if two corks can rise and fall on the same ocean wave, correlation can prove the two motions are connected, but one cork is not causing the other to move.

Correlation can be described mathematically, with a 1 correlation being the highest, and −1 showing a perfect negative correlation.

Weighting

Weighting is the technique of multiplying a variable by a constant to make it more or less relevant to an equation or aggregation. Weighting is almost always a form of editorializing, essentially attaching adjectives (value terms) to numbers.

Getting the weights right on a Sim usually involves significant calibration. Both amplifying and damping a number are forms of weighting.

Amplify

To amplify something is to increase the output in some way that correlates, either linearly or geometrically, with the input.

For example, one activity of a corporate communications process is to amplify the voice of senior management. In an act of leadership, the president of a country may point out an exemplary individual to amplify that person's voice.

Damp. To damp something is decrease the output in some way that correlates, either linearly or geometrically, with the input. For example, one activity of a PR department or process is to damp any bad news.

Zero-Sum

A zero-sum system is one in which value can neither be created nor destroyed; it can only be shifted or transformed.

Zero-sum is also called win-lose (one or more units can win only if others lose an equal amount), in contrast to situations that are win-win or lose-lose.

The law of conservation of energy is a zero-sum law. Most sports are zero-sum, whereby necessarily some players win and others lose. Gambling is zero-sum, although there may be an element of infrastructure friction (that is, the house always wins in the long run).

Zero-sum often creates conflict and competitors.

Aggregation

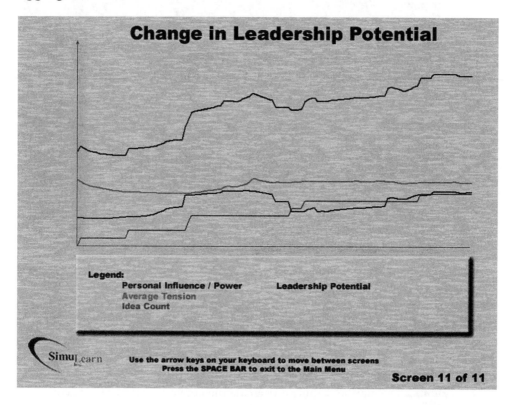

Aggregation is the combination of multiple variables in a single, higher-level variable. It can also include the amplifying or damping of variables, making some more relevant than others.

The grades in schools represent aggregations of variables, including test scores, homework, and participation. Two students, for example, could be ranked differently in relationship to each other if two instructors put different priorities on the various pieces. Likewise, any score produced by a simulation to evaluate student performance involves significant aggregations, necessarily including editorial weightings.

Aggregation can also be done to simplify an equation. If the movement of a large number of variables can be replaced by a single variable, it is computationally more efficient to do so.

Any attribute is, at some level, an aggregation.

Delay

Delay refers to the time it takes for a change of input to result in a change of output. In a system with significant delay, users might not understand the correlation between input and output.

Oftentimes if there is a delay, users have trouble calibrating, and as a result overcompensate. For example, if it takes thirty minutes between putting food in one's mouth and feeling satiation, one could easily overeat. If it takes three minutes between adjusting the temperature of the water and the shower to reflect the new temperature, bathers might go through cycles of getting the shower too hot and then too cold.

Other times, especially if the input has a high cost, users might give up. If spending money on advertising doesn't result in immediate increased traffic, a business might give up, despite the eventual increase that would have been realized had it continued.

One game element is to reduce the delay in a simulation. Another game element is to have a built-in delay, and to have participants get the hang of compensating for the delay. For other game elements, see Chapter Sixteen.

Delay is also called *lag time* or *latency*.

Analog

Analog information is continuous across time, not falling into neat number labels (technically, not discrete numbers). The speed of a car, pressure on a gas pedal, outdoor temperature, amount of interest of a potential customer, food in a bird feeder, pi, and number of acres of forests in Connecticut are all examples of analog information.

Analog information may be represented using a meter or graph, either dynamically on a heads-up display, or statically in an after action review.

Throttles and steering wheels provide examples of analog input. In some simulations, users can hold a button for various amounts of time to create an analog input.

Opposite of "Discrete," "Digital," and "All-or-Nothing" in this chapter, and "Binary" in Chapter Eleven.

Analog

Discrete

Discrete information falls into neat, whole-number categories, such as 1, 5, or −3, or items that can be presented as all-or-nothing and self-contained, such as choices in a branching story or units on a map.

"You are either with us or against us," said President George W. Bush in November 2001, paraphrasing an account of Jesus Christ described in Matthew 12:30: "He who is not with me is against me, and he who does not gather with me scatters."

See also "All-or-Nothing" and "Digital" in this chapter, and "Binary" in Chapter Eleven.

Digital

Digital can refer either to a simple system with only two states, on and off, or to information made up purely of discrete numbers (including computer programs and "digitized" movies and music). Digital information can be transported with almost no cost of travel and without corruption or mutation.

See also "All-or-Nothing" and "Discrete" in this chapter, and "Binary" in Chapter Eleven.

Opposite of *analog.*

Cap

A cap is an artificial restriction on how high or low a number can go.

Speed limits and quotas on fish caught, imports allowed, or even types of students admitted are examples of real-world caps. Prices, for example, can be capped at the high end (in legal terms, a price ceiling) or capped at the low end (in legal terms, a price floor).

In some simulations, players might set quotas themselves as an action, using text windows or sliders as the basic input. The units within the Sim would then react differently based on these settings.

When scoring is normalized around academic grade ranges, capping high scores at 100 percent and low scores at 55 percent comforts the user. Selective capping can also minimize "gaming the system."

Attributes are almost always capped.

Random

Randomness is a system property of being unpredictable. For example, a variable might have a shifting and unpredictable value or a situation might have an unpredictable outcome.

Despite its unpredictable nature, randomness can have boundaries, probabilities, and predictable patterns of distribution and aggregation.

Imagine rolling a pair of dice and adding up the value. The range has a low of two and a high of twelve. But the numbers in the middle, six, seven, and eight, are much more likely to come up than the numbers at the extreme.

Some simulations can generate a map that is random but still adheres to certain rules.

Sometimes events appear random, but there is really an underlining pattern. The study of chaos involves both trying to predict the patterns and understanding where prediction is not possible.

Randomness makes a Sim much harder to debug. If, for example, a Sim has three possible outcomes, one often has to play through it five or six times to experience all three of the possibilities. It also makes a Sim hard to present to a group. It's like acting with kids or animals. The Sim can play out in an unpredictable way, forcing you, in front of a roomful of people, to explain why a low-probability event happened when a higher-probability event is the more logical chain of events.

Randomness also doesn't always provide variety. If a Sim, for example, pulls a sound randomly from twenty potential options each turn, one sound will sometimes play at least twice in a row, most likely every fifteen turns.

A gambler who plays a perfect game of chance will have winning streaks, losing streaks, and periods of equilibrium.

Randomness can also make it harder to write walk-throughs. Too much randomness in a game or Sim, even if accurate, is frustrating (just as in real life). Managers often start from the premise that randomness is to be eliminated; the "Quality" movement in manufacturing, for example, has meant the attempt to eliminate all randomness (deviation from specifications) in producing a finished good. On the other hand, randomness also allows emergence of new outcomes, so it has some uses:

- Randomness, and specifically random mutation, is a critical component of evolution. One can increase the amount of mutation (of genetic randomness) by increasing radiation levels.
- Randomness is a tool to counter bias, especially in exploring the unknown. Suppose Brown University accepted one random applicant for every nine who were filtered by the traditional administration process. If the 10 percent of random students did as well as the 90 percent who were filtered, Brown could assume its filtering process was not worth the resources.
- In some educational simulations, users get lucky and get a great outcome the first time they try. But they cannot repeat that performance, and become frustrated (see "Accidental Success" in Chapter Eighteen). That causes a perceived credibility problem for the educational simulation deployer. Yet it happens all the time in real life—I can think of several managers who were lucky, got promoted, and then never repeated the success.

Related topic: "Noise" in Chapter Seventeen.

Probability

In a systems model, probability is the likelihood of something happening, or the percentage of times something happens.

Probabilities are ratios of "target action"/"all possible actions."

For example, when one rolls a standard, random, six-sided die, the probability of any number between one and six appearing is one in six.

In some situations, only two outcomes are possible, often distributed into the two categories: hit or miss. Obviously, just because a situation has two possible outcomes does not mean the percentage of each is 50 percent. In a lottery, for example, the chance of winning a million dollars (the hit) may well be one in two million.

The percentage of hits is called the hit rate. In many situations, real-world and simulated, one can increase or decrease probabilities (wearing a seat-belt decreases probability of death in a car accident), while never fully controlling the outcome (some seat-belted individuals still die).

Permutation

In game development, *permutation* refers to a selection of specific combinations from a larger set.

If a Sim has ten possible power-ups, and a participant can use up to three (that is, zero, one, two, or three at a time, with no duplication, making eleven possible power-up elements) to impact a level of core gameplay in the execution phase, that level now has (anyone, anyone?) 165 permutations: $(11 - 10 - 9)/(3 - 2 - 1)$.

Distribution

A distribution is a taxonomy organized by number of occurrences.

One can toss a coin and organize the results by heads and tails. One would assume an equal distribution of heads and tails over many iterations, but that would obviously be impossible if one just flipped a coin once.

One classic distribution is the *bell curve*, a pattern that fits predictable situations in which most members have only slight deviations from a norm, but a few deviate from the norm significantly. The norm is also called the mean or arithmetic average.

A bell curve. The attributes of many organic systems follow a bell curve, such as the height of fifteen-year-olds.

Explosion

An explosion is a sudden and dramatic increase in any quantity.

Explosions in an ecosystem can be the result of

- A chain reaction, such as acquisitions in the social networking space
- A time in a cycle (such as spring or payday)
- A new process, path, attractor, source, or dispenser, such as a bird feeder or airport

Explosions can often follow the degradation of one or more balancing loops.

Spike

A spike is a flurry of activity, followed by a drop in activity. The point of highest activity is called the *peak*.

Peak

The peak is the relative high point on a graph (or of any variable over time), followed by a decline. In economic terms, a peak might be followed be a recession.
Opposite of trough.

Crash

A crash is a sudden and unexpected reduction in any quantity.

Decay

Decay is the reduction or breaking down of value (including capability), often over time or when exposed to certain conditions.
Incremental, analog decay can lead to a sudden all-or-nothing failure.

Decay in Formal Learning. Most knowledge decays if not used, including combat readiness, as shown in the chart of bombing accuracy. As a result, students cram for tests the day before or even the same morning in the hope that their awareness won't decay before they are required to write down the information.

Decay in the Natural World. In nature, politics, and business, structures form out of building-block units, hold together for a while, and then decay. Plants grow from sun and soil, and then break back down into soil and energy. A smart computer programmer might get hired by IBM, downsized, and hired by Microsoft, downsized, and then hired by Google. A political party becomes compelling, attracts new constituents, and then decays, releasing the loyalty of the constituents to new people and parties.

Decay

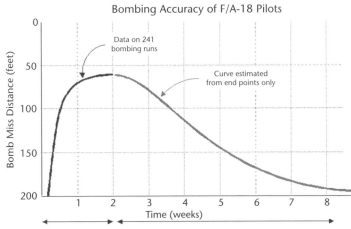

Bombing Accuracy of F/A-18 Pilots

Data on 241
bombing runs

Curve estimated
from end points only

Bomb Miss Distance (feet)

Time (weeks)

Air-to-Ground Training at NAS Fallon,   Weeks After Leaving NAS Fallon
U.S. Navy "Strike University"

(total 14 flying hours)

Pendulum Cycle

A pendulum is a type of system with attributes that move between two states, in an analog and predictable way (physical pendulums are perfectly predictable, unlike social and biological pendulums).

For example, day follows night and night follows day. Organizations may swing back and forth between centralizing and decentralizing functions. Countries may swing between nationalism and globalism. Forests may have rampant growth and then massive fires. Game designers may alternate between honing existing genres and creating new ones.

In some cases the swing may be nothing more than style or fashion, such as a preference for shorter or longer hair. But in most cases, the swing is necessary for long-term equilibrium or healthy growth. For example, one political party may come to power, make valued changes, stagnate, and then provide an opportunity for the other political party to come to power and make new changes.

Sometimes the swings are more nuanced. For example, an organization may start with a broad tax on the business units to fund technology services like computers, Internet access, and business applications. This model encourages unlimited consumption and funds research and development, but it also increases cost. Then the organization might switch to a charge-back model, which forces users to set their own priorities based on what services are valued. After the efficiencies are gained and costs are lowered, the charge-back model then appears too cumbersome, and the organization returns to a broad tax model, often to regain economies of scale.

Multiple pendulums may interact, causing increasingly complex behavior.

Recursion

In a systems model, recursion describes larger patterns that are made up of smaller, similar patterns: the original "mini-me."

The term *recursion* comes from math and computer science, but the phenomenon also applies to language, biology, and even art.

Imagine a typically hierarchical organization, such as a large nonprofit foundation. A CEO at the top has a team of executive vice presidents as direct reports, with metrics for success. Then each executive vice president has a team of senior vice presidents, with metrics for success. Each senior vice president has a team of directors, with metrics for success. Each director has a team of supervisors, and so on.

Because of a recursive organizational structure, every employee in a 5,000-person organization might have one boss, a team of peers, a set metrics for success, and a group of subordinates. Only the one at the top and those in the bottom layer have less than the full set.

Vector

A vector is made up of two pieces, direction and strength. Vectors, such as wind, influence any on-screen movement of units (where wind is a vector, by the way, a windsock icon can be used to visualize it).

13

WORK PROCESS

Work processes are, in models of work, sets of repeatable structured activities that add predictable value, while consuming costs budgetable to an enterprise. Examples include creation, refinement, transportation, and marketing.

Work processes, just as big skills (described in the next chapter), are examples of higher-level systems. Their successful modeling requires the use of other techniques, including map-based (Chapter Eight) or state-based (Chapter Eleven).

Characteristics of Processes

Processes can involve transforming ideas, money, people, and products, delivering a service or message, branching to alternative processes, or triggering an action. They often feature the movement and enrichment of some container of value, whether a widget to be painted or a form to be approved (or kicked back) or a technology to be researched.

Processes often have an owner who takes responsibility for them. Managing a process often requires the application of middle skills and big skills. Some actions simultaneously impact processes and big skills to opposite ends. A manager may force an employee to follow an established bureaucratic process (saving the company a bit of money), while crippling that employee's creativity and costing extra time (that may have otherwise been spent inventing new value for the organization, making money).

Some processes are core, while others are tangential. Processes can be ongoing (infrastructure), or triggered by an event.

Processes also might produce unwanted and perhaps unintended outputs, beyond their cost. The refinement, reorganization, or elimination of processes is a high-value activity in many organizations, often called process reengineering. And as with other systems, the optimization of one process without looking at its interdependencies can be suboptimal or even counterproductive. Improvements can also be made within a process (as with business process redesign).

Processes can be simple or complex, and need to be connected to other processes, sometimes through paths. Processes can also be done in parallel. And the integration between processes is called the "process fit," something that can be as strategically significant as the process itself. Business processes maps are also called business process diagrams.

Processes often need units and resources and can be represented on maps by structures. Processes can be automated.

A process can be

- Done internally (retailer employees stock shelves)
- Outsourced (retailer hires independent workers to stock shelves)
- Transferred completely to another organization (retailer asks vendors to stock shelves, or retailer becomes online retailer and asks vendors to ship directly to customers)

Typically, the more important the process, the more ownership the enterprise wants to have. New processes can also have a disruptive effect.

In many charts, both processes and activities are represented by rectangles with rounded corners. The completion of some processes, typically more complex and unique ones, is considered a milestone. Business processes should be evaluated against balanced scorecards.

The concept of *process* contrasts and overlaps with *activity*, including internal (high-control) activities and external (low-control) activities.

Activity

In models of work, activities are functions or tasks that have valued results when completed, and that consume resources such as time, facilities, attention, and money to create and use. These resources may be significant or insignificant in amount, but some demand is inevitable.

Activities are almost always repeated, either many times by a few people, or a few times by many people. In a Sim, most player and AI actions are done in the context of activities (the action is the what, the activity is the why), which then might shape the interface. Collections of activities can form processes. Mental states can also change activities pursued.

Activities, both in Sims and the real world, can be made up of smaller activities, such as commuting to work, delivering packages, producing a dinner in a restaurant, or assigning people to work on a movie.

Activities can also be simple and stand-alone, such as finding a piece of information through a single click in a Web page. (And if enough people want that information, a good designer might remove that activity by making the information accessible in the preceding page.) Activities can be in different stages of completion, from not yet started to started, and varying percentages done to finished.

Some collections of activities, typically internal, are completely under the control of an organization. Widgets, paperwork, or ideas flow through prescribed activities.

Other collections of activities, especially those involving customers, have to allow for more self-direction. Customers choose to engage activities. If activities require too much expenditure of resources, or too much deviation from another flow of activities, customers complain or choose alternatives.

Consume

In models of work, consumption refers to use of the resources needed to build units, to maintain units, to upgrade units, or for units to perform specific activities. When resources are consumed, they are lost.

Cost

A cost is something that results in a loss of resources or other forms of value.

Increasing the cost typically lowers the demand (by various units) for something, or decreases the likelihood that something will happen. Ideally, costs are budgeted.

Consume

Cost

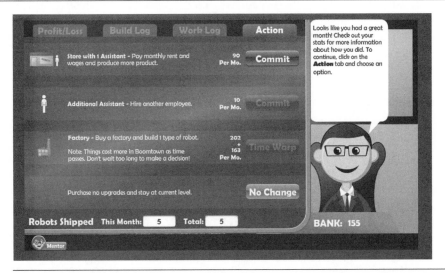

Source: Acton Foundation for Entrepreneurial Excellence

Economies of Scale

Economies of scale are benefits or cost reductions that increase as a system increases the number of times it does the same thing.

Achieving economies of scale is a critical component of both value creation and cost reduction.

Author's note: The issue of economies of scale is at the core of educational simulations, and maybe all of formal learning. Clive Shepherd said it well: "What I am having trouble getting my mind around is how the quality of Sims can be kept as high as possible, with all the intellectual effort that this entails, without the whole process becoming unrealistically expensive and disenfranchising learning and development professionals who have to subcontract all this work to outsiders."

Most people buy many things, such as clothes, pain remedies, and cars, instead of making their own. Every book published uses economies of scale. Of course, this tapping in of scale involves some sacrifice of ego and fit. Products that leverage economies of scale often include the ability to configure (that is, allow for mass customization), a more scalable framework than customizing.

A trip to the doctor's office ideally represents a combination of personalization, with a doctor who examines you, and a tapping of economies of scale, with the creation of a configured or customized prescription that applies highly researched mass-produced pharmaceuticals that fit into your biology and lifestyle.

Boards and advisers can connect individuals or organizations to existing economies of scale. Applying economic, value, and governing models requires an understanding of scales involved. Economies of scale change budgeting allocations.

Economies of scale can create natural monopolies, situations in which an organization can control most market share, not because of anti-competitive practices, but because of efficiencies.

Opposite of club, where the value corresponds to exclusivity rather than accessibility.

Edited, Processed, Refined, Augmented

Edited and the other terms in the heading refer to the anticipated higher value of having been selected, filtered, or assembled, as opposed to occurring organically.

A random home photograph or movie might be slightly edited, with decisions around when and where to shoot. An advertisement for a new vodka is almost inevitably highly edited, with everything from characters and settings reflecting very careful choice and placement.

Locations themselves can also be highly edited, such as Disney World, or more organic, such as a mountain top. The notion of being edited is recursive. One can take a casual photograph of Russia's Hermitage Museum.

Editing is also called *bias*.

Related topics: "Story" in Chapter Fifteen, and "Situational Awareness" in Chapter Nineteen.

Milestone

In models of work, a milestone is an alert using a marker on a path that shows how far one has come, or how far one has to go.

Milestones

Originally referring to a literal stone placed every mile along a road, the term *milestone* has been generalized to refer to specific, recognizable achievements in a project, process, or life cycle.

Procedure

In Old Sturbridge Village (Massachusetts), the procedures of running a small New England town are preserved.

In models of work, a procedure is a series of actions that must be done in a linear sequence. To follow a procedure, a participant might also react to feedback and choose between simple branches.

Most repeated activities in an enterprise have corresponding procedures, whether captured in a knowledge asset or not.

See also "Procedural Knowledge" in Chapter Twenty-Two.

Process Map

A process map is a form of map that uses a state-based model to show the connections among actions, procedures, activities, or processes.

Revenue

Revenue is a desired result of having a reliable stream of money and customers for the product or service in question—for example, to sponsor learning programs over the course of a planning horizon.

The metric of revenue is more important than the metric of funding for a group, but less important than profitability.

Role

Following a role is a way to be productive in, create, and follow an explicit or implied script. Each role has its own actions, activities, and processes and is evaluated against different balanced scorecards or primary variables.

Some other examples:

- Roles among family and friends: Spouse; child; parent; listener; "the fun one."
- Roles at work: Engineer; innovator; documenter; problem solver; whistleblower.
- Roles in learning: Participant; instructor; expert; audience member; coach or facilitator; buddy.
- Roles in society: Steward; producer; consumer.
- Roles in stories: Mentor, supervisor, or guide; villain; innocent bystander; instigator; hero.

Other characteristics:

- Different types of units might have certain inherent roles and also might be assigned to roles.
- Some roles are mutually exclusive, and some role compete.
- Occupying a role includes following scripts and using technical skills. Roles often have a hierarchy of tasks. (See "AI States" in Chapter Ten.)

A Process Map

PDD00344: Contract Management - Handover and Execute Agreement

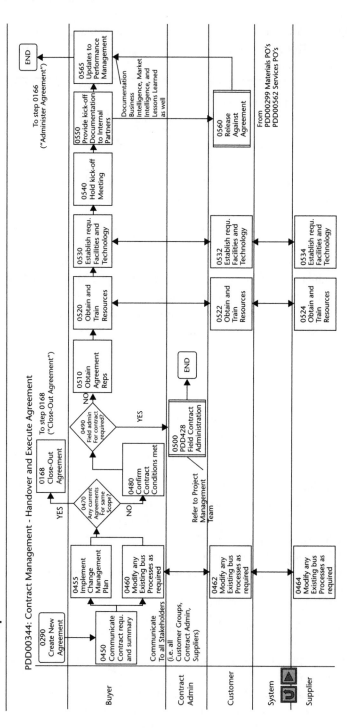

• A form of aligning strategies and tactics would be assigning the right person to the right role.

Related topic: "Assigning Roles" in Chapter Five.

Span of Control

The volume of processes and units under the ownership of a single individual is referred to as *span of control*. A high span of control can be an attribute of a unit depicting its power. The personality or priorities of unit can impact attributes of all other processes or units. For example, managers with a focus on short-term revenue at the expense of maintenance will impact everything under their spans of control in a way that is different from managers who focus on customer satisfaction or innovation.

Value Chain

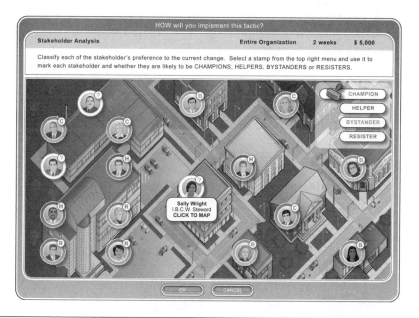

Source: Tactic execution for ExperienceChange: SkyTech. © 2009 ExperiencePoint Inc.

Revenue: Structures require and can enable revenue.

Role

A value chain is a linked string of processes that includes every activity under an organization's control that leads to a consumer's receiving and paying for some value. In City Interactive's Beauty Factory, the four steps in the value chain are research and development, manufacturing, sales and marketing, and office management.

Engine

In organizational terms, an engine is anything that continually, effectively, predictably, and positively impacts a critical metric or provides a critical service, with little maintenance when necessary inputs are met. An organization with a well-honed marketing engine may be effective at promoting every new product or service. An organization may choose to identify and hone just such an engine if it is in its long-term interests. Likewise, an organization may not understand that an effective engine is already in place and inadvertently disrupt it, causing a huge and sometimes irreversible negative impact.

14

BIG SKILLS

The Most Important Twenty-First-Century Skills

The tragedy of corporations and universities alike, is that big skills—also called *soft skills* or *organizational skills*—are the most valued nontechnical skills a person can have, but they are rarely taught. This includes leadership, along with nurturing and stewardship, communication, relationship management, and all the common skills that give people the most control over their lives. These skills represent a system, either explicitly or via a community, and they necessarily balance technical skill.

Given that, in the context of serious games and simulations, big skills have many roles. I discuss them in detail in this part of the book, which addresses systems, because each big skill is a special type of complex system, something that technically comes between action and result. Big skills can be used by an AI player to act realistically, but big skills are also desired results of many formal learning programs (or at least they should be). Designers have to create and visualize systems whereby only the correct understanding and application of big skills by a player can result in success. So big skills could also be in the Introduction, as they represent failures of linear content, or in the Conclusion, as the North Star for Sims. To many they seem mystical—at once too important and too nebulous to define in practical terms. Therefore one challenge of this section is to start to deconstruct them. For example, these skills share critical qualities:

- They are simultaneously relevant for individuals, work groups, families, organizations, even industries, states, and countries.
- They have to be practiced. It is not sufficient to be intellectually aware of what they involve.
- They often require the application of middle skills, such as directing people and containment.

- They can be honed, in some form or another, almost every day.
- They involve improvisation and knowledge of systems, not just processes.
- They are characteristically applied most effectively by the top organizations in the world.

Developing big skills requires participants to experience cycles of frustration and resolution (discussed in more detail in Chapter Twenty-Eight).

The Core of Any Curricula

In educational simulations, big skills are applied through the use of actions and middle skills. Developing big skills in people will most likely not happen predictably by accident, or in big multiplayer environments. Instead, these skills require not only practice environments but often entirely new genres. Because simulations are not perfectly predictive, the learning goal for a big skill is often "how to avoid doing the wrong thing" as opposed to "how to do the right thing."

Big skills can be measured through 360-degree feedback, and they can lead to actualization. Their rigorous development is very difficult through simply raising awareness, although that might be an important first step. It almost necessarily involves the role of a coach, a way of practicing, and the target's keeping of a journal or blog.

Schools and many corporations have not focused directly on developing big skills. Schools develop them indirectly, through extracurricular activities such as sports, while corporations hire or promote people who display these skills rather than attempting to develop them deliberately.

Adaptation

Adaptation is the big skill of changing incrementally, including the ability to develop or strengthen new capabilities and wither old, to meet the needs of

Adaptation. This picture includes at least seven individuals of the same type of large mammal. Find them.

(or increase one's suitability for) a new ecosystem. Adaptations can be made through altering attributes or reassembling building blocks.

Adaptation requires the ability to change, the opportunity to change, and the availability of good feedback.

Applying Economic, Value, and Governing Models

Applying the right models, including governing, economic, and value models, to your role is a big skill in its own right. It includes an intellectual component, understanding the different options, and a doing component, successfully selecting and implementing the appropriate one.

Model choices apply to individuals as well as organizations and countries. Possibilities include

- Economic (how you are paid for your value and other funding models): Pay-per-use, commons, sales tax, income tax, buy, rent, high-end, low-end, retainer, steal, by hour, by deliverable, front loaded, back loaded.

- Governing (how people work together): Democracy, communism, dictatorship, franchise, public company, private business.
- Value (what others get from you): Infrastructure, high-innovation and research, low-cost, high-service, relationship-based, path of least resistance, power-based, addictive, mold to customer, mold to vendor, delighting customers, problem-solving, sales or other paths, trains-run-on-time efficiency, distribution, high customer satisfaction, licensing.
- Success may be 1 percent inspiration, 50 percent perspiration, and 49 percent finding the right business, sustainability, and monetization model.
- Kurt Potter, the Gartner analyst, maintains that IT departments go through a perpetual financial loop:

  1. IT departments start by charging the corporation some sort of broad tax.
  2. Then, to be more fair, they begin charging more to departments that use more computer and other IT services.
  3. To be even more fair, they get more and more specific in their charge-back strategy, down to charging per person, per job role, or even per use or direct cost.
  4. Finally, they become buried in paperwork, and to simplify and cut costs, they go back to 1.

  Applying the right model is a big skill.

Budgeting

Budgeting is the middle skill of planning the amount and cost of resources needed at various times in the process.

Budgeting. Users of Virtual University both create budgets and compare actual expenses against forecasts.

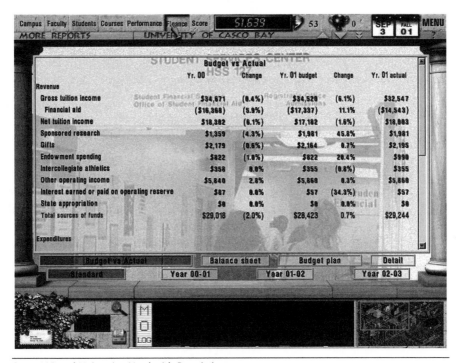

Source: Virtual University. Used with Permission.

Creating budgets typically happens at the beginning of a process, although the budgets may be calibrated during the course of the project. Budgeting is appropriate for infrastructure or one-off activities, as well as planning hours spent during the course of a day.

Budgets may need to be approved by boards or advisers.

Some budget issues can be allocation-based. (For example, given five competing categories and X hours, how do you allocate time?) Some can be blank check issues (How much will you need to accomplish X?), and some can be growth issues. (If you commit to doubling your money, how much will you borrow?) Some budget issues can involve inventory and caching. (Given that you only have three donkeys or two boats, which supplies will you bring? Can you prepare other supplies for scheduled air drops?)

Budgeting is often a critical component of the interactive spreadsheet simulation genre. Budgeting also means balancing inputs.

Budget units are a measurement used to quantify budget items. For example, the unit for people might be hour or day. The unit for rent might be month. The unit for topsoil might be cubic yard.

Related topics: "Cost-Benefit Analysis," later in this chapter, and "Economies of Scale" in Chapter Thirteen.

Communication

At its core, communication is the big skill of moving information between a transmitter (including a broadcaster or narrowcaster) and one or more receivers.

More broadly, most person-to-person communication strives to increase awareness, explain actions, direct people, comment to answer questions or correct perceived mistakes, change the alignment between people and ideas, and increase the attractiveness of the information source. It includes the ability to express oneself effectively through various and appropriate media (writing, speaking, charts, even graphic novels). Communication includes understanding audience and target requirements, needs and pain points, and knowledge and also listening effectively as others express themselves.

Part of communication is knowing what is in it for the audience. All communication also has a credibility component. The right communication sets off a chain reaction.

Communication strategies often have to be created before an urgent need for them appears. Having a weekly open house to combat a rampant rumor mill might be critical. As organizations and teams become more distributed, ad hoc (so-called water-cooler) communication becomes less reliable, and so formal communication techniques need to be established.

Picking the right genre is important. Letters have different requirements from those of e-mail. In fact, the best way to trash someone's career is to circulate a colleague's instant-messaging comments reformatted as a letter. Videoconferencing is more formal; webcams are more casual.

Dynamically customizing the content is critical. This could be based on audience questions or, for self-paced content, providing alternative branches through the content by setting up a variety of links.

An effective communication strategy might involve having the audience do some exercises to internalize the information. This could be everything from taking notes at a lecture to playing a marketing mini game around the release of a new soft drink or movie.

Building on existing alignments can also be critical. Politicians use the icon of the U.S. flag. Computer games might tie into famous athletes or movies. Advertisements shamelessly use idealized models, professions, or roles (showing a mother buckling up her children in a minivan while talking about some new fast food product). Create a verbal label for a complicated idea, and you shape the perception of the idea.

There are legal requirements for communications, especially around product recalls and shareholder information. Organizations often have different uses of (and budget differently for) the processes of public relations and advertising.

Some communication is passive. Clothing and hairstyle choices broadcast your affiliations and even aspirations. Corporations choose colors and fonts carefully.

Some communication strategies are malicious. It's possible to spread a lie through so many channels that it becomes thought of as a truth. An ethically challenged leader leaks a lie to a newspaper anonymously, and then publicly refers to the article as a source of credibility. Some communication is designed to overload a receptor.

Conceptual Dead Reckoning

Conceptual dead reckoning may have a funny name, but it's a life-defining activity. It is a big skill that leaders use for accomplishment. It is analogous to physical navigation without reference to specific landmarks.

The term *dead reckoning* migrated from steering ships at sea to aviation, and then to animal research and orienteering. But it also describes what professionals do all the time. In the professional's case, the map is conceptual, the destination is a goal (the creation of a product, the closing of a sale, the solving of a complex problem), and the options and barriers are procedural and not physical, but the model, much more adaptive and dynamic than the milestone approach, is the same.

To understand the behavior of people in challenging situations, it is critical to understand the conceptual map that the leaders see and then to recognize their strategy for identifying a destination.

Conceptual maps, complete with large dark spots labeled "unknown," can include

- Differing governing models for a new nation
- Different combinations of chemicals and therapy that may cure Parkinson's disease
- Differing drama genres for conveying a complex idea

Once the maps are roughed out, leaders commit to a destination, then create a vector based on understanding of current and destination location, and finally make a series of short-term decisions based on reconciling the vector against real options available on a map. More specifically, these are the steps:

1. Rough out a conceptual map. Ask, "what are all the possibilities available in the relevant area?" Parts of the map will be labeled "unknown."
2. Identify the "as is" current position, region controlled, or area of competency on the conceptual map.
3. Identify the "to be" position or region—the one you desire to reach. It can be ambitious and far away or conservative and close, and in part determined by the cost of travel. Then make a commitment to get there.
4. Make a series of very short-term decisions and actions to get closer to the destination point, often using a compass for direction. It doesn't matter how quickly you wish to reach the ultimate destination, the resulting path is inevitably winding and full of branches, like lightning forking to reach the ground.

Conflict Management

Conflict management is the big skill of resolving an adversarial situation with the minimum expenditure of force necessary to achieve a satisfactory outcome.

Conflict is often, but not necessarily, a failure of conflict management. When conflict does occur in the context of a successful conflict management approach, it is either more contained and productive than either no conflict or a larger conflict, or it supports other agendas, including political ones.

In some environments, certain types of conflicts represent automatic failure of conflict management strategies, including physical, in most workplaces, and certain types of chemical or nuclear conflict between nations.

Strategies for conflict management include listening, negotiation, leadership, communication, adapting, involving a third party for mediation, and establishing ground rules. They can also involve proactively dismantling sources of potential conflict before conflict occurs.

Conflict management can also include a "cold war" scenario. That is, two or more parties can live with long-term hostilities that never resolve and that divert resources, but that do not result in full-scale force either.

Ironically, but consistent with conceptual dead reckoning, preparation for successful conflict management can include building force.

Cost-Benefit Analysis

Cost-benefit analysis is the big skill of evaluating past and future actions, activities, and processes based on the relationship between gains and losses.

For simulation examples, see "Costs, and Budgeting Costs for Simulation" in Chapter Twenty-Three and "Return on Investment" in Chapter Seven.

These are the relevant questions in a cost-benefit analysis:

* How much will it cost? How will the costs be budgeted?
* How much of the possible benefit will be realized at each milestone?
* What is the range of possible costs, and what makes the costs increase or decrease? How will costs be contained?
* At what cost will the project in question no longer be worthwhile?
* How will we know, once we are into it, when to back off or when to "stay the course"?
* What other things could we do with the resources that might be better (and thus represent opportunity costs for the current project)?

Just because something is good, that doesn't mean it should be done. Likewise, just because it's possible to get rid of something that is bad, that doesn't mean the required action is the best one to take. The same cost-benefit questions apply.

It's a good idea to do a cost-benefit analysis (using a balanced scorecard) every day for yourself personally, as well as for every project, everything your work group is doing, and what your organization and even your industry is doing.

Author's note: There are at least two traps with cost-benefit analysis.

Plenty of so-called leaders try to circumvent the cost-benefit analysis and present activities as things that "have to be done no matter what" or "have to be stopped no matter what."

Others, typically staffers, often cheat their jobs by using cost-benefit analysis as an excuse not to do something that makes sense to do; to support the easy, seemingly no-risk status quo (one classic obstructionist staff technique is to apply a much higher standard on justifying new activities than on justifying existing activities—including their own pay—to give themselves a reason to let something fail rather than do the hard work necessary for success.

Creating and Using Boards and Advisers

It is a big skill to use a group of diverse individuals to provide short- and long-term guidance and oversight.

Boards provide metrics, defining balanced scorecards. They perform after action reviews. They help in all aspects of conceptual dead reckoning.

Corporations, universities, and nonprofits have boards of directors (or trustees). The Federal Reserve, for example, is led by seven governors appointed by the current president to staggered terms.

But individuals use advisers all the time, albeit less formally. People surround themselves with opinionated experts:

- Doctors
- Ethicists or religious leaders
- Academic advisers
- Parents
- Accountants
- Personal trainers, coaches, or facilitators
- Spouses
- Best friends
- Bosses

And these experts often give conflicting advice.

Key activities in exercising this skill include forming a board, based on balancing needs, vision, and diversity, and then organizing and compensating that board, reconciling differing opinions and even conflicts, using the board's advice, and aligning strategies and tactics.

Some people go as far as creating virtual "dream boards" of heroes, drawn from throughout the ages. This allows them to ask, for example, "What would Einstein do?"

Creating New Tools

It is a big skill to recognize a situation in which current approaches are not sufficient, then design, prototype, pilot test, and roll out new approaches.

Decision Making

Decision making is the big skill of, in a rigorous and trackable process, understanding all options and choosing the best.

Ethics

Ethics is the big skill of abiding by both universal and cultural rules, expectations, and goals. (It can be assessed with a balanced scorecard.)

Ethical actions have a net positive addition to an ecosystem, rather than extracting value from it. Ethical behavior likewise tends to result in strengthen-by-using relationships.

Following ethical behavior can be at odds with short-term gains, often precludes gaming a system, and can involve the selective enforcement or breaking of rules.

Can You Make an Educational Simulation Around Ethics or Sexual Harassment?

In theory, it should be feasible. One point of a Sim is to make an experience that allows people to see the consequences of their actions in a safe environment.

If you made a pure "ethics" Sim, however, then of course students would just always "do the right thing." It would be as useful as the official Enron *Ethics Handbook*.

Rather, my own thinking goes, one would build a life Sim, or a business Sim. One would challenge students to some realistic activity, and then toss in some ethical problems along the way.

But then what? Would it be a challenge to recognize ethical problems, or would they be obvious? If they were obvious, is the best gameplay thing to always do the right thing, to accept an "ethics" friction? Or would they somehow represent interesting choices?

Would you ever make people go bankrupt for making ethical decisions? Would you ever create a situation in which people made some ethical compromises and were better off for it? Would the ideal strategy to be a little immoral? What is the role of realism versus learning objectives?

Can karma have the properties of an accumulator, where one might be able to work off debts? Can this moral ambiguity exist in an environment supported by corporations, for whom ethics have to be black and white?

Can one's negative actions create indestructible demons waiting to spring upon one, perhaps visualized in a heads-up display? (In WILL Interactive's branching story on sexually transmitted diseases, drinking too much eliminates options for getting out of a high-pressure situation; in Tropico, where you are the president of an island-state, you can put off elections, but that increases discontent of your people, who might rise up in arms.)

And would the simulation designer want to seduce people into becoming bad? Would you engage in moral entrapment? Would you want to pull people to the dark side, and then surprise them with a mirror of themselves?

Is this a matter of aligning strategies and tactics? Does degree of morality become a strategy that has to work into a larger context ? Cheat, but only in certain industries?

Would the ethical problem really be just a single-solution puzzle, like the beer game? Would students go through it once, be tricked, and then never be fooled again? Would older students tell younger students "the solution"?

Likewise, how might one deal with ethical violations in others? What if a great salesperson committed slight moral breaches? Do ethical violations spread in a chain reaction if not stopped? Are ethical violations contagions to be caught and spread? Or is there a balancing loop? Might one set up a containment strategy around a necessarily or incurably corrupt group? And how do you even find ethical violations? Does it require an act of probing?

And if you were a manager, would you be concerned if an employee playing the Sim engaged in highly unethical behavior? Aren't Sims supposed to be safe places?

All this talk is academic, to some degree. The most important design consideration is that corporate sponsors can't even acknowledge that breaches of morality might have anything but bad consequences. It might be a paradox of this industry that in areas where Sims could do the most good, they might not be able to do anything at all.

Presenting Choices to Users

Source: Copyright Atari, Chris Sawyer

In Roller Coaster Tycoon, players must lay out activities, in the form of rides, lines, and food stalls connected by paths, to direct the unpredictable on-screen movement of thousands of guests, all pursuing their own goals. For example, many guests walk down a path. They all see a ride, and the ones who have the interest and the inclination (that is, they're not hungry, don't have to go the bathroom, do have enough money, and don't mind the line), branch off and (activity a) get in line, (activity b) get their ticket, and (activity c) get on the ride, while others continue. Guests don't generate any revenue while just walking, so having rides close together makes sense. Guests also only generate revenue when they see something that meets their needs, so making sure they are exposed to a variety of opportunities to spend also makes sense.

Innovation

Innovation is a matter of stopping a current process and implementing a new, better process.

The concept of innovation has to be nurtured in the context of leadership. If an organization says that it values innovation, does that mean that it values

- Coming up with a good idea? (Action level)
- Creating an ecosystem where good ideas are sought after and nurtured, and attracting creative people? Or forcing different approaches? (System level)
- Successfully launching products, services, and activities that are different from in the past? (Results level)

Innovation requires research.

Leadership

Leadership is the big skill of getting groups of people to complete the right work.

As with all big skills, leadership is an organizational skill as well as a personal skill, and also must be understood at three levels simultaneously:

- The results level
- The actions level
- The system level

Results. The results of leadership are the organizational or personal completed work that is successfully evaluated against a balanced scorecard. It takes leadership to change either organizational or personal priorities.

Actions. Leaders have a collection of distinct leadership actions available. They can direct people, supporting and opposing them, and they can support and oppose work themselves.

A Model of Leadership, Identifying Actions, Systems, and Results.

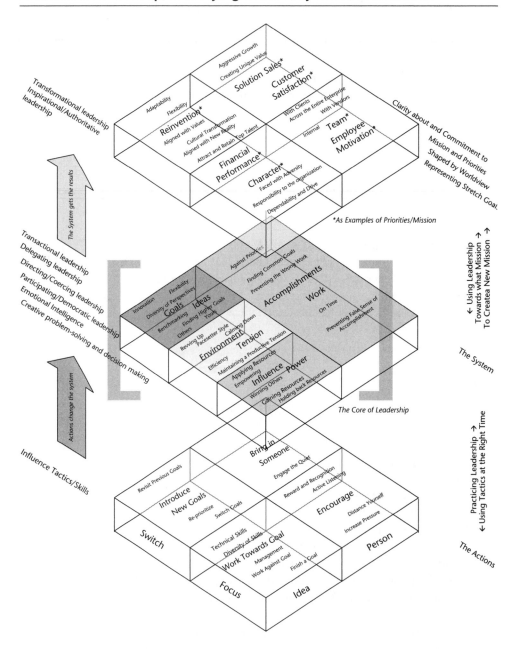

System. Naive (and soon to be frustrated) leaders just look at actions and results. They think that by getting more work done, for example, they will better meet organizational priorities. Or that by praising people, a good team will form.

However, actions don't impact results directly. Instead, there is a system in the middle. Actions impact the system; the system gets the results.

In leadership, the middle, invisible system has four parts: power, tension, ideas, and work.

- Power is the ability to influence other people through alignment. If you have power, other people will lean toward your ideas, just because you support them. Power can be accumulated.
- Tension is the environment. If tension is too high or too low, people don't get much work done. It is only when tension is moderated that a productive environment is formed.
- Ideas are the grist for the mill. If your group does not have a steady stream of new ideas, you cannot innovate.
- Work is the ability to get things done. At the end of the day, it is only what is completed that positively impacts results.

Again, the actions impact the system, and the system impacts the results. So an effective leader, to increase the amount of work completed, might reduce the tension in an unproductively tense environment by talking to people and listening to them.

Or to get new ideas on the table, an effective leader might engage the quietest person in the room.

This sometimes involves conceptual dead reckoning, but the more one understands the middle system, the more intuitive are the steps of the effective leader.

Negotiation

Negotiation is the big skill that drives the process of coming to an agreement, with at least one side trying to get the most possible value out of the agreement.

Negotiation. In Sid Meier's Alpha Centauri, players negotiate with the AI characters for control of the world.

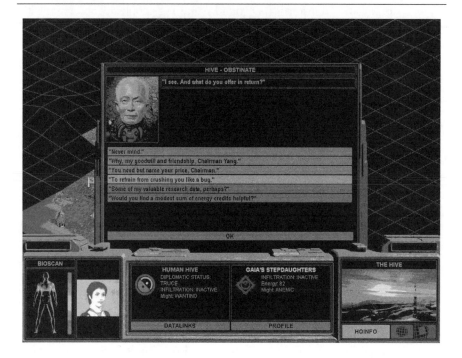

Negotiation, can include (roughly in order):

- *Leadership*, sometimes just to get the v to the table.
- *Gathering evidence*, to better understand the situation.
- *Communication*, to both hear and be heard.
- *Changing the level of alignment*, either strengthening the relationship between the two parties to build trust and rapport or weakening the relationships that a party might have with another who could be interfering with the negotiation.
- *Innovation*, creating new approaches and solutions.
- *Finding the right fit* between the two parties.
- *Splitting up a map*, allowing each party to take ownership of a zero-sum resource.
- *Performing a cost-benefit analysis* of the various options.
- *Project management*, to plan next steps.

Nurturing and Stewardship

Source: Cisco Systems. Used with permission.

If you don't take care of the land, the land won't take care of you.

—FARMER ADAGE

Stewardship means committing oneself to the growth, maintenance, and success of someone or something. In many ways, it is the skill most missing in organizations today.

Whether for a pet, a child, a parcel of land, a start-up nonprofit organization, or a Fortune 500 company, stewardship can include funding (or in other ways meeting the need to consume), performing hands-on maintenance activities, instituting processes, and perhaps serving as a coach or adviser.

Stewardship often means managing an internal ecosystem and establishing a role with an external ecosystem. Stewards initially provide containment and protection, and then carefully introduce competition and even conflict, to support adaptation and the achievement of a mastery level.

Failure of nurturing often leads to premature death or rampant mutation.

Rewards for stewardship are often back loaded.

A microcosm for nurturing is growing a garden or taking care of a pet.

Related topics: "Leadership," earlier in this chapter, and "Constituent," in Chapter Twenty.

Author's note: What is funny (and the result of the tyranny of linear thinking) is that having a ten-year-old grow and care for a plant (an action of stewardship) only registers on an academic's radar if a paper can then be written about it.

Process Reengineering

Process reengineering is the big skill of completely rethinking or reconceptualizing how groups of processes (see "Process Map" in Chapter Thirteen) are constructed, a value is delivered, or even the value itself. Reengineering is often enabled by the advent of new processes, such as those involving technology, or philosophies such as environmentalism.

Process reengineering is different from process improvement, which involves incrementally refining current processes.

Project Management

Project management is the big skill of organizing and managing the successful completion of a complex deliverable or other value.

Project management includes

- The distribution of ownership
- Fit
- Throttling up or down the distribution of resources
- Procurement
- Scheduling
- Cost reduction
- Sourcing
- Long-term planning
- Selective enforcement or breaking of rules
- Estimating costs and estimating benefits

Tracking a project may include using a progress meter.

Relationship Management

Relationship management is the big skill of strengthening by using the value of contacts over time. This can occur within a role or even expanding roles.

Relationship management includes

- Creating positive associations
- Fit
- Containment (for example, safeguarding privileged information)

See also "Nurturing and Stewardship," earlier in this chapter.

Risk Analysis and Management

Risk analysis and management is a matter of optimizing a situation given the existence of risks—events that might have a relevant negative impact on one or more critical areas (or primary variables).

Risk analysis and management has multiple parts:

- Identifying the risks (which may involve probing and long-term planning)
- Determining the probability of the risk happening
- Determining the risk's probable impact if it does happen
- Determining what control an organization has
- Estimating the cost of mitigation that fits with the current environment
- Determining the cost-effectiveness of mitigation (asking whether the cure is better than the disease)
- Implementing a solution

Security

Security is the big skill of creating and maintaining an appropriate containment around things of value, quarantining anything that gets past the containment, and possibly taking steps to reduce the chances of anything even trying to get through the containment.

Security also includes fraud control.

Security exists in an environment where all sides adapt. Long-term security also has to withstand a cost-benefit analysis.

Solutions Sales

Solutions sales involves combining, customizing, configuring, and regionalizing building block units and services to fit a need at a price or cost the sponsor is willing and able to pay.

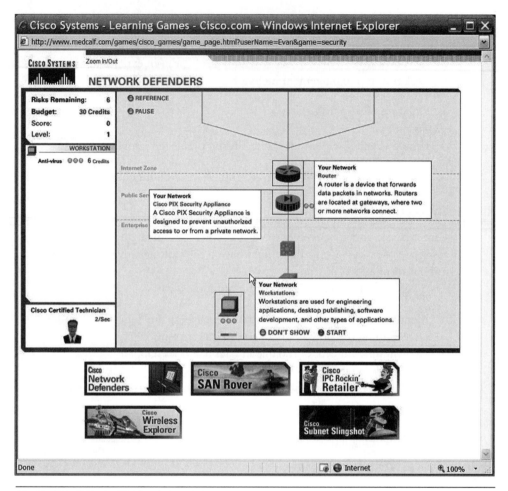

Source: Cisco Systems. Used with permission.

In some cases, this includes the appropriate substitution of items and the estimation of benefits.

Can Schools Teach Leadership?

If so, why don't they? If not, are schools doomed?

Can schools teach leadership? I often ask this question of schools I visit.

The first naive reaction is no. Schools have classes on biology, calculus, history, and English literature, to name just a few. The goal of schools is to teach specific cultural literacy and thinking skills. A student who fails history or

English is held back, because those are required. If someone fails leadership, nothing happens.

The next response, meanwhile, from any marketing-savvy school professional is, "We provide opportunities for students to learn leadership in all activities, especially extracurricular activities." But this has its own problems. Providing a microcosm for developing a skill is different from actually teaching it, measuring it, and subsequently calibrating a program to better teach it. Further, a student can be, say, in charge of a school paper and be a dictator, exclusively using pressure and dictatorial tactics, and actually learn bad practices not good ones.

Finally, most school professionals will honestly say, "Our goal really is to make sure that students do well in the next grade. We prepare third graders for fourth grade, high school juniors to be high school seniors, and college seniors to be grad school students."

Now, superficially, this seems a little problematic. Most parents want their students to be better leaders (and project managers, innovators, stewards, just to name a few of the big skills). And schools know this is what parents really want, which is why any prep school uses words like leadership all over its brochure.

But this is not just a problem of curriculum priorities or even the inward focus of a monopoly. At a deeper level, schools are governed by a fundamental law that supersedes budgets and politics: "What is taught is governed by what can be taught."

So even if you talk to business schools with dedicated classes on leadership, the focus is on "studying" leadership, not practicing it. Further, you can talk to corporate officers who desperately want better development of leaders, and even spend significant money on classes, but few organizations have great results. This is because there is a big difference between watching someone else drive and driving yourself.

The real rate-limiting step is that today, and probably forever going forward, almost all formal learning programs are media dependent. Currently, programs rely on case studies, time lines, analysis, and tests via books, video clips, presentations, posters, and handouts. Media naturally require media authoring, and that typically means word processors, PowerPoint, and video editing suites. Media also comes packaged in genres, such as narrative history, pop quiz, essay question, or book report, which not only shape (and are shaped by) the tools but also provide precedents and role models for future authors.

So at this point in the history of our collective civilization, through a series of flukes, educational media are biased toward presenting inner monologues, analysis, images, and time lines, rather than teaching actions and presenting supportive practice environments. When going to almost any library in the world, it is easier to find a history of a thousand years' of a culture's important milestones than a media program that, when experienced, will impart knowledge of how to play a piano, drive a car, or speak another language. (Although, as with leadership and project management, there may be books and audio programs that provide overviews or begin the process.) Many school theorists have even created a defense mechanism whereby teaching any actions is "vocational" and thus somehow beneath their charter, but clearly that defense falls apart when talking about the most valued big skills a person can have.

This is an existential–caliber problem. As long as both schools and corporate training programs can't teach people how to do, educators will be trapped in a ghetto of being increasingly irrelevant, having to spin or misstate their results, justify an irrelevant curriculum, and live with less and less funding and other forms of social support.

There are, however, two early sources of hope. First, some places today do have a culture and track record for rigorously teaching actions: sports programs and military services. Both have escaped the reliance on media, and despite the considerable costs, both use coaches and practice fields. And second, one of today's scalable media does focus on learning to do rather than just learning to know: computer games that begin with single-player play to learn best practices, and then introduce multiplayer (and massively multiplayer) scenarios where people can apply their new skills in increasingly dynamic situations.

Having said this, both the sports/military model and the computer games represent structural approaches, not solutions. There are no shortcuts to the tremendous work ahead. Schools can't just assign two hours of World of Warcraft and use in-game Guild status to determine effectiveness and grade. But by first using the design philosophies of computer games to rethink leadership—and project management, stewardship, innovation, security, relationship management, and other real-world skills—and build these skills into new genres of supported practice environments, and then using coaching techniques to help students use them well, education can once again be the most sublime of careers and institutions.

In other words, the fate of all formal learning programs is ultimately tied to how well some can develop leadership in their students.

BUILDING INTERACTIVE ENVIRONMENTS

Building successful interactive environments requires building the pure simulation elements described in Parts Two and Three. But, a Sim consisting of just simulation elements by themselves can be both dry and disorienting.

There is an apocryphal story of an Army general and a simulation designer. The general believed in simulations, but he hated the thought of computer games. He ordered the designer to create a simulation for the role of a guard to be as accurate as possible. The designer went off to carry out this mission. The designer returned, and the general eagerly started the Sim. Playing the role of an on-screen guard, the general stood at his post. The Sim continued for minutes. Nothing happened. The general looked at his watch, and then at the Sim designer, who was smiling proudly. Then the Sim went on with nothing happening for fifteen minutes, then thirty, then an entire hour. The general's face got red. Still, he stayed at the Sim. Another hour passed. The general turned angrily at the Sim designer, who was still proudly looking at his creation. "When is something going to happen?" the general exploded.

"Oh, not for at least seventy-four more hours," said the Sim designer. "But probably longer. You said you wanted this to be realistic."

Simulation elements need support. By themselves, things take a very long time to play out. Further, students don't always know what is going on. They may fail in the experience and not know why, or—much, much worse—they may succeed and not know why (failing upward may be a common path for corporate types, but the same lucky sods resent un-understood success in a Sim).

In other words, Sims are like life, but not quite. Therefore, in a good Sim, the simulation elements are mixed with:

- *Game elements*, techniques that motivate people to want to engage an experience, beyond any intrinsic motivation. Game elements can include a beautiful campus in a virtual world or a giant explosion. They can include awards or situations with no pressure, chases, the ability to adjust the difficulty level, choosing an on-screen character's appearance, compelling contexts, cool graphics, high scores, treasure hunts, or a futuristic design.
- *Pedagogical elements* (also called *didactic elements*), techniques and elements that surround an experience, ensuring that a participant's time is spent productively. Pedagogical elements in real life range from one-way street signs and labels on food packaging to a helpful neighbor who knows more about electricity than you do. They represent the codification of and access to context-specific knowledge.
- *Tasks and levels*, which create incrementally more challenging practice environments. Typically progressing to the next level requires successfully demonstrating some mastery in the last.
- *A community*, including coaches, peers, and sometimes allies and opponents, for help and motivation.

Part Four addresses how to go from a simulation to a Sim.

15

LINEAR CONTENT

Linear content is content where the only interactivity, if you can call it that, is to choose to go forward or backward along a path. Which isn't to say it isn't valuable; linear content has stood on its own for generations, and must be used to augment a Sim.

Historically, mass-produced media have been linear, including books (see Chapter 4) and full-motion video. As a result, culturally we have developed a deep understanding and incredibly nuanced body of techniques for linear content. Most audiences understand, for example, the use of an inner monologue, foreshadowing, or an establishing shot.

Further, many schools and other formal learning programs rely on the linear form of lecture. Still, understanding linear content can only be done in context of non-linear.

Linear content can meet more traditional learning goals, such as awareness and procedural knowledge, and provide a context for learning analysis.

Linear Content in Sims

Any good Sim uses significant linear content, including every type I've mentioned so far. Linear content can be used to establish a character and backdrop. Sims often use death, the ultimate linear content. And linear content is presented as cut scenes and sets.

However, in the context of an educational simulation, linear content that does not support action is often filtered out by the user as noise. Further, repetition also necessarily prohibits the use of long (as in more than ten seconds) canned, prerecorded, ready-rendered rendered material, either video or even audio, in the core gameplay, unless it can easily be skipped. Hearing something the first time is engaging and fun. By the fifth time, it can be staggeringly numbing. Here are some linear constructs.

Anecdote

An anecdote is a short first-person story or example from real life, often designed to increase awareness. Anecdotes are the core of social networking, such as blogs, and can add color to case studies. Typically, experts adapt and refine anecdotes into inspirational examples or best practices, often highlighting the role of a hero.

Anecdotes can be used to evaluate a formal learning program by "showing" that a learning goal has been met, although many criticize their subjective nature (preferring measurable results). Still, for the measurement of the development of big skills, they might be more persuasive than even improvements in 360-degree feedback measurements, and they are certainly quicker to assemble.

Appendix

Appendixes are special, designated chapters at the back of a book. Appendix material is usually considered either too technical or perhaps tangential and distracting from the main theme of a book. An appendix may contain case studies.

The equivalent to an appendix in a simulation is the associated supporting material. See "Instructor Manual" in Chapter Twenty-Six.

Backdrop

The backdrop is the setting and context for a story or experience.

In a story, the backdrop first establishes time (for example, 1812, last Thursday, or even a dystopian future). The backdrop then establishes location (such as Burbank, Los Angeles, a generic corporation, or Vladivostok). Finally, it can establish a specific, shared event, such as the first day on a job or the Russian Revolution.

Originally, and still, *backdrop* is a theater term that designates a large, static, two-dimensional illustration used behind the actors and props to add to the illusion of place. Many computer games and simulations also use a static backdrop illustration in mini games or behind dynamic three-dimensional props, sets, and characters.

Related topic: "Setting" in Chapter Sixteen.

Backstory

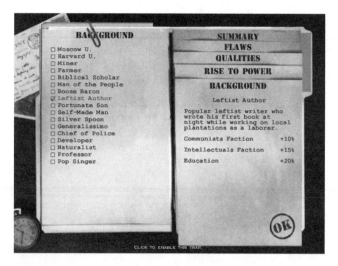

The backstory comes before the story, that is, it's what has happened before the player joins in. Backstories provide motivation for many characters and explanations for any out-of-the-ordinary starting conditions. They are often written early on in the development process and are stored in the project's story bible.

Most backstories for Sims, if directly shared with players at all, are static and told in cut scenes or browsable documents. But in cold-war dictator Sim Tropico, players choose their own backstory for bonuses. For example, if players choose their dictator to have risen to power through a CIA coup, the dictator begins with a better relationship with the United States. In the figure that illustrates this section, the dictator-to-be starts as a leftist author, which provides a better starting alignment with certain communist and worker factions, as well as other perks.

The backstory of a hero in a hero's journey is, by design, mundane.

Similar to background, see also "Backdrop," earlier in this chapter.

Exposition

Exposition is the delivery, sometimes forced, of backstory that participants need to understand and care about to follow the plot, including story and characters.

Bullet Point

Bullet points are a type of linear content that presents or summarizes information in a series of short, presumably unambiguous statements.

Bullets tend to present active behavior. They often give tasks to an audience. Most of the time in a Sim, the briefing section should present the goal of the player in a series of bullet points. Meanwhile, the current goal of the player in any part of a Sim might be presented as a highlighted bullet point on a set written in the upper right of the screen.

Cut Scene

Source: Halo. Microsoft product screen shot reprinted with permission from Microsoft corporation.

A cut scene consists of full-motion video triggered to present backstories, awards, briefings, and end-of-level resolution, as well as other level milestones.

In cut scenes, the participant loses all control except the option to skip the scene.

Care must be given to make sure cut scenes are task-relevant, not task-redundant. Cut scenes work best when short—less than a minute.

If the same game engine is used to render the cut scene as the core gameplay, and the cut scene happens in the middle of a task, black bars conventionally appear at the top and bottom of the screen to give a letterbox, wide-screen appearance and differentiate the sequence from the interactive portions of the Sim.

Epilogue

The epilogue is the chapter or cut scene after the primary story arc is completed, putting the story in context, drawing conclusions, or following up on characters or events.

In a Sim, the epilogue may be related by the character serving as a guide. A Sim might have multiple possible epilogues, of which one is selected or generated based on the player's actions during the Sim.

Flashback

In the Sim display, a flashback is the presentation of some part of a backstory, often presented as a memory of a character.

Flashbacks are often signified cinematically by a ripple dissolve, a sound cue, a different color scheme, or rapid fade out/fade in.

Foreshadowing

Foreshadowing involves presenting an event that is a microcosm or other early indicator of something that will happen later.

For example, a newly hired chief scientist walks into the building on the first day and sees one technician crying and two others arguing about breaches in ethics. This foreshadows some significant problems.

Related topic: "Recursion," in Chapter Twelve.

Source: Sid Meier's Civilization IV Screenshots Courtesy of Firaxis Games and Take-Two Interactive Software, Inc.

Full-Motion Video

In the Sim display, full-motion video (FMV) is a scripted series of pictures shown in rapid succession to simulate movement. It can also include an audio track. The educational simulation genre of branching story uses FMV almost completely.

Traditional FMV. FMVs feature cinematic effects. They can stand alone, as in a movie or television program, or can be part of a Sim. FMVs used in Sims can serve as noninteractive cut scenes.

Where there is interactivity in full-motion video, it is primarily limited to multiple-choice decisions (although sometimes it requires finding a hot spot on the screen). This interactivity can either branch to more FMVs or change a condition in the task.

Full-motion videos are judged by their production and artistic quality, their Sim, game, or pedagogical success, their frames-per-second rate (often referred to as *fps*), and their resolution. Usually, the FMV is of higher quality than any fully interactive portions.

FMVs may be storyboarded, or even replaced if budget is an issue, by comics. FMVs significantly increase the cost of a simulation.

Full-Motion Video in the Age of Social Networking. In the age of You Tube, and cell phones with video capture, FMV (albeit of lower quality) is presented and treated increasingly as any other post, including the more traditional text and pictures.

Inner Monologue

An inner monologue is a written or spoken account of the thoughts of a character who is experiencing a situation, doing an analysis, or perhaps applying a big skill, making a decision, or receiving feedback. Inner monologues are the core of many books, including most fiction, but they work less well in Sims, as they turn participants into passive audience members.

Inspirational Example

An inspirational example is a short, often spoken story, presented as true by an identified expert. It typically describes target behavior in a character, causing surprising and desirable effects.

Inspirational examples derive from anecdotes. They typically follow story arcs, are tools to raise awareness, and present goal behavior and societal expectations. Further, audiences love inspirational examples.

The actual inspiration from inspirational examples, however, decays quickly. Audience members feel a buzz of warm support, and then do nothing differently. For the most part, such stories are useless lies—the primary output of so-called gurus.

When embedded in a Sim, in fact, most inspirational examples are actually considered task-redundant.

Lecture and Lecturer

Lecture is the pedagogical technique of getting key information to an audience through the presentation of prepared materials by an instructor, coach, or expert, in order to raise awareness (such as of theoretical principles and models), demonstrate analysis, and present processes, including compliance requirements. In many corporations, and distributed classrooms, lectures are done remotely through webinars. Many traditional freshman classes are taught in 300-student lecture halls.

Lectures can sometimes be interactive, but more often they feign interactivity. For example, a lecturer may ask what seems like an open-ended question (say, "what is the most important quality of a security process?"), but only accept as correct the student answers that predict aspects of the prepared material. This is the "guess what I am thinking" phenomenon, and quickly disempowers students.

Within a Sim deployment, lectures can present background material and briefing before a Sim and kick off an after action review at the end.

Montage

A montage is a cinematic technique of using series of quick video clips to collapse weeks or months of activity and progress into a short sequence, often with music in the background. A montage in a Sim is presented in a cut scene.

Plot

The plot is the highest-level frustration-resolution pair in a story (see Chapter Twenty-Eight).

Plots are typically made up of tensions and resolution arcs, nested together. This diagram shows one framework, with the top to bottom height corresponding to relative narrative importance.

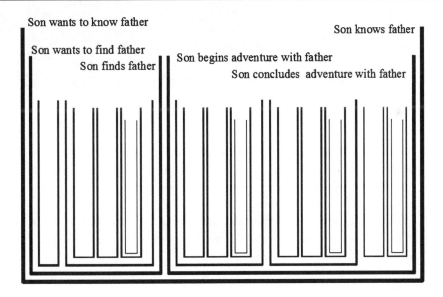

Most stories, such as in movies, are recursive. They start with an initial large problem or mystery. To solve this large issue, characters must deal with smaller problems, microcosms, and mysteries, which themselves are made up of smaller problems and mysteries.

Puzzle

This looks like some kind of industrial mechanism, although there's a hole in the centre, and no way to operate it.

Source: Penumbra. Copyright © 2007-2009 Frictional Games.

A puzzle is a situation that requires the participant to manipulate some part of the virtual world and often use some inventory items, applying perceptions of the situation and knowledge of properties to get past a level or part of a level. Solving puzzles often involves some sort of insight.

While some puzzles are simple and others are very challenging, most tend to have a single solution (meaning they have little or no replay value), and most answers, when discovered, feel obvious.

So while puzzles are examples of frustration-resolution pairs, they are more diagnostic than skill developing. The only exception would be if a smaller puzzle were a microcosm of a larger puzzle.

Puzzles are often used in certification programs and adventure games, and occasionally to demonstrate analysis.

Some mini games, such as Tetris or Bejeweled, are called puzzle games, although they do not represent a single-solution puzzle.

Quote

Quote. In Operation Flashpoint, a player's failure is punctuated by one of dozens of quotes about war and death.

Quotes are a form of linear content consisting of a short statement, often considered profound or funny, and often attributed to someone well known.

Quotes can be used or triggered at any time in a Sim to add humor and gravitas and are commonly used in briefings, milestones, or after action reviews.

Quotes suffer the same instructional drawbacks as inspirational examples, but thankfully take up less time. While they trigger a neural pleasure response, they seldom help in any actual accomplishments. It is not hard to find contradictory quotes in any given field.

Related topic: "Mentor, Supervisor, or Guide," in Chapter Seventeen.

Story

A story is a presented sequence of events.

Stories take place in, and often transform, a story world. They follow arcs, often driven by plots and the development of big skills by key characters, and often with further frustration-resolution pairs recursively embedded. One larger story may also consist of several smaller story lines. There is often a story before the story, called the backstory.

Anecdotes are stories taken from the real world. Inspirational examples are anecdotes that have been highly, highly processed, to a point where they are often unrecognizable to the people who inspired them.

Stories are supported in Sims by cut scenes and other scripts.

Story Arc

The path of beginning, middle, and end (the "acts") through which a story progresses, often driven by plot, is called the story arc.

- Most story arcs begin with a frustration the main character tries to resolve.
- Some story arcs include a journey over a map.
- Some arcs include the development of big skills and middle skills.
- Some characters try to solve a mystery or otherwise reveal obstructed information.

Story World

A story world is the collection of backdrops, characters, backstories, technologies, items, even sound cues used in one or more stories. A story world can intersect, partially or completely, with the real world.

All movie-based game franchises, such as Spider-Man, Jurassic Park, and Star Wars, are built on story worlds.

Story Line

A story line is one of the independent but sometimes intersecting smaller stories that make up a larger story. Often, story line "a" is the primary story, and story line "b" (sometimes called a subplot) is less emphasized and often character-driven. Short-term story lines may give the audience a sense of completion and resolution and be interspersed with longer story lines that build more slowly and dramatically.

What's the Problem with Purely Linear Content?

The enduring criticism of linear content is that it is massively incomplete to nurture any of the most important skills. Further, the "if it's knowledge, then capture it in a book" mentality has tragically distorted and lost most of our culture's wisdom.

Author's note. The last fifteen years have been about digitizing information. Scanners, digital cameras, word processors, optical character recognition programs, Web pages, blogs, and Google have all become commonplace. We fill up servers and hard disks with gigs of content. This has built nicely on our heritage of linear content, including books, movies, and paintings. We have standards, genres, tools, and approaches. We have, of course, a common vocabulary. We talk comfortably about paragraphs, bullets, photographs, indents, commas, movie credits, PowerPoint slides, book pages and chapters, underlined words, footnotes, short stories, novels, newspaper articles, and the evening news. We have dictionaries, thesauruses, *Gregg's Reference Handbook*, the *Writer's Market*, and Strunk and White's *Elements of Style*.

We are most familiar with linear content. Here we present learners with inevitable sequences, with one event or step following the next. Striking a match produces fire. World War I came before World War II.

And even the most interactive of experiences tend to have some level of linear content, including backstory, triggers, and cinematic sequences.

(Continued)

But the business model behind linear content is becoming increasingly strained. For example, we are witnessing the collapse of the business model around linear content as the dominant form of educational material. The best lectures will be available for free as podcasts. Wikipedia, essentially open-source content, and its children will decimate the market for textbooks. Blogs change the definition of class participation. The walls between academics and enterprises are becoming more permeable every day.

16

GAME ELEMENTS

A Spoonful of Sugar If You Can Avoid Hypoglycemic Shock

Game elements are techniques that motivate people to want to engage an experience, outside of any intrinsic motivation. They include fantasy, whimsy, competition, beauty, and a great story. It is a game element, for example, that positions the participant as the sole hero in any game.

Game elements can do a lot of good in serious games or educational simulations, driving engagement and making boring material much more tolerable. They can build goodwill, which is often then transferred to the content itself. They can lower tension (so using a game show Sim for assessment might actually be more accurate than using a written test). In fact, the genres of frame games and mini games are the result of almost pure examples of game elements, although any Sim genre uses some game elements.

But game elements are also very controversial, for a variety of reasons:

- Game elements surround and dilute the learning. They take up both developer time and end-learner time, ultimately diverting resources from the primary content.
- They are subjective. What is fun for one person, such as gambling or a treasure hunt, can be tedious for someone else. When the potential audience includes different cultures, ages, genders, experiences, and needs, it creates complex demands on the designer.
- Game elements can also sometimes subvert the learning. A developer can make things happen faster, or more dramatically (see "Exaggerated Response" in Chapter Seventeen), or skip tedious steps, which increases the fun at the expense of accuracy.
- Elements added to enhance the fun can often also be leveraged by a learner to "game" the Sim—to win on its terms without actually mastering the intended content.
- Certain game elements, like competition, can focus users on getting a high score rather than on learning the material.

Having too few game elements results in a boring, dry experience, and having too many game elements creates something that is silly and distracting. As a rule, the more participants care about content, the more intrusive game elements become. If the orphanage is burning and you need to learn how to put out the fire, the last thing you want is to play Wheel of Fortune to get the information.

The most challenging problem is the subjective factor: as noted, what is fun for one person is not necessarily fun for another. Some people love fixing cars, or shopping, and others hate it. As with being a student in high school, you can envy the fun someone else is having but know that, if you were in the same situation, you would not be having any fun at all.

An Alphabetical List of Techniques

Balancing simulation elements, game elements, and pedagogical elements is unquestionably an art, not a science. But understanding the trade-offs is critical to aligning sponsor, developer, implementer, and student.

The following sections list the essential terms and concepts.

Advanced Graphics

It's possible to increase engagement through the game element of advanced graphics: using a higher level of visual detail and smoothness of graphic elements and richer animation in the display than what is necessary for educational, immersion, and game-play objectives.

The standard of visual detail and smoothness rises over time, so what constitutes advanced graphics one year may be standard the next. The highest level of graphics is photorealism. Also known as eye candy, advanced graphics increase the cost for a simulation.

Compare with "Comics," later in this chapter, and with "Illustration," in Chapter Seventeen.

Award

Graphic from the Xerox Documents at Work series.

An award is something of value earned by meeting formal (although not always stated) criteria.

Awards can be symbolic, such as represented by trophies, certificates, certifications, grades, and diplomas. In a Sim (as in the real world), they can have immediate utility, opening up or unlocking, new levels, including optional or hidden levels, new processes or activities or units, or even increasing attributes of existing units.

Awards are often all-or-nothing, but they can also be analog, such as earning virtual money that can be spent on future upgrades or points toward a total score. Awards can also rank participants, such as "first prize" or "green ribbon." Accomplishment of an award might trigger an alert.

Awards can reward *style*, the way a player accomplishes something, as well as *substance*, what the player accomplished. One style award, for example, might be

"If the player gets three grants of more than $10,000 each, the player gets a morale bonus, where all researchers are 25 percent more effective for two years." In an educational simulation, any learning objective should have a corresponding award.

Tasks are a special type of award that are required to progress. Other awards are optional and can be earned in any order.

Finally, awards and tasks can work together. It might be a task to be awarded first or second prize in a race. Other bonus awards are given for completing a task exceptionally well.

In some Sims, having the player create and calibrate awards to attract people-units toward certain behaviors is a desired action.

Also called *achievements*.

Beauty

Sheer beauty—using attractive people, objects, or locations—can increase the appeal of the experience or message and enhance player engagement. Like any game element, using beauty is risky; what is appealing to one person might be distracting culturally bias or even insulting to another. Advertisers hope that using beauty will create a positive alignment with their products.

Then guess what? Maybe you'll get a little vacation. I'll even come with you.

Source: Eidos Interactive

Beauty often comes at the cost of accuracy. Eidos' Just Cause uses characters and locations designed to be attractive to people in its target market.

Chase

Chase elements increase engagement through using situations in which the player either tries to beat, get, or tag something, or someone or something tries to beat, get, or tag the player, using speed, movement, and strategy. Many movies rely on chase.

See "Racing Games" in Chapter Three.

Cheat

To cheat is to purposefully subvert the intent and design of the experience.

Some cheats are sanctioned by the developers, as when cheat codes are built in as Easter eggs (discussed later in this chapter). Some, such as walk-throughs, bug exploits, and other forms of gaming are not part of the designers' intent, and steps can often be taken to prevent such behavior through randomness and subsequent patches.

Cheating often reduces the effectiveness of a Sim in helping participants to reach learning goals.

Many artificial intelligence (AI) players are built to cheat to compensate for the designers' inability to build them with the capacity for long-term strategy.

Choosing Appearance or Voice for an On-Screen Character

Source: The Sims 2 and SimCity 4 Images © 2009 Electronic Arts Inc. The Sims and SimCity 4 are trademarks or registered trademarks of Electronic Arts Inc in US and/or other countries.

Many Sims try to increase engagement through allowing participants to alter aspects of their virtual representation (or avatar) in the Sim display, such as in this example from The Sims 2.

The range of choice can be simpler, such as selecting gender, race, or color of clothes.

Related topic: "Backstory," in Chapter Fifteen.

Given the ability to modify their appearance, most players won't aim for realistic representations of themselves, but rather more fantastical or idealistic.

—TIM HOLT

Choosing an appearance can be a form of configuring the Sim, or it can be an award. Choosing an on-screen appearance can support the learning goal of "learning to be."

Clicking Quickly and Accurately

It can enhance a Sim to present a sequence that requires fast reflexes and near-constant action. The need to click as quickly as possible can help users focus, without being distracted by thoughts of anything outside the Sim.

Collecting

Collecting can be as engaging in a Sim as in the real world, so designers often present a challenge and opportunity to get all, or as many as possible, of a given set. A player might try to earn all possible awards or find all statues hidden in a map.

Colloquialisms

Using a regional, colorful, and overly casual speech pattern can amuse players and help lower tension. For example, when a Texan AI is asked about meeting someone, it might respond "We've howdied but we ain't shook."

Colloquialisms help define a character.

Comics

Source: Copyright Dingo Games, used with permission.

Comics use a style of linear content that involves panels, pictures, and word balloons. Comics are often associated with superheroes or with newspaper "funnies" such as Dilbert or Doonesbury, although the genre has also taken on more weighty topics such as the Holocaust and 9/11.

Comics can be a game element if they are used to entertain and lower tension. Comics can also be pedagogical if they highlight key points that might be less clear in a photograph or even a scientific illustration, such as on an airplane emergency card.

Competition

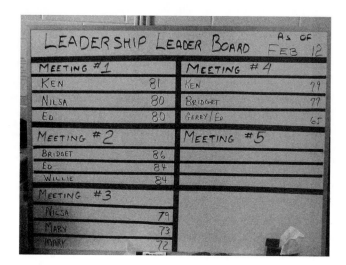

Players, including students, can be both motivated and evaluated by comparing them against other students. This can be done via direct competition (possibly asynchronously), such as competing in an arena, or indirectly, through artifacts including high-score lists and grades.

The top players may win an award.

While competition motivates, it also encourages participants to cheat or otherwise game the experience, rather than learn from it and reflect how it applies to real life. When students feel they are falling behind, they take greater risks.

Competition can also be against AI players or agents.

Related topic: "Scores and Grades," later in this chapter.

Destroy

Source: Far Cry.

Destruction is engaging, and many Sims provide opportunities to break things beyond repair. In a social setting, a "destroy" element might include the ability to criticize or tell people off.

Easter Egg

An Easter egg is a piece of bonus content that is in some way hidden, and yet still accessible by a user, in interactive media, such as a computer game or DVD. The content can be a message, a hidden level, even designer art.

The Easter egg is initially found by accident by a casual user or deliberately by a determined user, through entering certain key codes or going to obscure places on a map, and then made public on chat rooms or forums. Easter eggs were originally the work of programmers trying to sneak content into the finished product under the radar of the publisher; they are now included deliberately as an extra game activity to build the user community.

Easter egg. Some public art, such as this painted cow in the Amsterdam international airport, serves as a real-world Easter egg: a happy artifact to be stumbled upon.

Fantasy

In Half Life 2, participants get to operate giant pieces of equipment, such as this crane.

Source: © Valve.

Fantasy gives players the opportunity in a virtual world to do something that they want to do but would not or could not do in the real world.

Futuristic

Futuristic designs are elements that invoke or represent, in style or substance, things that may exist in the future. Futuristic elements can be engaging, but they can also date a Sim if the real world passes them by, so they look quaint or retro rather than ultramodern.

Gambling

Gambling gives players opportunities to spend some value, risking loss, in the hope of getting more back in return, based on some combination of randomness and skill.

Often the reward and risk are at least correlated, and some of the time they are mathematically balanced (such as doubling your money on the toss of a coin).

See also "Mastering an Action," later in this chapter.

Gambling

Gaming

Gaming isn't just playing a game; it's a form of cheating by manipulating an imperfection in the rules or software to get a better score in a program or experience than by playing in the spirit of the program. Gaming a Sim often takes advantage of game elements, and it subverts any learning goals.

For example, in the MMORGP Battlefield 1942, players can use wingwalking, a technique by which they can carry more than a plane is supposed to hold by having an infantry unit stand on the wings.

Meanwhile, here is an actual cheat for Roller Coaster Tycoon:

> To increase park ratings, find all of the guests who are unhappy or angry. Drown them. Eventually your park rating will go up 100 to 200 points.

Author's note: When showing a great simulation to an instructor, I often get back the following response: "Well," the instructor says slowly, "I don't like it. It seems like students could game this." Then the instructor leans back, smiling triumphantly, as if having delivered the killing blow.

I stammer back, "The simulation represents about 15 hours of student time. Sure, if they wanted to put in an additional 15 or 20 hours, they could probably get a better score," I reply. "But that would almost necessarily come after they learned quite a bit."

The instructor shakes his or her head. "The whole gaming thing troubles me. We need to have a higher level of integrity in any kind of grading or scoring. Gaming is the antithesis of that. Sorry."

Here is what I really want to say:

"Listen. I have been gaming classrooms for my entire life to get better evaluations, comments, grades, or certification scores. I have been:

Dressing appropriately . . .

Feigning interest in topics that bore me beyond belief . . .

Cramming for tests in a way that gives my command of the information a half-life measurable in hours, desperately hoping that I forget the information moments after I write it down and not moments before . . .

Skimming tangential sources to ask the one question that makes me seem much more knowledgeable than I really am . . .

Interviewing past students to see what will be on the test . . .

Playing back what the instructor said without understanding it at all . . .

Pretending to take notes when I am really designing a biosphere in the margin . . .

You want to talk about gaming? What do you think all your students are doing all the time?"

Hero

The hero is the character who, often uniquely, can bring about success in an experience. The appeal of being a hero is as genetically compelling as fire and shelter.

Whole literature genres, including myths and inspirational examples, center on the hero's journey. These genres include specific character archetypes such as mentor or guide, gatekeeper, and villain or boss; specific moments such as gaining possession of a rare and powerful item or battling in an arena; and even acts such as introduction, establishment of problem, resolution of problem.

In single-player computer games and serious games, the player becomes the person, represented by an avatar, who has the power to save the day or make all the decisions. This is a standard game element across all game genres.

But this role of hero is less appropriate in many educational simulations. Programming the user to be the hero has fidelity issues. Should a designer give the participant the unique power to make a difference?

- If yes, the Sim feels false.
- If no, the Sim is unsatisfying.

Finally, should formal learning programs encourage people to be heroes? Heroes often break rules, something that every centralized department hates. Yet every good organization rewards heroes with praise, even if it is along the narrow definition of performing a traditional activity with unusual vigor.

Here, perhaps, the model of massively multiplayer online role-playing games (MMORPGs) becomes the best. Teams come together to overcome tough obstacles by fitting together to accomplish goals. This not only works from a gameplay standpoint, but it also works in real life.

Jeopardy

Jeopardy is an attribute of an environment where failure is both likely and has significant negative consequences for the player. For example, if failure to complete a task means that a person is three minutes late to a movie, which would result in missing the advertisement for the concession stand, there is not much jeopardy. But if the failure to complete a task means that a person is three minutes late for an airplane, thus missing it, and thereby missing an interview, and thereby not getting the perfect job—the one that would have made it possible to continue with cancer research that was on the verge of a breakthrough, justifying a lifelong quest into a type of science scorned by colleagues and creating a bridge to an estranged father, the sense of jeopardy can be extreme.

Mastering an Action

Through practicing, players become increasingly able to complete a sequence of kinesthetic gestures or actions to gain immediate positive feedback, such as throwing a card into a hat or a basketball into a hoop, or driving a golf cart.

In the virtual world, gestures involved in mastering an action can include such basic inputs as clicking, dragging, hovering, holding, moving, using different buttons, and flicking.

See "Best of Both Worlds?" in Chapter Two.

Mystery

A mystery factor increases engagement by presenting a situation in which an important or desired piece of information is obviously missing or obstructed, with the promise that throughout the experience, the missing information will be provided.

For example:

• Two people with whom you work are having an affair. Which two?

- A character is dead. Why?
- Customers are buying your type of product from a competitor. What is causing them to go there?
- A piece of software isn't working. What is preventing it?

Mysteries are at the core of the plot of several types of book genres, where the mystery is a type of passive frustration-resolution pair around a backstory.

Solving a mystery can include probing, gathering evidence, and finding the right fit, middle skills discussed in Chapter Six.

New Sets and Settings

Regularly changing the surroundings by providing new sets and settings can help hold people's interest. Organizations do this regularly with retreats, off-site meetings, and conferences. Physical classrooms are expensive to change around and therefore stay pretty much the same week after week and even year after year, which reduces their effectiveness as a teaching environment.

In Sims, new sets and settings can occur at every level, or even more often. In first-person shooters, players move through a steady stream of new backdrops, which is one reason for the genre's popularity. New sets, obviously, increase the cost of creating a simulation.

Variations on this game element include introducing new characters, items, plot devices, or cut scenes.

Cognitively speaking, changing sets reduces habituation and saturation. You can see this for yourself if you try this experiment: stare at one spot on the wall; the details of the room will start to fade.

Pet

Including pets in a Sim increases engagement through giving the participants ownership over a creature to nurture, train, use, and engage.

For example, the toy sensation Tamagotchi gave participants a little critter and the following actions: "feed," "play with," "give rewards to," "discipline," and "clean up after."

Pets almost always have some character.

Raising a pet allows participants to reflect their own nature, much like choosing an on-screen character's appearance or voice.

Pet. In the Black and White series, players not only raised pets, but the pets became reflections of the players. The pets, called *creatures*, mimicked their masters' actions and became increasingly good or evil based on what the masters did.

Source: Microsoft product screen shot reprinted with permission from Microsoft Corporation.

Poll

A poll asks questions of participants to determine their opinions or context. Polls are often in the form of a multiple-choice question, and the results of the poll may then be displayed, showing a histogram of different responses.

Polls can also be open-ended questions. Polls tend to measure learning to be more than learning to know.

Power-Ups

Power-ups increase engagement through using items, such as cards, that can be spent to give a player or side a temporary advantage.

These items can be part of initial conditions, bought, or awarded after a victory. Power-ups can be obstructed, either from other players or even from the player before being bought or traded. Using a hidden power-up can (but won't necessarily) reveal it to the other players.

Source: Rise of Nations. Microsoft product screen shot reprinted with permission from Microsoft Corporation.

Parker Brothers' Monopoly is the game with the world's single most famous power-up, the "Get Out of Jail Free" card.

Certain genres have standard power-ups. In a racing game, for example, a conventional power-up provides the ability to go faster for a short period of time, often called nitro or turbo.

References to Culture

Making a reference to "high culture" or "pop culture"—that is, to anything primarily known to a subgroup, such as people who have achieved a given education level—flatters the participants who get it, aligning them with something important or enjoyable and making them feel part of the same club as the designer.

Pretensions can have their cost, of course. Harvard's "VE RI TAS" looks to those in the club as a sign of high culture, but to most other people looks like one syllable short of "VERY TASTY."

Rubber Banding

Rubber banding is a technique to increase engagement by allowing AI-controlled competitors to bend the rules to keep things exciting and "close" for the real player. The term comes from racing games, where one can imagine a giant rubber band extending out from the player's car to pull lagging cars forward and winning cars back.

Rubber banding, as with many game elements, makes an experience more engaging, in this case at the expense of accuracy.

Author's note: Designers of educational simulations are bound to debate this technique, so it's useful to look at some very specific examples of using rubber banding in racing situations.

If the racing educational simulation is intended to build familiarity with a map (travelers racing around a foreign city to get comfortable with the layout, students racing through a functioning ancient city), or to become aware of principles (driving tiny vehicles through magnetic fields), because the learning objective is not winning a race, "rubber banding" would increase interest without undermining the learning experience.

If the course was on winning a race, be it chariot, NASCAR, or UPS truck, the same technique would cripple the learning.

Scores and Grades

It is a mainstay of computer games, sports, classrooms, even standardized tests—the score. The score (called a grade in school) is the single number that allows easy comparison and ranking (see "Ease of Deployment" in Chapter Twenty-Three). It is, however, not without controversy.

Scores Increase Engagement. Having scores unquestionably increases usage and focus. Every Sim should have them. Scoring can motivate, as it allows benchmarking against oneself and others (see "Player Comparison Panel" in

Chapter Nineteen). Persistent high scores also allow an asynchronous multi-player aspect, or at least social bragging rights.

Scoring can also have a practical value for a participant, such as gaining compliance or certification credit or even just additional lives in an arcade game.

But if overemphasized, scores and grades encourage gaming while subverting learning. The greater the reliance on scores for motivation, the more students will worry less about learning the material and more about gaming the system, making the scores actually subvert the learning rather than supporting it.

Further, when students try to optimize scores and grades, they are also much less likely to try completely different approaches, and instead just calibrate their current approaches.

Range. Scores in Sims work best if they are built around the academic standard:

- 69 and below = D = unacceptable
- 70–79 = C = good try but plenty of room for improvement
- 80–89 = B = solid
- 90–100 = A = great

This seems natural to those on the outside and a good cultural feedback standard to follow. Otherwise, imagine the confusion of using the same (or even a different) immersive learning simulation three times, the first time getting a score of 24, the second time, 190, and the third time, −1.

Scores Necessarily Editorialize. But for Sim designers, aggregating the permutations of open-ended actions and outcomes into that single analog range of 59 to 100, with an acceptable distribution (typically bell curve), aligned difficulty levels, and even any artificial caps, requires the calibration of a yoga master. And just putting absolute numbers to actions should make anyone at least a little uncomfortable (try putting numeric values to the activities you did today); most find a balanced scorecard reflecting a set of primary variables more accurate and even helpful.

Points become associated intrinsically with an external value system, whether they're meant to or not. If no points are associated with an action, it is not worth doing. For example, in the old Atari game Asteroids, shooting a big asteroid is 50 points. Shooting a little asteroid is 100 points. Dodging an asteroid is worth nothing. Just as arbitrary, in some classes, term papers are worth 30 percent, in others, 70 percent. In some classes, classroom participation is worth 30 percent; in others—nada.

Further, as with all formal learning aspects, points demonstrate that what is measured is often what can be measured, not what should be measured.

Presentation of Scores. Scores and grades can be presented pedagogically, as a free-floating number that breaks the fourth wall, or as a simulation element, such as a research bonus in dollars, acres of property saved in an environmental program, numbers of votes received, or magnitude of promotion.

Usually the higher the score the better, although there are a few exceptions like golf.

Related topics: "Standardized Test Results," in Chapter Twenty-Nine, and "Return on Investment," in Chapter Seven.

Author's note: If you believe more in evaluation than in formal learning, you might shoot for a scoring system that follows a nice bell curve, with some winners, some losers, and most lumped in the middle.

We like to pretend that academic scores and grades are instructional and pedagogical, but really they are motivational game elements. The reason to work hard is to get a good score, as opposed to using the score to figure out how to improve (where an after action review, just one example, is so much more useful).

We also like to pretend that scores are scientific, when instead they represent a staggering editorial commentary on what is important, and by how much.

Setting

A setting is a compelling backdrop, including one that evokes strong associations from past experience, designed to increase involvement in any medium.

Examples of engaging settings include:

- Film noir
- A farm
- Comic books
- Some place of high luxury
- Somewhere exotic or foreign
- Somewhere privileged
- Somewhere bright and open
- Some place of fear or apprehension
- A seat of power, or place one would go if promoted
- Some futuristic place
- A shopping mall

The right setting might also provide an opportunity for a participant to explore a topical area. A traditional action movie might use the Kremlin, Iraq, or a dot-com to present an environment of interest.

As with many game elements, selecting a setting for its engagement qualities has fidelity issues, and what is fun for one participant may not be fun for another.

Related topics: "Backdrop," in Chapter Fifteen, "Set," in Chapter Nineteen, and "New Sets and Settings," earlier in this chapter.

Shopping, Virtual

Shopping elements—enabling participants to acquire items and services with virtual money or other resources they have earned, often as a variation of a score—can serve as a reward for activities or accomplishments.

Shopping can also lead to investing in better equipment to make subsequent levels easier, which compounds successes and failures in any campaign.

Increasingly, "buying things" can include customizing your avatar (see "Choosing Appearance or Voice for an On-Screen Character," earlier in this chapter) and settings (such as shopping for your virtual apartment) for self-definition and status. Ever since players discovered they could buy a giant plasma television in The Sims, the floodgates have opened. Today, walking onto a multiplayer golf course with $1,000 virtual sunglasses sends a message to the other golfers as to your status.

Buying better equipment.

Source: The Sims 2 and SimCity 4 Images © 2009 Electronic Arts Inc. The Sims and SimCity 4 are trademarks or registered trademarks of Elecronic Arts Inc. in US and/or other countries.

Infrastructure and access to customers and resources can be bought.

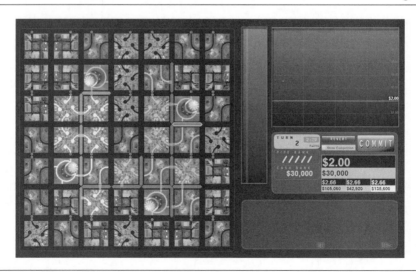

Source: © 2009 ACTON FOUNDATION FOR ENTREPRENEURIAL EXCELLENCE. Developed by GamesThatWork.com.

The wall between real and virtual in online worlds grows more permeable as buyers can, in real time, convert real money into virtual to buy virtual goods that some vendor spent real time creating, and then the vendor can turn the virtual money back to real money to pay real bills.

Related topics: "Hero," earlier in this chapter; "Budgeting," in Chapter Fourteen; "Student" and "Buddies," in Chapter Twenty; "Virtual Adviser," in Chapter Seventeen; and "Inventory," in Chapter Nine.

Timer

A timer provides a visible countdown to a trigger.

The timer reaching the zero might equal failure, unless the player accomplishes something, or success, if the player keeps something from happening.

Source: Cisco Systems. Used with permission.

While timers are an integral part of game shows, and time pressure is indeed a game element, nonetheless simply putting time pressure on a test does not a serious game make. Likewise, putting a timer around a decision on a branching story does not make it real-time, let alone practiceware.

Author's note: I used a Tetris-style game in one educational simulation, where to break up the intensity of the simulation and to review key points I had falling quotes that the students had to identify in one of six categories before they reached the bottom of the screen. A few evaluators of the simulation just couldn't understand that part. "Why is there a timer? What is the educational value of having students have to identify the quote in four or five seconds?" Part of my answer was, "It's a game element," but the other part was, "Don't people have time limits for exams? Doesn't that same logic apply to one as applies to the other, just in a smaller chunk?"

Wish Fulfillment

Wish fulfillment is the technique of putting the participants in a situation that they had previously desired. Some people may want a certain type of person, such as an arrogant peer, to get his or her comeuppance. Others may want to see what it feels like to acquire huge amounts of wealth.

17

PEDAGOGICAL ELEMENTS

Learn Faster and Better

Pedagogy. Street signs represent real-world pedagogy.

Pedagogical (also called *didactic*) techniques and elements generally surround a learning experience, ensuring that participants spend their time productively. Pedagogical elements can capture and present expert knowledge. In real life, for instance, presenting expert knowledge of a locale can range from street signs to GPS data. Pedagogical information can also support behavior, as with speedometers and caller ID readouts. Finally, pedagogical elements can be mentors, supervisors, or guides that might break complex tasks into simpler tasks, as well as providing expert commentary as needed.

In Sims, pedagogical elements can include in-game tips and directions, graphs, highlights, forced moments of reflection, and bread crumbs. These elements are often called *scaffolding*, and they are discussed later in this chapter. Related topics: "Background Material" and "After Action Review," in Chapter Eighteen, and "Coach or Facilitator," in Chapter Twenty.

Pedagogical elements provide a balance to the Sim elements (which are there to model reality) and the game elements (which are there to make the experience engaging). See "Venn Diagram" later in this chapter for a sketch of the relationships among these elements.

The Role of Pedagogy in Sims

In educational experiences, pedagogical elements help the learners:

- Know what to do
- Know how to use the interface
- Avoid developing superstitious behavior, such as believing they are influencing something by a particular action that really has no effect
- See relationships faster
- Work through frustration-resolution pairs
- Try different approaches
- Apply lessons to the real world

Pedagogical elements have to balance the challenge of giving neither too much nor too little help. They take the place of the wise instructor (and could in fact be programmed to take the form of a virtual mentor, supervisor, or guide), watching, commenting, pointing out key relationships, and knowing when not to say anything. The assumption is often that the earliest levels have a lot of pedagogical elements, but that the amount of support will shrink dramatically throughout the program.

> *Author's note:* At the highest level, pedagogical elements also refer to what information is modeled at all.

Sound Cue

A sound cue is a consistent sound that accompanies a character, cinematic technique, theme, or action.

For example, a movie might use the same flashbulb sound whenever a flashback is introduced. Or chirping noises whenever a character is using a computer (computers are much louder in movies than in the real world).

A Sim, meanwhile, might use an airplane or wind noise if a participant zoomed out sufficiently from a map. Or a location on a Sim map, such as an office, might have an associated sound cue, such as people talking on phones.

Mentor, Supervisor, or Guide

A mentor is an individual, typically a role model, coach or facilitator, or expert who has accepted some increased responsibility for another's development, including helping that person achieve mastery level in middle skills or big skills. Such an individual may perform tasks including after action reviews and may help understand processes.

Within a Sim, a mentor is a partially or completely scripted character who provides exposition and instruction (see "In-Game Tips and Directions" later in this chapter) through alerts and cut scenes, but unlike a coach, does not break the fourth wall.

In a traditional hero's journey, the mentor or guide is a critical enabler of the hero, giving both advice and also exotic items. Often the mentor either dies before the end of the journey or betrays the hero.

Mentor. A single virtual character can be used to provide instruction and guidance, even praise, throughout a program.

Author's note: In corporate-sponsored educational simulation, the role of the guide is often defined as a benign and helpful supervisor.

Abstraction

Abstraction is the process of taking out details or repetitive actions.

For example, a simulation designer might abstract the many actions involved in getting into a car and preparing to drive "grab door handle, unlatch door, open door, sit down, close door, put keys in ignition, press brake pedal, turn key, release brake" to just one "press (spacebar) to get in car." A radar screen or mini map is an abstraction.

For an educational simulation on child-proofing a house, for example, the designer might abstract that into a situation where a baby crawls from one side of the house to the other, past the stove, the detergent, the ironing board, the glass table, and the mean cat. The player has to move things and put on soft things to prevent the li'l darlin' from killing itself on that one pass.

Is chess an abstraction of war? Is Monopoly an abstraction of commerce? Is SimCity an abstraction of being a mayor? Are all games abstractions?

Related topics: "Comics," in Chapter Sixteen, and "Illustration," later in this chapter.

Simplified Interfaces

A simplified interface is a form of abstraction. It takes steps, choices, or information away from the player that would be required in the real-life activity. Designers build simplified interfaces for the sake of increasing engagement.

Noise

Noise is a system property of having random, out of place, or ambient inputs to and outputs from a system.

Noise can make understanding and learning from a situation more time-consuming. For example, a politician makes a speech and popularity figures go up. A company rolls out a new advertising campaign and sales climb. An organization curbs travel and costs drop. Are these cause and effect or just noise? Or a combination?

High-fidelity models of a situation must include noise; dealing with randomness is part of real-world analysis. Even so, a popular game element is to reduce noise to make cause and effect more direct.

Noise suppression (also known as signal enhancement) can be a value of business processes. For example, a competitive analysis or due diligence function could filter through the magazines, newspapers, and other press and interviews to find the real story. Potentially, a (presumably different) process could also generate noise to confuse an opponent.

Organic systems almost always have noise, but the systems either compensate for the noise or have balancing loops. Meanwhile, feedback loops are the result of noise (an output) being fed (input) back into a system, with the effect of amplifying the noise.

Related topics: "Probing," in Chapter Six, "Mutate," in Chapter Nine, and "Fog of War," in Chapter Eight.

Often, so-called random noise is really just an exogenous input. (Check an online dictionary to find out what *exogenous* means, because I didn't know either. . . .)

Author's note: Noise is one of those topics that no one thinks about until he or she actually builds a simulation. Is it all right to include noise? Experts say yes. Students say, "Oh please no!"

Acrostic

An acrostic can be used as a pedagogical technique, triggering a memorable phrase that helps students remember something; it's a type of mnemonic device.

For example, Please Excuse My Dear Aunt Sally is an acrostic to help students remember the order of doing equations—Parentheses, Exponents, then Multiplication and Division, then Addition and Subtraction. Obviously, the acrostic should not be harder to remember than the information it invokes.

Auto-Journal

The auto-journal is a place where the Sim automatically records key pieces of information, passwords, open tasks, actions, and awards, available to the participant on demand.

Auto-journals make sense when participants have to juggle multiple tasks and information.

Compare with "Bread Crumbs," later in this chapter.

Difficulty Adjustment

Players of the computer game Splinter Cell can self-select how hard they want the single-player campaign to be.

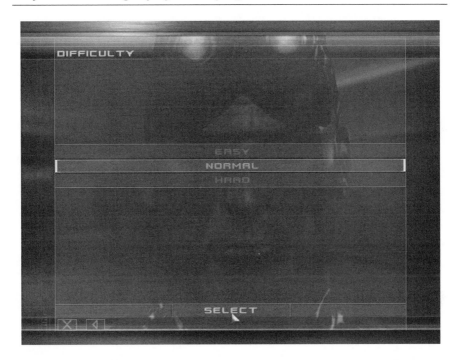

Difficulty adjustment is a way of increasing engagement through enabling participants to configure a campaign to make it easier or harder, based on their interest, time, and past experience.

Difficulty can typically be adjusted at the beginning, but in some experiences it can be changed at any time. Finally, some experiences automate the difficulty adjustment process, constantly changing it to keep the participant challenged.

As with other game elements, some changes in difficulty subvert the experience and learning (by taking out important steps or sequences that require difficult skills, for example, or by including more coaching and more live graphs and charts), and still other changes simply increase the time to complete the experience (such as by having more remedial levels or more encouragement).

Changes in difficulty can adjust any final score, with harder difficulty levels enabling higher scores than easier difficulty levels.

Here are some techniques that allow the designer to increase difficulty:

- Reduce pedagogy, including less transparency and less active role of any coach or facilitator.
- Make the artificial intelligence (AI) opponents more smart and crafty.
- Make the AI opponents cheat more.
- Skip levels.
- Reduce the amount of helpful resources.
- Change attributes to make the player less powerful, either permanently or one time.
- Change attributes to make the opponents more powerful, either permanently or one time.
- Reduce game elements.

Techniques to decrease difficulty include
- Add more pedagogy, including more transparency and more active role of coach.
- Make the AI opponents less smart and crafty.
- Make the AI opponents cheat less.
- Add more remedial levels.
- Increase the amount of useful resources.
- Change attributes to make the player more powerful, either permanently or one time.
- Change attributes to make the opponents less powerful, either permanently or one time.
- Add more game elements.

Automated adjusters should decrease difficulty if the participant is constantly failing in a mission. Contrariwise, automated adjusters should increase difficulty if the participant is passing all missions on the first attempt.

Speed-Up or Slow-Down Switch

In Sims where reaction time is not a critical element, it can be useful to give the user the ability to increase or decrease the reference speed of the core gameplay to take advantage of quick reflexes or reduce the need for them.

The ability to speed up or slow down the reference time may be constrained to a training level or practice level. In some Sims, such as The Sims, the program defaults to speed up time during a less interesting game interval, such as when a character sleeps.

Alert

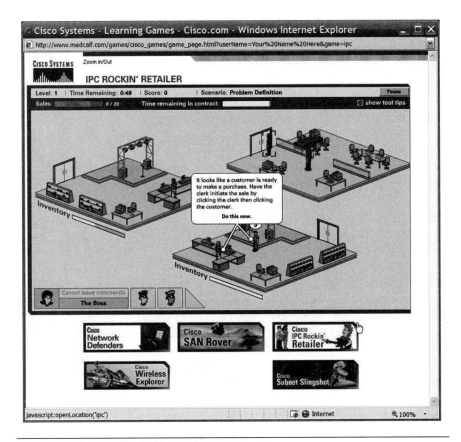

Source: Cisco Systems. Used with permission.

An alert is an obvious signal to the participant that something relevant has happened.

The signal could be purely pedagogical, such as putting up one of these elements:

- New window
- Text block
- Comment from a virtual coach
- Icon

The signal might be accompanied with a flashing halo, highlight, or sound cue. Or the signal could employ simulation elements, perhaps a phone answering machine, a newspaper headline, or an avatar's comment. Fire alarms are real-world alerts.

An alert may also solicit simple information from the participant, possibly pausing everything else until information is given, actions are taken, or an acknowledgment is input.

Alerts are a form of just-in-time knowledge.

Design questions:

- What triggers an alert?
- What form does the alert take?

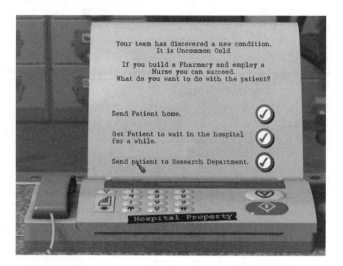

An alert can ask the player for a decision. In Bullfrog's Theme Hospital, for example, a player who has a diagnostic facility (that is, can perform the diagnostic activity) can discover new conditions. When this occurs, a link is made available and an alert is placed on the bottom of the display. When the player clicks on the alert, the real-time aspect of the game stops, and the player is given information on what has just occurred and what needs to happen, and also some immediate choices. When a choice is made, the game returns to real time.

Exaggerated Response

Designers often find it useful to exaggerate the response of a Sim, so that reactions to participant actions happen sooner, bigger, and with less outside interference than they would in real life. For example, the designers of the military Sim Full Spectrum Warrior, in which soldiers try to bring order to an urban environment, built two modes—one for soldiers as a simulation and one for casual gamers. In the casual version of the Sim, smoke canisters filled more space more quickly than in the soldier version, enhancing fun at the expense of fidelity.

Bread Crumbs

In the Sim display, bread crumbs are indicators of where a participant has already been. For example, people leave tracks in the snow, and active links change colors when traversed.

Online retailers such as Amazon.com present "recently viewed items" lists as a form of bread crumbs.

Bread crumbs abound in the real world. Ants leave chemical bread crumbs to lead other ants to a food source. Corporations have career ladders to help employees see how other people have successfully been promoted to senior positions. Many animals with a strong sense of smell can track the paths taken by other animals who inadvertently left their scents.

Mouse-Over

A mouse-over is an interface or basic input: a trigger that is activated by a participant's positioning a cursor, often controlled by a mouse, over a hot spot. Mouse-overs often invoke simple, noninvasive pedagogical activities such as text boxes and bubble help or highlights, but also might activate a video clip in a banner advertisement.

Mini games use a lot of mouse-overs to make them easier to use.

In any first-person perspective, the functionality of a mouse-over can be invoked based on where the participant is looking.

Also called *roll-over*.

Libraries of Plays

A library of plays is a collection of video clips or other records of past participants' performances in a Sim level.

In Sims, these past plays should be organized both by style (the approach of the participant) and by record of success.

For example, the first level of vLeader includes media files like these, each about five minutes long:

- A "directive" play, where the player is too forceful of her own agenda and doesn't listen enough to her subordinate.
- A "delegative" play, where the player is too weak in pushing her own agenda and cedes control to her subordinate.
- A strong play, where the player listens, firmly pushes her own agenda, and uncovers a great idea that meets everyone's needs.

Depending on the situation, accessing libraries of plays can be a cheat.

Mixed Scales

Sid Meier's Civilization IV uses different scales for units, structures, and countries.

Source: Sid Meier's Civilization IV Screenshots Courtesy of Firaxis Games and Take-Two Interactive Software, Inc.

Mixed scales are multiple frames of reference in use at the same time. In the real world, they are often used for mapping. That is, some three-dimensional maps have a vertical scale (height of mountains, depth of canyons) that is exaggerated at twice the horizontal scale to make the topology more dramatic.

Similarly, many instructional diagrams of Earth's solar system use planets scaled to each other and planets' orbits likewise scaled to each other, while the planets and orbits use quite different scales. This makes it feasible to present the solar system on a useful piece of paper—at the same scale, the orbits would fall off the page or the planets would be invisibly small.

Mixed scales in Sims, including educational simulations, computer games, and serious games, are around maps, time, and money. They enhance gameplay, but they're not realistic, which is another reason why experts tend to oppose the best simulations.

Graphic Elements. Often on maps, the distances between towns are truncated, people are smaller than cars, but only slightly, and cars are smaller than buildings, but only slightly.

Under the Covers. How fast time moves, with cycles of day and night for example, is almost always faster than real-world time. But the speed of other cycles, be they weeks, seasons, or generations, potentially provide a third and even fourth time scale.

Here is an example from Hasbro's Monopoly Tycoon:

- 24 game hours = 5 game years = 10 minutes' real-world time
- 1 decade = 48 game hours = 2 game days = 20 minutes' real-world time

Meanwhile, on-screen characters in Monopoly Tycoon walk at what looks to be a normal, real-time pace.

Money, like time, often exists at multiple scales (money has to have mixed scales if time does). Tickets for an amusement ride might cost three dollars (aligned with real-world prices), but new rides might only cost a few hundred dollars to build.

This, as with other game elements, is problematic for experts, but helps participants grasp the totality of situations and understand complex systems.

List of Tasks

It is often useful to maintain a constant list of core tasks (that is, goals and quests), with updates on little steps either completed or that need to be completed.

This little piece of pedagogy is especially useful when there are more than two quests going on at a time, as the figure illustrates from Fallout 3.

See also "Auto-Journal," earlier in this chapter.

Virtual Adviser

In SimCity 4, players are given suggestions by a cast of characters.

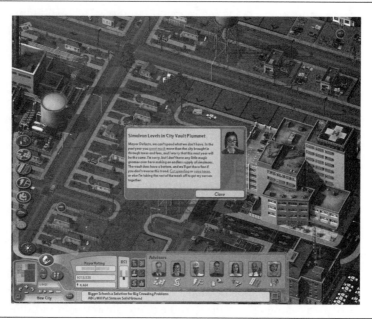

In a simulation, a virtual adviser is a character who seeks to influence your actions.

Unlike the mentor, supervisor, or guide, the virtual adviser is not perfect, trusted, or without a potentially self-serving agenda; even well-meaning virtual advisers may give contradictory advice. Balancing, filtering, and even seeking out contradictory advice is a critical part of the big skills of leadership and creating and using boards and advisers. One of the main lessons they teach is that you will never be president if you don't learn how to ignore some advice.

A virtual adviser may also:

- Be a constituent (or a proxy for one), such as a voter or board member, so keeping advisers happy may be a necessary strategy even if you don't agree with them, like them, or even respect them.
- Be the ombudsman for a single primary variable or work process.
- Simply produce noise.
- Be activated by triggers.
- Reveal obstructed information.
- Be a competitor.
- Be more trusted if there is a higher personal alignment or alignment with the current strategy.
- Take different forms, such as an expert or a newspaper editorial.

The task of building a virtual adviser puts less pressure on the Sim designer than that of building a mentor. Because the character does not have to be perfect, the designer needn't do a perfectly thorough analysis of the situation.

Redo

An immersive learning simulation or computer game may include a redo command in its processes to either offer the ability, encourage, or force participants to return to a saved or bookmarked point. Redo allows a participant to

- Make different choices or apply different tactics.
- Try new styles (such as going after specific awards).
- Spend more time practicing (to reinforce the learning or avoid an accidental success).

Death and other types of level-ending or failure feedback force a redo through loading a saved game. Typically, practiceware requires more redos than branching stories or interactive spreadsheets.

Sim designers often debate what to do when a Sim participant makes a small procedural omission. Does one slam everything to a stop, give some slight clue, or ignore it but write it up in an after action review?

Finally, in a redo situation, how differently should the environment play out, even if the participant actions are the same? (See "Random Map" in Chapter Eight.) Can you step in the same river twice?

Replay Option

In some games and simulations, players can passively watch plays after they are over.

A replay option is a process that allows participants to passively watch some core gameplay as a cut scene, either right after it happened or as part of an after action review—for analysis or just for fun. Replay options typically show the event from different points of view. Replays may use media controls, including" "Slow Motion Replay," discussed later in this chapter, or "Skip Chapter," discussed in Chapter Twenty-One.

Replays might be triggered automatically.
See also "Recording" in Chapter Twenty.

Save

Saving is a technique of recording enough information about a situation in a Sim to enable the participant to return to those same conditions in the future.

Accessing saved games allows players to leave the Sim and come back later, creating a pause of infinite length, or redo from the saved point, presumably to try new tactics or strategies, or maybe even relive a great sequence.

Saving a game (and the corresponding "three lives" granted in an arcade-style game) represents some fairly significant departures from fidelity:

- It necessarily breaks the illusion of the experience.
- It changes behaviors, rewarding high-risk behavior. (Funnily enough, in the old arcade games, there was a real financial consequence to dying.)
- It is also a different experience from playing a game or Sim the first time, where everything is a surprise. The second and third time through, everything is expected and success is just a matter of reacting the right way.

Yet entertainment-oriented simulations require the contrivance, and even the purest simulation-hawk would advocate practicing in a Sim by replaying over and over to master an action, as one might with a tennis backboard or batting cage.

Some other notes:

- Some strategy games, like Rise of Nations, have campaign modes that do not allow players to backtrack via saved games. Players have to live with the consequences of their actions, increasing the sense of jeopardy.
- Some science fiction games, such as System Shock 2, have tried to work the notion of save games into the story using reincarnation machines when the player dies.
- The more open-ended a game is, the larger the save file.
- Randomizing after a save point reduces the cheating that saving can represent.

Related topics: "Autosave Trigger" and "Save Blackouts," in Chapter Eighteen; "Bookmark," in Chapter Twenty-One; and "Redo," earlier in this chapter.

Removal of Scaffolding

Reducing Sim-embedded pedagogy, or scaffolding, as participants demonstrate competency is itself a pedagogical element. Scaffolding can also be reduced as participants move through a Sim, or even at the request of the participant.

Removing scaffolding could also be done not in absolute terms in a Sim, but around each new skill as it is developed. (See Chapter Twenty-Two, especially the "Mastery Level" section.)

Scaffolding simultaneously reduces the depth of frustration and the height of resolution that a participant experiences. See also *profile* and *difficulty adjustment*.

Slow Motion Replay

A slow motion replay presents a record of a participant's actions in more than real time, allowing a student to observe everything in more detail. Students can see nuances, such as body language of any avatars or locations of relevant objects, more clearly. Sometimes in a slow motion replay students can also change the camera angle or direction. Slow motion replay helps develop situational awareness (described in Chapter Nineteen).

Related topic: "Replay Option," earlier in this chapter.

Taxonomies

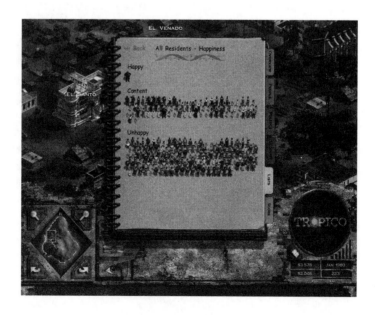

Taxonomies encourage the viewer to see objects or information as being members of discrete categories.

Applying a taxonomy can be useful to understand and visualize data. The game Tropico allows players to view all of their citizens grouped into happy, content, and unhappy.

Applying a taxonomy can also involve persuasion and editorializing. A proposed bill in Congress might be subjected to one taxonomy by one party (moral versus immoral) and another taxonomy by the other party (big government versus freedom).

Imagine some kind of crazy Sim world where labeling the exact same complex immigration bill as amnesty or not amnesty changed the constituents' approval of it! Or just labeling the same person as an enemy combatant or communist rather than criminal suspect changes that person's legal status. . . .

Chapters in a book present a taxonomy, as do job titles such as vice president. Creating a taxonomy requires sensors and edge enhancement. Still, taxonomies are always incomplete in some way. Designers often have to force something that could be in multiple categories into just one (in contrast to a Venn diagram, which allows for an overlap). Participants should be able to switch taxonomies easily.

Related topics: "Conceptual Maps," in Chapter Eight; "After Action Review," in Chapter Eighteen; and "Venn Diagram" and "Time Line" in this chapter.

Time Line

A time line is typically a two-dimensional visualization of the change in activities, variables, or milestones over time, either documenting a past or current event or predicting or planning a future event.

Time lines include trails.

In Sim Pedagogy. A time line can be a chart with the beginning of a game, Sim, or level on the left side and the end at the right side, showing milestones and shifting values of key variables.

Time lines can be shown in a heads-up display during the core gameplay or can be used in an after action review, and they can form an abstraction of the more detailed recorded plays.

In Development. A time line can also be used as a project management tool for developers to map all elements.

In a Procedure. In capturing or presenting a procedure, a time line might dictate when to do what activity.

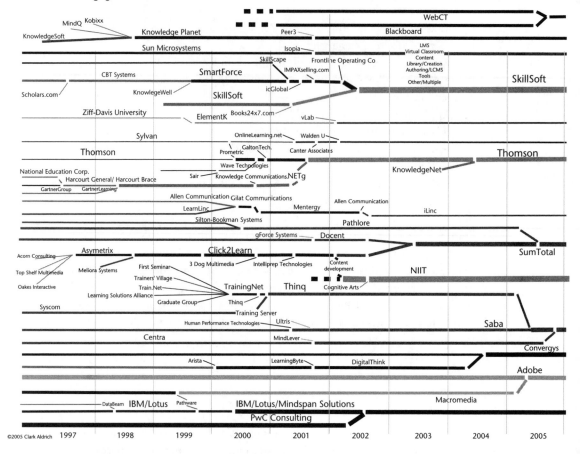

©2005 Clark Aldrich

Different Forms. A time line might take a variety of forms:

- A process map, branching tree, or other state-based model
- A set of time-lapse photographs
- A graph, such as a change in aggregate variables, scores, and attributes over time
- A rich progress meter

If part of a Sim system, a time line might trigger certain events (see "Table-Based Triggers" in Chapter Eight).

Minard's map of Napoleon's march is a famous example of a rich time line.

Time to Core Gameplay or First Decision

The time that a participant spends in a Sim before engaging in the core gameplay can also be a pedagogical element.

The interval may be spent absorbing backstories, briefings, even splash screens. Information can be presented in cut scenes or, in some cases, lectures. Most participants tend to skip through this kind of material as quickly as possible, no matter how important the designers may believe it to be, as it decreases their engagement and satisfaction if they're forced to go through it in detail.

Many developers of immersive learning simulation believe that because a real-world activity requires deep researching, so too should the Sim. This almost always makes the time to core gameplay too long to hold participants' interest.

Trail

The pedagogical technique of using trails can be integrated with simulation elements, such as this real-world vapor trail, making it easier to see the jet and where it is going.

A trail embodies the pedagogical technique of presenting a persistent indicator of where a unit or variable has been or how it has changed over time.

Trails, like blurs of fast-moving objects, snapshots, strobe light images, and lines on graphs, make it easier to see patterns. Trails can also lessen the need for mixed scales. Hospital EKG machines are classic examples of trails.

Compare with "Bread Crumbs," earlier in this chapter.

Venn Diagram

Venn diagram on basic differences and similarities between game, simulation, and pedagogy.

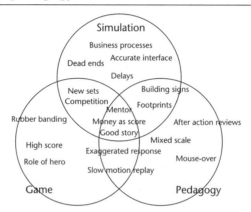

A Venn diagram is a pedagogical technique of organizing elements into three overlapping categories by using overlapping circles and labels. Venn diagrams avoid some of the artificial edge enhancement found in pure taxonomies such as book chapters or static definitions.

Sims combine simulation, game, and pedagogical elements, although many elements fall in two or even all three categories.

Related topic: "Conceptual Maps," in Chapter Eight.

Walk-Through

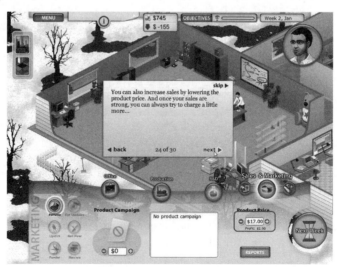

A walk-through is a set of step-by-step instructions on how to successfully engage an experience.

Walk-throughs, typically in the form of Web pages, are often sufficient support for real-world procedures.

In a Sim, walk-throughs of a training level may be provided by a coach or facilitator or embedded in the program (such as this example from City Interactive's Beauty Factory). But walk-throughs of all levels may also be posted by other participants in places including fan sites; these unofficial walk-throughs are thought of as cheats by program sponsors or coaches. Puzzles, standardized tests, and other linear experiences are easily ruined by walk-throughs, but practice-centric Sims are not.

Walk-throughs may be called demonstrations or "show me" levels.

Pace Setter

A pace setter is something or someone that establishes a level of desired accomplishment (often as measured against a primary variable). For example, people at a higher organization level set the pace for everything from work hours to ethical norms for employees at a lower level. People might use siblings or classmates to compare their own progress in everything from financial success to positive impact on the world. Scores and grades convey a pace, with B's conveying to students that their pace is, on average, about right. The success of the stock market (or a specific industry) provides the context to measure a specific company's progress.

Different pace settings include

- Low threshold: What is minimally required so as not to fail, such as a thirty-minute guarantee for delivering pizza, or a D in a class for getting credit.
- Average level: What peers or the "average" competitors are doing.
- Stretch goal: What is possible with strong effort, or what the leading competitor is doing.

Pace setting in a Sim can take different forms, including a player comparison panel. A coach or mentor might superimpose an artificial pace during a practice session.

Juxtaposition

Juxtaposition involves the comparison of any two significantly different frames of reference for comedic, dramatic, or educational effect.

For example:

- A superhero's suit shows a cranberry stain.
- A plumber gets to ride on Air Force One.
- In the middle of a war, a woman gives some food to an orphan.
- A very small house is built next to a very large house.
- A genius-level professor can't operate a telephone answering machine.

A Sim may use traditional juxtaposition to make a comparison, such as in a linear briefing. More effectively, a Sim may compare the outcomes of two or more student plays, noting how (traditionally small) differences in approaches resulted in significantly different outcomes. For example, saving a small amount of money each turn might result in a war chest magnified by compound interest. Listening first instead of talking first in a relationship management situation may make the difference between an enduring friendship and a meaningless transaction. Calling some colleagues on their small ethical lapses may avoid a subsequent major scandal. When members of a class are each going through a single-player Sim, a coach might compare their various results, tracing back differences in their approach.

Forced Moments of Reflection

Forcing a moment of reflection means stopping after the core gameplay or execution phase and asking the participant to think about and articulate strategies and tactics and their application to the real world. This pedagogical technique can also be introduced at any time during a level.

Forced moments of reflection can interrupt engagement, but they are nonetheless critical for aligning strategies and tactics, understanding complex systems, and application of new content.

Forced moments of reflection are often initiated by a mentor, supervisor or guide, an instructor, a buddy, or a coach or facilitator.

Related topic: "After Action Review," in Chapter Eighteen.

Graph

A Sim display can use a graph for the pedagogical element of displaying the movement of aggregate variables and attributes over time.

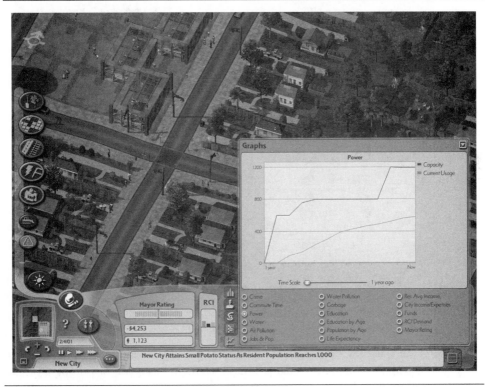

Source: The Sims 2 and SimCity 4 Images © 2009 Electronic Arts Inc. The Sims and SimCity 4 are trademarks or registered trademarks of Electronic Arts Inc in US and/or other countries.

Graphs can be superimposed during the core gameplay, can be available to be pulled up during the core gameplay, or shown in the after action review after gameplay is compete.

Two or three lines tend to be more interesting than just one. Seeing how several lines move together is a major component of intellectually understanding complex systems.

Author's note: We put a little graph in the upper-right corner of the Virtual Leader screen as a debugging tool. We ended up liking it so much we just decided to keep it.

Highlight

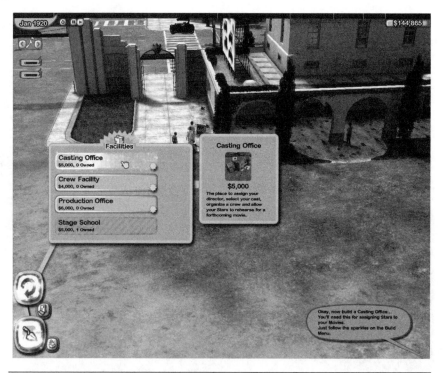

Source: Microsoft product screen shot reprinted with permission from Microsoft Corporation.

In a Sim display, highlighting is the pedagogical technique of drawing attention to a graphic element by making it flash, changing its color, or putting a bright, contrasting background color around it.

Highlights are often used in

- An alert
- A script (such as teaching the participant how to use the Sim)
- A view filter (such as looking at a nation-state through the lens of birth rates)
- Reaction to the player mouse-overing or looking at something (such as a hot spot, menu, or potential responses in a multiple choice question)

Bullfrog's The Movies uses these highlights:

- Sparkles for things that need immediate action
- Red highlight bubbles for things that need attention the next chance the player has
- Red dots for long-term issues

In the real world, people highlight by pointing something out by using a laser pointer, a finger, or even a quick glance. The role of emotions can be to highlight real-world objects or situations.

Illustration

Illustration is the pedagogical technique of using a drawing or computer-generated image to both capture reality and also highlight certain information and filter out other information. Illustrations are almost inevitably stylized, intentionally or not, and abstracted.

Illustrations are often more useful and instructional than photographs, which is in part why they are used for most airplane emergency cards. They may include mixed scales.

Quick lab: Go to Amazon.com and look up the bird guides. How many of the best-selling ones use photographs and how many use illustrations?

Scientific illustrations stress fidelity.
Related topic: "Comics," in Chapter Sixteen.

In-Game Tips and Directions

Source: Tomb Raider Series © Eidos Interactive.

The use of in-game tips and directions is the pedagogical technique of proactively getting key helpful information, in the form of alerts and highlights, close to the point of need, and activating them by some trigger. They can be essential for successful gameplay, even for things that seem obvious to the designer. As a rule of thumb, assume you will need ten times as many as you think.

In-game tips are used extensively in the first level.
Tips can be given by a guide.
Compare to "Load-Up Screen Tips" in Chapter Eighteen.

Fourth Wall

Source: The Movies. Microsoft product screen shot reprinted with permission from Microsoft Corporation.

The "fourth wall" is a concept from the theater world, referring to the open side of the stage, which actors generally treat as impervious—allowing them to behave as though they had privacy for their on-stage discussions—but occasionally "break" to address the audience directly. Thus it refers to maintaining or deliberately stepping outside of the illusion of the story or the virtual environment and connecting to some part of the real world.

Some pedagogical techniques, such as a narrator, can break the fourth wall.

> *Author's note:* Most casinos and shopping malls (as well as the inside of theaters) have no windows and no clocks, to maintain a type of "fourth wall."

Related topic: "Bubble World Calibration," in Chapter Six.

Superstition

Sim participants easily fall into superstition, the belief that it is possible to influence a system or result in an experience through an action, activity, or process that really has no effect.

Superstition can be the result of assumptions brought into an immersive learning simulation or coincidences during the simulation.

Superstition can lead to accidental success and can be reduced through using pedagogical elements.

Forcing Different Approaches

It can be a pedagogical goal to encourage or force participants to retry the same or similar situations using a new way to solve the same problem or meet the same goal.

Unless steps are taken, most participants will replay each chunk exactly the same way, just refining their own tactics and better anticipating obstacles. Getting people to try new approaches requires either explicit instructions and rails or, more challenging in an educational Sim, putting a huge obstacle in the way and being content for participants to bang against it again and again until they get so frustrated they finally realize a new approach is needed. Awards can be used.

Forcing different approaches is especially important when participants have access to difficulty adjustment, as they can make the Sim easier and get away with using their old skills married with a gaming approach.

This kind of roadblock can interrupt engagement, but is critical for developing new approaches in participants.

Sims and the Nature of Math

If in other sciences we should arrive at certainty without doubt and truth without error, it behooves us to place the foundations of knowledge in mathematics.

—Roger Bacon (*Opus Majus*, book 1, chapter 4)

The computer game Civilization IV quotes this compelling observation, and I was thinking about it the other day, when a foundation head asked me how I would use Sims to teach math.

To answer that question, it's first necessary to ask, What is math, anyway? (And by the way, I use math every day, quite a bit, and it is essential to create most simulations.)

And maybe the second part of the question is whether, as the Bacon quote suggests, math really is perfect. After all, 1 + 1 always equals 2. And 5! (that is,

5 factorial, or $5 \times 4 \times 3 \times 2 \times 1$) always equals 120. Isn't that perfection? It seems like it.

Except, what if the symbols and numbers of math are a form of pedagogy (including taxonomies, graphs, and abstractions)? What if math is best seen as a layer of content on top of, and augmenting, real experiences? In that case, the question of the "perfection" of math rests not just on the self-referential math-to-math manipulations (where math becomes a bubble world), but also the real-life-to-math, or math-to-real-life transitions.

Here's a simple example: if I drive 60 miles per hour for three hours, I will have traveled 180 miles. That is a perfect statement. But does that perfectly translate to real life? Probably not, because no one drives exactly 60 miles per hour, and, perhaps, few people drive for exactly three hours. The math is sloppy and inaccurate, but good enough to be helpful.

Or a simpler example: If I combine two piles of hay, what do I get? One pile of hay!

So, beneath a faux self-defined perfection, in fact, math is sloppy and inaccurate, if asked as on- and off-ramps to the real world. Likewise, in an academic setting, the learning about math requires the systematic stepping back from, even repudiation of, reality.

Is there a point to the math observation? Maybe.

Only if math is better defined as a tool for improving our relationship with the real world, not just as the rules of an insular, perfect little pocket world, then we can create simulations to make people great at using math, instead of creating simulations that help people become great at knowing math.

Furthermore, multiple levels of self-referential systems ("the point of second grade is to prepare a student for third grade," or "the stock market will go up because it has gone up," or "if you beat the simulation, you know how to use the skill in the real world") are the signs of an impending fall.

But breaking the perfect pocket world requires a view of math that is at odds with current schools, textbooks, standardized testing, and in fact our educational establishment's entire philosophy of being. The odds of changing all that are not so good. Especially because, quoting Roger Bacon, math is perfect.

18

TASKS AND LEVELS

Tasks are mini-goals that a player is asked to complete in a Sim. Similarly, levels are a chunking of tasks into the simulation equivalent of chapters.

Sims are made up of these tasks and levels, in order to present the content in a productive form. Most Sims have common designs both within levels and connecting levels, all surrounding and supporting the core gameplay.

Inter-Level Structure

Within a level, Sims begin with a fairly non-interactive briefing, where story and task, objectives, and missions are introduced.

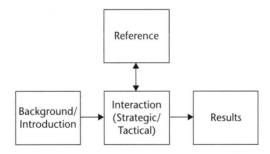

The participant than progresses to the interaction phase of the level, which may require an initial strategic decision. This may include where on the map to go next, what items or units to bring, or what power-ups, if any, to use. (This enables a later opportunity of aligning strategies and tactics.)

Then the core gameplay begins. Throughout this phase, the participant may have constant access to reference material. Finally, at the end of a level, there may be a harder challenge such as a boss (not a real-world supervisor but a particularly strong opponent, discussed later in this chapter).

This is followed, where appropriate, by formal feedback such as an after, action review.

The following sections cover the aspects of task and level design in more detail.

Entice Mode

The entice mode shows combinations of annotated gameplay, cut scenes, and explanations of core concepts in a screen-saver type of looping video. The entire entice mode may be between three and ten minutes, and it often runs when the Sim is first launched, or if the player is inactive for ten minutes or more. This mode is the evolution of the sequences that coin-operated arcade games ran to attract the quarters of passers-by and is designed to engender comfort and excitement. For Sims designed for organizational use, the entice mode may be muted, so as not to bother coworkers if left on auto-run.

Background Material

Background material is designed to give students enough information to go on with before they engage the full simulation, both self-paced and coach-deployed. It can include case studies, visual and text representations of systems models, and descriptions of interfaces to be encountered (such as how to execute actions using basic inputs of the type described in Chapter Twenty-One).

Background material might be tiered. Very complicated simulations, such as military flight simulators, often use simplified flight simulators or control panels as background material, and these in turn might use articles or screen shots as background material.

Contrast with "Backstory" in Chapter Fifteen and "Briefing" in this chapter.

Briefing

Briefing is the pedagogical technique of presenting information immediately before the core gameplay or execution phase that introduces tasks and the situation. The information is presented by a coach, mentor, supervisor, or guide. Where necessary, briefings also cover how success will be measured, such as through a balanced scorecard.

If canned and part of a Sim, the briefing is presented in a cut scene.

A briefing may include some backstory, descriptions of new actions available or suggested techniques, descriptions of awards available, and links to

Briefing. A screen shot from SimuLearn's vLeader 2007.

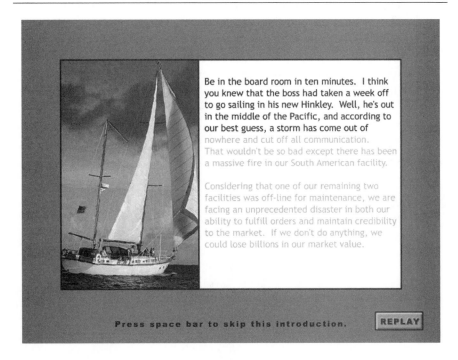

Be in the board room in ten minutes. I think you knew that the boss had taken a week off to go sailing in his new Hinkley. Well, he's out in the middle of the Pacific, and according to our best guess, a storm has come out of nowhere and cut off all communication. That wouldn't be so bad except there has been a massive fire in our South American facility.

Considering that one of our remaining two facilities was off-line for maintenance, we are facing an unprecedented disaster in both our ability to fulfill orders and maintain credibility to the market. If we don't do anything, we could lose billions in our market value.

Press space bar to skip this introduction.

REPLAY

background material. In many Sims, the information in the briefing turns out to be incomplete.

Briefings (and the Sim itself) can help align the current emotions of players with the emotions of their future selves in the context that will require the skills developed in the Sim. For example, a WILL Interactive simulation on sexually transmitted diseases puts the player in a relaxed and even aroused state when making some critical decisions, assuming that will be the state when the person will be making real-life decisions.

Contrast to "After Action Review" later in this chapter.

Black Box

A black box is a system where one knows the input and the output, but does not know exactly how the input was turned into the output. All real-world physics represents black boxes, with increasingly precise approximations being defined. Any sufficiently complex system, even if one knows the mechanics, has properties of being a black box.

It is a matter of debate, when a live or virtual coach or facilitator is presenting a simulation to students, how much of the Sim's systems should be black box. Should the learning activity involve figuring out what the system is? Or should it be a matter of practicing connecting actions to link systems to results? Or simply developing increasing awareness that a system exists at all and recognizing to what broad extent it interconnects areas that originally appeared distinct?

Said another way, how much does a great tennis player have to know physics?

It is also a point of continual struggle to know when to present "the model." Some argue that it should be before students engage it, and others argue that it should be after.

Objective

An objective is an activity, sometimes made up of tasks that, if completed, brings a participant closer to completing a mission. As with the terms *tactical* and *strategic*, or even action and middle skills, it can be used to encompass different scales by different people, making it a vague if mildly useful term.

Strategic Decision, or Load Out

A strategic decision point is a place in a Sim, typically before a core gameplay, where a player has to make decisions, typically turn-based rather than real time, that significantly impact both the core gameplay and the ability of the player to win the campaign.

For example, in Microsoft's "Age of . . . " series, players choose which countries to attack and what resources to bring to bear on the attack, with the actual battle being conducted during the core gameplay. In a leadership Sim, a CEO may decide where to have a critical meeting, and whom to invite, during this strategic step before the real-time meeting occurs.

Load-Up Screen Tips

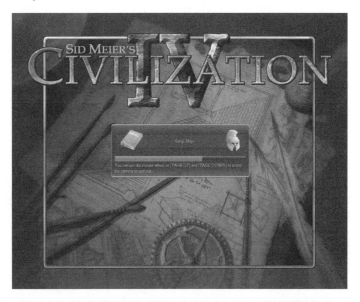

Source: Sid Meier's Civilization IV Screenshots Courtesy of Firaxis Games and Take-Two Interactive Software, Inc.

Action Gate. In Fallout 3, players must demonstrate they can move and open a simple gate before they can access the rest of the game.

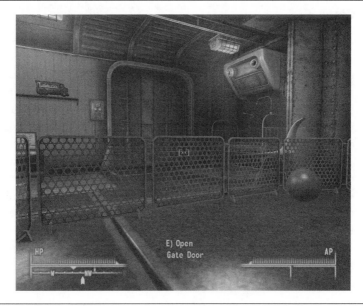

Source: Fallout ® 3 © 2008 Bethesda Software LLC, a ZeniMax Media company. All Rights Reserved.

Information such as game-play suggestions can be presented on the load-up screen. Often, these tips will rotate, and they may be specific to the level that is loading.

Compare to "In-Game Tips and Directions" in Chapter Seventeen.

Core Gameplay

"Core gameplay" refers to the most interactive part of a Sim level, typically conducted in real time.

Core gameplay can be to set up by a briefing, interrupted by forced moments of reflection, and followed by an after action review.

When participants engage a Sim, especially for the first time, they anticipate the core gameplay. When they have to sit through significant setup, either in the form of an extended briefing (such as cut scenes) or required pre-work, such as research or planning, most participants lose engagement. If an extended setup is required, the designers may elect to have a brief moment of core gameplay to relieve that tension.

If the level is part of a campaign, then past decisions make the core gameplay easier or harder and may require aligning strategies and tactics.

In a formal learning program, the core gameplay has to support implicit knowledge, and it is where skills are developed. It can include mastering simple actions.

Also called *execution phase* or *core interaction*.

Action Gates

In Sim level design, action gates are places where the players have to demonstrate mastery of a single necessary action before they can continue. The action gates are used to help players learn both what abilities are possible and how to engage them using the interface. For example, a player in the first level of a first-person Sim may be trapped in a room and allowed to continue only after demonstrating the ability to open a door. (This skill of opening doors presumably would be required for later success in the Sim.)

Typically, the action gate traps players and leaves them very few other options, such as confining them in a fairly small area, so that people do not waste much time trying to circumvent the gate. And depending on the Sim, there may also be some kind of explicit directions, either on-screen text ("Press the x button to crawl"), a flashing icon, or words spoken by another character. Finally, action gates may be preceded by some visualization of either what to avoid or what to do. Action gates are ideally integrated into the story, but may also be extrinsic in some kind of training level.

Action gates are the tips of any skill cones. The action required may be slightly more complex in later levels.

Purists of discovery-based learning models may find action gates manipulative and overly leading. Like any pedagogy, however, action gates can save frustration and increase the productivity and the flow of the experience.

Save Points

With save points in use, participants can save their progress only at established locations, such as after a completed task or at a home base, rather than whenever they want.

This increases the suspense and the sense of jeopardy and minimizes the possibility of accidental success, but can lead to frustration if the participant has to replay a sequence over and over again, especially if the sequence includes some linear aspects (especially pedagogical elements) or easy, extended repetitive play before the much tougher play that forms the stumbling block.

Educational simulations have stricter save-game philosophies than computer games, restricting access to save points with a view to making sure the desired learning occurs and progress isn't the result of a strung-together series of lucky actions.

Autosave Trigger

An autosave trigger is a preset location on a maze-style map that launches a process to automatically save the player's place. This might be before a difficult encounter; after a linear story element, including a cut scene or a briefing, has been played; or right after a new level has been loaded.

Automatic save points do not preclude open-ended saving options.

Save Blackouts

A save blackout is a part of a Sim where the player cannot save the game. This increases the sense of jeopardy and tension and requires a more comprehensive application of procedural knowledge.

End of Level

The end is the part of a level that, when completed, will allow the participant to access the next level (if there is one) or the end of the Sim (if there is not).

The end of level often includes a significantly heightened challenge. This might include solving a complex puzzle, defeating a large number of opposing units, or dealing with one very powerful unit called a boss. Often the time pressure is greater, and the graphics are more advanced and intense. The challenge may tie into the story as well, giving some emotional payoff. The end-of-level challenge may be followed by a cut scene.

End-of-level challenges can cause significant frustration if they are too difficult, and can be a letdown if they are too easy. More important (and perhaps ideally), they require a player to demonstrate a certain level of developed skills that will be necessary for subsequent levels, which can reduce the chances of accidental success.

Similar to real-world testing certification processes.

Boss

A boss is a powerful end-of-level antagonistic unit.

The exaggerated attributes of bosses can include size, speed, and energy. The most powerful boss, sometimes called a big boss or master boss, is typically at the end of the last level of the Sim.

These bosses may also have significance in the plot, such as being recurring antagonists; thus their defeat moves the story along as well. The defeat of a boss is often followed by a cut scene.

Related topics: "Avatar," in Chapter Nineteen; "Character," in Chapter Nine; "Tests and Quizzes," in Chapter Twenty-Nine; and "Certification," in Chapter Twenty-Three.

After Action Review

After action review (AAR) is a pedagogical technique of using focused sessions, typically after the core gameplay or execution phase of an experience, to better understand what happened and what should have happened. This can include strategy review and action review.

Feedback in AARs can include

- Raw material, such as recorded plays and time lines
- Analysis (what happened and why at a thematic level)
- Coaching (how to get better results next time, and perhaps how to transfer the experience to real-life situations, from the perspective of an expert or a peer)
- Evaluation for certification (how ready the player is to handle any real situation)
- Comparisons to norms, including game elements like a high score or rewards and recognition to spur competition and repetition of the level

AAR. Some after action reviews are simple and just show basic results; others provide assessment and advice.

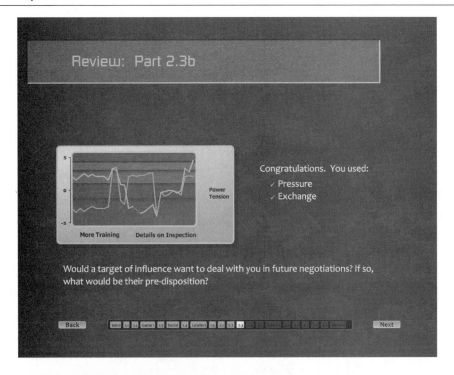

AARs in a Sim ultimately require a combination of human and computer intervention, but one or the other can do in a pinch. Ideally, the participants might give the first analysis of their own performance, before any coach. AARs risk being either too positive or too negative. Parts of the military use a "thumbs up, thumbs down" system in AARs, meaning, "here is one positive thing and here is one thing to change."

In a Sim context, AARs should also be used often enough to force users to think about performance, and then give them the opportunity to try again.

And like all pedagogy that supports Sims, they also should be used in the real world. For example, AARs might be held several weeks after a final deliverable with the team to evaluate what went well and what did not.

Also called *postmortems* or *debriefings*.

Sim Structure

The levels in a Sim are surrounded and organized by common structures. When first launched, the Sim might show a producer splash screen and a developer splash screen. Then the main menu provides the participant with access to the Sim features.

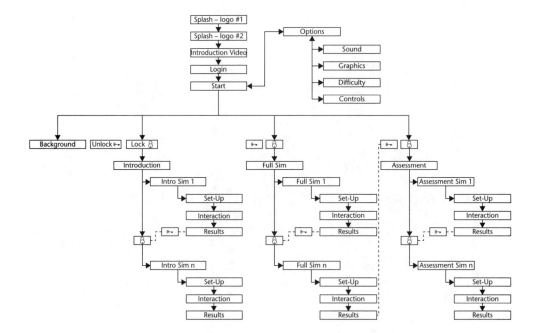

A participant might have the ability to configure the Sim.

The core gameplay is launched using some type of campaign structure, taking participants from the first level to the final level. After the final level, a program sponsor may be notified. There may also be an instant action and multiplayer experience.

Here are the elements in more detail.

Technology Test Page

A technology test page is a Web page that diagnoses the user's computer and settings for compatibility of all of the technology, networking capabilities, and security access needed for the successful use of a Sim. Before entering a simulation, students might go to this page and find any problems.

Typically, these types of areas are tested:

1. The presence of Adobe Flash (or the expected version of Adobe Flash)
2. Ability to communicate with external servers (for instant messaging or multiplayer interaction)
3. Screen size and resolution
4. Sound capability, such as presence of headphones, speakers, microphone (if needed), and sound levels
5. Adequate graphic card, sound card, and DirectX drivers (if needed)
6. Graphic card memory size
7. Hard disk size
8. Whether installed game is up-to-date or in need of any patches
9. Whether hard disk is sufficiently defragged

A good technology test page may also provide solutions and workarounds, such as links to driver homepages (Flash, for example), or launch an HTML instead of Flash version of the Sim or communication tools.

This page will offload some or all of the technical support needed to run the Sim.

Goals and Objectives of the Program

In an educational simulation, the goals and objectives list the learning objectives for the entire program. This section may also include requirements for credit and instructions on how to use the Sim.

Training Level

A training level is a self-paced level, often the first core gameplay encountered, that is structured to help the participant learn how to use the Sim.

In the computer game The Movies, the training level requires the player build a necessary structure before continuing.

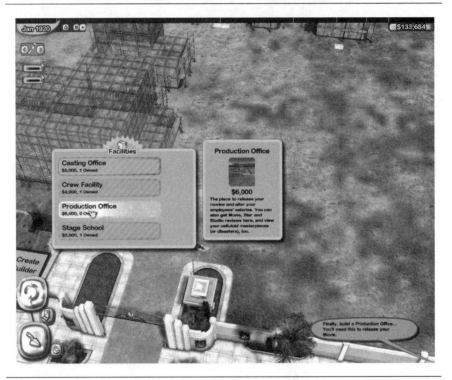

Source: Microsoft product screen shot reprinted with permission from Microsoft Corporation.

Typically, the training level has a lot of trigger-based pedagogical elements, including voice-overs, the active use of a mentor, supervisor, or guide, in-game tips and directions, highlights, walk-throughs, some type of compass, filtering of basic inputs, and alerts. It offers fewer opportunities for a participant to make strategic choices.

The training level may also be seamlessly integrated into a story, where it may not break the fourth wall, or it may be separate (and perhaps optional, although few participants will take an optional training level). The training level is often accessible via the main menu, although often best called "the first level."

Typically, the more a Sim varies from established genre interfaces, the more detailed a training level has to be.

Oftentimes, the training level is also the first level. Contrast with "Sandbox Level," later in this chapter.

First Level

The first level provides the participant's initial exposure to the core gameplay of a campaign.

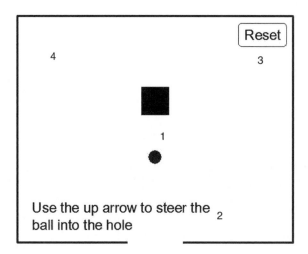

Creating the first level of any Sim is harrowing. It has to be impossible to fail yet still deep enough to entice. If you don't get it right, any deployer has to waste significantly more time getting students interested. And a great many educational simulations get this wrong.

Here are four rules:

- Players must be able to finish the first level quickly (in less than one minute).
- The directions and goals of a first level must be unambiguous, with immediate feedback and a clear sense of success or failure. It should be set up through a brief cut scene and include very high feedback, such as in-game tips and directions.
- The first level must have a reset button (to encourage exploration and reduce fear of failure).
- The first level must have room for some exploration and a promise of more interesting things to come. It has to be so easy as to be intuitive to use, but also must deliver a slight learning payoff and foreshadowing of the experience to come.

Typically, a disproportionate amount of developer time (but not end-user time) is (or should be) spent on the first level of a Sim. It needs to include a lot of verbal and text directions.

One of the biggest traps of first levels in serious games or educational simulations is making them have a strong educational goal. Rather, if a user engages the interface and meets with success in a very short time, the goal of the level should be considered met. The deeper learning should begin at level 2.

The first level may be explicitly a training level (especially in a complex game), but it can also just as easily not, especially for a mini game. The first level can also be a demonstration level (discussed later in this chapter).

Accidental Success

Accidental success is a phenomenon that occurs when a participant succeeds at an experience and is promoted without knowing how it happened or being able to repeat the success. This causes significant problems. In some cases, players are promoted to the next level, where everything is harder, and they are doubly unprepared. Players also get very suspicious of a program that tells them they have won when they don't feel like they should have, nor have they learned anything.

Levels designed to minimize accidental success tend to risk being tedious or linear and overly procedural. One solace for a coach or deployer is that, sadly, accidental success also happens all the time in the real world.

Practice Level

A practice level is a place in a Sim where participants can leave the Sim's story and repeatedly try difficult activities with feedback to improve skills, such as mastering an action. A practice level does not have consequences on the users' campaign performance, but may still be required either for everyone or as a remedial intervention for those struggling with the main Sim.

A practice level may have available higher levels of pedagogical elements.

Final Level

The final level in the Sim has many aspects found at each end of level, including story, graphics, and learning objectives, but ratcheted up still further in intensity. (See "End of Level," earlier in this chapter.) The final challenge may be followed by a cut scene showing the end of the story arc, and possibly an epilogue.

Conclusion

In an educational simulation, the conclusion is a section that reviews key lessons learned. It often repeats some of the information found in the goals section.

Campaign

A campaign is a series of discrete and often arena-style challenges connected by a larger context, such as a story or control of a map. The results of one challenge (gains, losses, changes in supplies, and so on) are frequently carried over to, or even enable, the next one.

Campaigns add increased strategy and jeopardy to the core gameplay and execution phase.

An entire campaign might take between two and twenty hours, resulting in either a complete win, partial win, or complete loss.

Campaigns can be linear and single-player, branching, or open-ended.

Compare with "Career Mode," later in this chapter.

Linear Campaign

A linear campaign is a single-player variation where a participant progresses through a scripted sequence of levels (maps and arenas), often connected by a story.

Typically, the participant makes few or no strategic decisions between the episodes of core gameplay.

Creating supporting pedagogy for linear campaigns, including rigorously developing skills in the simulation and moderating frustration-resolution pairs, is easier in a linear campaign than in an open-ended campaign, but participants take less ownership for the results.

Linear campaigns are launched through the main menu, often simply referred to as single-player games.

Open-Ended Campaign

An open-ended campaign is one in which two or more participants compete for control of territories of a large map, often using a series of arena-style challenges to determine control of smaller regions.

Campaigns can be around anything:

- Military and financial forces struggling for control of territory and population

Campaign. In Microsoft's Rise of Nations, players decide which region to invade. Successful attacks on strong countries are possible only with past successes.

Source: Microsoft product screen shot reprinted with permission from Microsoft Corporation.

- University professors battling each other over a new field of study for intellectual credit and grants
- Corporate officers battling over budgets
- Sports players battling for media attention and sponsorship dollars

Success requires an alignment of strategies and tactics, successfully engaging in conflict, performing ad hoc cost-benefit analysis and ad hoc budgeting, using containment strategies, and using conceptual dead reckoning.

Campaigns end either after a time limit or when one side wins. Unlike their role in a more linear campaign, participants have a significant depth and span of strategic decisions. This is in part because

- The strategic map is state-based.
- Some areas are more valuable than others. This might be intrinsically (any European war is going to go through Poland, or a lot of people are

going to watch the Super Bowl), or due to an attached award going to the
player who controls a given area.

- Past successes or failures make future actions easier or harder.
- Participants can decide where to commit offensive, defensive, and support
  resources both long term and short, in part based on the moves of other
  players. A participant may use a power-up before a specific battle.
- Participants can contain less defended regions with more heavily defended ones.
- Participants can decide whether to engage in negotiation or conflict.
- Participants are constrained by movement restrictions.

Open-ended campaign.

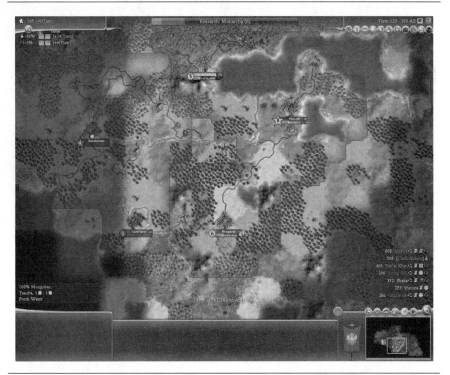

Source: Sid Meier's Civilization IV Screenshots Courtesy of Firaxis Games and Take-Two
Interactive Software, Inc.

For example, a lemonade stand campaign might consist of a participant
starting with one lemonade stand in a neighborhood with three or four competitors. The participant would choose, block by block, to open lemonade stands
and compete with local competitors for dominance. Players might hold off
before challenging a tough player until they have strong cash flow from other
blocks. Success is defined as establishing a monopoly.

Open-ended campaigns can be engaged by real players or AIs, or both, and have a high replay value.

Career Mode

Source: Microsoft product screen shot reprinted with permission from Microsoft Corporation.

Career mode is a type of single-player campaign where players make open-ended professional decisions for their characters, building up reputation, skills, and resources that impact a series of instant-action challenges between their first entry and their retirement.

Related topic: "Open-Ended Campaign," earlier in this chapter.

Open-Ended Level or Game

An open-ended level or game is a part of a Sim in which a player is restricted not by formal levels but by more subtle structures designed to create an environment that feels unrestricted.

Typically, these levels feature large maps with units and structures. This can increase player engagement and perceived fidelity.

Unlike sandbox levels (see below), such games often still have formal and linear level design constructs, where completion of tasks open up sections of the map. This can be explicit, such as getting a key or permission to gain access to a building's door, or more subtle, such as hearing on the radio, after the completion of some activity, that a bridge is fixed (as used in some of the Grand Theft Auto series) or a new apartment complex has been opened.

They may also have less formal design constraints. For example, a section of a map may be accessible only when the player has earned enough of a resource such as money (acquired in any of many different ways) to buy a ticket or has earned enough rank to access restricted areas.

Certain areas of a map may be inhospitable unless certain conditions are met, either absolutely, such as the need for oxygen making it useless to bring a burning torch into a vacuum, or all-but-absolute, such the need for shelter making it difficult to keep a torch burning in a rainstorm. Fallout 3, for example, uses radiation levels.

Finally, the level design may be informal and almost happenstance. Certain locations may be almost impossible to find without specific instructions. Certain neighborhoods may be so tough that to be there after dark without the right chaperone or street cred is very challenging. Locations can be so far that walking takes too long and one needs a car.

Typically, open-ended level design allows for back-tracking.

Open-ended Sims may not use briefings or after action reviews, or use them more subtly. They also typically use a list of tasks.

Instant Action

Instant action is a process in a Sim allowing participants to assemble and play their own level, typically configuring a map or arena, available resources, opposition (including AIs or real people), difficulty level, and victory conditions and variations.

An instant-action level might take between ten minutes and several hours to build and play.

Instant-action capability tends to add significant replay value to a Sim. A campaign or career mode puts further layers of strategy and consequences around a series of instant-action levels.

See also "Mini Games—Best of Both Worlds?" in Chapter Two.

Sandbox Level

A sandbox is a stand-alone level with no formal tasks or goals, no direct competitors, and no end point. It is designed to encourage emergent learning and ownership. A sandbox level may, however, include awards.

Custom game. In Sid Meier's Civilization IV, players can set parameters for a configured game.

Source: Sid Meier's Civilization IV Screenshots Courtesy of Firaxis Games and Take-Two Interactive Software, Inc.

Sandbox option. Many Sim games, such as Zoo Tycoon 2, give players the option to play in a sandbox mode.

Source: Microsoft product screen shot reprinted with permission from Microsoft Corporation.

In some ways, a sandbox level is the purest expression of the Sim's core gameplay. Some games, such as SimCity and The Sims, are played entirely in sandbox mode.

Sandbox mode is typically not part of any larger campaign. Participants are often able to select a map and difficulty level (at the easiest level, participants may not have to worry about resources at all). A sandbox level is almost always single player, and if available, is accessible through the main menu.

Also called *free-form level*.

Demonstration Level

A demonstration level is a stand-alone level that shows off many of the features of the Sim. Computer games often have demonstration levels (called *demos*) that can be downloaded for free to drive sales of the full game.

When designing an immersive learning simulation, imagine the forty-five-minute conversation with prospective clients or sponsors and what part of the Sim you would show to them: that's your demo level. Unfortunately, before funding, any investor expects to see the demo level—and that tends to be tough because it is often the last thing produced.

Often a demonstration level has two parts, the first level for training and access, and a more advanced level to demonstrate some of the complexity and need for strategy.

Other Task and Level Definitions

The successful design and trouble-shooting of tasks and levels requires an understanding and use of many specific concepts. Here they are in more detail.

Initial Value

The starting point for a variable at the beginning of a level of a game or Sim is called its initial value. This can include

- Campaign settings
- Global condition or capability
- Individual attributes
- Current element

The concept is similar to the position of chess pieces on the board at the beginning of each match.

Some Sims apply some randomization of initial values (within ranges), which increases the fidelity of the situation but also increases the difficulty of debugging the code and makes it harder for the participants to deliberately try different strategies. (It makes less sense to ask "What if I had done x instead of y?" when the conditions confronting the player at the beginning of each game are not the same.)

Front Loading

Front loading means giving participants a lot of resources at the beginning, for consumption throughout the game. The experience focuses on judicious use and hoarding of resources.

The board game Monopoly is front-loaded. Front loading compensation for a job would include large signing bonuses and moving stipends.

Opposite of *back loading*.

Back Loading

Back loading means limiting participants' starting resources so that they have to invest wisely to build up much greater resources. The experience focuses, in part, on wealth creation. Real-time strategy games are examples of back-loaded Sims.

Back loading compensation for a job would include milestone payouts and completion bonuses. For Microsoft and Sony, the expense of game consoles is front loaded and the revenue from them is back loaded.

Opposite of *front loading*.

Task

A task is an activity that, if completed once, brings a participant closer to completing an objective, milestone, or mission.

Tasks are usually evaluated on an all-or-nothing criterion, as opposed to the more nuanced *mission*, which is more often evaluated against a balanced scorecard.

Participants may have multiple open, or incomplete, tasks. Some Sims maintain lists of tasks.

Related topic: "Goals," in Chapter Nine.

Failure

Failure is a type of feedback indicating that the player has not met the requirements of a situation. Presentation of failure is critical for developing skills in a simulation.

Big Failure. Big failures stop progress on the current level and can only be recovered using a "start over" or "load saved game" option.

Wrong Way. Wrong-way failures are setbacks (like the real-world situation where someone yawns at your idea when you are talking to him or her) that require a series of small corrections and a different path (see "Conceptual Dead

Reckoning" in Chapter Fourteen). Going the wrong way for long enough can lead to a big failure, a puzzle failure, or a deep hole failure.

Little Blows. Some little failures cause small shocks to your system. Enough small shocks, without corresponding successes, lead to a big failure.

Puzzle Failure. Some failures come not from the elimination of a primary attribute but from the inability to make progress. Participants are in no immediate jeopardy, but they cannot figure out how to move forward. This can sometimes be the most frustrating sort of failure, and it is the result of a challenging puzzle.

Procedural Omission. Some failures come out of not following the right steps. What to do with this type of failure is not always obvious for a Sim designer. With a procedural failure, the simulation can be built to execute a number of options:

- Stop.
- Force the participant to fix the problem before moving on.
- Give the participant a "second chance" through a simulation element, such as having someone else walking by throw a glance or puzzled look.
- Play out the natural consequences of the failure, even if there happen not to be any in the current situation.
- Make the rest of the mission slightly harder using natural or contrived logic.
- Highlight the failure to the participant right then.
- Note the failure in the after action review.

Deep Hole Failure. A deep hole is a failure that comes if the participant is in a situation where, through previous bad decisions, the chance of success is zero. What should a Sim do? Should the Sim abruptly end, or should it let the participant fully embrace the natural, prolonged results of the failure? The more open-ended a Sim is, the greater the chance of a deep hole failure. Deep hole failures can feel like puzzle failures.

Wrong or Incomplete Answer. When demonstrating awareness, such as on a test, presenting a wrong or incomplete answer constitutes a type of failure. This is closest to the procedural failure.

The Ecosystem of Success and Failure. In many Sims, some form of energy or primary attribute, such as health or wealth, is a repository of constant feedback. Big failure is all-or-nothing, causing a major change in Sim flow, while little failures are analog. For example, if the goal was to create a nonprofit organization, all-or-nothing feedback would be things like the cessation of all activities due to bankruptcy, and analog feedback might be the loss of a key employee or failure of an important project. Constant negative analog feedback would eventually result in an all-or-nothing failure.

Author's note: Nothing is more boring than playing a computer game "perfectly"—that is, without failing—the first time.

Game designers need to spend a whole lot of time thinking about failure. What are different types of failures? What do they look like? How can one learn from them?

Most training people, meanwhile, focus on one brittle path to success. Focusing just on success is faster, after all. One can cover more ground. It is easier and more "positive" as well. Meanwhile, failures are harder to research, as most subject-matter experts, from salespeople to engineers, hate thinking about and dwelling on failure. Ironically, of course, sticking to the brittle path of success is what makes so many training programs fail to achieve real behavioral transformation.

Task-Redundant, Extraneous Details

Sims tend to contain information that does not help someone accomplish tasks, objectives, goals, or the mission. Stories, and especially cut scenes, in the context of a simulation risk being skipped because they are task-redundant.

Task-Relevant

Task-relevant information helps someone accomplish tasks, objectives, goals, or the mission. The perfect task-relevant information is presented as close to the need as possible. For example, as a player approaches a door, the information on how to open it may flash on the screen. When a player gets stuck somewhere and appears to be floundering, the Sim may present some helpful suggestions. Or in a cut scene, a movie may provide some critical information on how to finish the level.

Level Length

The length is the average amount of time it takes participants to complete a level. Typically, an entire sim has between ten and twenty levels (but of course, your mileage may vary), with the earlier levels taking between one-tenth and one-third as long as later levels. Level length can be measured by how fast the best player can finish it or how fast the average player can finish it.

Chunking Levels

Chunking levels involves creating natural break points that are an appropriate length to best entertain or educate.

There are different types of chunking. If the goal is for a student to replay a simulation level, it should be less than fifteen minutes in a corporate environment, thirty minutes in an academic environment, and two hours in a military environment. Regardless of the intended environment, designers should build in natural places for students to feel some accomplishment and take a break from the simulator altogether. These breaks should come every forty-five minutes for corporate employees, two hours for academic students, and four hours for military personnel.

Books are chunked into chapters. Words are chunked into sentences and paragraphs. Finishing a chunk provides a feeling of accomplishment.

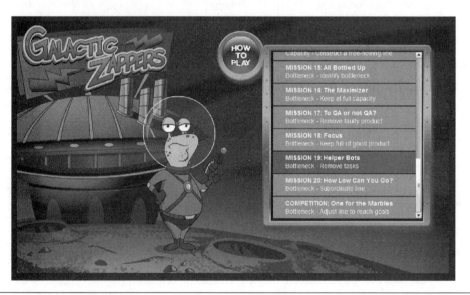

Source: Action Foundation for Entrepreneurial Excellence.

Menu Structure

The home screen for most players in most Sims presents a menu of options. This menu sets the tone for the entire experience, both in terms of look and feel and of functionality.

Producer Splash Screen

The producer splash screen is a still picture or full-motion video showing what organizations funded and distributed the Sim. It is often the first thing that a participant sees when loading a Sim.

The participant might then see a developer splash screen or the Sim title. Typically, pressing the space bar or other key might skip to the main menu.

Developer Splash Screen

VSTEP, a developer of computer games, includes its name in animated form at the beginning of its Sims.

A developer splash screen is a still picture or full-motion video of the organization that developed the Sim. It often comes after the producer splash screen and before the Sim title and main menu. It often can be skipped by pressing the space bar.

Main Menu or Start Screen

The main menu or start screen is the screen from which a participant can launch the main elements of the game. These may include any of the following:

- Single-player campaign
- Multiplayer game
- Previous saved games
- Practice level
- Sandbox level
- Training level
- Open-ended campaign
- Instant action
- Career mode
- Any background material
- Difficulty adjustment
- Option configuration

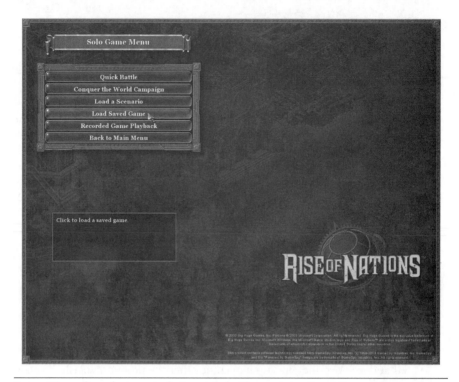

Source: Microsoft product screen shot reprinted with permission from Microsoft Corporation.

The participant can also quit the Sim from this menu.

Random Access

Random access makes it possible to access a repository of content at many different places and, locations. Novels are books that tend not to welcome random access (although they still allow it), while dictionaries encourage it by providing running heads and page tabs.

Sound Options

On the configuration menu, sound options allow a user to change settings. The player may choose a mute mode, calling up subtitles so it is possible to continue even on a computer with no speakers or located in a crowded workplace. The player may also choose to balance sound between quality and gameplay if complicated sound effects such as Doppler are used. Certain sound options, such as surround sound, may be hardware dependent as well.

Configure

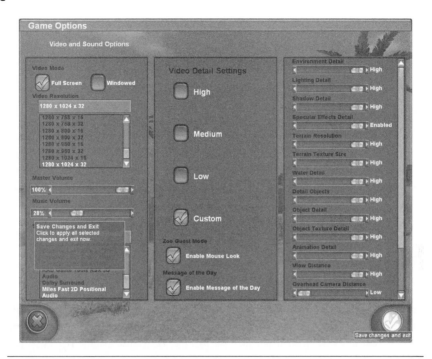

Source: Microsoft product screen shot reprinted with permission from Microsoft Corporation.

To configure a game is to use built-in processes and technology to improve the fit of a mass-produced product or mass-delivered service.

In a Sim, configuring might include changing the screen resolution, sound options, and difficulty level. In buying a shirt, it might include picking out the sky blue as opposed to the navy blue.

Configuring software is easy, and it allows seamless upgrades to future versions, unlike customizing.

"Washing Out" Technology Incompetents Before They Judge Your Sim

One of the most frustrating things for a developer is to show a new simulation to a senior decision-influencer, and have the influencer get confused by it and then give up. This is hard on two fronts: first, some support for the simulation goes away, and two, it sends you back to the drawing board to spend more resources on making it easier.

Obviously, some of the time these observations of interface miscues are invaluable to the Sim's successful evolution. But here's a tip. I believe any simulation that is facing a wide audience should have an early, fun, trivial test game. The test game should require some basic use of action and thought, but in no way should it line up with the interface and content of the subsequent real simulation.

Most Sim participants will blow through the game, hopefully in a minute or two. But some people will not be able to pass it, and will therefore be prevented from moving on—and that is the point. If you don't weed those technology incompetents out, they will fail in the simulation and blame it rather than themselves. If they wash out in the pre-game, the real reason for failure can be appropriately identified.

There is a purer point. So much content is judged by formal learning professionals in terms of how well it meets their own aesthetics; hopefully, eventually, they will build the instinct of first looking at the reaction of the (often younger) target audience.

This natural hubris will only cause more problems in the immediate future and has to be overcome. We are entering an era in which the best content for students is often intellectually foreign to many instructors, and the most comfortable content from instructors is equally foreign to the students.

19

DISPLAY

Source: Sid Meier's Civilization IV Screenshots Courtesy of Firaxis Games and Take-two Interactive Software, Inc.

The display presents the information that the user sees. Beyond the issues of accuracy, fluidity, and advanced graphics, a display represents multiple levels of information and options. (For example, see "Augmented View" later in this chapter). Display issues are also defined by level and genres.

In the core gameplay or broader execution phase of a level, the display includes the factors discussed in the following sections.

Simulation Elements

Simulation elements focus on the part of the virtual world the participant sees. This includes perspective, including partial versus complete view, and point of view (including isometric view or first person). If the Sim is on stewardship using the microcosm of a salt marsh, the display might include a first-person walk-through or a third-person flyover.

Context

Collectively, the specific environment or situation that changes or invokes specific or acceptable ethical actions, systems, and, or desired results is referred to as the *context*. A core justification for educational simulations is that knowledge is only useful in context. Ideally, virtual environments provide a context similar to the one in which the content will eventually be used. Abstract displays lose context.

Inputs

A display typically includes some basic input options, discussed in more detail in Chapter Twenty-One. On-screen buttons, icons, menus, mouse-overs, and hot spots all add touch-screen functionality. An on-screen cursor, whether controlled by a mouse or other input device, acts as a surrogate finger.

Pedagogy

Displays also include pedagogical elements, including heads-up display (HUD) features such as radars, mixed scales, and filters. These highlight certain visual elements and add layers of visualization and analysis to the system's content and input options during the interaction. In our salt marsh Sim, the display might show key variables such as population diversity, and perhaps extrapolations of the current flight of a bird or tags on each species.

Cut Scenes

Before, after, or during the core gameplay there may be cut scenes—recorded video sequences. At one extreme, cut scenes can be used to move along any story and reward the player with some exciting visuals. These might employ cinematic techniques such as a montage or flashback. At the other extreme, they may be used to show the player how to perform some technical action, either in the Sim or in the real world.

Briefings or Debriefings

Briefings and debriefings (after action reviews) bookend a Sim. Briefings are fairly static, with information about upcoming goals and challenges. Debriefings are significantly more complicated. A Sim may have three or more basic debriefings for fail, low pass, and high pass, based on student performance. The debriefing may also have highly customized information, such as time lines, scores, or objectives met. Finally, the Sim may present various forms of analysis, driven by customized comments. (See Chapter Eighteen.)

Avatar

Source: Virtual Heroes, a Division of Applied Research Associates.

In the Sim display, an abstracted or virtual representation of a person or other character is referred to as an *avatar*.

Related topics: "Artificial Intelligence (AI) Player-Agent" (all of Chapter Ten), along with "Player's Avatar," in Chapter Twenty, and "Character, in Chapter Nine.

Body Language

Source: Sid Meier's Civilization IV Screenshots Courtesy of Firaxis Games and Take-Two Interactive Software, Inc.

Body language is the use of the movement or stance of any avatars to express emotional states. As more serious games are created, the study and use of body language will increase. And we will see a growing use of dynamic body language generators.

Specifically, the body language generators will take a few analog variables, such as tension (high to low) and alignment with player or current topic (high to low), and output the appropriate body language. So in this case, if both alignment and tension were high, the computer character might be excited and express the corresponding behavior to the player.

Civilization IV uses one dimension, "feels toward the player," to generate body language animations, including happiness on one extreme and anger at the other.

Likewise, the generator must also take into account a few other, longer-term attributes such as culture, position, props, and "last thing done." Thus an Iraqi police officer standing up with a weapon will respond differently from a female reporter sitting in Chicago.

The need for body language is not unique to serious games. But in the same way that computer games over the years have built up increasingly rich libraries of animations (and language) around combat, movement, and interacting with on-screen objects, so now must serious games build up libraries of people in tight, dynamic, real-time first-person interpersonal situations. Here, nuances of expression will be as meaningful as an enemy taking cover in a first-person shooter.

Motion Capture

Here I am during a motion-capture session.

To some extent, body language can be imported from real life, via motion-capture equipment. It will be challenging to create dynamic body language generators, but still far easier than the subsequent challenge of making dynamic language generators.

Point of View

In the Sim display, the part of the virtual world that a participant sees is governed by point of view (POV). The POV may be a partial or a complete view, and may change constantly.

The POV can be used to make the camera part of the action. In part inspired by reality shows and documentaries, it is hard to watch television or movies these days without seeing the deliberate (and even artificially rendered) techniques such as "shaky cams," "mounted cams," or even "dirty cams," in part inspired by reality shows and documentaries. A camera might go out of focus during an action scene.

Likewise, computer games and other Sims are increasingly simulating the use of physical cameras in the artificial world to add both reality and a cinematic quality. One of the earliest techniques on this path was the "lens flare," which simulated the real-world phenomenon of the reflection of light in a physical camera lens.

Today, such effects are everywhere. As we speed in virtual cars, the camera bounces as we hit bumps or as other cars whoosh by. Images blur. As we negotiate in Civilization IV, the avatar to whom we are talking might smack the camera, shaking up our view. In Fallout 3, as we fight, dirt and blood might spatter and cover the camera lens for a few seconds.

Fallout 3. Blood and dirt obscure the player's first-person view.

Source: Fallout ® 3 © 2008 Bethesda Software LLC, a ZeniMax Media company. All Rights Reserved.

These techniques become more important in immersive learning simulations. One of the value propositions for educational Sims is mapping context. While this superficially means mapping the look and feel of the situation that requires the application of the content to the training for the content, it goes much deeper.

Simulations in big skills must map to emotional context as much as physical. In Sims that focus on conflict management, we might hear a pounding heartbeat and see the display tinged with red during a tense moment. During emergencies, smoke or debris may obscure what we see. Financial poor performance might turn the world sepia, while success may make our view more vivid and high-def. In public speaking, if we don't connect with our audience, our perspective might be more jerky. Drips of sweat might slide down the corner of our view.

As with a mouse-over, moving the point of view can serve as a basic input for a player: where one is looking can impact where one moves, the reactions of other characters (looking at a character might make that character look back at the participant, even ask a question), or invoke a menu.

Changing POV can reveal obstructed information.

A POV can be described in position, direction, angle, and type of lens (such as wide-angle), resulting in terms such as first-person, third-person, overhead, isometric, fisheye, zoom in, zoom out, cinematic view, complete view, partial view, and obstructed, all described in the following sections.

Point of view is also known as *camera* or *view*, and includes *field of view* (FOV).

First-Person

Source: Her Interactive - Nancy Drew ® The White Wolf of Icicle Creek.

In the Sim display, a first-person point of view or field of view lets the participant see the virtual world through the eyes of an avatar. A first-person view in a Sim is often augmented with a HUD. This perspective feels natural, but it limits the scale of what the player can see. In a first-person Sim, participants can see their own avatars only during a cut scene or if looking onto a reflective surface such as a mirror or body of water.

Overhead

Players of Hard Truck Tycoon must strategically plan routes and manage assets.

In the Sim display, an overhead view puts the point of view above the virtual world, that is, looking straight down, as if from a helicopter.

Ideally, an overhead view provides a strategic, contextual view.

Also called *top-down* or *down shot*.

Isometric View

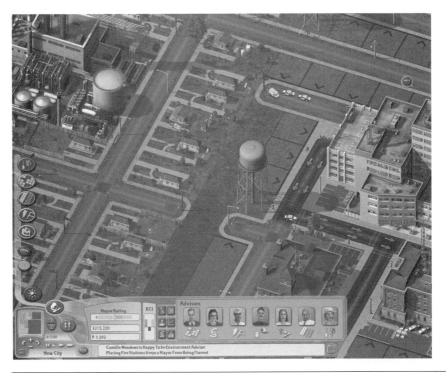

Source: The Sims 2 and SimCity 4 Images © 2009 Electronic Arts Inc. The Sims and SimCity 4 are trademarks or registered trademarks of Electronic Arts Inc in US and/or other countries.

In a Sim display, an isometric view puts the participant's point of view in the world somewhere between first-person and overhead view—between God and man—much the way fans watch a football game from the bleachers.

Ideally, an isometric view captures some of the excitement of being there, and some of the perspective of seeing a strategic, contextual view.

Also known as *three-quarter view*.

Third-Person

In the Sim display, third-person view lets the participant see the virtual world from just behind and above the avatar. A third-person view in a Sim is often augmented with a HUD.

This perspective has many of the benefits of first-person view, including a sense of being there. At the same time, third-person can focus more on establishing the avatar as a character independent of the participant. For example, the appearance of the avatar, including the way it moves and what it wears, is

Isometric View

Third-Person view

Source: Credit: Collaberation in Fortera Systems' OLIVE virtual word software.

always part of the display. The avatar might swagger when walking, or limp if hurt, or look around if idle.

Third-person allows the participant to see a little bit more around the avatar, providing a wider field of view. This can add more context, such as by allowing the participant to see more of the environment, but also be pragmatically useful, allowing details such as how close the participant's car is to another car when racing.

Fisheye

In the Sim display, fisheye is a distortion of a point of view that zooms in on the center while zooming out at the edges. A fisheye perspective allows both focus and peripheral (or contextual) information.

A fisheye lens can be applied toward any perspective, including first-person.

Zoom In

In the Sim display, zooming in is a distortion of a point of view that makes every simulation graphic element in the center larger, forcing the exclusion of more surrounding information.

Zooming in can increase the amount of noise.

Opposite of zoom out.

Zoom Out

In the Sim display, zooming out is a distortion of a point of view that makes every simulation graphic element smaller, allowing the inclusion of more surrounding information. Zooming out, as one might do after getting a big promotion, may involve automating functions, as things that the participant would otherwise micromanage now are below the radar.

Opposite of zoom in.

Complete View

In the Sim display, a complete view fits the entire virtual world into a player's field of view display. In the game of chess, for example, players have a complete view of the chessboard and all the units on it.

Partial View

In the Sim display, a partial view allows the player to only see part of a situation or virtual world at a time.

A partial view is often a concession to the size of a display (that is, the computer screen), and the participant can be supported with graphic elements such as a HUD, with a radar or mini map and a compass.

The partial view can also be a Sim or game element, with deliberately obstructed information such as a fog of war.

Obstructed

In the Sim display, relevant information can be obstructed, that is, hidden or otherwise made unavailable.

For example, in many card games, certain players' cards are obstructed, whereas in chess, no information is obstructed.

Real-world examples:

- Thousands of effective new drugs and other technologies are theoretically possible, but not found yet.
- New business processes are always being developed.
- Marketers like to say, "you've never tasted your favorite cereal." In real life, people often don't know what they don't know.

Obstructed view. In SimuLearn's Virtual Leader, important ideas are obstructed (shown here by blank idea bars) until certain conditions are met, such as a character feels engaged or the tension is lowered or raised.

In any situation, information might be obstructed by fog of war, point of view, or noise, and sometimes deliberately by an opponent. Some obstructions can be revealed through probing.

Sims can make the existence of obstructed space obvious by measures such as leaving dark spots on maps or blank idea bars like the ones in Virtual Leader. Sim designers can make the act of probing an obvious one, marking spots on the screen "press here to probe," or they can require a bit more of the sort of finessing typical in real life.

Map locations can have three states:

- Known
- Unknown
- Once known but now uncertain

A well-designed Sim in almost any big skill area should make people constantly think, "What am I missing?" A partial view may be the result of obstruction or a limitation of the display.

Cinematic Views

In the Sim display, cinematic views are a matter of using the dramatic and expository techniques found in movies. These views are often temporary and non-interactive. Designers tend to use full-motion video in cut scenes to introduce a task or scene or to replay a moment of drama.

Establishing Shot

In the Sim display, an establishing shot is a quick, exterior cinematic shot before cutting to an interior shot.

As in movies or situation comedies, exterior shots might show the outside of a real office building, but what is shown after the cut is a set of an office interior.

Reveal

In the Sim display, a reveal introduces a new and relevant piece of visual information or graphic element that had previously been obstructed.

This can be through moving the camera point of view, fading in, appearing, shifting the focus, or removing fog of war. Reveals can be used to introduce main characters or key pieces of information.

Establishing Shot.

Fade In

In video, fading in is the cinematic effect of starting at black and slowly moving to full exposure. In audio, it is starting with silence and slowly moving to full volume.

Fade Out

In video, fading out is the cinematic effect of starting at full exposure and moving slowly to black. In audio, it is starting with full sound levels and moving to silence.

Ripple Dissolve

In a Sim display, a ripple dissolve uses the cinematic technique of distorting a transition between two full motion video scenes through a series of concurrent waves, as if the viewer is looking through moving water.

Ripple dissolves, especially when accompanied by a music cue, often indicate the transition to or from an inserted dream sequence or flashback.

Pedagogy

The Sim display can involve a number of techniques designed to enhance the learning experience. As with all pedagogy, these are artificial from a purist's view, but helpful. Having said that, many real-life environments, including military gear and car dashboards, have versions of pedagogy built in.

Augmented View

In a display, an augmented view combines the real world, a virtual world, and (optionally) a HUD.

For example, doctors might operate on patients using video goggles that present an aggregated view of internal organs, computer-generated blood flow, and primary variables such as heart rate.

Player Comparison Panel

Player comparison panel from Civilization IV.

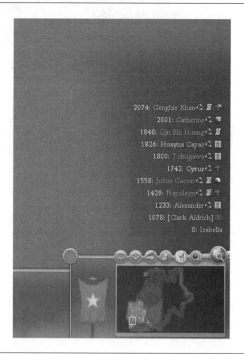

Source: Sid Meier's Civilization IV Screenshots Courtesy of Firaxis Games and Take-Two Interactive Software, Inc.

In a multiplayer Sim display, a player comparison panel presents one or more primary variables about each player to each player.

Player comparison panels increase awareness and competition. They are also pedagogical, letting the players know whether if it is necessary to calibrate their strategy.

A variation or augmentation is to announce to each player when another player reaches key milestones.

Stock tickers are real-world comparison tools.

Rankings at any one time are always a bit arbitrary, as they count on some scoring algorithm, and ranking order can change quickly.

Author's note: In a conversation I had with him, Thiagi told me that he noticed that when people are doing less well than others, they take more risks.

Radar or Mini-Map

A mini-map is a graphic element in a HUD that shows a small abstraction of the map. Where relevant, it can be presented as a radar screen.

A radar is located in the bottom left of the screen of cold-war dictator Sim Tropico. The white box on the radar shows the section that is zoomed in on for the larger display.

This cinematic view can include units or walls, but can apply filters as well. Information on a radar might be obstructed, and the radar itself might represent a partial view.

You Are Here

In this real-world display for the Century Hyatt Tokyo, a small arrow (at the bottom) shows where the reader currently is in relation to the map.

A "You Are Here" (generally called a "YAH") is a graphic element on a mini-map that shows the current location of the user. Sometimes it employs a device such as an arrowhead to indicate the current point of view.

Compass

In the Sim display, a compass uses an arrow to point in a specific direction, no matter the orientation of the possessor.

A compass can provide absolute bearings on a map (for example, showing that your character is facing north by north-east), or toward an objective of value (a door, a key). Compasses may be part of a HUD, usually at the top of the display, or appear on a mini-map.

Maintaining a calibrated compass is a component of dead reckoning. Most people have a moral compass to alert them when they go astray.

Progress Bar, Navigation Bar, Progress Meter

Various graphic elements show the percentage of an activity that is currently complete. This can include computer activities (such as software installation), a media clip (such as a song being played), or even the amount of an e-learning course finished.

A participant, by watching the speed of the change in percentage, can get a feel for how long until the operation is complete. Where an actual bar is used, typically it is a slim, horizontal rectangle that fills with a contrasting color from left to right.

This feature intuitively replaces the "thickness" feature of a book, where a reader can instantly see (or feel) how many pages have been read and how many pages are left to go.

Progress meters, sometimes in the form of progress bars, are used explicitly in any task that either is thought of as undesirable, such as filling out a shipping label, installing software, or some formal learning programs, or has a timer or other high-pressure component, such as defeating an end-of-level boss.

For example, this navigation bar above, visualized throughout a Sim, has the following features:

- First, it provides a quick visual indicator of how far through the simulation a player has come, in this case, about halfway.
- Through the text in the buttons, it provides a high-level outline of the order of the material.
- It provides one-mouse-click access to all previously completed content.
- For a player considering going back to review or replay material, it visualizes both the player's current status and how much progress the player has made.

Subtitles

As in the movies, subtitles superimpose text on the display that captures what is being spoken. Subtitles can also present regionalized translations. Often turning on or off subtitles is a configuration option for a Sim.

Also called *closed captions*.

Energy Bar, or Health Bar

In the first-person shooter FarCry, players see their health (top), armor (center, but gone here), and stamina (bottom) in bars positioned at lower right.

In the Sim display, an energy bar or health bar is a graphic element in the HUD visualizing how much energy (or more than one type of reserve, if the game involves several kinds of energy) a player currently has.

If the Sim uses health, that information is almost invariably shown most prominently.

Also called a *power bar*.

Interface

A Sim interface is a synthesis of display, basic inputs, actions, and pedagogy.

Interface (and interactivity in an application) is greatly influenced by genres.

One of the big "ahas" of the next generation of content designers is that the interface is a significant piece of the content, not just a conduit to the content. The interface should line up to the real-life activity at some level, high or low, to enable transferability of content.

Heads-Up Display

From Ship Simulator 2008.

On the screen, the heads-up display (HUD) superimposes information on a first-person POV, creating an augmented view.

The information can be about the avatar's internal state, such as energy, including health. It may include a list of tasks.

The information can be about the external world, such as a compass, clock, signal strength of wireless networks, bread crumbs, and locations of and distance to objectives, friends, buddies, or foes.

It can provide access to alternative points of view, such as overhead, and present these either in a toggled full screen or in an embedded radar, with photographic or abstract quality.

It can also potentially use different lenses and filters, such as infrared, X-ray, or motion sensitive.

HUD elements also might do some analysis, such as calculating enemy units' probable location in five seconds based on current movement, identification of landmarks, facial recognition, ETA to next coordinates, or other situational awareness.

In Sims. In a Sim, a HUD—unlike a coach or facilitator—doesn't overtly break the fourth wall. It can also include scores.

Some Sims or games allow users to configure what information their HUD presents, the amount of transparency, and sometimes even the color scheme. Many Sims allow participants to toggle between different HUD levels (full, light, and off), and individual elements.

The designers of Dreamworks' Trespasser tried not to use any HUD, as they felt it ruined the fidelity of the experience. Instead, the main character would say key pieces of information, such as "Hmm, I'd better climb up that hill," as if talking to herself, which ruined the fidelity of the experience.

Because HUD graphic elements light up one part of the display for a long period of time, they increase the chance of burn-in on a monitor.

Related topics: "Sensors," in Chapter Ten, and "The Role of Pedagogy in Sims," in Chapter Seventeen.

What we do . . . . What we know shapes what we see. And what we do is shaped by what we see.

Situational Awareness

As discussed in the introduction, one of the best educational opportunities of a simulation is to force people to develop a situational awareness, to see the world differently by focusing on different cues. This is often done at the display level.

In the dictator Sim Tropico, one view of the island-nation uses highlighting (in green) to show the regions that tourists would find desirable. Thinking of the island in this way is critical to making the right investments in structures and advertising to build up a good tourist trade. (The game designers also could have used nothing but pure simulation elements as well, having tourists or focus groups themselves go to the best spots.) Either way, it would force users to develop a situational awareness of geography and tourism to be successful.

It is also possible to model impaired situational awareness. One simulation from Second Life captures what it is to have some mental ailments, with other characters screaming at them and demonic images appearing on the walls. Meanwhile, some driving simulations capture the sensation of being drunk, showing the reduced reaction time. Variations of this theme are very significant, as many people in many situations find that what they do not see is more defining than what they do see.

Icon

In a Sim display, an icon is an interface: consisting of a small picture used instead of words as a label for an alert, menu, or button. If the icon is on a button, pressing it may change how it looks.

Filter

In SimCity 4, players can filter out the pipes and just see the city that is above ground, or they can filter out the city and just see the pipes that are underground.

Source: The Sims 2 and SimCity 4 Images © 2009 Electronic Arts Inc. The Sims and SimCity 4 are trademarks or registered trademarks of Electronic Arts Inc in US and/or other countries.

In a Sim display, a filter renders certain elements invisible or muted and highlights other elements, making it easier to focus on the relevant information. Filtering also works on a radar or mini-map.

Filtering can also reduce noise.

Examples of filters for business processes might be customer satisfaction or environmentalism. Leaders always filter information; some just do it effectively and others, not so well. Leaders sometimes use filters that only pass information that agrees with their own positions.

Filtering takes energy. One can live in a disruptive environment and be used to the chaos, but be unconsciously spending energy in filtering.

Allocation Triangle

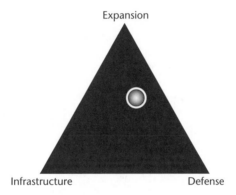

An allocation triangle is an interface or basic input in the form of an abstract panel that allows participants to drag a token to allocate analog resources in real time among three competing categories.

If the token is in the middle of the triangle, resources are allocated equally to each of the three categories. Moving the token closer to or farther from one category has a corresponding boosting or draining effect.

Allocation is a component of budgeting and project management.

Cursor

A cursor is a graphic element, often an arrow, that is controlled by some basic input device such as a mouse, and that acts as a virtual finger or hand with the ability to impact something represented on the display.

The cursor may change shape if over a hot spot, as a way of telling the participant that the program is busy (by turning into an hourglass), or if some new default action is available.

In a typical real-time strategy game, for example, the player may select a unit, such as a lion, by moving the cursor over it and left clicking on it. Then, with that unit selected, the cursor may change shape as the player moves it across the screen. If the player is hovering in a location that is inaccessible to the lion, the cursor may change to a red X. If the player hovers over a lamb, the cursor may change into a pounce icon. If the player then right-clicks, the lion will do that default action and pounce on the lamb. By contrast, left-clicking might switch the selection to the lamb, in the same motion unselecting the lion.

Basics

Some other basic terminology is important to keep in mind. These words all become adjectives when discussing display issues.

Real Estate

In the Sim display, the amount of space on a computer screen is finite; it is referred to as *real estate* as a reminder of its value. Any interface or HUD graphic elements compete for real estate.

Green

Green is the color used for graphic elements (including highlights) to represent any of the following conditions:

- A situation lacks danger and poses no imminent threat.
- A process or unit is running and functioning properly.
- A character is happy.
- Significant levels of energy are available.
- No alerts currently need to be attended to.

If the color green is used in a button, it gives the participant the ability to start a process or, in a social simulation, agree.

Contrast with *red* and *yellow*.

Red

Red is the color used for graphic elements (including highlights) to represent any of the following conditions:

- A situation is dangerous and poses an imminent threat.
- A process or unit is stopped (or about to stop).

- A permanent and consequential decision is about to be made.
- An energy level or capability has been highly reduced or exhausted.
- A character is angry.
- A general alert needs to be attended to.
- An infrared filter is revealing the presence of heat.

The combination of red and flashing, sometimes accompanied by a sound cue, represents an alert that needs immediate attention or requires new actions.

If the color red is used in a button, it gives the participant the ability to stop a process or, in a social simulation, disagree.

Yellow

Yellow is the color used for graphic elements (including highlights) to represent any of the following conditions:

- The threat level is moderate.
- A process or unit is paused.
- An energy level or capability has been somewhat reduced.
- A general alert is active and needs to be attended to eventually.

If the color yellow is used in a button, it gives the participant the ability to pause a process or, in a social simulation, ask a question.

Polygon

In the Sim display, surfaces are defined by small, flat shapes known as polygons, each specified by a series of points. As shown in the previous figure, quite complex 3-D objects can be constructed from polygons. The number of polygons a character or scene has often correlates with the quality of the scene, with a larger number of polygons resulting in a higher-quality scene. Thousands or tens of thousands of polygons can be used for one object.

Polygons are covered by a mesh to create objects. They are often appropriately lighted and textured in the rendering process.

Frames Per Second

In the Sim display, the frames per second (fps) rate is the number of still, distinct images displayed each second to trick the viewer's eyes into believing objects are moving. Also called *frame rate*, fps is a metric of fluidity.

A normal U.S. television show (NTSC TV) is broadcast at 30 fps. PAL (phase alternating lines) TV is 25 fps. Movies are shown at 24 fps. A rate of 20 fps is considered by many to be the minimum to trick the eye, and is the minimum to enable the simulation genre known as practiceware. Higher frame rates (like 60 fps) result in more appealing animation, and some console games sacrifice other elements to maintain this level.

Lower fps rates result from system limitations, poor programming, other applications consuming system resources (such as AI), and detail of image, including screen resolution and complexity of objects (high polygon count), and lighting.

There is a difference between average and low fps rate. If 20 frames per second is the minimum (and to some, that is a pretty big if), then the average might be 40, and it only drops to 20 fps during a busy scene.

Related topics: "Advanced Graphics," in Chapter Sixteen; "Full-Motion Video," in Chapter Fifteen.

Set

A set is an artificial construction, whether virtual or real, of a location. Computer-generated sets typically have limited interactivity and are often drawn flat first and then created in 3-D.

Sets and locations can be more than static in a Sim. For example:

- In The Sims franchise, players design their sets ("houses") for aesthetics and functionality. They might make one room optimized for cooking and another for relaxing with friends.

- Sets can display feedback on a participant's performance. Cracks in the wall and dead plants might convey a needed message.
- A leader might decide where to have an important meeting: the board room, the parking lot, or the golf course.

Related topics: "Backdrop," in Chapter Fifteen; "Fourth Wall," in Chapter Seventeen; and "New Sets and Settings," in Chapter Sixteen.

Graphic Element

In a display, the individual components that are visualized, including pedagogical and simulation components, are referred to as graphic elements.

In a Sim, graphic elements might have different appearances under different filters or highlights. They may serve as basic inputs when moused-over or clicked. Graphic elements may use mixed scales for clarity.

Related topics: "Full-Motion Video," in Chapter Fifteen, and "Frames Per Second," earlier in this chapter.

20

COMMUNITY

Acommunity is a group of people who see mutual benefit in communicating, playing, or working together, or at least people who are part of an organization that sees such a benefit. The benefits of a community can include the creation of knowledge, relationships, or reflection.

Unlike audiences, communities participate. They generate content as well as consume it. They inevitably shape the experience. Ultimately, at least some of the members of a community have *presence*. That is, they are seen as individuals (or at least characters), and people form relationships with and to them.

Members also tend to have fluid roles in communities. There might even be exclusive subsections, informally or formally (such as in a club).

The Network Effect of Education

An old joke talks about how lonely it must have been to be the first person to have a Facebook account (or an e-mail account or fax machine before that). That is because of something called "the network effect."

The network effect states that, if five people are on a network, the power is not five times greater than one person, but 2 to the fifth ($2 \times 2 \times 2 \times 2 \times 2 = 32$), because you realize value each connection.

Anyone who obsesses about behavior change realizes that a network effect is active in education. The effort to learn to speak Chinese or use leadership by yourself is absurd. Likewise, if you really want your child to learn to play a musical instrument, you might also learn to play at the same time. If you want to stop smoking or drinking, a supportive community makes a big difference.

This phenomenon has plenty of reasons. It is always hard to be an outlier. Meanwhile, you can also ask people around you for help when you are supported by a common vocabulary. Also, because people have the same situational awareness, being part of a group makes it less likely that you will slip into old habits.

What are the network effect's implications for anyone creating a formal learning program?

- Students using e-learning by themselves in any of the big skills (such as project management or security) will probably fail.
- If you want to pilot a program, don't pull together people from different parts of the organization. Instead, take at least five or six people from one work team.
- Academic students must do projects together, in environments that closely resemble the ones where the content will be applied beyond the specific school programs. It is fair to assume that learning of big skills will be subsequently applied in sports or other extracurricular activities.
- The closer together in time that skills are learned by a large community, the more effective they will be. Having a formal learning program touch one thousand connected people in one week is much more effective than having the same program touch two thousand connected people over six months. Call this the zeitgeist effect.

Community and Support for Formal Learning

Formal learning programs include at least two different types of roles. There are participants, and there are a variety of people supporting the experience, including coaches and facilitators and technical support, even sponsors and vendors.

Computer games have driven and modeled online virtual communities, and educational simulations will have to go even further. Technologies that have to be considered for any good collaborative educational Sim include message boards or forums, chat rooms, instant messaging, application sharing, calendaring tools, and other control tools for the facilitator, if present.

Inappropriately collaborating with fellow students is a form of cheating.

Belonging to a community to compare, share, collaborate, and brag is a game element.

Communities in Social Networking

For social networking, it is the users, not professionals, who are the writers and editors. The role between coach and student narrows and overlaps.

The primary elements in social networking sites, including articles, pictures, and sometimes sound and videos, are created and submitted by users of the site, instead of paid editors and writers, as was the case in early 1999 through 2001 (now-called Web 1.0 models). The content is real, relevant, recent, and raw. Content creators feel published, heard, and uncensored. Content creators, when younger people, actively experiment with their own identities.

Users also view the sites as communities to be nurtured. They rate content. They comment on content. They highlight one another's content. They sometimes form personal relationships with other members. They feel ownership of the site, often anonymously shaping it.

Multiple Roles

In a community around a learning program, the same real person has different roles, depending on whether you are looking at the context of the virtual world, the classroom, or the real world. For example, a person can be a hero in the context of the Sim, a student in the context of the class, and a project manager or steward in the context of the enterprise.

Likewise, *coach* can refer to an embedded, scripted avatar or a real person—or both.

Real roles. The same person might have many roles, depending on the context.

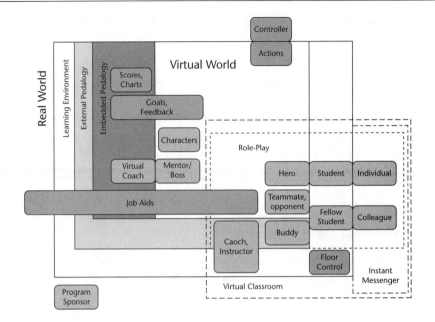

Characters in the Sim might exist only in the Sim (such as a boss), or be controlled by other students. A colleague of yours (context: real world) can help you either by being a teammate (context: virtual world) or a buddy (context: classroom). (The difference being that a teammate helps you in the Sim, while a buddy helps you understand the Sim.)

Here are the different roles:

Player

A player is someone or something that influences a game or Sim at the highest level.

When referred to as *a* player, this can be:

- A human participant in a solo experience
- A human in a multiplayer experience
- An AI-controlled entity taking the role of a human in a multiplayer experience.

When referred to as *the* player, it tends to be a human, often in a single-player campaign.

There is debate as to whether to call a participant in an immersive learning simulation a player, which suggests the experience is a game rather than a learning experience.

PC is often short for player character (see "Player's Avatar," later in this chapter).

Newbie

A person who is new to a technology in general, or to a specific genre, application, or computer game, is generally referred to as a *newbie*. The term is used as a designation in, and relative to, a community such as in a chat room or multiplayer game. It can either be derisive ("you are such a newbie") or self-effacing ("I know I am a newbie, but I can't figure out . . . "). In some environments, newbies are prey for more advanced players.

With experience, newbies become full participants and players.

Also called *novice*, *n00b*, or *nub*.

Opponent

The opponent is a character against whom a participant competes or who represents a puzzle for a participant to solve, either for enjoyment or to increase a participant's mastery of the skills involved in the Sim.

An opponent can sometimes be turned into an ally.

In a game, rubber banding (discussed in Chapter Sixteen) might be used to calibrate an opponent's skill level.

Competitor

A competitor is a player, real or virtual, who wants the same limited or zero-sum resources that another does. Players might compete in a multiplayer environment such as an arena. Competition might lead to conflict.

Priorities or activities can also compete, as in "A provost has to allocate time between three competing activities, fundraising, fundraising, or fundraising."

Related topics: "Competition," in Chapter Sixteen, and "Opponent," earlier in this chapter.

Buddy

The buddy role is one in which two or three participants agree to help each other out during the course of an educational experience, or a small team is formed for mutual support.

The buddy relationship can be short term: players might watch each other use the simulation and provide feedback and comments. In some cases, they might buddy up just long enough to help each other figure out basic inputs and actions.

The buddy relationship can also last weeks or even months: buddies can follow up with each other virtually to make sure they are completing assignments, applying the material, and providing a constant muse. They can read and comment on each other's blog entries.

The buddy relationship can also be informal or formal. The more important the material learned, especially when big skills are being covered, the more important the role and responsibility of buddies. On the other hand, inappropriately collaborating with fellow students is a form of cheating.

User tip: Bring headphone splitters if using buddies in a classroom situation.

Ally

An ally is a character, either virtual or human, with whom a participant has a predictable and productive relationship, including mutual support on accomplishing work or results.

Audience

An audience is a passive group of consumers of educational or entertainment content. Audiences have to meet access requirements.

Anonymous and passive audience members in a group whose members are invited to participate are called *lurkers*.

Contrast with "Participant," later in this chapter. An audience is not a community.

Subject-Matter Expert

The various experts in a formal learning program are called *subject-matter experts*. They play the following roles:

As Designer. A subject-matter expert provides content (as opposed to structure, design, or technology) for a formal learning program to define and support learning goals. The best subject-matter experts provide content at three levels: what actions are available in a situation, how the actions impact relevant systems, and how those systems produce feedback and results. A subject-matter expert should also be able to talk about both situational awareness and conceptual dead reckoning, as well as related soft skills, big skills, and middle skills.

If nothing else, subject-matter experts can provide a series of anecdotes. Subject-matter experts who have been retired for a while, especially those who have given a lot of lectures, usually talk about entertaining but content-useless inspirational examples.

Subject-matter experts should evaluate the accuracy of any content.

In Groups. Subject-matter experts can also present material live as speakers or instructors, or coach or facilitate students, including performing after action reviews.

The acronym for the role, SME, tends to get confused with the more common business definition, Small and Medium Enterprise.

Speaker

The speaker is the one person in a synchronous community given the tools and authority to talk. In a hierarchical setting, such as a classroom, the primary speaker is often the instructor or an expert, but the role can also be given temporarily to a student or audience member.

In some communities, groups use a "talking stick," which is a token passed around the group, and only the person currently holding the token can talk, forcing everyone else to listen.

It is a leadership action to "call on" quiet members to get them to be speakers.

Related topic: "Lecture and Lecturer," in Chapter Fifteen.

Sponsor

The sponsor is the person or organization that commits the resources to pay for the development, purchase, or deployment of a program. Sponsors usually have multiple success criteria that have to be achieved (see Chapter Seven, especially the "Balanced Scorecard" section).

For many immersive learning simulations, the sponsor is different from the target audience, although for computer games, the sponsor is often the same as the target audience.

Related topics: "Evaluation Strategies and the Analysis of Learning" (Chapter Twenty-Nine) and "Measurable Results," in Chapter Twenty-Three.

Student

A student is a participant who attends a formal learning program, usually with the goal of completing the program for credit or compliance.

Students themselves are usually trapped, with little control over the often large, inwardly focused monopolies in which they must perform because of the blurred lines between desired results and learning goals. They also suffer as a result of the system, whereby their fees are paid (and subsidized) by a complicated web of sponsors that further obscures ownership. Students (and parents of students) often develop a Stockholm Syndrome relationship with their instructors.

Related topic: "Scores and Grades," in Chapter Sixteen.

Coach or Facilitator

Graham Courtney works one-on-one with a student using a simulation, focusing on real-world applicability and examples.

Coach or facilitator is a role in which a human or avatar helps participants make the most of an experience, in a way that breaks the fourth wall of any virtual situation.

Coaches add pedagogy and motivation. They have to present some background (often through lectures), pace the individual or group during the experience, sometimes forcing different approaches, and conduct after action reviews. They are even involved in presenting and interpreting pre- and post-360-degree review results.

The constant dance of a coach is not solving the frustration of the user, but helping the user solve it independently. Coaches also have to deal with the bottom 20 percent—the students who either don't want to take part in the program or lack the ability to do so.

Coaches are often the face of a program, taking on technical support, scheduling, or logistical issues for students as well. In addition, some students (in the role of buddies) can temporarily take on the role of one-on-one coach.

Most simulation producers must support the role of coach. The coach is most often directly responsible for the program's learning and other goals. The rigorous development of any complex skill (such as big skills) almost certainly requires a coach.

Having said that, some genres, such as branching stories, need little or no coaching.

A coach is sometimes called a *trainer*.

Constituent

In Tropico, players must win elections to stay in power by meeting the needs of a majority of units.

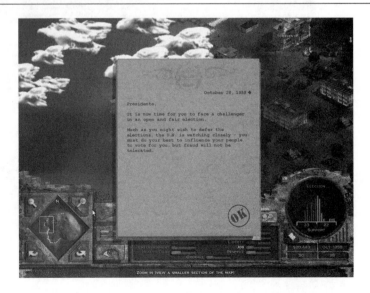

A constituent is a unit (or another player) that has supported or can support someone with a vote. A leader does not have to meet the needs of all constituents or groups, just an aggregated majority.

A constituent's opinion of a candidate may be analog, but the vote is all-or-nothing.

A constituent's loyalty or affection may have various degrees of capacity— sometimes enough to help weather any storm.

Related topic: "Nurturing and Stewardship," in Chapter Fourteen.

Majority

A majority is an opinion held by 50 percent plus one of a category of units.

Participant

In a community, a participant is a person engaged in, influencing, and feeling some ownership for an experience. In computer games, participants are called *players*. In formal learning programs, participants (and audience members) are called *students*.

Participation may be necessary for learning:

> In a famous experiment, [researchers] exposed two kittens to nearly identical visual information. This was done by placing one of the kittens (the passive kitten) in a little gondola, and linking it up to a harness worn by the other (active) kitten so that, as the active kitten moved about and explored its environment, the passive kitten was moved in exactly the same manner. The result was that only the active kitten developed normal depth perception. The passive kitten, even though its sensory input was nearly identical, did not. (See http://mind .ucsd.edu/papers/pisml/pismlhtml/pisml-text.html.)

Participants have to meet access requirements.

Related topic: "Engagement," in Chapter Twenty-Three.

> *Author's note:* People can switch between being members of an audience and participants. Typically, participants lean forward, and audience members lean back. Look around any working meeting, no matter how big—chances are you'll see that no more than six people are participating, and the rest, possibly dozens, are audience.

Fans

Fans are third parties who, in their free time, support a Sim. Fans might produce and share mods, cheat codes, home-made walk-throughs (another form of cheating), reviews, and previews, often through Web pages called *fan sites*. Fan sites are often nonprofit, but may include am advertising-supported model that might provide patches. (See "Cost Per Thousand Views" later in this chapter.)

Fan sites are often supported by game manufacturers, but if and when they spring up around educational simulations, such as those used for certification, they threaten the integrity of the Sims. Fans might also follow a group in Facebook or an individual in Twitter.

Expert

An expert is someone who has recognized mastery with certain experiences or has performed deep and respected analysis. If an expert is used in a formal learning program, the title is expanded to subject-matter expert, as discussed earlier in this chapter.

Gamer

People who play games for enjoyment are referred to as *gamers;* the term applies to computer games or whatever games (including board games) are under discussion.

There are different types of computer gamers:

- Hard core: People for whom computer games are part of their lifestyle and who spend more than twenty hours a week playing, and at least another five keeping up with gaming news. They often prefer the lowest level of abstraction.
- Casual: People who play about ten hours a week.
- Peripheral: People who play fewer than five hours, and mostly solitaire or free online games.

Different people, and even different generations, have different media of choice that shape how they view entertainment, communication, and formal learning. Some examples, from oldest to newest:

- Books
- Movies
- Rock and roll
- Television
- Magazines
- Single-player computer games
- Multiplayer computer games
- Massively multiplayer online role-playing games (MMORPGs)
- Social networking

Multiplayer

A multiplayer environment can be a game, electronic space, or online forum that involves more than one participant.

Many multiplayer environments are synchronous—the players engage each other in real time. The players can simply coexist and communicate, or they can compete with each other, form teams that compete with each other, or collaborate.

Players are often represented by avatars. In some situations, an AI-controlled player can take the place of a real player. A first-time or inexperienced player in a multiplayer environment is called a newbie.

An administrator sets up certain attributes, such as victory conditions, maps or arenas, passwords, and population size. Then participants might wait in a lobby, before everyone joins in. In an educational environment, the sponsors hope that learning will then ensue and be consistent across groups—but they generally have no way of making sure that it does.

Some servers or hosts have matchmaking abilities to bring together players of similar skill levels.

Massively multiplayer online role-playing games, in contrast, use persistent environments.

Even a multiplayer Sim needs a single-player training level.

The opportunities and risk of multiplayer participation in educational simulation can be understood in microcosm by looking at the issue of directing people. In a multiplayer Sim, participants can communicate with other real participants naturally, via open-ended speech or text. But the pedagogical opportunity to shape how and why participants talk to each other can occur only in the briefing and debriefing, so the situation reinforce bad habits.

Instructors

The instructors are the individuals responsible for interacting with students or participants and ensuring formal learning program objectives are met. Instructors can deliver lectures and serve as coaches and facilitators.

Followers

Followers are community members who perform a role under the guidance of a leader. The role of follower is much less sexy than that of a leader, but hugely important. Despite recent media coverage, a follower who has a unique technical skill may be significantly more valuable to a community than the person leading the group. Further, a follower may take on a temporary role as leader in a specific situation.

Faction

A faction is a group to which people are aligned or associated.

Flags or other public displays are often associated with a faction. Factions are typically larger than teams. As a result, they help organize large groups in multiplayer environments.

Also known as *gangs*.

Technical Support

Technical support is a person or organization tasked with keeping an organization's technology working, such as ensuring access to a Sim. Technical support does not have the role of answering content questions.

A coach often has to assume the role of technical support. Technical support is often included in any "per user" cost for a simulation. Technical support may also set up a large Sim deployment to deal with participants within the Sim.

Tools

Successful communities also use one or more tools. These tools may include a subsection of instructor tools, as well as general access community tools.

Massively Multiplayer Online Environments

Many people enjoy persistent virtual worlds, combining varying degrees of social networking and Sim participation. Current massively multiplayer online environments (MMOs) and role-playing games (MMORPGs) are capable of hosting hundreds (and often thousands, or tens of thousands) of real people at the same time, and participants can both enter and exit in an open-ended manner and can meaningfully interact (including instant message, perform tasks, pursue objectives and goals, carry out missions, trade, and create artifacts) with each other and with the environment. Participants are often represented as avatars.

MMOs can include unstructured environments, such as Second Life, and games, called MMORPGs, such as World of Warcraft. Even an MMO requires a single-player training level.

As with real role-plays, the ability of MMOs to serve as educational simulations and produce specific learning goals is completely dependent on the activities of the participants. Creating two sides, say cowboys and Indians, is only valid if the participants on the cowboy side actually behave as real cowboys, and the players on the Indian side actually behave as real Indians. Otherwise, the result could just as easily be negative training.

Having said that, some participants in MMOs will develop some middle skills and big skills.

Contrast with "Multiplayer" earlier in this chapter.

MMOs may also be called *virtual interactive environments*.

Commentary: Top Ten Missing Features of Second Life as an Educational Simulation Platform

Second Life truly is a phenomenon. It is exactly what the name and vision imply: an example of a parallel "multiverse." People will learn much in it, as they might alternatively learn via participating on a real-world sports team, running a real-world lemonade stand, or walking around a great real-world city.

Perhaps most important, participants "learn to be" through expressing themselves, including building elaborate sets and exploring alternative groups with which to interact. Meanwhile, corporations set up shop in Second Life, as in Facebook and Twitter, to be where the kids are in an attempt to speak their language and get some eyeballs.

But when people talk about Second Life as a platform for educational simulations, I am less excited. Here are my list of top ten missing features from Second Life:

1. Support for a good scripted story
2. Support for after action reviews
3. HUD to support specific learning goals, as opposed to navigation
4. Interfaces that map to real-world actions
5. Dynamic AI characters, with which participants can repeatedly try new behavior to see how they react, and any form of interesting computer-controlled scriptable units for a player to influence

6. The modeling of functional work processes
7. Levels, tasks, and milestones
8. Dynamic systems, with interacting primary variables and secondary variables tied to actions
9. Supporting mentors, supervisors, or guides
10. Any direct support of big skills or middle skills (in a way that is richer than real life)

Access

Access refers to the infrastructure, configuration, license, or location to view or use an experience. For example, in the area of minimum system requirements, potential participants might need a graphics card or broadband Internet service to run a type of simulation. The license, meanwhile, can be acquired through paying the cost of a simulation.

Sometimes access is not so all-or-nothing. A participant might need to download a free browser add-on but be prohibited from doing so by an IT department, or only have access to bandwidth during off-hours. Meanwhile, access to some mod-based simulations is restricted to those who bought the original, vanilla game. Access can also require physical actions that may exclude people with certain handicaps.

When calculating the potential targets for a program globally, one has to use "access percent" as a multiplier. If two hundred people would want to use the program, but only 30 percent can get access, the potential target group is now just sixty. Further, in a corporate or otherwise centralized environment, if access of a group drops below a certain number, often around 80 percent, then the entire program is scrapped.

Access, in this definition, is not reduced by the presence of people who do not know that a simulation exists and is available, or who know but are not motivated to use it—those people all *have* access, they just for one reason or another aren't using it.

Related topics: "Target Audience" in Chapter Twenty-Four, and "Ownership," in Chapter Six.

Control Tools

Control tools come in two types. One type involves technology and processes that enable the person in charge of a virtual classroom session to perform a variety of tasks:

• Call on community members
• Cut community members off
• Poll the community

- Enable or disable chat rooms
- Share applications or slides, images, and white boards
- Change the mode, for example from lecture mode to practice mode
- Change the group member who is designated speaker

The other type are the *floor control tools*, that is, technology and processes that enable a coach or facilitator in charge of one or more simulations to perform the following tasks:

- Restart a simulation
- Increase or decrease pedagogy in a simulation
- Form or disband teams
- Automate or skip certain activities
- View the players in a Sim and a snapshot summary of each player's experience

Instructor Dashboard

An instructor dashboard is a centralized tool to aggregate and summarize all student performances metrics, such as completion rate, number of plays, and number of different approaches used. It also provides the ability to zoom into individual student plays.

Player's Avatar

Screenshot courtesy of Persuasive Games LLC.

The avatar is the player's on-screen presence in the game world or play space. The avatar can be the form of an abstracted person, vehicle, animal, or even a completely abstract token. The avatar, often some form of character, is almost always capable of movement.

The avatar is usually cast as the hero of a story that provides context and motivation for specific tasks or quests. The location of the avatar on a map or the relationship to another unit can activate a context-specific trigger, such as in-game tips or directions, the sound of traffic if the avatar is near a road, or a context-specific menu, such as the opportunity to talk if the avatar is near another character, or even make a copy of a document if the avatar is near a copier. Often the object of a game is to get the avatar to certain key locations.

The camera's point of view in a virtual world tends to be governed by the position of the player's avatar, either first-person, third-person, overhead, or isometric. Being able to see your avatar during the course of the simulation enables more complex actions, and it also creates a stronger sense of character.

The avatar can be customized in many ways. The look of the avatar can be customized as a game element to add levels of "buy-in." This includes changing wardrobe, face, even importing a photograph.

The avatar has certain attributes, such as speed, health, and persuasiveness. The abilities of the avatar can often be increased or decreased, either permanently or temporarily, through various activities, including the use of found power-ups and the accomplishment of certain quests. In role-playing frameworks, the player might have choices in terms of development opportunities, such as between increasing sales skills or technical skills.

The avatar might also have a limited or unlimited inventory, granting further capabilities.

An avatar can also represent a person in a chat room or other community tools.

In many tycoon games, god games, and strategy games, however, the player is not represented by an avatar.

Application Sharing Tools

Application sharing tools are technology and processes that enable multiple virtual participants to see and interact with a software-based tool on the facilitator's computer (or some other centralized machine).

Some game-based simulations might use application sharing rather than slide sharing (the sharing of pictures) to engage all of the participants.

Calendaring Tools

Calendaring tools are processes that allow Sim organizers to automatically schedule participants for group activities and maintain and present updated calendars with relevant commitments. They typically are built into a course management tool such as Moodle, but also may send out information to popular calendaring software such as Microsoft Outlook or Google Calendar, or use industry standard formats like iCalendar.

Minimum System Requirements

The minimum system requirements are the lowest level of technology able to run a Sim or other environment, and a component of user access.

Technology specifications for a complex game cover several criteria:

- Computer processor and speed
- Operating system
- Memory size
- Hard disk space
- Video card capacity
- Sound card

Typically, the participant needs to meet all of the minimum requirements (an example of balanced inputs). Often, the more cutting-edge the simulation, the more specialized the configuration required to run it (See also "Frames Per Second" in Chapter Nineteen and "Advanced Graphics" in Chapter Sixteen). Users may also have to have recent drivers for their hardware.

For mini games, in contrast, the minimum requirements might just be having a recent Flash plug-in for a browser.

The percentage of people who meet the minimum requirements for a program increases if one calculates home as well as work or school computers. Using floating labs can also significantly increase access for certain populations.

The minimum requirements are different from the recommended requirements.

Directory

A directory is a centralized collection of members. The directory often includes some or all information from a community member's profile. An instructor's directory may have more information than a student's directory.

Profile

A profile is a description of a participant either for the sake of configuring a Sim or making available biographical material.

Some aspects of a profile may be editable by the participant or not, viewable by the participant or not, or private from other members or not. Profiles are critical for creating presence online. A picture recorded in a profile may appear in every one of the subject's post entries.

- Examples of participant-editable content: Pictures, videos, bio description, interests
- Examples of participant-viewable (but not editable) content: Number of plays or posts, success rate, computer operating system.
- Examples of content hidden from participant: Strengths and weaknesses, trustworthiness.

Club

Clubs increase engagement through providing the opportunity to get to or belong to a desired place (virtual or real world) where membership is limited and members share one or more interests.

Earning a club membership may be an award of a program. Entrance into a club may be restricted by levels of containment.

Cost Per Thousand Views

Cost per thousand views (CPM) is the cost to an advertiser for a Web site to show an image or impression one thousand times (the M in CPM standing for the Latin word for one thousand), paid to the site owner.

The range of prices per CPM range from $0.05 to $30.00 or more.

Things that increase CPM:

- Smaller number of impressions per page (average is between 2 and 6)
- Size of impression
- Position on page of impression
- Richness of media (video is more expensive than Flash, which is more expensive than text)
- Average length of time the viewer spends on the page
- Depth of alignment between advertisement message and demographic, including general interests, specific interest in page, age, location, and gender
- Broader business relationship (a sponsor can buy all images for a site for a week)

Sites tend not to fill all available space with premium impressions ($3.00 to $30.00), and sometimes sell what is left at remnant placements and prices ($0.05 to $0.15).

CPM motivates sites to attract the largest possible community. Predicting CPM revenue is a critical step in determining economic value and governing models for a social networking site. A certain volume of traffic, and the realization of CPM revenue, requires that persistent social networks realize certain economies of scale. This model of revenue generating may support fan sites and even mini-game development.

Related topic: "Click Throughs," in Chapter Twenty-Nine.

Instant Messaging Tools

Instant messaging tools enable text-based synchronous communication.

Recency

Recency reflects the higher value to a community of a post or comment published closer to the present time than one that was published further from the present time. In the environment of social networking, all other things being equal, a post from two hours ago is considered more valuable than a post from two days ago.

Community-Created Content

Members of communities produce content. Inevitably, what is created is shaped by what can be created. In a formal learning context, any of this content can be graded.

Blog

A Web log—or *blog*—is an online journal, updated regularly, often with links to other items on the Internet, with the goal of reflection, self-reflection, or sharing thoughts and peer reviews. Blog authors often allow others to comment.

Increasingly, students are asked to keep blogs in conjunction with courses that involve significant "outside the classroom" experience. This is both to get credit for time spent and also reflect on their experiences. For example, if, throughout a course, students are asked to explore Second Life on their own, they might write on it once a week. Or, if a students were learning leadership or project management or other big skills, they might use the skills in real-life situations, and reflect in their blog how successful or not they have been.

Blogs may be regularly reviewed by an instructor or buddy.

Chat Rooms

Chat rooms are sets of tools and processes for online, persistent, asynchronous conversations, accessible by a community. Typically, a user posts an article or question, and other users post comments.

Chat rooms maintained by a vendor can be used to provide technical and other help to users of a simulation. This help can be differentiated between help to students and help to instructors, and the instructors' help might in some way be locked to prevent student access and cheating.

Chat rooms can also be part of a class. Here, students' participation may be graded. Also, in a virtual class setting, instructors may use the chat room as a gauge of any individual student's participation level.

Especially in more social networking environments, the content in chat rooms is immediate, and there is a tremendous social premium put on recent information. This is in part because users return often, they want the newest information. The newest entries are listed first by default. Even if users choose to look for the highest-rated content, it is still often within the context of the preceding twenty-four hours or week.

In some environments, users get points for posting. Pictures or other forms of avatar might accompany each post.

Also called message boards and *forum tools*.

Post

A post is a short article, video, or other element created by a participant of a community and published to a blog, chat room, or other site for sharing.

A post's perceived value increases if

- It is rated favorably.
- Other people link to it (creating buzz).
- Other people comment on it.
- It was published recently.

Comment

A comment is a piece of communication (often text but also video) in response to someone else's post (such as in a blog or chat room), linked to the original post.

Points

Online community participants earn points through doing various activities, typically involving maintenance or content creation, and can spend them for certain benefits. Students may earn points for every post, for example, and spend points on customizing their avatars.

Rating

In a community, a rating is either an evaluation by a participant, often in the form of one to five stars, of a post, comment, product, or other element, or the aggregate of all ratings given to a specific post, product, or other element.

A participant might get points for rating another's post. Ratings provide a way to filter content.

Related topics: "Player Comparison Panel," in Chapter Nineteen, and "Competition," in Chapter Sixteen.

Recording

Recording is a process for capturing events as they are happening for future use.

For example, lawyers may record the sequence of word changes to an important document. A supermarket may record the activities in a parking lot via video. An interviewer may write down everything being said. Recording may be used in an after action review, to solve a mystery, as input for multimedia projects, to create simulation elements, and as evidence.

It even comes in handy for homework, where students can use machinima—the process of using traditional film editing techniques on clips recorded from virtual environments—to put together a composite work. For example, a student may explore Second Life, use the built-in video capture tool or an external program like Fraps, and then edit together the video clips into a five- or six-minute film, often with music and titles, to turn in in class. It's also possible to go further and create entirely new sets, characters, and animations, and set up elaborate camera shots.

Recordings are limited by sensors and storage capacity.

In a Sim, the recording may also be used for a library of plays.

Related topic: "Replay Option," in Chapter Seventeen.

Mod

A mod is a miniature program that changes aspects of a commercial off-the-shelf computer game. The word *mod* is short for custom modification.

Mods can add or change levels, skins and models, items available, cheats, special effects, interface options, and game balancing. Mods cannot change the underlying game genre.

In some situations, serious games, although seldom educational simulations, can be created by modding computer games.

The Culture of Modding. Mods are created by people called *modders*. The act of creating a mod is called *modding*. Modders are often very dedicated to their activities and can work in elaborate teams and spend more time modding than on their day jobs. Some modders aspire to be professional game developers.

Mods can increase the value of a computer game, and they are often encouraged by the game developer and distributor. Mods can be downloaded from fan sites. In cultures around games that are heavily modded, a non-modded version of the game is called a *vanilla version*.

Web-delivered applications cannot be modded, but can be hacked.

Modding and the Future of Learning. Modding will enable a role for students as content creators, not just consumers. They might take an existing historical Sim built on a project management genre engine (say, constructing a barn in colonial New England) and rebuild it to apply to their sports team's fundraiser, or the characters of a movie executing a plan to take over the world, or whatever interests them. Building and modding Sims, and even evolving open-source genre engines, will be a critical job for schools.

A Backlash Against Modding. Computer game companies may reduce the ability of users to mod their games. This is a reaction against the users who have been creating and distributing antisocial mods, such as "nude" skins for The Sims or Oblivion and the infamous Grand Theft Auto: San Andreas Hot Coffee Mod, and against the way the public, press, and politicians have been holding game companies responsible for third-party mods.

21

BASIC INPUTS

Basic inputs are devices and techniques for transferring participant actions from the real world to the virtual world. Everything participants want to do in a Sim must be enacted through basic inputs.

Basic inputs include

- Devices and controllers: buttons, joysticks, keyboards, or pointing devices (mouse, touchpad, trackball)
- Motions: click, drag, and tap
- On-screen tools: menus, text boxes, checklists and radio buttons

Some basic design considerations apply to input decisions in general:

- *Real-time or turn-based:* Buttons and joysticks tend to be real-time (the computer does not stop and wait for the player), while text windows and deep menu structures tend to be turn-based (the computer waits for input before proceeding). Books, for comparison, are turn-based.

- *Role of magnitude and timing:* For example, tapping a key or button sends a simple, all-or-nothing signal. Holding down a button for one, two, or three or more seconds sends an analog signal.

- *Number of options at any given time:* Simple multiple-choice basic inputs typically present just three all-or-nothing options. In an elaborate real-time computer game, players might have dozens of options, many with analog aspects.

- *Abstract or specific:* To submit a proposal to a committee, how many steps should a player have to go through? One button, or hundreds? Should repetitive or tedious tasks be included? How much is automated? If it is an educational simulation, the level of abstraction should correlate with the learning objectives.

- *Adherence to existing genre:* Any existing computer game genre, like real-time strategy or first-person shooter, has established sets of basic inputs.

- *Used in isolation or combination:* Should combinations of basic inputs be enabled? In early first-person games, players had to press a dedicated "up" button to climb a ladder. In more recent games, players have to approach a ladder, look up, and press the forward button. This combination takes a bit of practice, but once mastered becomes more fluid and ultimately intuitive.

Input Devices

All basic input conversations are framed by a choice to use machine-standard equipment—that is, equipment that comes with the computer such as a keyboard, or any optional add-ons, such as for a PC, a webcam or joystick. Using standard equipment increases the number of people who can use a Sim, while using specialized equipment can make the experience richer and easier for the participants.

Joystick

A joystick is a device that provides basic input in the form of vectors (absolute direction and amplitude).

These vectors can translate to movement of a player's avatar or selection of a menu. When a menu is involved, the items may be placed in a circle to correspond with movements of the joystick at various angles from the center.

A joystick is simpler than a mouse or keyboard to use. It is often more intuitive, and it does not need a stationary surface.

Keyboard

A keyboard is a device that provides basic input in the form of numbers and letters.

Keyboards enable rich and diverse communication, but can be confusing to use, especially in a real-time environment.

A keyboard can serve as a four-way joystick, often by using the w-a-s-d keys for up, left, down, and right, respectively.

Controller

Controller is a general term for any hardware device for translating user actions in the real world to a virtual world. It can refer to a keyboard or touch screen, but more often indicates a mouse, a joystick, or a gamepad.

Mouse

A mouse is a device that provides basic input in the form of decisions about the exact placement of a cursor on a surface.

A mouse might control

- Where a player's avatar is looking
- The use of a drawing tool
- The selection of icons or text, such as organized through menus

A mouse is intuitive and accurate, but requires a hard surface, typically a desk, to use.

> *Author's note:* In this day, it is easy to assume that every computer has a mouse. However, many computers, especially laptops, use instead touchpads—small built-in rectangles that use finger gestures to move the cursor. This changes the design considerably. A game that would be fun with a mouse is tedious and frustrating if the user only has a touchpad.

Left-Click. Left-clicking is the basic input of using the primary mouse button (placed by default on the left), often to select, use, or launch.

Right-Click. Right-clicking is the basic input of using the secondary mouse button (placed by default on the right), often to either pull up a menu, move a selected unit, or to perform a different default actions.

Double-Click. Double-clicking is the basic input of pressing a button (usually the left one) on a controller twice, quickly, often to launch or open.

Drag. Dragging is the basic input of depressing a mouse button (or other controller), and, while continuing to hold down the mouse button, moving the mouse, and finally, at the right time, releasing the mouse button.

Dragging can be for any of three related reasons:

- Move or copy an on-screen object (drag and drop) and (usually with the right button) set its direction
- Link two objects
- Select co-located objects

Button

A button is an easily accessible input device that typically sends one binary signal when pressed; a second, this time analog, signal when held, and a third signal, binary, when released.

This simple input provides a variety of outputs:

- Some buttons, such as the [shift lock] key, turn on when pressed (often indicated by a light), and then turn off when pressed again.
- Some buttons send a different signal when double-clicked.
- Some buttons activate toggles. The first time the button is pressed, the signal is A. The second time, the signal is B. The third time, the signal is C. The fourth time, the signal is A again.
- Buttons can also be de facto throttles, sending an analog signal so that the longer they are held, the greater the effect.

Keyboards are collections of specialized buttons.

Accelerometer

An accelerometer is a basic input device that transfers the user's three-dimensional movement, including speed and direction at any given moment, into the program. These have been popularized with both the Apple iPhone and Nintendo Wii.

Microphone

A microphone is a device for inputting voice into the Sim. It may be used for talking to other players in a multiplayer environment, or it may be used to give instructions, including short, one-word commands and more natural sentences that can be parsed and (with luck) understood by the computer.

Gamepad

A gamepad is an input device optimized for entertainment, with collections of buttons, sliders, and joysticks. Gamepads are usually used with game consoles, such as Xbox 360 or PlayStation 3.

Dance Pad

A dance pad is a basic input device consisting of buttons embedded in a floor mat that are optimized for quick and discrete foot movement to trigger on-screen actions.

Throttle

Ship Simulator 2008.

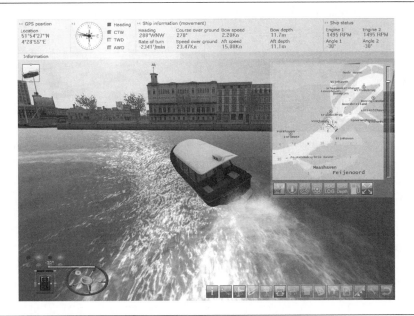

Source: Ship Simulator 2008.

A throttle is a basic input device that enables the participant to enter an analog input into a system, often to produce a corresponding analog output.

For example, the harder a driver presses on the gas pedal, the more fuel goes into the engine, and then the faster the car goes (unless it is out of gas, or hits a tree, or is capping out, or overheats, or some other fuel-related problem intervenes).

Throttles allow some sort of calibration of actions. Most people use management throttles every day:

- How hard to push the underperforming employee?
- How much money or time to put toward a project?
- How much time to spend responding to a critical e-mail?
- How active to be on that conference call?
- How hard to push a security initiative?
- How much to invest in this new, unproven technology?
- How hard to look for nutritious food, and not just settle for what is at the buffet table?
- How much care and thought to put into a job?

In capturing domain expertise, the throttle is an input mechanism, and it must have a defined relationship to one or more simulation systems.

Related topic: "Allocation Triangle," in Chapter Nineteen.

Second Layer Inputs

Sometimes specialized hardware is used in a Sim, such as a mechanical throttle to help control an airplane. More likely, the input devices are generic (sometimes called commercial off-the-shelf, or COTS), and therefore have to control various program features indirectly. While this increases potential access to the Sim, it may also require some supporting pedagogy. Here are examples of second-layer basic inputs.

Media Controls

Media controls consist of virtual buttons to play, stop, record, fast forward, skip chapter, rewind, and repeat chapter, with an interactive progress bar.

These buttons can influence any type of media, such as full-motion video, and also can influence any simulation action.

In most Sims, the spacebar is the default "skip chapter" button for cut scenes.

Open-Ended Interface

An open-ended interface limits, leads, or guides participants' basic input as little as possible.

For example, a text box is considered open-ended, while a multiple-choice question or menu is not. As a rule, the more open-ended the interface, the more supporting pedagogy such as in-game tips and directions the designer needs to include. In theory, with a truly open-ended interface, all actions and communications are possible.

Prospective participants in a Sim tend to want open-ended interfaces. After all, they say, the real world is open-ended.

However, the more open-ended the interface in an educational simulation, the more easily the Sim can spiral out of control. By using raw text or speech in directing people, as in a multiplayer environment, the Sim designer is pushing the instructional responsibility to the coach or buddies—or more likely, to no one at all. Besides, nothing is completely open-ended. In a car, you can drive where you want, but you can't fly. Likewise, you can type any letters or numbers in a text box, but you can't transfer the pressure of a breeze off of the Cape of Good Hope, or the smell of grapefruit burning, or the sounds of dolphins fighting.

The interface always guides and shapes the response.

Combo Move

Capcom's fighting games had "hidden" combo moves that players could discover and use.

Source: Capcom Entertainment, Inc. Used with permission.

A combo move is a set of three or four actions that, when done quickly and in the right order, magnify the impact of each or create an entirely new effect, to produce a much larger impact than any action or unplanned combination of actions.

For example, in a leadership situation, criticizing someone's work and then praising the individual (or the other way around) keeps the person motivated and engaged, while encouraging him or her to try a new approach. Strongly supporting and building upon an idea for three or four multiple turns can build momentum without giving any opposition a chance to organize.

The term moved to Sims and serious games from fighting games such as Mortal Kombat. In some games, certain complex combo moves cannot be blocked.

Short for *combination* move.

In the Sim Army Influence, combo moves translate basic intentions into specific actions. Here is a player's cheat sheet:

- A *Pressure* technique: To use this technique in the Sim, after you introduce an idea and hear resistance from the target, support the idea once, and then again. You will be saying a variation of: "Do it. Do it now."
- A *Legitimate requests* technique: To use this technique in the Sim, after hearing resistance from the target, support the idea once, and then again when you have authority. You will be saying a variation of: "Do it, because I am in charge."
- *Rational persuasion:* In the Sim, after hearing resistance from the target, support the idea first neutrally in the middle, then strongly in the green. You will be saying a variation of: "I don't have all the answers, but it is the best alternative."
- *Apprising:* In the Sim, after hearing resistance from the target, support the idea first strongly in the green, then the person strongly in the green. You will be saying a variation of: "Here's the idea, and here's why it benefits you."
- *Exchange* technique: In the Sim, after hearing resistance from the target, support the exchange idea strongly in the green. You will be saying a variation of: "If you do this for me, I will do that for you."
- *Participation:* In the Sim, after hearing resistance from the target, support the person, then support the person. You will be saying a variation of: "I trust you. How would you do it?"
- *Collaboration:* In the Sim, after hearing resistance from the target, support the idea first neutrally in the middle, then the character strongly in the green. You will be saying a variation of: "I don't have all of the answers so I need your help."
- *Personal appeal* technique: In the Sim, after hearing resistance from the target, support the person strongly in the green and then the idea strongly in the green. You will be saying a variation of: "I trust you, and need you to do this for me."
- *Inspiration* technique: In the Sim, after hearing resistance from the target, support the inspiring idea strongly in the green. You will be saying a variation of: "We all share the same goals, and this will help."

Combo moves can also be called *routines, arrangements, blends, collections, sequences,* and *reflexes.*

Bookmark

A bookmark is a record that enables a user to note the current location in the game, Web, Sim, globe geocaching, or other static or semi-static experience, for the sake of returning to or sharing the location. Saved games represent a type of bookmark.

Related topics: "Autosave Trigger" and "Chunking Levels" in Chapter Eighteen; "Redo" in Chapter Seventeen.

Compare with "Bread Crumbs" in Chapter Seventeen.

Perspective Control

Perspective control is a basic input enabling the participant to change the point of view in a 3-D environment. This is often done by pressing the middle button in a mouse, and then using mouse movement.

Cheat Code

A cheat code is a basic input consisting of sequences of keyboard or game controller commands that enable the player to force the game or Sim to provide favorable results.

Cheat codes are programmed in by the game developers, often originally to help them debug. For example, a programmer might make the main character invincible to enable better examination of animation in a sequence. Or a developer might skip to a specific bookmarked level or moment. Or to trick the game or Sim into thinking a mission had been accomplished to make sure the right subsequent briefing plays.

Sometimes developers take out all the cheat codes when they're done with them, but sometimes they just rename them, or even leave them in as is to enable cheating as a game element.

Cheat codes are nonintuitive by design, and therefore the easiest way to find them is to tap into a game-specific chat room or forum.

Related topic: "Easter Egg," in Chapter Sixteen.

Multiple Choice

In a multiple-choice input, participants are presented with a menu of two or more options, and they must pick one from the list to continue. Multiple choices are associated with state-based systems, including branches or links and elements.

As a Sim Interface. In a branching story, multiple choice is the default basic input, and each option is a discrete action.

Multiple Choice: Like Life, Except for the Life Part

You are a new manager, and you are meeting a legacy employee for the first time. After you exchange pleasantries, do you first:

a) Immediately ask her to do a job for you that you need done.
b) Ask her what is on her mind.
c) Pause and see what she says.

A multiple-choice set might also be used for an alert asking the player for a decision.

Branching interfaces raise awareness, of both options and consequences.

As an Assessment Interface. Multiple-choice tests greatly facilitate standardized evaluations, where students are presented one right answer with one or more wrong answers. Because standardized tests only consider awareness and light analysis, they are useful but not sufficient for evaluating implicit knowledge, certification, or mastery level.

Menu

A menu is a list of three or more discrete options for basic input, with each option clearly labeled, often by a button.

While menus traditionally are organized sequentially, when options are to be selected by a joystick they may be organized in a circle, where they are called a pie or radial menu.

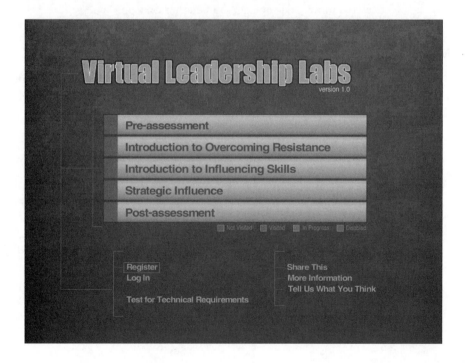

Menus might be presented as alerts, or might need to be invoked. Menus are a form of nested input.

Real Time

A real-time interface does not stop and wait for the participant's input before continuing, as a turn-based Sim might. Said another way, if the user does not do anything, the simulation takes that as the action.

The core gameplay of almost all computer games involves real-time action. Some consider real-time immersive learning simulations to be more realistic, engaging, and educational for a variety of reasons:

- They have greater fidelity because many real-life target situations, from flying to negotiating, are real time.
- They also create pressure that mimics the pressure found in situations that aren't inherently turn-based.
- They are more engaging, in that they require intense awareness and impose the constant requirement to deal with surprising situations.
- They also might prevent people from overanalyzing their activities.
- They are educational, but they also make it easier to see fluid patterns play out.

Despite all these advantages, very little of any learning program today is in real time (other than artificial timers on tests or due dates on papers).

Of course, even educational simulation real-time zealots (people who would argue for a real-time simulation even if the target use of the content is not in real time) would still argue for forced moments of reflection, such as an after action review.

It is finally worth noting that real time is not synonymous with twitch speed (where quick response at the neuron level gives some people a huge advantage over others whose nerves and muscles respond more slowly to their perceptions). A good real-time immersive learning simulation, unlike a twitch game, could still be of significant educational value if played as a turn-based game.

Related topic: "Practiceware," in Chapter Two.

Skip Chapter

A skip chapter media control allows the user to move instantly past the current chunk of linear content. This may be to the next piece of full-motion video, such as in a DVD, or past a cut scene, or through a Sim replay.

Slider

A slider is an input device that returns a value to a system depending on where a movable object lies on a bar. Users can change the value given by the slider by dragging the movable object.

Text Box

A text box is a place and prompt for players to type strings of characters. A text box is an open-ended interface, used for communicating in a variety of situations:

- MMO and MMORPG environments
- Interactive spreadsheets (in which participants tend to submit allocation levels)
- Instant messaging tools
- Blogs, posts, and chat rooms

Text boxes are used in virtual communities and can also contain expressions of emotions such as flagged written words (*grins*) or emoticons (:-).

See the sidebar "Directing People (in an Educational Sim)" later in this chapter.

Text Window

A text window is a panel with written information, such as page of a novel or a subtitle. Discrete text windows can also serve as a button or link, as discussed later in this chapter.

Parser

A parser is a technique for converting text (such as entered into a text box) into a basic input by identifying key words or phrases and associating them with actions. For example, if a participant types "go forward," "move forward," or "advance, a parser might convert that into moving to the next available location.

Click on Text (Hypertext)

Text or a text window can be used as a button. The term *hypertext* is often used when some of a larger number of displayed words or pictures serve as links to other content, typically of the Web page genre. Hypertext increases the inter-activity (and presumably customization) of otherwise linear content through better navigation and access.

Fast Forward Button

The fast forward button is a basic input control that allows the user to increase the amount of virtual time per real-world time to more than 1:1, so-called fast time.

Click on text. In most branching stories, players are given a series of possible statements or actions, and they choose the one they want their character to say or do. If a text window acts as a button, it often is highlighted if the participant mouses over it.

Source: Courtesy of Minerva Software and Blueline Simulations.

Author's note: For many authors, hypertext represents the furthest extension of their comfort level with interactivity, including Web pages and branching stories. Meanwhile, in movies, flashbacks are a type of editor-controlled hypertext.

The fast forward button might be a toggle, perhaps geometric, with options including 2x, 4x, then 8x, and then back to 1x. The 1x setting is considered real time.

If possible, the fast forward option might be automatically triggered *on*, and separately automatically triggered *off*, by in-game events. For example, in The Sims, time speeds up when your character falls asleep, and then slows back to real time when your character wakes up (or a crisis—such as a burglar or a fire—appears).

Hierarchy Arrows

Hierarchy arrows are a basic input consisting of buttons to collapse and expand hierarchical information. A right-facing arrow next to a parent indicates that the child elements are obstructed, while a down arrow indicates the child elements are visible.

Sometimes plus and minus signs are used instead of arrows.

Hot Spot

A hot spot is a graphic element that is interactive, launching some kind of response when either moused over or clicked on. The hot spot might expand the information a participant sees, or it might activate a link.

Interactive

Interactive content requires or reacts to input from the user. In a real-time interactive situation, no input is still an input.

Directing People (in an Educational Sim): A Case Study in Balancing "Open-Ended" with Helpful

Directing people is a middle skill of changing what other people do by using actions and activities. This includes giving orders, direction, goals, advising, and other forms of communication. Given the open-endedness of direction, how have Sims enabled it? Computer games and simulations have dealt, at various degrees of nuance, with the issue of directing bots in a dynamic environment.

Branching stories, an educational simulation genre, create discrete, direct, if highly scripted, options.

Command: Star Trek: Bridge Commander presents the player with dozens of possible one word commands to give the crew at any time, organized by the five different crew members. The commands can be highly specific, or they can be high-level enough to let the AI do at least some planning on its own.

Negotiate: Sid Meier's turn-based Civilization IV requires that you negotiate with other leaders. You might make a transaction trade, where you have to figure out what is a good "deal," but you also have to manage a long-term relationship based on past favors and even aligned goals, such as religion and domestic agenda.

Discuss: Virtual Leader, simultaneously and in real time, presents dozens of options, organized by supporting or opposing people or ideas.

Entice: Finally, in The Sims, in both building relationships and sales, players indirectly control bots by buying and placing objects to meet their needs and creating opportunities to build common bonds.

Asking for Information.

Source: Interview module for ExperienceChange: Lakeview. © 2008 ExperiencePoint Inc.

Negotiation

Source: Sid Meier's Civilization IV Screenshots Courtesy of Firaxis Games and Take-Two Interactive Software, Inc.

Discuss

Channeling Expectations

Participants in a game or Sim want open-ended communication with others. After all, they say, in the real world, or even in a chat room, they can just talk to people. However, giving in to this desire is often a cop-out on the part of the Sim designer. It pushes the instructional responsibility of shaping, framing, organizing, and appreciating options in communication to the coach or facilitator or to buddies, or to no one at all.

Also, pragmatically, given that interacting with artificial intelligence (AI) players is critical for learning in a formal structure (as it allows participants to practice), creating real-time, unambiguous interfaces requires a distillation of possible actions (both good and bad).

Ultimately, the opportunity of the interface is to shape how end-learners look at their strategic options in a situation. This is more true, and in some cases more controversial, when dealing with characters than when learning how to drive a car.

PART FIVE

FORMAL LEARNING PROGRAM

A formal learning program is designed to increase the capacity of students through their adoption of specific learning goals, such as application of new content or achieving mastery level. The purpose of such a program often involves delivering specific desired results for a sponsor, such as measurable compliance (including graduation rate) or better results as measured against the organization's balanced scorecard. Simultaneously, a program needs to meet program goals, such as low cost, self- or community pacing, ease of delivery, high student engagement, and effective use of student time.

Any formal learning program has the roles of sponsors, producers, and students, and often other community members. Formal learning programs can be aimed at specific groups, such as freshmen, new members, or high-potential employees.

Formal learning programs can involve and often start with linear content such as lectures, then can progress to nonlinear scalable content such as immersive learning simulations, and some *can* conclude with nonlinear, nonscalable experiences such as microcosms.

Delivery of formal learning programs is the primary activity of academic institutions and certain vendors, and it is critical to both military and corporate organizations.

22

LEARNING GOALS

Learning to Be, Learning to Do, Learning to Know

Learning goals are the ambitions of any formal learning program. Likewise, the *identification* of learning goals (including the assessment methodology) is the first step of creating any formal learning program.

The concepts I describe here are intertwined. The desired result of a Sim includes exercise of the big and middle skills it presents, and their acquisition is the learning goal of a formal learning program. For example, successfully negotiating (a big skill) with avatars in a Sim might be the desired result of a certain educational simulation, and the successful application of negotiating in the real world is the learning goal of the formal learning program that includes it.

The definition of learning goals gets more interesting as instructional designers see more types of content available. With the explosion of media available, including Web 2.0 and computer games, people now assume they will achieve three overlapping learning goals in everything from life to high school to the first day on the new job: first, learning to be; then, learning to do; finally, learning to know.

Learning to be is the students' quest to find out who they are, including their preferences as to companions and the nature of their various roles in different communities. (The funny one, the creative one, the problem solver, the risk taker, the good-looking one?)

Learning to do is the students' quest to develop and increase their own capabilities (including leadership, project management, design, innovation, sports, and art), and to pass a level of competence.

Learning to know is the students' quest to see themselves in a bigger context, both across space and across time (including other cultures, history, place in a food web, ancestors).

Social Networks and Communities—Learning to Be

In learning to be, participants experiment with and discover who they are. They might experiment with choosing their appearance or voice in a community (including community of practice). They might experiment by participating in different social communities altogether, and even by taking on different roles within groups.

They share anecdotes and comment on others' contributions to establish themselves.

Core questions for participants to answer:

- Who are the people I tend to like?
- Who are the people who like me?
- What do I like to do and talk about?
- What do I do for fun? What is fun for me?
- How do I dress, and what is my brand?
- What is my role in a group? The funny one? The brave one? The stylish one?
- Who are my preferred leisure companions?
- How do I dress (or otherwise appear), and what is my brand?

Learning to be might be greatly influenced by a great novel or even, in a professional sense, a branching story.

Educational Simulation and Microcosms—Learning to Do

In *learning to do*, participants learn and practice how to influence and change their surroundings. They learn how to apply big skills (such as adapting, leadership, nurturing and stewardship, communication) and middle skills (such as moderating ownership and containment), and of course, technical skills, even how to play football.

Participants focus on goals and missions, and they learn about unintended consequences and the need to evaluate success against a complete balanced scorecard, not just one criterion. They have a constant opportunity to understand and apply actions and activities, including the ability to calibrate many different throttles. Participants develop mastery levels and increase their professional value.

Core questions for participants to answer:

- How can I impact the world? How can I bring about change?
- How can I practice in virtual environments, and then transfer that to microcosms and real environments?

- How can I add value to a situation? What can I do for a living? How can I increase my control?
- How do I know whether I did the right thing or the wrong thing?

Books and Lectures—Learning to Know

In *learning to know*, participants begin to increase their awareness of their place in the universe. They make sense of the world they inherited. They understand connections to what came before them and what might come after.

They hear stories, and they learn to tell stories themselves. They are briefed on anecdotes, background material, and case studies.

Core questions for participants to answer:

- How can I make people care about outcomes?
- Can I evaluate the work of others?
- Why are things the way they are? What are the rules?
- What is a good life?
- What did my parents do? And their parents? What is my ancestry?
- What are the labels of things? How can I process my knowledge to make it easier to broadly communicate?
- How do I describe characters?

The tragedy is that the staggering success of the old technology of books has made learning to know the cornerstone of schools and training programs (at least what is formally taught, practiced, graded, and recorded). But until people first learn to be and learn to do, learning to know is not only useless, but it is impossible.

From Simple to Complex

In the development of a Sim, the first question is always *What learning goals do we need to deliver?* Related questions: What are performance objectives? What are the "aha" moments? What false assumptions is the audience likely to have? Some specific types of learning goals are described in the following sections, roughly in order of learning from the students' point of view.

Awareness

Awareness is the learning goal of having an overview knowledge of the topic and its context.

Awareness is often accomplished through linear content such as books, inspirational examples, case studies, even advertising, or by serious games, and can be contained in backdrops. The amount of awareness retained by a participant is often evaluated through writing papers and taking linear tests. Unless reinforced, awareness has a very steep decay rate.

Awareness is a first step toward application of new content, ideally creating an intrinsic desire to learn more about a topic, and it might be sufficient for new members, employees, freshmen, or recruits. But awareness is in no way sufficient by itself. Web pages and search engines, for example, support awareness rather than directly supporting action. In a Sim deployment, awareness can focus on background material.

Meanwhile, self-awareness can be facilitated by keeping a blog and using a coach.

Compare with "Mastery Level," later in this chapter.

Explicit Knowledge

Information that can be explained is called *explicit knowledge*. This is learning-to-know content, and it can be delivered though a low-pedagogy simulation in a formal learning program. Books and slides, by definition, are made up of explicit knowledge. Many tests ask for students to recite facts and other forms of explicit knowledge, although some tests in contrast might ask students to perform some analysis on a set of data. Typically, a novice's knowledge of how to do something is explicit (he can recite the steps), while experts' knowledge on how to do something is implicit (they don't know how they do something, they just do it).

Application of New Content

Application of new content is the learning goal of doing different or specific actions as a result of a learning program, in accordance with the material covered. The ability to apply new content decays quickly unless reinforced, either by real-life demands or by a high-fidelity simulation.

While content that seeks to drive application of new content must focus on actions, it must also focus on all simulation elements. This is because actions don't produce results directly, but only through an intervening system.

The adoption of simple actions can be best measured by observing active behavior. If more complex systems are involved, the evaluation might include 360-degree measurements.

Application of New Content

Procedural Knowledge

Procedural Knowledge

Procedural knowledge is the learning goal of being able to appropriately apply or perform a procedure. Successfully completing activities often requires a combination of procedural knowledge, middle skills, and big skills.

Coping Without Choking

Choking under pressure. Some people, when faced with new situations of perceived high importance, experience a significant damping of capability.

Coping without choking is the learning goal of building the ability to intelligently improvise, even when an event is regarded as extremely important. People at a mastery or expert level can be counted on not to choke under pressure.

Content to support the learning goal of avoiding choking under pressure must focus on real-time actions.

Evaluations of choking under pressure can be accomplished through observations of active behavior in real life and, to a lesser degree, behavior in a simulation.

Some people might practice in high-tension, low-consequence activities, such as in a mini game.

Implicit Knowledge

With implicit knowledge, people have a "habit of mind" that allows them to take appropriate action, even when unaware of their own behavior or application of any governing rules.

For example, it's possible to have the implicit knowledge of speaking grammatically correctly (or at least consistently), without ever having learned or being able to state any formal rules. Individuals are said to possess the target implicit knowledge if they almost always apply the same actions or middle skills in a given context. For example, one might always

- Study someone else's ideas in detail.
- Put on a seat belt without thinking about it.
- Ask the quiet person in the room for an opinion.
- Cut fat from a budget.
- Ask presenters tough questions.

Implicit knowledge comes from engaging in multiple experiences. As with all habits, those stemming from implicit knowledge run the risk of being used in the wrong situations as well as in the right ones.

In a formal learning program, a learning goal in the form of implicit knowledge can be more powerful but less satisfying to the student. This is because students do not feel it immediately. The unconscious awareness only really begins to kick in when a situation similar to the experience in a Sim presents itself. Then, and only then, comes the flood of new awareness and control.

Muscle Memory

Muscle memory is knowledge of actions stored at the real reflex level. Muscle memory can automate certain activities, which is why driving your own car feels so much more comfortable than driving a rental with a different layout of controls and indicators.

Understanding Complex Systems

Learning goals often include development of an awareness of the existence and behavior of complex system, including the role of time and interdependencies in its operation.

The material can be as basic as the general properties of all systems or as specific as the behavior of one target system (such as a big skill or collection of business processes).

Understanding complex systems is often taught through interactive spreadsheets. Learning how to apply complex systems leads to mastery level.

Conviction

A conviction is a strong belief in an invisible system that may not be apparent to other people. Someone who has convictions will look at short-term failure of his or her strategy as a sign he or she needs to try another approach, not that the strategy is wrong. Through playing a well-designed Sim, participants don't just learn a set of rules, they gain a strong and intuitive belief in relationships. For example, if one learns via a simulation that sugar spikes the body's insulin levels, this new perspective can stay with the person longer and more strongly impact subsequent decisions.

Mastery Level

Mastery level is the learning goal of developing the ability to apply the right content in a variety of real-world situations to get the right results, including through improvising.

Mastery level can be for mechanical tasks such as driving a car or big skills such as project management, and it often leads to increased professional value.

Mastery level requires success in the real world, which may be aided by high-fidelity educational simulations, microcosms, and working with a coach.

Some organizations live as hunter-gatherers when it comes to mastery, attempting to hire people with the competencies they need. Others are more like farmers, cultivating essential competencies in the people they already have.

Increased Professional Value

It is often a desired result to have participants be more valuable to any organization (as measured by given professional responsibility) after going through an activity such as a formal learning program.

Increased professional value is a significantly higher-level learning goal than awareness or analysis, and often requires mastery level, including success in a microcosm, or at least certification. Curricula can include both technical material and big skills.

Universities strive to increase the professional value of students, especially in graduate programs.

In an organization, the rigorous development of professional skills should be budgeted on a per-person basis proportional to salary level, on average around 2 percent to 6 percent, or 4 to 14 days per year. While an organization faces some risk of employees leaving after increasing their value, increasing professional value is a cornerstone of employee nurturing and stewardship. These programs can, in part, be considered a perk.

Increasing overall professional value is different from skilling-up for an organization's context-specific strategic goal.

Actualization

Actualization is becoming all we can be. Actualization almost certainly requires a mastery level of many of the big skills. In many ways it is the highest level of any of an individual's learning goals. On one hand, the appeal is undeniable. On the other, it defies traditional metrics of most learning programs. It is often associated with the American psychologist Abraham Maslow.

Combining the Three Goals

I was giving a speech the other day on the different learning goals—learning to be, learning to do, learning to know. But it was clear that a handful of professors in the audience were not on board with what I was saying. They did not understand the distinctions I was trying to make. Only in talking to them afterward did I realize why.

For the top students, these three categories of be, do, and know completely overlap. Schools are primarily focused on learning to know. But the top students then define themselves as the top students (honor roll, teacher's favorite, the person with all the academic answers) by their mastery of learning-to-know skills. And correspondingly, the top students' primary activity is learning and practicing the skills to be the top students (note taking, asking good questions in class, researching, writing papers, test prep and test taking).

When most people think back over their education, they tend to remember their best 5 percent of teachers. Meanwhile the people who have the most control over schools (today's teachers and politicians) tend to be the 5 percent for whom school represented the best organic alignment of be, do, know. Meanwhile, most academic institutions have the goal of being just like the top 5 percent of academic institutions.

But perhaps the reinforcing super-student loop (school defined as being for, by, and about the most pure students) has so much blurred the boundaries of the different learning goals that we don't even realize how different they are. But by being able to at least talk about them, we can finally address them and make schools relevant for the other 95 percent. It is only in action-based contexts of post-academic life that the chickens of "learning to know" as the be-all and end-all finally come home to roost.

23

PROGRAM GOALS

A formal learning program generally has requirements *outside* its learning goals. Together, program goals and learning goals are designed to produce any desired results.

For example, a specific program might have these program goals:

- Measurable results
- A high level of student engagement
- A certain cost ceiling
- Ease of deployment
- A high completion rate

With many programs, these program goals are more important than the learning goals, but there are exceptions. Some environments truly value formal development programs. These are the groups that say (in a riff on the more famous phrase) "train hard, manage easy." That seems better than "if you pretend to teach me, I will pretend to learn."

Basic Program Goals

Program goals include a variety of issues, some obscure and others instantly apparent.

Asynchronous Versus Synchronous

Some distance learning programs require that programs be asynchronous (turn-based and not requiring a same-time community) as part of their deployment and organizational philosophy, which can obviously be a deal killer for a synchronous program.

Increased Access

Many programs seek to employ processes that take an existing experience and make it available to many more individuals, greatly increasing the practical target group or target market.

Increased access and cost reduction for formal learning programs were early motivators for e-learning.

Certification

A certification program defines successful participants as those who can pass a certain knowledge or skill threshold. Certification programs provide more benefit (but typically require more work) for those further from the threshold, and less benefit (and less work) for those closer to the threshold.

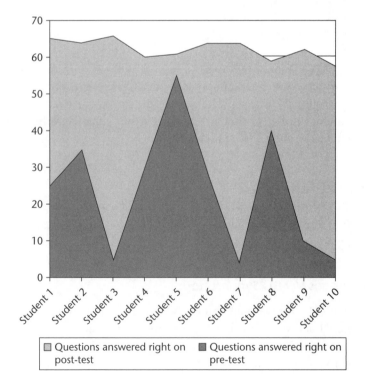

Questions answered right on post-test   Questions answered right on pre-test

As a program goal, certification can involve

- Getting all members of a target group up to a specific competency level no matter where they start off (a learning goal)
- Validating that competency level (an evaluation goal)
- Giving those who have had the competency validated access to a broader brand or reputation (a desired result)

While some certification programs have been early adopters of simulations, many still focus on teaching and testing around linear content.

> *Author's note:* One result of "No Child Left Behind" is that it has forced schools to reduce or eliminate programs on helping intellectually advanced children to excel and to spend the money instead on helping less intellectually advanced children get to a minimum threshold. This is a classic certification pattern.

Compliance

As a goal, compliance is the ability to meet legally or institutionally defined standards for

- Awareness and behavior or application of new content (learning objectives)
- Measurable completion rate supported by access (program objectives)

Compare to "Certification," earlier in this chapter.

One Contact Point

Having one contact point—a single Web portal from which all formal learning content is available, including course suggestions, requirements, and tracking—increases access and the amount of content started or launched (although not completed). However, a mandate of "one contact point" often forces the Web page to forgo more dynamic content for variations of Web pages.

Commercial off-the-shelf computer games and most military simulators, as well as ad hoc and e-mail conversations, conference attendance, podcasts, and classroom experience, fail the necessary attributes of being integrated, tracked, bookmarkable, and Web deployable.

One contact point is measured by calculating "student hours of content deployed through the portal" out of "all student hours consumed." One contact point can also increase the ease of deployment. While highly process-centric organizations will embrace this approach, highly creative and innovative organizations will eschew it.

Reducing the Cost of Formal Learning

Organizations can reduce the cost of formal learning programs by

- Automating processes wherever possible (for example, by using a learning management system)
- Centralizing management
- Using e-learning
- Using off-the-shelf content
- Creating one contact point
- Consolidating vendors, renegotiating, or finding cheaper sources

They can also use formal learning to reduce the cost of other organizational activities. Achieving economies of scale is often a critical theme.

Costs, and Budgeting Costs for Simulation

The cost that organizations have to spend to access an educational simulation, either by commissioning custom software or licensing it on an "off-the-shelf, per named user" basis.

Here are some examples of costs for access by corporations:

Branching Story. A branching story is a simulation in which students make a series of decisions via a multiple-choice interface to progress through and impact an event.

- Custom short (less than ten minutes): $30K
- Custom medium (between ten minutes and thirty minutes): $100K
- Custom long (between thirty minutes and two hours): $500K
- Off-the-shelf short (per user): $30
- Off-the-shelf medium (per user): $100
- Off-the-shelf long (per user): $500

Interactive Spreadsheets. An interactive spreadsheet is a simulation in which students typically try to impact critical metrics by allocating resources among competing categories and getting feedback on their decisions through graphs and charts.

- Custom short (less than one hour): $30K+
- Custom medium (between one hour and four hours): $100K+
- Custom long (between four and eight hours): $500K+
- Off-the-shelf short (per user): $30*
- Off-the-shelf medium (per user): $100*
- Off-the-shelf long (per user): $500*

*The cost of facilitation needs to be added to the price of off-the-shelf content.

Mini Games. Mini games are small, easy-to-access games built to be simple and addictive. They often focus on mastering an action and can provide awareness of more complicated issues.

- Custom short (five minutes): $10K
- Custom medium (ten minutes): $15K
- Custom long (thirty minutes): $40K
- Off-the-shelf short (per user): n/a
- Off-the-shelf medium (per user): n/a
- Off-the-shelf (per user): n/a

Virtual Product or Virtual Lab. Sims can present series of challenges and puzzles to be solved using on-screen representations of real-world objects and software.

- Custom short (thirty minutes): $30K
- Custom medium (one hour): $75K
- Custom long (four hours): $150K
- Off-the-shelf short (per user): $10
- Off-the-shelf (per user): $30
- Off-the-shelf long (per user): $100

Practiceware. Practiceware is offered in real-time, often 3-D Sims that encourage participants to repeat actions in high-fidelity situations until the skills become natural in the real-world counterpart.

- Custom short (one hour): $100K+
- Custom medium (five hours): $500K+
- Custom long (twenty hours): $1,000K+
- Off-the-shelf short (per user): $100*
- Off-the-shelf medium (per user): $400*
- Off-the-shelf long (per user): $1,000*

*The cost of facilitation needs to be added to the price of off-the-shelf content.

Increasing Cost

Here are some items that typically and significantly increase costs:

- Full-motion video (many Sims instead use comics or illustrations)
- Advanced graphics
- Calibrating units, maps, processes, and other parts of relevant systems
- Creating a new genre
- Having a totally self-paced and asynchronous deployment
- Customizing or building software instead of configuring or using off-the-shelf software
- Allowing for distance-deployed multiplayer play
- Building a complex game

Typical Sim Conversation

Instructor: I can't do simulations. They are too expensive.

Me: Not necessarily. There are many simple models. There are branching stories, virtual products, interactive spreadsheets, frame games, just to name a few.

Instructor: And are these more effective in achieving learning goals?

Me: Yes. They have very impressive long-term productivity benefits.

Instructor: Those are great. But how about multiplayer? Do you have any examples of multiplayer?

Me: OK. Here they are.

Instructor: Those are cool. But do you have any with better scoring and coaching built in as well?

Me: Sure. Here are a few other examples.

Instructor: Animations and advanced graphics are really important to me. Do you have any examples of Sims also with really great, smooth animation?

Me: Yup, I have a few right here.

Instructor: Our corporate colors are blue and red? Is it possible to customize it?

Me: Yes.

Instructor: Wow, that is so fantastic. That really blows me away. It's too bad, really.

Me: What is?

Instructor: I can't do simulations. They are too expensive.

Credit

Certification for completing an academic program that contributes toward a degree, but often is not enough in and of itself, is referred to as *credit*. Different academic programs may have different amounts of credit, in part dependent on their required time commitment.

Customize

Customizing involves changing between 5 percent and 20 percent of the off-the-shelf version to meet the needs of a specific demographic, organization, or individual.

Changes to a simulation program can include (from hard to easy) recoding some of a simulation, modding, and making changes in the facilitation and workbook.

Customization adds cost to any program and can be done by the simulation vendor, a third party, the implementing organization, or even a student as part of an advanced program.

And savvy organizations use caution: customizing any software often makes it difficult to take advantage of later vendor upgrades.

A coach or facilitator can also "customize" a program by using new words or changing the flow of the sessions to focus in on the most appropriate skills.

Compare with "Configure," in Chapter Eighteen.

Author's note: Upon seeing any simulation, many training people's first question is, "Can I customize this?" Training organizations have a perpetual desire to change things. In many cases, the changes suggested do not have a meaningful impact on the learning objectives.

Ease of Deployment

With ease of deployment, the threshold of effort required by an implementing educational organization to deploy a program is low. In most cases, managers of formal learning programs will forsake other program goals, learning goals, and results to maintain a high level of ease of deployment.

In March 2007, eLearning Guild's landmark report *Immersive Learning Simulations* presented live data that illustrated this point. Managers of educational programs, both academic and corporate, were asked about relative importance of various factors in a simulation program. They ranked "ease of deployment" over every other category, including "provides a strong return on investment" and "fun and exciting for participants." (Raw figures: 57.4 percent said ease of deployment was very important and 37.2 said it was important; 34.6 percent said return on investment was very important and 41.4 percent

important; and 50.2 percent regarded fun as very important, while 28.4 percent rated it important.)

The desire for ease is best modeled by the one-contact-point strategy. The easier genres to deploy include books, branching stories, and mini games.

The harder genres to deploy include backboards, batting cages, and other practice environments, as well as case study, interactive spreadsheets, labs, microcosms, practiceware, real-time strategy games, tycoon games, and virtual experience space.

Runs in the Students' Environment

It is necessary for a Sim to be able to run on the technology platform used by the target audience. At a broad level, the four choices are Apple/MAC, PC, Linux, or Web deployed. Beyond the platform, other hardware considerations, including processor speed, availability and power of graphic cards and sound, and (less winnowing) browser type, may make it easier or harder to reach this goal.

Typically, the state of the student environment is pretty well known and determined by other factors. However, it is possible to perform a technology survey if you want to know for sure what kind of platform students are using. Further, there are many free, small, and easy-to-download programs that students can run to see whether their environments are sufficiently powerful. Once the high-level criteria are met, the biggest stumbling block seems to be network access.

Engagement

Engagement is a condition whereby participants happily spend more time than required in an activity, often in a *flow* state.

Engagement is the reason for existence of any entertainment, including computer games, and a key aspect of anything designed for formal learning. In a Sim, engagement can be the result of the right combination of game elements and gameplay. (When speaking to prospective sponsors, *engagement* is a better term to use than *fun*, even if they are often used interchangeably in the design process.)

Engagement can also result in "addictive" behavior. This addictiveness can be problematic. Even when they are enjoying the simulation, corporate employees will still complain if they felt the extra time was required or expected to achieve learning goals, program goals, or results. Meanwhile, parents become concerned when any one program is occupying too much of a young student's time.

Intense engagement in a simulation can also leave a participant drained. Just twenty minutes in a Sim can leave someone shaking with exhaustion, especially when it requires complete engagement and imposes consequences for failure. This further can reduce naive participants' immediate satisfaction with the program, as a fifteen-hour course with significant engagement takes up much more mental energy than the equivalent in listening to lectures or watching videos.

Engagement is broken when participants hit walls, as when they cannot do something they think they should be able to do, or during pedagogical interruptions.

Introducing new sets and settings (discussed in Chapter Sixteen) is a technique often used for increasing engagement.

Increased Number of Opportunities

Making links available to students increases the number of options they have, both during the program and after its completion. In formal learning programs, a student goal often involves having more career paths available after completing the program, both within a sponsoring organization and outside it.

To the chagrin of Baby Boomers, for high-potential Gen Xers, increasing student opportunity is often more important than increasing professional value within the enterprise, and even promotion. This is in part, for example, why Gen Xers value the right to post to their own blogs more than playing internal corporate politics.

Increasing student opportunity requires a number of elements:

- The opportunity for creating objectively measured value in a microcosm
- Making critical contacts, including with the press and other parts of the outside-the-enterprise world
- Gaining an outside accredited certification

Obviously, increasing student opportunity can hurt corporate retention. In contrast, not increasing student opportunity can hurt corporate retention.

Measurable Results

Measurable results are data from a formal learning program that, objectively and rigorously, show that either a learning goal has been met or there has been progress toward a desired result.

Measurable results can be tactical or strategic, and can be based around things that are important or unimportant. They can be used for financially justifying a program by being associated with value and then divided by the cost. They can also be indicators for greater value delivered and can include contrasting measurements taken before any formal learning program.

In some cases, just measuring active behavior can change its occurrence rate independently of any formal learning program.

Programs that have rigorous and complete measurement requirements cannot be used to develop big skills or middle skills. The requirement of measurable results changes what can be taught.

Time Commitment

The time commitment is the minimum amount of time that a student should plan to put into a formal learning program, including any synchronous classroom time, any lab time, any self-paced homework, and even any required *informal learning* component. The amount of actual time might end up being less or more.

Most students think of time commitment in terms of the default lectures, writing papers, and studying for tests. It has other dimensions as well:

- Adding game elements increases the time while increasing engagement as well (a trade-off that some are willing to make and others are not).
- Every frustration-resolution pair increases the amount of mind commitment, which increases the perceived time spent by the student (and decreases the ability to do other activities like e-mail), but not the actual time commitment.
- Getting a top grade might require more time than getting a passing (certification) grade.
- Microcosm and informal learning are much less predictable than more formal learning programs in terms of time commitment, while also often providing richer learning.
- Some Sim genres, such as interactive spreadsheets, typically increase the necessary time commitment for covering the same material, while other Sim genres, such as virtual labs, can decrease the necessary time commitment.
- Virtual labs can reduce the time commitment over real equipment by 75 percent.

In a corporate setting, a miscommunication about time commitment or mind commitment lowers completion rate. In academic environments, the amount of credit for a program often depends on the time commitment required rather than the amount of material covered.

24

TARGET AUDIENCES AND
CORRESPONDING LEARNING
AND PROGRAM GOALS

Most formal learning programs bring together multiple pieces, including learning goals, program goals, desired results, methodology and genres, and evaluation strategies. All of these are shaped to some extent by the characteristics of the group the sponsors wish to engage: the target audience.

A Contrast of Two Target Audiences

The target audience consists of the group of people who either will use a Sim, should use a Sim, or potentially could use a Sim. Participants need access (including resources), awareness, and motivation (both intrinsic and through game elements). They also must make the necessary time commitment.

For target audiences for computer games, see "Gamer" in Chapter Twenty.

Meanwhile, designers of formal learning programs also have to be aware of current skill levels, prerequisites, and learning goals of the target audience.

Newcomers

People who are (or are about to be) "learning to be" in a new but established environment—new members, new employees, freshmen, recruits—need orientation to the existing organization or community of practice.

Engaging new people quickly (often called *onboarding*) is critical. In many situations, if people are not feeling good about their decision to join an organization in three or four days, their productivity and alignment will drop significantly. The transfer of people from academic to production environments is especially challenging culturally, as they must focus on actions, not knowledge.

A formal learning program for newcomers should have the following:

Learning Goals

- Awareness of (including history and backstory), mission, available resources, procedures, values, tone, frequently asked questions, and familiarity with the real experience
- Procedural knowledge

Program Goals

- Engagement with the program
- Increased access and ease of deployment (to get to a new person as quickly as possible)
- Cost reduction (see "Costs, and Budgeting Costs for Simulation," discussed in Chapter Twenty-Three)
- Compliance (proof that a person went through the program, to meet any ethics or sexual harassment policies and laws)
- Certification (in some cases, required to remain with the organization)

Desired Results

- Engagement with the enterprise (make people happy to be there)
- Compliance

- Individual improvements as measured against the organization's metrics and balanced scorecard
- Avoid choking under pressure
- Productive retention

Methodology and Genres

- Lecture (to present an overview, attach a person to the organization, and immediately answer questions)
- Community and buddies
- Branching stories and (if aligned to the tone of the culture) mini games and game-based models
- Coach or facilitator

Evaluation Strategies

- Anecdotes
- Surveys given to managers and students
- Percentage of employees who stay more than eighteen months.

Related topic: "Newbie," in Chapter Twenty.

High Potentials

Some people join an organization already classified as "high potentials." They often come in from business schools and are known (or at least expected) to be dedicated, hardworking, and creative. Others are quickly identified from the employee pool. These are the people with the greatest chance of getting either multiple promotions throughout their careers or one or two significant promotions, jumping intervening steps.

Many will be young stars with little deep management and leadership experience, who nonetheless have been very successful in everything they have done. They can also be longer-term managers who have slowly earned incredible respect and a long list of accomplishments.

In any case, it would be a significant blow to the organization of any of these people left. It would be a red flag to an organization if many left, and learning programs can be part of the strategy for keeping them.

A formal learning program for high potentials should have the following:

Learning Goals

- Mastery level in multiple big skills
- Analysis
- Relevant processes

Program Goals

- Completion rate (high-potential managers are always busy, so completion rate is especially significant)

Desired Results

- Individual and departmental improvements as measured against the organization's balanced scorecard
- Exposure to an organization's leaders
- Retention

Methodology and Genres

- A coherent community
- Coach or facilitator
- Mentor, supervisor, or guide
- Virtual experience space
- Practiceware
- Interactive spreadsheets

Evaluation Strategies

- Group performance and individual improvements as measured against the organization's balanced scorecard
- Competition between learners
- Anecdotes
- Retention
- Promotion

Great care must be taken so that the peers of high-potential people aren't demoralized by the attention and investment lavished on one of their own, as it can have a serious demotivating effect.

Experienced managers will tend to resist simulation-based training, thinking that they already know it all. In some cases, a 360-degree feedback system will increase their honesty level.

25

WHEN TO USE SIMS

Meeting Both Learning and Program Goals

So when should you use Sims rather than linear content? (This is the same statement, if more accurate and less weasel-worded, as "What is the right mix of the two?") And of course the answers will overlap here as well. Given that, this chapter describes some key places to use simulations.

Where the *Use* of the Content Is Critical

The first and easiest answer is, one should always use educational simulations when the successful application of the content is critical. This is always been the case with pilots, nuclear power plant operators, and Wall Street traders. Where failure is not an option, and the situation can be simulated, instructors will probably already be using simulators.

This recommendation can also be broadened: Educational simulations should be used when content is designed to be applied beyond the classroom but currently is not. For example, if an organizational behavior class is striving to drive real changes in the behavior of the students once they leave the classroom but the students all go back to their former practices, then again simulations might be a good opportunity.

This need can be determined by simply interviewing students six months after content has been delivered. One can also survey instructors with the following question: What existing programs are thought critical from a content perspective, but ineffective from a delivery perspective?

Improved Access Needed

A second area to use Sims, and perhaps the simplest argument to make for them, is if physical tools are too expensive, dangerous, inaccessible, or fragile, or a location is too remote or even fantastic (such as a literary world). When you can't afford real-world practice time, or such practice is difficult or impossible to arrange, then simulations make a lot of sense to save money and enable greater use and immersion.

Seeking Increased Engagement

Next, simulations are powerful when students need to be engaged more than they are. Clearly, this is an area in which distributed classrooms have suffered, as death by PowerPoint has not just been refined in many programs but almost weaponized to military specifications.

When students are not expressing any interest in the content presented, using a good simulation can attract and engage them. And students are not just engaged but actually grateful. This may ultimately be either the weakest argument or the strongest argument for adopting Sims.

It may be the most relevant if the goal is to engage younger people more substantially, by reforming content and introducing a needed first-person and visual framework to static content trapped in a passive learning environment.

There are two big risks, however. The first is that instructors will think they are speaking in the students' native medium, when in fact they are speaking in their own native medium. Different people, and even different generations, have different media of choice that shape how they view entertainment, communication, and formal learning.

Some examples, from oldest to newest:

- Books (launching textbooks)
- Movies (launching documentaries)
- Television (launching PBS)
- Rock and roll (launching *Schoolhouse Rock*)
- Magazines (launching job aids)
- Single-player computer games (launching edutainment titles such as Math Blaster and Leapfrog)
- Multiplayer computer games (launching online role-plays)
- Massively multiplayer online role-playing games (MMORPGs) (launching the corporate adoption of Second Life and other virtual worlds)
- Social networking (launching internal social programs and even human topology programs)

Just as every cognitive scientist ends up describing the human brain in terms of the newest technology, so too do leading instructors try to reimagine content through the media on which they grew up.

The second big risk is that teachers will try to communicate in the fast-moving target of the students' native media, and do it clumsily. Some teachers today end up drafting popular culture, forever playing catch-up, and like dogs chasing cars, seldom catching new media nor knowing what to do if they do.

Dynamic Content

Another area where simulations are appropriate is when the content itself is inherently dynamic, that is, the content is made up of the three layers characteristic of flight simulators:

- Actions (which transfer to the interface of the Sim)
- Results (where there is a goal to be accomplished)
- One or more systems that connect the two

This is in contrast to the time lines or inner monologues stressed by linear content, and it could be relevant for everything from project management to chemistry or even history. The key questions are: Where are students not understanding the content, and Where has the content become so abstract that it doesn't meet the original learning intent?

Typically, surfacing the need for simulations comes from questions to instructors and curriculum designers such as these:

- Across all areas, what are the most difficult topics to learn? What topics are most frustrating to master? What training topics would be best covered with repeated practice and repetition?
- What existing programs are critical from a content perspective but ineffective from a delivery perspective?
- What are areas that you would like to incorporate into a curriculum, but have not? Are there classes, curriculum, or topics that would be best if the learner could act as an apprentice to a more senior person? Are there areas identified by stakeholders that are not currently being met?

Depth of Knowledge Required

If students need a deep and rich knowledge base, one in which they can improvise to a variety of surprise situations, simulations work well. The more they truly need to understand a topic, the more simple rules and processes are insufficient. Again, when applying simple processes or time lines is insufficient, simulations make sense.

Availability of Sims

The last part of the "when are simulations better" checklist is perhaps the least satisfying. People who cannot build their own simulations or hire someone to do it must use simulations that already exist. Given the relative paucity of existing simulations (at least compared to textbooks), even if a simulation is in theory appropriate, it will not be feasible to use one if none is available.

The fundamental question is: Where do simulations come from? There are several answers, each with its own trade-offs. Fairly or unfairly, the source of a Sim has an impact on how and whether students are asked to pay for it directly.

Commercial Off-the-Shelf Games

For some lucky professors and students, computer games built for entertainment and bought through retail channels provide a deep enough and sufficiently curriculum-aligned experience for classroom use.

A screen shot from Civilization IV.

Source: Sid Meier's Civilization IV Screenshots Courtesy of Firaxis Games and Take-Two Interactive Software, Inc.

The two most famous classroom-ready games are the Civilization and SimCity series. The pros are that these experiences have reasonable per-student costs (around $40), very high production values, and at least some element of fun built into them. The biggest con is that only a few such games exist. Further, both deans and parents can be uncomfortable having the students spend their class time playing off-the-shelf games. These games can also be awkward to install. Students typically directly bear this cost in academics.

Using computer games in a formal learning environment can be risky. This is because, obviously, computer games were not built to be accurate. But as Richard N. Van Eck, an associate professor and graduate director or instructional design and technology at the University of North Dakota, points out, "Errors and inaccuracies are in fact teachable moments."

Free Foundation-, Cause-, or Corporation-Sponsored Sims

A lot of free Sims, typically Adobe Flash–based, have been created in the last few years by various organizations. They represent some of the most successful and innovative examples of serious games. Examples include Cisco's Binary Numbers and American Public Media Budget Hero.

American Public Media Budget Hero.

Source: Budget Hero™ screenshot © 2008 American Public Media. Used with permission.

Where these Sims fit, they can be perfect. The pros are that they are free and typically easy to access. The cons are that they are short, often shallow, and often editorially skewed. They represent a position that could easily be wrong or even offensive (blatant stereotypes in Sims really get people mad). Further, a specific Sim that is interesting and relevant may not be around next week if the sponsor changes its mind or gets sued.

Off-the-Shelf Educational Simulations

Some vendors sell prepackaged simulations. The pros are that these products tend to be rich and detailed educational experiences. They have technical support. They also have instructional support—notes for how to use them in a classroom environment. They may have gone through several generations of modification and refinement. And often the best supporting documentation has been rigorously gathered from other users. But they still have cons: the licensing is often restrictive, and the costs tend to be three or four times as much as a computer game, since the audience is so much smaller. Students typically directly bear this cost in academics.

Harvard Business Publishing's Pricing Sim.

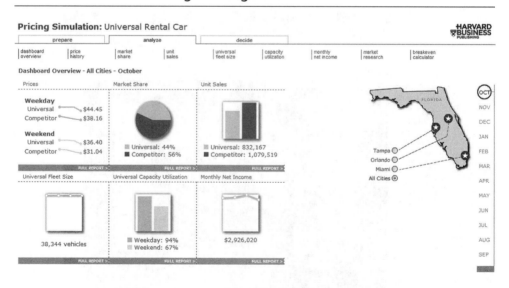

Source: Reprinted with permission of Harvard Business School Publishing, Universal Rental Car pricing simulation, no 2093, John T. Gourville, Tom Nagle, John Hogan Copyright © 2009 by the President and Fellow of Harvard College.

Many off-the-shelf educational simulations have configurable attributes, including custom configurations for different environments such as undergraduate, graduate, and executive education, as well as corporate use. Some simulations even provide access to variables in the models so that professors can customize the systems to align with their own curricula.

For off-the-shelf educational simulations that include them, the supporting manuals themselves often become a sales tool to raise awareness in the professor. Therefore the first step in pilot testing such a Sim is to review the printed material.

Internal Development House

Some institutions have a staff (usually between one and twenty people) dedicated to building simulations to support internal classes. The good news is that these people are focused, have the requisite skills, and are aligned with the goals of the institution. Once built, the content they produce can most likely be infinitely reused and shared. The cons are that often the experiences that result are dry, and they take three or four times longer to build than expected. Internal development groups often fight with the subject-matter experts (the professors) from whom they have to draw content. Who funds these groups is also up for grabs from budget cycle to budget cycle, sometimes minimizing long-term continuity.

One other alternative for internal development is to use grad students or gaming students. These can be very useful resources, and the price is right.

Professor-Created Simulations

We are seeing an explosion of technology-savvy academic hobbyists creating simulations to support their own classes, developed in their free time. (It was professor hobbyists who also created the educational simulation genre of interactive spreadsheets decades ago, and it is still thriving today.) The pros are that these tend to be perfectly aligned with content and to be deep and nuanced. They can also be freely shared. The cons are the simulations are often makeshift, with kludgy interfaces. They also tend to be more labs than finished Sims. Knowledge of how they were built, the assumptions built into them, and the ways to best deploy them tend not to be recorded.

Some professors decide to change existing computer games to make them appropriate for their classes. These bundles of changes are called *mods*. The pros are that, for not much money, professors can access very rich environments. The cons are that students still have to buy the original computer game, and often compromises must be made to shoehorn the changes into the computer game, resulting in a suboptimal or even unstable experience. (For more info, see "Mod" in Chapter Twenty.)

Otherwise Free Simulations

Finally, for whatever reason or business model, some simulations are just free. For example, joining and interacting in Second Life (a massive virtual world run by Linden Labs in which people create avatars, explore, meet, and build rooms and buildings) is free, though it costs money to buy real estate or the intellectual property of other people. Second Life continues to be synonymous with virtual worlds in popular literature because it is both an early leader and a bellwether for the industry. World of Warcraft is free for a trial period, often long enough for classroom engagement, but not enough to get to Level 70.

It is worth noting the pricing models one more time. Imagine that the cost of accessing a thousand units of a Sim is $50,000. If the Sim is structured to be sold per seat, often by an external vendor, then students typically have to pay for access, much as they would buy textbooks. But if the cost is spent in a lump sum or in salaries, it tends to be the department that picks up the tab. Fair? No. But predictable.

26

EDUCATIONAL SIMULATION CREATION AND MILESTONES PART 1

An Overview of Key Steps

The biggest and most important confusion in curriculum design today is between when to use Sims and when to use linear content such as lectures and reading and writing assignments.

To make this conversation easier, let me stipulate up front that educational simulations are harder to build and deploy than linear content, and will continue to be harder at least for the next few years. This means pragmatically that, when Sims and linear content are equally well suited for a learning objective, linear content is the way to go. It may also mean that simulations can only be brought into an organization when traditional approaches have failed in some way.

Development Steps

Here are critical steps, roughly in chronological order:

1. Identify target audience (see Chapters 20 and 24).
2. Identify learning goals and project goals (see Chapters 22 and 23).
3. Define current formal learning processes and shortcomings.
4. Create assessment (see Chapter 29).
5. Identify best practices and subject-matter experts.
6. Interview subject-matter experts.
7. Assess participants' current access to technology and knowledge.
8. Staff the game's development effort.
9. Define elements for the simulation, including game, pedagogy, and structural content, story, and level design (see Parts 2, 3, and 4).
10. Prepare a design document, story bible, and storyboard.
11. Play test and pilot test.

12. Prepare an instructor manual.
13. Patch the Sim—and expect to keep on patching it.

The subsequent sections describe those steps not covered in other aspects of the book.

Define Current Formal Learning Processes and Shortcomings

Sound Sim development requires identifying all current formal learning processes in the target area and understanding where the successes have been and what the failures are.

Care has to be taken to look at real learning objectives, strengths, and weaknesses rather than linearly biased learning objectives, strengths, and weaknesses. For example, evaluating a project management program based on scores on multiple-choice tests may not accurately reflect the success of the program in the field.

Identify Best Practices and Subject-Matter Experts

The most understood, predictable, efficient, and scalable way of accomplishing a desired result given a certain starting place or resources is to find out what is already being done that works.

Best practices are often derived from multiple case studies. They are often used as an input into any kind of formal learning program. Traditionally, formal learning programs aim to change participant behavior to better match the best practice case. Because a program is only as good as that input, if the desired results are not achieved, it may be because the formal learning program was not effective, or it may be because the identified best practice was not a real best practice.

Interview Subject-Matter Experts

It is challenging to interview subject-matter experts for simulation design. Most SMEs think in terms of case studies—polished snippets of success (the cultural result of growing up in the Gutenberg era). And that is good enough for most formal learning programs. But you need several distinct lines of questioning to build a good Sim.

The following goals tax the good will of any expert, but are critical part of the conversation:

Consider Wrong Approaches. Subject-matter experts are, well, experts, and asking them to explore the wrong path often gets looks of scorn. (Interviewer: What if you criticized the boss in front of the CEO? SME: Well, I wouldn't. Interviewer: But what would happen if you did? SME: There is no way I would because that would be idiotic.) This also forces the interviewee to guess rather than recount, and also sometimes to bring up personal failures, which is much harder.

But capturing the consequences of failure is critical. Not only is it critical for learning, but it turns out that allowing players to fail is also a game element. Players love deliberately doing the wrong thing, if just because they can.

It is funny that most formal learning programs focus primarily on a single brittle path of success, while most computer game designers are much more focused on player failure.

I have noticed a few things as I work through these challenges. The first is that the only experts who are of much value are those straight from the field. The gurus, people who have stepped out of the reality and who have focused on polishing stories, have remarkably little to add. (Pity the poor Sim designer who relies on teachers and authors.)

Second, while the interviewing process is hard, most SMEs, once they get it, then become frustrated with traditional interviews. They learn, as most students who go through Sims also learn, that these models work better, not because of magic, but because of increased rigor.

Finally, because it does stress SMEs, some Sim designers short-change this tough interviewing by filling in all of the holes themselves. This solution is common—and ultimately tragic.

Consider All Approaches. Part of the process is the rigor and tedium of considering all approaches that a player might use. This means considering not only complete failure but also short-term failure. It means considering not only total success but also mild success.

On one extreme, it might involve building a branching tree. This is exhausting because the designer has to keep going forward and back to cover every branch.

This process of considering all approaches is even harder when building equation-based systems. Now not only do SMEs have to validate interactions, but they have to translate between mathematics and reaction.

Consider Actions and Feedback the Context of a Microcosm. Finally, while some simulations cast the player as a CEO managing a balance sheet over decades, I like microcosms and an interpersonal time scale (in other words: first person and real time).

But this means that all short-term feedback (the kind of feedback that players can actually react to, as opposed to the after action review feedback) has to be immediate. This is not always realistic. (Interviewer: How would you know that was the wrong thing to say? SME: The next day the person might quit. Interviewer: But what would you see immediately to let you know that you had done the wrong thing? SME: Probably nothing. Those meetings are pretty quiet.)

Identify and Eliminate Negative Training.   Negative training is when a formal learning program produces students who are less prepared rather than more prepared for the target real-world activities.

Negative training can propagate dated content, inaccurate content, bloated content, or superstitions or encourage bad habits and sloppy procedural knowledge. The term *negative training* does not refer to useless training, such as linear abstractions, but to training with clearly damaging effects.

The better and more precise formal learning programs become, the greater the risk of negative training. If training is the equivalent of warm tea and minty candy, it does not do much good, nor can it hurt much. If training is the equivalent of a targeted pharmaceutical, it is very powerful in some situations, and absolutely wrong in others. Sims are so powerful that their aim must be carefully calibrated.

Assess Participant Technology and Knowledge

Designing a Sim requires knowledge of the prospective participants. In particular, you need to identify the most powerful common technology platform and distribution process to which at least 80 percent can easily get access. You also need to assess the target audience's current level of understanding and attitudes about the learning goals. These can be done through surveys or interviews of sample sets.

Finding Employees to Fill Serious Games Positions

As the conversation has shifted from "Should I do serious games?" to "How do I do serious games?" people have been asking where to find talent.

The easiest answer: check out the schools that graduate game designers. Lists can be found at both IGDA and Gamasutra. Some of the most notable in the United States are

- DeVry
- DigiPen
- Full Sail
- Guild Hall at Southern Methodist University
- Southern Michigan University
- University of Central Florida—master's and doctoral degrees in modeling and simulation
- Old Dominion University—master's in modeling and simulation—College of Engineering
- Rochester Institute of Technology—game design and development
- Ohio University—digital media
- University of Baltimore—simulation and digital entertainment
- Michigan State University

There are also slightly less direct paths.

- Game-centric job boards, such as GameJobs, and recruiters, such as GameRecruiters
- Advertisements in game magazines and game sites
- Social networking sites, such as LinkedIn, game blogs, and game industry specific–forums, again such as IGDA or Gamasutra

Finally, look at indie game producers. They know how to pinch a penny and can focus on highly interactive experiences.

The biggest caveat is that a game designer does not necessarily make a great *serious games* designer. First, make sure the experience matches the proposed solution. If you want to make Flash-based games, for example, don't bring aboard someone used to working in Triple-A level 3-D environments. Then, make sure the passion is aligned. Someone who wants to create games where heroes save the world may not want to work on serious games. But for someone who really wants to *be* a hero and save the world, this might be perfect.

Define the Game

Lay out the simulation elements, including actions, system content, and desired results. Define as many low level, simple relationships as possible (virus spreads via saliva) and high level patterns (a single infected host can infect an entire community in less than a week). Ideally, the emergent behavior of the aggregate low level relationships organically matches to the high level patterns. Where they don't, you can always use triggers. Add game elements, pedagogical elements and placeholders, and structural content, including story and level design.

Regionalization is the customization of a Sim to better meet the needs of a country, culture, or language.

During this process, specify the amount of regionalization you plan. Sims can be built to be easier to customize, including regionalize, through using XML sheets and other easy-to-access data outside the core engine.

Related topic: "Configure," in Chapter Eighteen.

Design Document

The design document is a very detailed description of every aspect of a game or simulation. It includes screen mock-ups, user interfaces, basic gameplay, art and animation assets, state charts, character descriptions and artwork, storyboards, level designs, minimum system requirements, platforms targeted, and high-level equations and relationships. It specifies the level of abstraction or fidelity the product will maintain, along with the toolsets, game engine, and instructor controls.

It is not a marketing document, but it may include a summary of the goals of the Sim. The design document for a complex game, one for an Xbox 360, for example, is around five hundred pages. There is also a technical design document that explains how items in the design document will be implemented, a story bible, and a design guide. The design document needs to be approved by any boards or advisers.

Designers may use spreadsheets to rough out equations, PowerPoint for screen shots, magazine photographs for character stand-ins, and other artifacts. Many educational simulation classes require a mock design document as a final assignment.

For examples of areas covered by a design document, see "Campaign" in Chapter Eighteen. Chapter Twenty-Two, especially the "Mastery Level" section, is also relevant. Also called *functional specifications.*

Has Dr. Seuss Overinfluenced Sim Design?

Many Sim designers make up some new species and ecosystem. You know what I mean: "The glorms are just like humans, but all they need to live is a single food protein, sunlight, and water."

The argument for the Seussian approach is compelling. It mostly follows two correct trains of thought and one wrong one:

First, Seussian Sim characters are obviously abstracted. They can focus the participant on a few key issues. They also get around the language issue.

Second, Seussian characters don't have to be perfect. One of the most common statements from Sim students is, "Oh, people don't act that way." By creating your own world, you make the rules, and you can short-circuit this common complaint.

Third, and this reason is less defensible, Seussian characters can be "fun." Now the problem with this, of course, as with all game elements, is that what is fun for one person is not fun for another.

While I think these reasons all need to be addressed, ultimately the Seussian approach causes more problems than it solves.

First, it puts off a lot of people. Feeding a planet of snicklewhacks (or whatever) puts a level of contrivance that simply doesn't resonate with enough people. Any game element, almost by definition, appeals to some while turning off others.

Second, it takes up too many resources that should be spent on making a better product. Creatures need body language, even culture, and all of that distracts from the core goal. Let's say that I need body language to suggest my creature is sick. I would rather the designer research the real-world body language than make up new ones. ("The juntiopians turn blue and spotted when sick. . . . ") The nice thing about using real is that other subsequent designers can build off of each other's work.

Third, it does take the designer off the hook. It allows the modelers to ignore reality. If one argues that content is there to drive intelligent actions, then Seussian settings interrupt the application of the content post-Sim.

Ultimately, I think the Seussian approach is a great but distracting shorthand. I would hope that a Sim program instead can make explicit the limitations and the abstractions of the Sim. (For example: "This Sim will look at the relationship between short-term and long-term use of land. It focuses on the cost of food as a factor of the health of the soil, but does not take into account cost as the result of the actions of other countries." Or "These are obviously not real people. But they will respond in a way that will align with at least some of your own experiences. By learning to manage these simulated people, you will better manage real people.")

Having said that, the level of systems abstraction (mathematical or otherwise) should align with the level of visual abstraction. In other words, graphics should not be photo-realistic if the AI (or other underlying mechanism) is much more simplistic.

I believe a good short-term goal for visual fidelity in the whole "big skills" area (project management, stewardship, relationship management, and so on) is about the level of a *New Yorker* cartoon. Real, but abstracted, including exaggerations and holes. The nice thing about that is that it provides an accurate representation of most systems as well. This is the level of The Sims, where "Sims" speak in their own Sim language and spend simoleons rather than dollars, but are still mostly human.

Sim designers have to walk a tightrope. If the goal is perfection, especially when dealing with models of human behavior, we all will be paralyzed by fear. But if the goal is Seussian, we may be letting ourselves a little too much off the hook. Worse, we may fall into the traps of traditional education with "it's not the specifics that matter, it is the very high-level lessons."

Story Bible. A story bible is a document that contains the most complete backstory for a story world. Some of this information may be presented to the audience, while other parts of the background might simply influence the developers' handling of the plot or characters, supporting consistency as further parts of the world are developed.

Storyboard. Developing a storyboard is a process to visualize, edit, and understand every shot, including point of view, backdrop, and characters, before the expensive final production, especially if that final production involves full-motion video.

Storyboards can be simple sequences of pictures and text, perhaps in PowerPoint, or computer-generated animatics (rough animations). Any linear sequence can be storyboarded.

A *New Yorker* level of graphics. This drawing is representative without being fanciful, and represents a good target for Sim designers.

Source: Title screen for ExperienceChange: GlobalTech. © 2007 ExperiencePoint Inc.

Storyboard

Related topics: "Branching Stories," in Chapter Two; "Comics," in Chapter Sixteen; and "Illustration," in Chapter Seventeen.

Fidelity. Fidelity is the accuracy of the virtual situation as compared to the real experience or context, often in terms of a percentage. Fidelity can measure sight, sounds, smell, interface, and consequences, just to name a few aspects of reality.

For educational Sims, fidelity does not completely correlate with educational value, and certainly not in engagement value. A completely "real" environment is not always the best initial learning environment, although it is necessary for mastery. It is apt to contain too much noise—not just sound but all sorts of random stimulation—to isolate the relationships that support the learning. Further, open-endedness, often enables the perpetuation of the same behavior. Finally, real life also takes a long time to play out, a step simulations try to condense.

As a result, game elements often reduce fidelity to increase the engagement of an experience, such as producing exaggerated responses. And pedagogical elements often reduce fidelity to increase the participant satisfaction and the transfer to the real world.

Fidelity might also be called a subset of reality.

Glibly, educational simulations can never be completely comprehensive and accurate. This is partially because once a perfect simulation model can be created, any activity can be automated, and therefore formal learning is not necessary.

Fidelity can include the participants' emotional state entering a situation. This can be achieved by backstory and other context.

Toolset. The toolset is the software that makes the development of content faster and cheaper, while requiring adherence to certain creation processes, user environments, standards, templates, or entire genres, and other preconditions and assumptions.

For example, Adobe Flash and Microsoft PowerPoint are toolsets.

Choosing and using a toolset involves trade-offs, typically between reducing the skill and time required to use them and offering a high degree of control over the finished artifact, and between providing a competitive differentiator and level of specialization for the needs of a specific subgroup and making it easy to distribute the final product easily and cheaply.

Toolsets share other features:

- Toolsets should produce content that is able to be integrated with content from other toolsets. A complex computer game may require the use of several

toolsets to create. For example, PowerPoint diagrams can be embedded in Word documents.
- Toolsets can vastly decrease the barrier to entry for a developer, level some playing fields between competitors, and increase access to the work of others.
- Some toolsets are open-source, while others are proprietary.
- Toolsets initially follow and generalize great examples of custom design. Historically, organizations that have tried to sell tools before great common references exist have failed.
- Popular toolsets gain de facto control of any content standards.

Game Engine. A game engine is a toolset, either bought from a third party or internally developed, that is used as the basis for building a Sim.

Games designers generally use one primary engine (the graphics engine, for movement, 3-D rendering, and resolution) and a few smaller engines that power other aspects of the game (AI, interface). Game engines, as with all toolsets, represent a trade-off between ease of use and diversity of possible experiences.

Elements a game engine should have include:

- Actions and basic inputs
- Display
- Linear content
- Maps
- Pedagogical elements
- Social networking
- Tasks and levels
- Units

Many game engines are optimized around one type of game genre, like first-person shooters or real-time strategy. This specialization compromises an engine's ability to enable educational simulations.

Author's note: Why are consoles so bad for serious games?

Many people believe consoles such as Xbox 360 or PlayStation 3 should be the perfect platform for serious games. After all, the argument goes, they are relatively cheap and even standardized. And currently a lot of them are out there in the hands of potential participants.

So where is the problem?

Console manufacturers lose money for every console they sell (Nintendo's Wii is an exception). They charge software developers for tools to create games, charge the developers to certify that the game is bug-free and completely compatible with the console, and then—the most important drawback—charge a per unit licensing fee for every game sold. This last category is where they make the real profit. Console manufacturers must have five or ten games sold for every console to make it a profitable transaction.

So with serious games, the fear of Sony or Microsoft is that consumers will buy just one serious game for every console bought. If there is a hospital management Sim, then the hospital will issue dedicated consoles just for running it. And the console manufacturer will lose money.

This is a problem even if a serious game manufacturer guarantees the sale of tens or even hundreds of thousands of units. The concern is that the serious games audience will still only buy one machine to run the one Sim.

Finally, there is the softer problem that the console manufacturers spend a lot of money on creating a countercultural brand, and selling "games that are good for you" might contradict that.

Instructor Controls. Some simulations give a centralized ability for the instructor to control or gate the progress of students in the simulation. For example, an instructor might assign students to access the preparation material and first practice level, but not move on to the rest of the simulation. With the right tools, the instructor could force that rather than just ask. Of course, reporting tools can give soft control—a student who knows that an unauthorized foray into level 2 will be reported back to the instructor may decide not to do it.

Educational Simulations Do Best to Produce Some Form of Artifact

Curriculum alignment and *ability to run in a given environment* may be the two absolutes for selecting simulation-based content. But there are some nice-to-haves as well.

When I was a cognitive science major at Brown University, my favorite professor had a funny complaint. He noted that, while he and his biology colleague could spend all day working in their respective labs, if they both were relatively unproductive, at least his biology colleague had a pile of dead animals to show for her work.

Likewise, when I talked to Will Wright about his success with The Sims, he told me how important it was that players could share artifacts, including houses and pictures, with each other. This made them feel like they were not wasting their time for the hours they put into the game.

Both educational simulation designers and the people who select them must likewise think about artifacts. What footprints in the digital sand are left behind, both deliberately and inevitably?

Some artifacts are fairly simple. Recorded grades and progress made are natural and traditional outputs of any learning program. But they are not enough.

Other artifacts can help a teacher or professor evaluate what the student did. This can include time lines or periodic screen snapshots. This is important—one instructor might supervise fifteen or twenty or even thirty students at a distance, so there is no way an instructor could watch everyone in real time. Some kind of summary of actions taken is essential.

Still other artifacts are more like The Sims. This gets closer to the social networking world. Players want to impress each other with their creativity. Where they did something unique or surprising, they want to show off. Now one form of this is just the high score. To be able to post that does increase engagement from the other students. In one academic deployment of SimuLearn's vLeader, teams of students carefully watched the highest score of other teams, and when breakthroughs were made, there was a flurry of activity from the competitive teams try to beat that. But as more creative approaches are captured and required by a simulation, the ability to share them with colleagues becomes ever more important.

At the simplest level, students can take screenshots to print or e-mail for credit. This can force an instructor to evaluate the mercurial but critical area of aesthetics.

One of the earliest complaints against e-learning was how unsatisfying it was to finish a program. So it is critical to note that social networking structures and rewards may provide a better motivation for accomplishment than pretty certificates or even an instructor's pat on the head.

Level Editor and Levels. A level editor is a utility for designers to efficiently build levels of a Sim. Level editors tend to import other assets, including art, animation, and music.

Level editors include the ability to combine:

- Animation
- Art assets
- AI
- Sound cues
- Physics models
- Scripts, including triggers and desired results and mission
- Units
- Items
- Attributes
- Maps
- Game mode

Smaller Sim projects may not bother with creating a level editor, and designers may instead just hard-code each level, but any complex game almost assuredly must take advantage of one.

Designers may also decide to release the level editor to a modding community.

Trust

Even if you attend a class at Wharton, a place oozing with prestige, the professors on the first day feel the need to build credibility as well. They may refer to a graduate who is a current successful CEO. They may refer to well-known alum whom they taught personally.

So if Wharton has that problem, you can imagine the challenge with Sims. Serious games and educational simulations must convince the player to work through the frustration, and any serious game must earn a certain degree of trust. This can come from a general sense of professionalism: the program behaves as it should, including loading, and it has no spelling errors or other red flags. Other techniques include prominently displaying logos and affiliations, or stating benefits.

Earning trust is the yin to the level design's yang. To both complement trust and reduce the need for it, good level design pulls the participants in, slowly teaching them necessary skills and always moderating the level of frustration to the appropriate level.

Play Testing

Play testing is the process of asking objective people to test a program while it is still in development.

Typically the test subjects are given goals to complete. The developers are not allowed to intervene, but they record all of the users' actions and might interview the users afterward. Preliminary rounds of play testing might involve developers and other subjective participants.

The developers take the input and modify the program, such as adding more pedagogical elements.

Also known as *usability testing.*

Author's note: I have found with any experiential and complex-systems–based learning program (such as one designed to teach project management), it is paramount to have the participants first get an exposure to the task, and then sleep on it before continuing. When students were not able to sleep on it, they were anxious and dissatisfied and learned less. In contrast, when the students did break up learning with sleep, their subconscious processed and assimilated the information, and they returned to the program the next morning without the trepidation they had shown the night before and in the control groups.

Said simply, the same program that took the same number of hours, if broken up with a good night's sleep, resulted in significantly better student enjoyment and, what is more important, organization and retention of the material.

The existence of this simple principle can hurt simulation deployments in at least three different ways. First, it can confound a training group's insistence on a "one-day" or "half-day" program, especially where students are unreliable in doing any pre-work (universities, thankfully, don't have this problem). It also can hurt some attempts to measure the effectiveness of simulations, as researchers often try to control all variables and shoe-horn an entire simulation experience into a single (often long) session. Finally, it can hurt the widespread adoption of a simulation if an evaluator tries to skim a simulation in a half-hour, and then "doesn't get it" and so doesn't support it.

As with a fine wine, authentic learning has to breathe a bit. A simple chunking process, where students experience at least thirty minutes to an hour of the interface in its entirety and at least some of the mechanics, even ideally getting a little stuck (which can be done as homework if the students are responsible and the deployers of the class have credibility), sleep on it, and then dive into harder levels, can be the difference between success and failure, between meaningful experience and frustration and confusion.

Bug List. A bug list is the current list of problems that have been identified in a computer program.

Typically, a bug list might include, for each bug identified, a ticket number, a severity level, and a description, as well as identification of a person or process to resolve it, classification of the type of problem, the person who reported it, the amount of resources it will take to resolve it, and current status.

Bug lists are maintained by the simulation developer. Resolving some bugs may involve a workaround.

Also called *defect report.*

Piloting. The final part of prep work is the pilot test. Simulations need to be piloted, that is, tested to hone the process of deployment. In fact, they need to be piloted twice. At a tighter and more constrained level, they need to be tested first to make sure all the technical bugs and process glitches are smoothed out. And then at a broader level, they need to be piloted conceptually with a class to make sure they do what they say they can do.

Technical Pilot. Actually, let me be more specific. A technical and process pilot will happen regardless of what you do. The only question is, do you want to pilot with a real class?

Technical pilots should, as close as possible, resemble the real-world environments in which the simulations will be deployed. It is not enough, for example, to test a deployment that will be international by testing it in different locations in the same building.

Different browsers should be used if the students will be using different browsers. If the simulation requires the use of a network, make sure that the different firewalls, including corporate if some students will access the Sim from their desks, will accept the network stream.

Stress testing is also critical. If thirty or fifty or a thousand students will be accessing the content simultaneously, then those are the conditions that need to be tested. Stress testing servers may be first done in one environment, and then distributed.

Also, in doing a pilot—especially with Web-based content—beware of caching. Caching is the process by which a local computer temporarily stores content that it pulls from the Internet, and it can be tricky for game developers because it conceals problems. For example, say the first time content is accessed remotely, the videos play choppily. The tech makes a few adjustments and thinks the problem has been solved. The remote test user plays the video a second time and it runs smooth as butter, so it seems as if the problem *is* solved. In fact, the performance only improved because the video is now cached in the local computer. When another student loads it up for the first time, the smoothness problems will recur. There are free tools such as CCleaner (www.ccleaner.com) that clean out all cookies and cached content, and it is often worth running one of those before any final technical test implementation.

A Quick Example and Warning

Cathy (a real person, but no last names will be given to protect the guilty) was an instructor who went to great lengths to troubleshoot a Sim deployment beforehand. She even used visualization before the event to plan ahead and think through all of the details. But, she mourns, "We did not do a pilot, which really meant that my first real group was the pilot. They were very patient as we worked through a lot of online issues, like the sound effects, so they lost out. We didn't do a pilot because of time, but we should have made the time for it."

Conceptual Pilots. The technical pilot is critical. Nonetheless, the pilot that more people will care about is the conceptual pilot. As the last step before a major rollout, take either a 10 percent or a thirty-person sample of representative participants (whichever is smaller), and run the program exactly as you intend the full program, but with a greater rigor in measuring the results at the end of the program.

The process of the conceptual pilot will map very closely, hopefully identically, to the final rollout. So in the spirit of recursiveness, imagine that a whole section is cut and pasted here.

The results of a pilot can be used either to support a go/no-go decision if an organization is evaluating a Sim, or to practice and calibrate the Sim before the full rollout (these are very different goals, by the way, and do impact the feel of the conceptual pilot if not the steps). If you make significant changes after calibrating the Sim, it's a really good idea to do another pilot deployment before a major rollout.

As a quick note, for reasons I will discuss later, when piloting a Sim, it is critical not to tell the participants what you're doing. "We are piloting this program; what do you think?" is the kiss of death. Instead, treat it as you expect to treat the major rollout, saying something along the lines of "This is a required program. Do your best."

Instructor Manual

Ideally a simulation comes with some type of instructor manual, facilitator guide, or other support (which may be online, and may be password protected). For the prospective purchaser, richer supporting content should tip the scale between two otherwise competing Sims. Typically, if a Sim is from a third-party vendor, it should come with significant support material. Meanwhile, if the community using the Sim is large enough, participants should have access to a forum where questions can be asked.

Here are some nice-to-have deliverables:

- *Slides and talking points:* Fully usable and editable decks of slides, with minimum formatting, that can be inserted into any class. This can include walkthroughs on how to install or access, use the interface, use any prepackaged self-evaluation tools, and submit results where necessary.
- *Details on the underlying system:* Simulations are often made up of rules and equations. Which rules are included should be documented, along with any relative weighting.
- *Technical support's Frequently Asked Questions list:* A list of the top twenty technical problems, with answers, culled from past deployments.

- *Examples of best, typical, and worst plays:* Either detailed screenshots and text or video clips showing a range of plays, with both annotations and analyses of actions.
- *Tips for debriefing:* A guide to how to debrief the simulation, if necessary. Typically, soft-skill simulations require two to three times the amount of space in the manual dedicated to helping instructors with debriefing than simulations focused on more technical skills do.
- *Cheat codes:* A list of keystrokes or other hidden ways for someone to evade the simulation's usual requirements, such as jump ahead, have unlimited resources, see equations or variables that are otherwise hidden, play any video clip, or see alternative paths.
- *Modding tips:* A list of places and examples where the simulation is easy to change.
- *Bibliography for the simulation:* The answer to the question, "How did you come up with the content for this thing?"
- *Further reading:* A list of books and articles where an interested person can go to get more information on the content overview in the Sim.
- *Examples of syllabi:* Three or four examples of places in typical course outlines where other professors have used the Sim. This material can typically be edited as well.

Harvard Business School Publishing's Denis Saulnier explains his philosophy in producing guides:

> They are meant to do two things. They are meant to be teaching notes, such as we use for HBSP's case studies. There are often no right or wrong answers to the Sims, so the guides list out the learning objectives, the most common and expected student outcomes, and ways of connecting them. We guard that content carefully and only give it out to authorized instructors (college faculty and corporate instructors, for example). But a second part of the guides are also the user's guide—akin to a software manual. This content should be, at least in theory, more readily available to anyone who's interested. But because they show so many screens from later on in the Sim, we have to be careful in their distribution as well.

Patch

A patch is a mini-application created and released by a publisher to fix problems and security with an application that has already been released and installed. Patches can also add additional content, similar to a mod.

Some programs check for updates automatically via the Web, while others require the user to find, download, and run (install) the patch. Some games have five to ten subsequent patches, especially games with advanced graphics or calibration and balancing requirements. Sims tend to be at the high end of patch needs, because in effect all Sims are beta software.

Patches can be viewed as continued support from a publisher, but also can prompt a publisher to release a buggy game with the plan to patch it later.

Web-based applications can be upgraded or improved without distributing a patch.

A Natural Process of Going from Educational Simulation to Game

Content may naturally follow four evolutionary steps. Here they are:

First, build a great model of content.

Second, build a great educational simulation. Put in all of the scaffolding and level design.

Third, build a great serious game. Watch and see what parts of the educational simulation are fun. Where do students put in extra time? Where do students explore the most? What parts are cool? Then, what steps are tedious and can be abstracted? Codify those changes and make the educational simulation into a serious game.

Fourth, build a pure game. Again, see where people spend the most time for fun. Further abstract the rules and settings. Put in graphics that are appropriate for the younger ages in your range.

27

EDUCATIONAL SIMULATION CREATION AND MILESTONES PART 2

Calibrating Skill Cones and Designing the Different Layers of Feedback

$\mathbf{S}$ims increase participants' ability to apply and combine the right actions throughout an experience. That is, participants in Sims are building a portfolio of skills and abilities as they travel through different levels and engage in different tasks and missions.

For each skill they:

- First learn about the skill, then
- Use the combination of actions in the right way, then
- Use the combination of actions in increasingly rigorous ways, trying to avoid failure, and then finally
- Combine them with other skills.

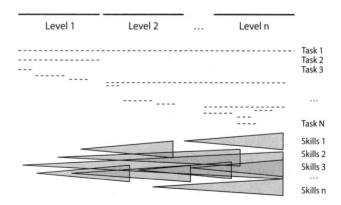

See the chart on the previous page. The cones represent skills, first as points, then getting broader as both the requirements of the situation and the ability of the participant increase, then mixing with others. The right use of skills cones minimizes the chance of accidental success. (The dashed lines represent tasks, with some tasks requiring many levels, and other less than a single level).

Skill Building and Feedback

Half Life 2, as one example, has ceiling-mounted creatures with long tongues that hang down and grab things to pull them up so they can eat them. One technique to inform the player might have been an encyclopedia-like screen giving some information about these creatures. Another would be to have a virtual colleague say something like, "Careful—those tongue creatures are hungry and once they grab you, it's over."

Instead, Half-Life 2 carefully builds the skills in the player, and then pushes it. The designers first show the player what these creatures do—in this case, by having an unwary crow get scooped up. Then they expose the player to a simple situation with a single creature. A few levels later, the player has to get through dozens of these creatures using increasingly clever techniques, including hybrid strategies learned from other parts of the game, and even enlisting the help of other characters.

This requires the careful use of feedback.

The following sections discuss some of the theories around feedback structures.

Emergent Learning

Emergent learning is a style of learning gained from trial and error, not reading manuals or books, listening to expert lectures, or other pedagogy-centric approaches. Emergent learning does not have to be ad hoc or left to chance; computer games rigorously develop emergent learning through level designs that require the development of specific skills.

Emergent learning requires practice in a low-cost-of-mistake and repeatable environment, such as a microcosm or educational simulation.

Constructivism

Constructivism is a theory of cognition that states that learning occurs when students build and calibrate their own models through performing actions, noting the results, and defining their own models of the system that connects them.

Designers of scalable formal learning experiences utilizing constructivism typically build some type of simulation of the target content or provide a relevant microcosm. Various degrees of pedagogy and coaching should still be used, especially giving participants the opportunity to redo and practice. Engaging the student is a high priority.

Feedback

In the context of learning, feedback is information regarding success or failure. At any given point, a participant in a Sim should be getting feedback on short-, medium-, and long-term actions, all simultaneously. These roughly translate to feedback on actions, feedback on strategic and systems performance (including units, maps, and processes), and feedback on results.

Action Feedback. Action feedback is designed to answer these questions for the player:

- Do I understand my options at any given moment?
- Can I map an action that I want to do or would do in real life to the virtual world?
- Do I know whether I did something really wrong?
- Do I know whether I did something really right?

Although students always want answers to the questions about getting things wrong or right, it isn't always practical to provide them. This is not really a problem, however, as that kind of information tends to be delayed or missing in real-world situations, too. Action feedback can fully meet these learning goals:

- Use of simple process
- Understanding options and tactics

Action feedback traditionally uses:

- Voices
- Graphics
- Cut scenes

Strategic and Systems Feedback. Systems feedback is much more difficult to provide than feedback around either actions or results. This is because the system is invisible and can often only be influenced indirectly.

Strategic and systems feedback may seek to answer these questions (depending on the learning objectives, content, and genre):

- Can I influence or optimize one (primary systems) variable?
- Do I know if I am on the right track?
- Do I know if I have blown any chance of success?
- Do I know where I am losing ground or need to triage?
- Do I know if I am doing something rather wrong?
- Do I know if I am doing something rather right?
- Do I know what my long-term goal is?
- How does what I do maximize some part of the system?
- How do I traverse some part of the map?
- How do I build some structure?
- How do I get some critical competency or tool?
- How do I control some territory?
- How do I build some important personal relationships?
- Given my strategy, am I executing against it?

Strategic and systems feedback meets these learning goals:

- How actions impact a system
- Executing complicated process

Strategic and systems feedback uses

- Triggers at milestones reached
- On-screen graphs and maps
- Cut scenes

Results Feedback. Completing any chunk of content delivers a result. Results feedback answers these player questions (depending on the learning objectives, content, or genre):

- Did I win?
- Can I optimize or influence many (primary systems) variables?
- Did I build what I wanted to build?
- Did I get to where I wanted to go?
- What does victory actually look like?
- Do I understand the trade-offs in my victory?

Results feedback meets these learning goals:

- Understanding complex systems
- Use of time
- Execution of complex strategy

Results feedback uses

- After action reviews
- Complex charts and graphs
- Multiple analyses of plays
- Advice for future plays
- Scores and aggregations
- Consequences of actions taken
- Cut scenes

When learners first engage the Sim (such as at the first level), they are focused on action feedback. But after a few iterations, either replaying or continuing on to advanced levels, the learners increasingly focus on results (which is especially true at the last level).

On Practice

It is one thing to remember, another to know. Remembering is merely safeguarding something entrusted to the memory; knowing means making everything your own. (Aliud autem est meminisse, allud scire. Meminisse est commissam memoriae custodire. At contra, scire est et sua facere.)

Seneca, *Epistulae ad Licilium*, Epis. cxx, sec iv.

Or, to paraphrase Abe Lincoln, who said "Give me six hours to chop down a tree and I will spend the first four sharpening the axe," I would say, "Give me six hours to learn something and I will spend the last four practicing."

Concepts that seem simple, narrow, and isolated when written are deep, complex, and extendable when modeled in simulations.

Consider these instructions: "When playing pinball, you can nudge the machine to keep the ball from going out of play. But if you push the machine too hard, you will tilt the machine, ending that play."

That is incredibly easy to write. It is incredibly easy for a student to "learn" that statement to the point of being able to write it on a test. But to nudge a pinball machine at the right time takes skill and practice. Even the best pinball player in the world cannot always do it perfectly. If you modified a machine to emphasize pinball nudging, any traditional instructor would say, "That seems like a lot of work to teach one simple statement." If you were becoming a pinball expert, however, you would absolutely need the deeper approach.

Now, few care that much about pinball. But all expertise has a nudge component (how hard and when do you push when inspiring your team to deliver, dealing with difficult people, getting the right amount of funding). Consider simple (from a linear perspective) statements like these: "Slow the boat down when approaching the dock" or "In the design process, solicit input from existing customers and potential customers."

Ken Kupersmith, co-founder at SimuLearn, notes, "Sometimes information alone is all that is needed. In basic sales training, learners should be reminded to 'ask for the business.' But when trying to decide when is the right time to ask for it, how much of the business to ask for, who are the most important decision makers and even what criteria are important to them, you might want to practice that complex behavior in many iterations with lots of variations."

"In the military, everyone talks about attacking from a flank," Robert Carpenter, deputy director of simulation development in Australia's Land Warfare Development Centre, gives as an example. "But actually setting up the conditions, taking into account the terrain and enemy actions, separates the great commanders from the rest."

Jake Stahl, director of client delivery systems at Purdue Pharma, puts it this way: "If Joe Montana said to me that throwing a football is simple, I would agree that from his perspective it is. But can he explain to me in words how to do it, or does he need to show me? Once he shows me, do I now know, or do I need to practice? Once I practice, have I perfected it or do I need to fine-tune?"

And finally, when is my skill good enough, or should I always be striving for improvement? Even professional baseball players have a spring training every year to practice and improve, and often they practice during the season when they do not schedule a game.

Simple theories take practice to use successfully, and the simplest rules when applied intuitively are more powerful than the broadest database or the most complex process. This inverts entire curricula.

28

THE NECESSARY STUDENT EXPERIENCE OF FRUSTRATION AND RESOLUTION

For a student, using a simulation is different from almost any other learning experience, except perhaps real life. In many ways, the experience is traumatic, as new mental muscles replace old.

Even when the class is over, students feel spent, mentally sore, but not always satisfied. They aren't sure what they have learned. They feel something, but not the buzz of motivation or the list of new facts they are used to carrying away. Even out in the real world, it is often peers, customers, and people above the student who see the biggest improvement in applied skills.

Therefore, the role of coaching and setting up a simulation is critical.

This chapter discusses the key concepts.

Frustration-Resolution Pair

Experience is the worst teacher because it gives you the test before the lesson.

—ATTRIBUTED TO MULTIPLE SOURCES

The frustration-resolution pair is a moment of learning that is marked first by being frustrated at not being able to do something that you want to do, and then resolving that frustration.

What is true of any transformation (from getting a big promotion to moving to a better house), is that things get worse before they get better, even when the transformation is sought after and desired. New clarity only follows frustration. New power comes from not being able to do things the way you have in the past.

When learning to ride a bike, or swim, or drive, or speak a foreign language, the process is uneven, filled with lows and highs, awkwardness and grace, frustrations and resolutions. This is more true, albeit plagued with noise, with big skills.

There are first moments when any learner wants to give up. Then there are "Aha!" moments when everything starts clicking together. The exaltation is then followed by another, more interesting frustration, and the cycle continues and the learner's capabilities increase. The frustration-resolution sensation is the sensation of new mental muscle forming, and means that the new learning will be around for a long time.

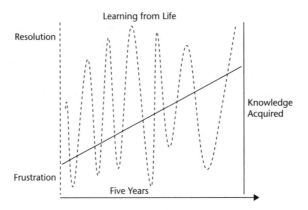

Students even have difficulty summing up what was learned, to themselves and to others. Words just trivialize the learning. But what we have learned through frustration and resolution sticks with us. Hence the knowledge of how to ride a bike is there forever, but knowledge of the year the Magna Carta was signed fades out five seconds before the next written test question calls for it.

Pedagogical elements can reduce the depths of frustration, but often at a cost of reducing the impact of the learning. Therefore, where the learning is just a gateway, such as how to use the interface, high pedagogy should be used. But where the learning corresponds with a learning objective, more restraint should be used.

Sims, and educational simulations is particular, only minimally smooth out the peaks and valleys of frustration and resolution. Instead, they compress them and make them more predictable.

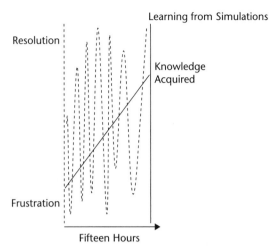

The valleys present a bit of problem, however, not in the learning (where they are critical), but in the expectation of the Sim experience. Some traditional areas of frustration are as follows:

- *Learning how to use the interface:* This is not just a way of accessing the program, but a whole new view of often familiar actions and processes. Worse, if the simulation is real-time, things happen very quickly and can be hard just to track.
- *Change:* Students often first want to do things in the Sim the way they do them in real life, and also have difficulty radically changing a pattern of actions that has worked so far in earlier levels.
- *Progress:* Students might try hard to get better results, doing things over and over again, but still hit walls. They reach a combination of simultaneous frustration and boredom.

Threshold to Quit

The *threshold to quit* is the point at which an individual will abandon a given education program.

This point differs for different end learners, but if the experience dips below the personal threshold, the learner will opt out of the course with a negative bias.

The threshold to quit is set deeper (that is, people are less likely to quit) when someone cares about the results, when the program is considered worthwhile, and when using the program is easy and entertaining.

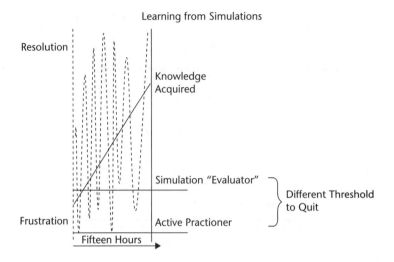

The threshold to quit is set less deep (that is, people are more likely to quit) when they are in evaluation mode, when they do not see the relevance of the effort, or when no one cares whether they complete the program. Some cultures, including the military, have an institutional deep threshold to quit.

Here are some of the factors that raise the threshold, making it more likely a student will quit:

- The student is evaluating or surveying the material.
- The program has little support.
- Expectations for the Sim experience have been poorly set.

And here are some factors that lower the threshold, making it less likely a student will quit:

- A live coach or facilitator is provided.
- The material is necessary for the students, and they understand that.
- The program has a lot of credibility.
- The students have a contract.
- The students are being graded in an academic setting or ordered to take it in a military setting.

Student Revolt

During a simulation deployment, often about halfway through, some students are likely to form a faction to reject the simulation, often on the grounds of perceived infidelity or inapplicability. Revolts are often initiated by people who define their value as having deeper knowledge of the topic, such as experts-turned-consultants.

Unlike the corrosive issues of the bottom 20 percent or the need to fail a participant discussed later in this chapter, a student revolt can be useful. It provides an opportunity to vent, and is an opportunity for coach or facilitator to show progress, restate goals, and map out the rest of the formal learning program.

Student Contract and Performance Expectations

A student contract is a document that contains a series of rules of behavior for participants in a formal learning program. Students might have to sign and commit to the rules as a condition of attending the program.

Typically any such contract has the following features:

- Ethical rules, for example, all work has to be one's own, and students will not harass other students.
- Time commitments for, example, students will spend six hours a week doing class preparation and will attend all classes.
- Grading rules.
- Process rules, for example, all assignments must be turned in on time, no e-mail is to be used during class.
- Cooperative effort rules, for example, information may be shared outside the program only under stated conditions.
- Waiver. Students acknowledge that they may stumble upon objectionable content (such as in online worlds).
- Participation expectations, for example, students will actively participate in group sessions.

In most cases, contracts are one-way. The requirements (input) of the students are very specific. The benefits to the students (output) of the program are vague or nonexistent.

The Bottom 20 Percent

In almost any program, some students—typically about 20 percent—do not buy into the learning experience. Instead, they mentally drop out. When asked a reasonable question, they don't know what is going on.

In a classroom, this group can sit (sometimes virtually) in the back, and most instructors quietly ignore them. They doodle or write e-mail. In an environment with simulations based on constant "doing," this group can become vocal opponents, criticizing the validity of the simulation.

In some programs, these bottom 20 percent are failing.

The common assumption from most designers is that this group needs more pedagogical elements. While this may be partially true, this increase may come at the cost of learning for the rest of the group. And about one-quarter of that 20 percent are students who want to be leaders, but do not see the opportunity in the simulation structure. These people, initially loud complainers, can be turned if put into a role of influence. The students in the bottom 20 percent have the option of persevering respectfully or being failed.

Failing a Participant

Failing a participant involves directing someone to stop attending a formal learning program and issuing no credit (or an "incomplete") for any work done up to that point.

Author's note: When should instructors fail (a.k.a. fire) students?

This is a more challenging issue in the corporate and government world, where training is more of a service, than in academia or the military, where it is a requirement.

This question also gets more interesting when simulations are introduced, and there is significantly more work required from a student than just showing up. Courses can also be several sessions, not just one.

To further muddy the waters, some people view completion rate as a critical metric. And any pure e-learning course never automatically jettisons a student.

But if students weakly approach a course, they go through the motions but don't push, then that messes up any ROI and 360-degree measurements. The passive students, the bottom 20 percent, also can become the biggest critics, resolving their own dissonance by lowering the view of the course instead of raising their own expectations for growth.

The Role of Honesty

Honesty: The ability to communicate about strengths and weaknesses across a relevant balanced scorecard ("the whole truth").

Honesty to and about self is necessary for the personal development of any big skills.

A shot of honesty, such as being the target of a 360-degree review, can be very helpful to some people—especially senior managers—in preparation for a formal learning program.

Author's note: I used to say that the most important ingredient in a formal learning program is motivation of the students. Having pored through thousands of results of recent big-skills programs, I think the most important ingredient is the honesty of the students.

I have also found that some cultures crush honesty. Some cultures pounce on any sign of weakness. Some people and groups are defensive. These cultures tend to evolve and grow the least, although they are busy in the short term.

29

EVALUATION STRATEGIES AND THE ANALYSIS OF LEARNING

Evaluation strategies are activities to analyze the success of formal learning programs. There are different approaches in creating an appropriate simulation evaluation strategy. Of course they should be around the core learning goals (one philosophy of instructional design is to create the test first, then the material to prepare for it) and program goals. But, pragmatically, they tend to be heavily influenced by some primary variables:

- Effectiveness and accuracy
- Cost (including political cost) and effort
- Caring about what a student *knows* differently or what a student *does* differently (or even, as in a certification program, whether a student knows enough or is able to do something sufficiently well)
- Whether the student follows the prescribed process or gets the right results
- Whether the student understands the content only in one context or can improvise and apply it outside of the context
- Whether to measure an end goal with many inputs or an intermediate goal with one single input (achieving a balanced and productive life; understanding Chaucer)
- Whether the aim is evaluation of the program or evaluation of the students
- Political and program expediency (so taking six months to evaluate a program may be necessary to show true effectiveness, but inappropriate for a course that has to make a difference to people in two months)

Here are some of the subsequent questions in designing an evaluation strategy:

- *Post only or also pre?* Do you evaluate what the students started off knowing, or just what they know after the end of the program? Any kind of certification program (programming, sexual harassment) just cares what the student knows at the end of the program. But any Sim program manager also wants to know what the magnitude of the shift is. P. S. Taking a pretest is miserable for some students.

- *Control group or just students?* Do you evaluate a group of people who did not go through the program, or just the students who did go through the program? Do you evaluate students who went through an alternative program? When multiple components (such as mentors and communities) are used, is the impact of each permutation measured? Note that any scientific validation requires a control group to create a baseline, but that often takes a lot of will on the part of the program manager.

- *Students only or people around students?* Do you just use the students' own knowledge or insights, or do you tap the knowledge and insights of the people around the student (so-called 360-degree reviews)? Students themselves tend to overvalue new knowledge and undervalue new actions, while the communities around the student are exactly the opposite.

- *Indicating or direct measurement?* Do you look at some sort of objective measure? Success of student? Retention of student? Promotion of student?

- *Evaluate right after the program, or weeks or months out?* Do you administer any post-program evaluation the moment the program is over? Again, this radically overemphasizes the fast-decaying new knowledge acquired, while making impossible the evaluation of new behavior (unless the program has occupied several weeks, so new behavior might have already shown up). The further out you go (one week, five weeks, five months), the greater the value of any recorded impact, but the harder it is to get results (compliance rate goes down), the harder it is to use those results to shape the evolution of the program itself, and the more other variables get in the way. The larger the group involved in evaluating the student (especially with 360-degree feedback), the more time you need (if someone only meets with the student twice a month, it takes longer for him or her to see real changes).

- *Standardized multiple choice or short answers?* Do you ask everyone the same multiple-choice questions? This makes it easy to compare results. Or do you allow short answers? This adds more personality and allows for factors beyond the standardized. It gathers anecdotes of success, which are great if (shudder) subjective.

- *Automated or done via interviewer?* Do you create an online test and questionnaire? Or do you have real people involved? The first is cheaper, but has a lower compliance rate, while the second is both more expensive and more nuanced.

- *Test versus reflection?* Do you ask questions like "What is the formal definition of ___?" Are you interested in making the students prove that they have learned something? While students who go through simulation experiences do understand the concepts very well, simpler programs may get the same result. One way is to ask for definitions, but another richer approach is to present mini situations and give the player the ability to decide what to do.

- *Knowledge versus behavior?* Or (and?) are you asking questions like "How good are you at   ?" and "How often in the last two weeks have you found yourself   ?"
- *Do you want students to look at their own experience and draw conclusions?* This subjective reflection in a pre- and post-situation can backfire. I have had students think they were a 4 out of 5 in leadership skills in the pre-test. Then they went through the program, learned a lot, but also realized- how much more they had to learn, and then in the post-test claim they were a 3 out of 5. Through the program, they seemingly lost a point of leadership skills! (One option around that is to have students re-evaluate their pre-program opinions in a post-test: Rather than just asking, "How good a leader are you?" in both the pre and post, I also like to ask in the post-test, "How good a leader were you before the program?" This can be compared against the respondent's original answer, often revealing interesting levels of change.)
- *Student opinion of the class?* Through years of schooling, we are very aware when we learn new facts. We are less aware when we increase our own abilities. It is very possible for a student to go through a Sim without learning any new facts—but developing skills that make it possible to apply that prior knowledge. Thus the student reviewing the program might say, "This was all pretty basic," while the student's colleagues see a new person.

Evaluating the Student

Student evaluations take a variety of forms. No one is right or wrong, but each fills in a specific role that may be required depending on the needs of the program.

Tests and Quizzes

One evaluation strategy involves tests and quizzes: formalized, typically timed and single-player activities that force students to demonstrate their short-term knowledge of learning goals in order to get a grade.

Tests and quizzes in a Sim can create forced moments of reflection. While most break any fourth wall, some questions can be asked in the form of an alert, or from the perspective of another character.

Related topics: "Standardized Test Results," later in this chapter; "Scores and Grades," in Chapter Sixteen; and "Frame Games," in Chapter Two.

Community Activity

Any community activity or community-created content can be graded.

Journals

If you have the students keep journals while they're playing the simulation, the journal itself can be graded for each student. The journal can discuss the experience in the simulation, including frustrations met and resolutions delivered. Ideally, the students may also discuss their experience in the real world as seen through the lens of the simulation. So, for example, if the simulation is on leadership, students may compare their experiences in the simulation to their experiences of a real leadership situation—on a sports team, at work, or in the community.

Written Reports

In some cases, students can write papers about their experience in a simulation after the fact. This is the most comfortable option for most professors. The papers themselves could be about why the players did what they did—justifying their actions. The students can also pull in traditional references to other literature, further making a comfortable fit into traditional academic environment. One variation of this is to have the students present to the class.

Evaluating the Program

Simulations and serious games need to be evaluated, too, and must pass certain thresholds. This evaluation can take any of the forms listed in this section.

Glint in the Eye

A formal learning program can be rated based on the expression of excitement and depth of knowledge in its students. The emotional tone after a rich instructional program is unmistakable. While hard to quantify, it may be the most telling metric.

Anecdote

Anecdotes can be used as part of an evaluation strategy (unlike inspirational examples). Consider this anecdote, which is an unedited comment from a real student, describing a moment of leadership learning:

While I am not a leader in the sense of management in my place of work, I recently used some lessons I learned from Virtual Leader in a department meeting. My department is managed by a powerless supervisor, who maintains little control in the actual organization and tends to micro-manage the department that she manages. She is very much so a directive leader. Our meetings follow an agenda, and little discussion is made about any topic. The meetings rarely produce any results, instead regurgitating previous topics and telling about upcoming events. Meetings wane between too relaxed or extremely tense, and no work is accomplished.

In the recent meeting, a recruiter was reporting about the high level of job vacancies in the organization. The manager wanted to know why there was such a high vacancy, but did so in a very accusatory way. The recruiter was taken aback, became very tense, as did others in the room. I was internally clicking on the red zone of the manager, but instead decided to literally click on the green zone of the recruiter. I complimented her on her ability to fill positions with qualified candidates in the past. I asked her what her approaches had been that made her successful, what the previous year's vacancy rate was. The recruiter relaxed a little, and she discussed what she had done in the past, we found that the previous year's vacancy at this time last year was also high.

As the entire group talked about the issue, the tension level leveled off into the productive range, and we began to discuss recruitment strategies and ways we could assist the recruiter. This is something that has never been discussed in a department meeting, only between the recruiter and manager.

By the end of the meeting, the group had come up with some great ideas, we all felt like we had all been a part of a successful meeting. Because my participative leadership style is very different from the manager's directive leadership style, under normal circumstances I may not have stepped out of my comfort zone and taken this approach, but decided this was the moment to put the lessons learned to use. I showed my manager that I do have the capability she thought I was lacking to be successful in the department.

DATA ENTRY TECHNICIAN

360-Degree Measurements

A 360-degree measurement is an aggregate profile of a person (called "the target") made up of interviews with or questions answered by people "all around" the target (thus the term 360-degree), including with positions of different authority. If the target is an employee, the input might come from supervisor, peers, subordinates, and customers. If the target is a student, the input might come from classmates, teammates, family, and instructors.

By taking two sets of 360-degree feedback six months apart, one can measure behavior changes. This is critical because students themselves rarely appreciate the extent of the transformation they have undertaken. It is only the people around them, the peers, customers, subordinates, and supervisors, who rate their change as transformational and comment most on the cessation of bad habits and the explosion of good ones.

This approach is helpful training senior managers or other individuals who might be hard to teach due to their strong, uh, self-confidence. The results from 360-degree measurement introduce a level of honesty and awareness of "holes" that is critical for growth, as targets learn they may not be perfect after all, despite their past success.

This represents one of the more advanced measurement techniques that reward application of middle skills and big skills.

Student Promotion

Formal learning programs can be evaluated based on the organizational advancement of participants after, and in part as a result of, the program. Promotion is a great metric if you can get credit for it.

Promotion of students often requires the learning goal of increased professional value or the desired result of achieving a certification level.

Using the metric of promotion of a student as a measurable result requires a longer time span than most other metrics.

Staff and Sponsor Promotion

Formal learning programs can also be evaluated externally based on the organizational advancement of the people (including sponsors, program managers, and instructors) responsible for delivering them.

Author's note: There is only one training metric that matters: the person responsible for the training program is promoted. Any other metric, be it smilesheets or increased organizational productivity or stock price, is only ammunition. Now, clearly we need to tap into pure research. We need to pilot. But there are at least three reasons why this is the critical metric.

1. You can't do any good if you get fired.
2. Your clients, be they sales teams or management, live in a world of results. That is the language they speak, and you are too removed from them if you are not speaking this language.
3. Getting yourself promoted is the ultimate form of accountability. I have known too many people who called themselves "purists" or "in it for the good of other people" or "researchers" or "visionaries" or "business partners" or who like to shake their fists at the gods, saying of everyone else that "they just don't get it" or "they are part of the old model," who really just soft-talked themselves out of sweating the details, worrying about the repeated, incrementally improved implementations, and delivering real value.

Click Throughs

The action of a participant in clicking on a link and going to a desired location can be evaluated as proof of interest and engagement.

For example, advertisers might pay a Web site for a click through to get potential customers to the advertiser's site, as opposed to simply exposing them to a message (such as cost per thousand views) as with television, or actually making a sale (with a commission-based fee).

Clicking through open-ended material is harder than just reading a book because more choices must be made, but potentially there is more ownership of the information. The steward of any Web site or other form of linked material might track participants' paths through the links they clicked.

Compare with "Mouse-Over" in Chapter Seventeen.

Related topics: "Cost Per Thousand Views," in Chapter Twenty; "Completion Rate," later in this chapter.

What Went into the Simulation

Some people, especially academics, prefer to measure a program by validating the inputs into the program. Thus they will endorse a simulation if the inputs are externally researched and proven effective. Footnotes ("it should work") trump results ("it seems to work") for some.

Both Evaluating the Student and Evaluating the Program

Some measures do both; they evaluate the student and the program. These are not inherently better than the more focused approaches already discussed, but they may suit certain programs. Again, choose your approach carefully.

Observation of Active Behavior

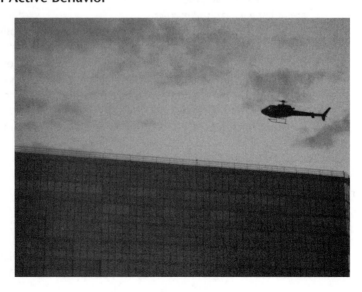

Actions that can be observed in a person, and specifically can be observed when changed, can provide an index as to what the program is accomplishing. As a result, recording the amount of either changes in active behavior or adherence to a procedure is a technique for evaluating a formal learning program.

For example, it might be easy to see whether a person is following a different research process, but hard to tell whether a person is listening differently.

Watching to see whether someone chokes or does not choke under pressure is an easy case of watching active behavior to see if learning occurred. (See "Coping Without Choking" in Chapter Twenty-Two.)

Standardized Test Results

Standardized tests strive to consistently and objectively evaluate awareness and analysis or declarative knowledge among students, often through presenting hundreds of multiple-choice questions. Standardized test results can be used to compare an instructor, a student or participant, or a whole formal learning program against larger populations.

Standardized test results support the program goal of measurable results, including in raw improvement, as well as certification and compliance (getting everyone up past a threshold level). Meanwhile, frame games can be used to reduce the inevitable tension that accompanies standardized tests.

Drawbacks of Standardized Tests

Most standardized tests today measure very little very well. They cannot measure procedural knowledge, middle skills, big skills, professional value, or mastery level. (But other than that. . . .) As a result, any instructor or administrator who wants to game the educational process for the sake of personal promotion would allocate time and resources away from the skills that matter most and toward skills that are most easily tested. Sound familiar?

Success as Success

Success within the Sim can be taken as an argument that real learning has occurred. (*Quis custodiet ipsos custodes* that, buddy.) Success itself can be an evaluation strategy, based on the argument that success within an immersive learning simulation is sufficient proof that learning goals have been met.

Two conditions encourage this philosophy within a formal learning program: fidelity of the Sim and lack of access to the real target experience. For example, a flight simulator might be at 99.4 percent fidelity and therefore be safely regarded as sufficient. Similarly, if the Sim is around handling a nuclear reactor meltdown or incident of workplace violence, it has to be regarded as sufficient because the target experiences are not accessible on demand—and everyone hopes they won't be accessible at all.

Of course, there is always the issue of ease of deployment as well. (I am not saying training people are necessarily lazy; some just have more important things to do than make sure the workforce is trained.)

Completion Rate

The completion rate—the number of people finishing a program, compared to either the number who started it or who were supposed to start it—is often used as a measurement of success. Students who do not complete a course may have left the program, or may have been failed. The completion rate is often tracked with a learning management system (referred to in the literature as an LMS).

It's possible to increase the completion rate in many ways:

- Make completion highly relevant to a job.
- Make completion highly relevant to an interest.

- Have the student work hard to get into the program.
- Use a great, charismatic instructor.
- Increase access.
- Make completion relevant to a future job or promotion.
- Make the program address a current pain.
- Increase the number of game elements (especially useful if the targets do not intrinsically care about the learning objectives).
- Make completion part of a certification program.
- Have a "higher-up" introduce the program and track the progress.
- Shorten the program.
- Make the program one classroom day.
- Reduce the intellectual burden.
- Make the "higher-ups" complete the program.
- Make the program mandatory.
- Reduce the number of other programs required.
- Use a coach.
- Pay people to take the program, or fine people who do not take it.
- Prevent people who might drop out from taking the course.

The metric of completion rate, according to many program sponsors, aggregates program relevancy, target satisfaction with the course and its methodology and conditions, and passive advocacy for others to take the program. When training meets a legal compliance requirement, completion rate is typically all that is necessary.

As a measure, completion rate has a number of problems:

- Many targets only need some of the content.
- The metric rewards a captive audience, not the successful achievement of any learning goals.
- There is almost always going to be a bottom 20 percent.
- Making the course accessible to everyone waters down the content, making it less useful and powerful to those that might need it most.

Simulations and other nonlinear content bring a different spin to the notion of completion rate. A student can go through a branching story two or three times, complete the course, but not access every permutation or link of the story.

Completion rate is also known as *sheep dipping, butts in seats,* and *retention rate.* It is the opposite of *drop-out rate.*

Author's note: Completion rate is a good, red-meat area for corporate training people. Most hate it, asking "Why measure completion rate," and I agree that it is problematic. On one hand, the highest compliment I can get on any of my books is that the reader finished it. To me, that means that I wrote something that was both relevant and fun to read. (As a comparison, the average book is read only for twenty-two pages.) On the other hand, I would not expect anyone to read this entire book. I would hope he or she would skim around, get what is needed, and move on.

A Higher Standard

It seems unfair that any new educational approach has to pass a bar that no traditional methodology could ever meet. Sims, for example, are asked to be free, cheat-proof, easy to use, and deliver transformational results, while being free of bias. Sometimes it seems that new approaches become the repository of all that people hope education should be. As unfair as that is, a well known adage in Silicon Valley is that any new technology has to be ten times better than the technology it seeks to replace. To me, that seems to make a lot more sense. I can't promise that Sims will turn us all into supermen, but ten times better than classroom alone—that I can handle.

30

CONCLUSION

Banishing Today's Classrooms, Curricula, Term Papers, Training Programs, Business Plans, and Linear Analysis to the Intellectual Slums and Backwaters to Which They So Richly Belong

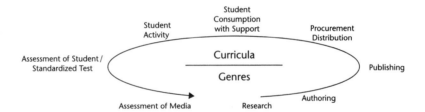

As I wrote in the Introduction, this book is designed to look like a helpful guide for a small group of simulation authors seeking to ply their craft, and I hope it is. Underneath that pleasant veneer, however, it is an attack on all of the educational and knowledge industries, from schools to book publishers to business analysis. The true implication of this material is nothing less than a manifesto for the overthrow of the intellectual legacy of civilization to date.

But, of course, this revolution is not going to be easy. We have a complex and interdependent network of processes optimized around linear and passive content. Parts of the phalanx include

- Authoring environments such as Microsoft Word, PowerPoint, and QuarkXPress
- Publishing models of books and magazines with text and pictures
- Online and traditional bookstores
- Students whose primary activity is writing
- Tests that ask only for facts and analysis

Any incursion into one of the pieces can be overwhelmed by the others.

Imagine a great new simulation: How will students buy it? How does it fit into the classroom model? How do teachers know how to support it? And how will it impact traditional test scores?

Imagine I am an author, and I want to build a simulation on stewardship or innovation. How do I tap others' knowledge and research? What existing research is even helpful? What genre do I use to shape the Sim? What authoring environment can I use? How do I test it? How do I sell it?

Two rotten cores hold the whole model together:

- The first core is curricula. Right now, schools teach history, analysis, and symbolic manipulation. This is because what is taught is limited by what can be taught.
- The second core is genres. The industrial education complex supports the genres of classroom lecture, books, papers, and tests.

Both are so ingrained that they are seldom questioned. By deconstructing the two cores of curricula and genres, education can evolve. As long as these pieces of the phalanx are firmly in place, education will remain in its current holding pattern. But at some time in the near future, one country is going to blow up the whole model and do it right.

The impact could be huge.

If Books Liberated us from Kings, can Sims Liberate us from CEOs?

Books and widespread literacy liberated people from kings (riffing on Jefferson). Part of the argument was that with literacy, kings and their priest supporters were no longer the only people who could read religious texts. Moreover, the middle class gained their own widespread access to both history and the inner monologues of others. Once the cat was out of the bag, so to speak, the context of civilization changed. People could understand kings, and therefore criticize kings, and ultimately bring down kings.

Fair enough. But can books liberate us from the CEOs? While kinglike in many ways, their power is based on more than texts. CEOs today are the people with the most contacts, the best reputations, and the greatest adeptness in certain critical skills and talents necessary to run large organizations. In thinking about CEOs, most of us go back and forth between admiration and resentment. But mostly, we are confused. What do they do all day? We can't judge them because we don't understand them. And reading Proust or even Thomas Watson Jr. won't help us.

So I wonder, will it be Sims that break down that wall? By playing at being CEOs and other leaders, will we better understand them? Will we empathize not with the person but with the performance in project management, leadership, and stewardship? Will we better see some CEOs as being masterful and others as being ham-fisted? And once that happens, will we become meaningfully intolerant of at least some CEOs?

Further, will Sims allow more people to both work and shop in a CEO-less environment? If I know how to create and deliver value, do I really need to swear fealty to my liege, I mean, sign away so many rights to a corporate structure?

Books and their ability to let people "learn to know" had their role in creating the modern concepts of freedom and democracy. What will Sims and learning-to-do next bring?

APPENDIX

SIMULATION CASE STUDIES

Do Sims Work Better Than Traditional Instruction?

A current critical question among those concerned with the future of education is, Do game-like Sims really teach? Beyond that, people ask, Do serious games have a social impact? How do immersive learning simulations compare to classroom lectures, Web pages, and books? Do educational simulations actually improve big skills, including what one knows and what one does? And is there a good case study for soft skills or leadership?

To help answer this question, one practiceware leadership simulation, SimuLearn's Virtual Leader (and the updated vLeader 2007) has been rigorously studied. To ensure the objectiveness of each piece of research, the leadership simulation was completely handed off to highly credible third-party evaluators, who did their own deployment, measurement, and analysis. Then the independent evaluators went public with their results, producing research papers, academic dissertations, published case studies, or speeches outside SimuLearn's influence.

This has now been done in academic, corporate, and military settings. The results are consistent—and surprising to proponents of traditional classroom training.

Across multiple third-party studies, statistically significant (and often unprecedented when compared to traditional models) research results show that, in learning leadership skills through Virtual Leader

- The students have become better at using their emotional intelligence. (See "A Sim Develops Emotional Intelligence" in this appendix.)

- The students do use the leadership skills they have learned when measured six months after they learned them in contrast to traditional examples of executive education content and delivery that are quickly forgotten. (See "Executives in Class—From 'Recalling' to 'Applying' New Knowledge" in this appendix.)
- The students have become about 20 percent more productive, through using their supervisory skills, when measured five months after the program, compared to their peers who did not go through the program. (See "Fortune 100 Company: An Extra Day Every Week of Work" in this appendix.)
- The non-context-specific but real-time practiceware is more effective than turn-based (but Army-specific) branching stories. (See "U.S. Military Academy—Self-Paced Practiceware Deployment Beats Traditional Approach" in this appendix.)

This validates the vision of game-like simulations teaching both old content better and entirely new types of content in significantly greater richness than traditional methods, and it paves the way for new generations of learning-to-do media.

A Sim Develops Emotional Intelligence

Stanley Michael Sidor (for a dissertation submitted in partial fulfillment of the requirements for the degree of doctor of education at the University of Central Florida) measured the emotional intelligence of three hundred students in a college introductory management class before and after participating in the Virtual Leader leadership simulation game.

Sidor's analysis of the measures of emotional intelligence revealed a statistically significant increase in respondent scores in three of the four subscales after the respondents participated in the simulation:

1. Self-emotion appraisal (SEA), $p = .031$ (I have a good understanding of my emotions, up 22.2 percent)
2. Others emotion appraisal (OEA), $p = .002$ (I have a good understanding of the emotions of people around me, up 62.85 percent)
3. Regulation of emotion (ROE), $p = .002$ (I have good control of my emotions, up 44.12 percent)

The emotional intelligence construct, use of emotion (UOE), $p = .061$ (I would always encourage myself to try my best, up 6.91 percent), also went up, but did not demonstrate statistical significance.

The percentage increase represents average increases in the "strongly agree" category of the survey.

Process

Potential student participants were invited to participate in the study and were given the informed consent document. Participant rights, voluntary consent, and the right to withdraw consent were explained to participants prior to distributing the Wong and Law Emotional Intelligence Survey (WLEIS). The survey instrument was presented to the students by the researcher and supporting faculty. Students electing to participate completed the first survey instrument in class and returned the instrument either in class or via a postage-paid return envelope.

After return of the completed survey, participants were given or mailed the disk for the Virtual Leader software. Upon receipt of the software, participants were assisted in installing the software to classroom computers and were provided with installation instructions for their home computers. Installation and simulation technical assistance was provided by the researcher via telephone and e-mail. Participants were instructed to complete each of the first four Levels of the Virtual Leader simulation one time and to complete each of the next five Levels three times each. Participants were provided e-mailed reminders by the researcher and an e-mailed acknowledgment of their progress by the researcher.

Upon completion of the simulation, participants completed a second administration of the WLEIS and returned it to the researcher through collection by the classroom instructor or via a postage-paid return envelope. Results of the survey were provided to any participant who requested the information.

Implications

This study focused upon measurement of learning gains in the leadership skills related to emotional intelligence as the result of participating in the Virtual Leader simulation. Those leadership and emotional intelligence skills related to relationship and influence development were individually practiced over multiple iterations in a computerized environment laden with workplace context. Participants demonstrated statistically significant gains in their emotional intelligence scores after participating in the simulation.

The participants' post-simulation gain in emotional intelligence has implications for educational leaders. Given the convenience of this computer-based simulation, an educational entity could use this tool to screen applicants for positions requiring the exercise of leadership skills. The Virtual Leader simulation can serve as a diagnostic tool to help an organization develop the correct training plan and methodology for new and existing employees. Participant performance in the simulation also could serve as an indicator of the need for more intensive training and mentoring for the rapid development of leadership skills.

This training tool also provides a means to standardize the leadership training experience, thus allowing a participant the ability to practice a skill set within the same set of simulated organizational conditions. These repeatable training conditions allow the participant to focus on a specific leadership skill set or situation without the distractions or changing context of the real-life experience.

Executives in Class—From "Recalling" to "Applying" New Knowledge

Dr. John Dunning, professor of organizational behavior (OB) at Troy University, discovered that despite the popularity and high marks given by students to a required capstone public administration OB class, when he surveyed multiple classes six months after the courses were over, the knowledge and theories that had been taught with a traditional lecture and term paper approach were not being applied in the workplace.

Process

John Dunning ran two organizational behavior classes. One class studied using the more traditional curriculum, and the other class used the practiceware Virtual Leader instead of reading some case studies and writing some papers.

The class that used Virtual Leader had the following characteristics:

- Number of students: 15
- Average age of students: 38
- Range of ages: 27 to 53
- Number of managers: 12
- Number of military personnel: 9
- Number having previous leadership of management training: 13
- Average number of graduate courses taken: 5

The class was broken up into three teams. These teams worked to support each other to complete each of the five scenarios using different leadership styles. Each team also competed with the other two teams.

Results

Six months after both classes were over, Dr. Dunning again polled the students. The differences between the two classes were significant. The traditional class

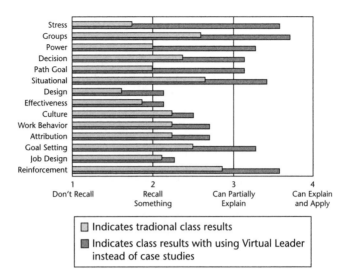

using case studies and reports, as was consistent with the earlier surveys, could recall some portion of class material.

But the students who went through the class that used SimuLearn's Virtual Leader had significantly greater occurrences of both being able to explain the material and, more important, being able to apply it.

Some of the contributors to this can be found in the after action review at the conclusion of the class. Dr. Dunning tallied the following statements:

- Fourteen of fifteen students supported the statement that simulations like Virtual Leader are the "future of learning."
- Thirteen of fifteen students supported the statement that Virtual Leader was a valuable tool for learning about theory.

The students and professor supported that observation that "Three to One" was a more accurate and useful leadership approach than more academic models, and that Virtual Leader supported much more than just the leadership segments of the OB course.

Summary

Using practiceware significantly increased retention and application, not just awareness of learned content.

Fortune 100 Company: An Extra Day Every Week of Work

A Fortune 100 company needed groups to relate better across departments, achieve desired meeting outcomes, better use time, and build healthy relationships.

To create "influential leaders," the division heads brought in Virtual Leader, an off-the-shelf leadership simulator from SimuLearn.

Process

A 360-degree pre-assessment was conducted for each of the participants. The managers themselves, their peers, their subordinates, and their supervisors were given an extensive questionnaire about the managers' performance.

The managers were then introduced to Virtual Leader, and were required to spend eight two-hour lab sessions practicing on the simulator, broken up over four weeks. The labs were available twice a week, allowing flexibility for the managers, and were staffed with a facilitator to answer questions and provide background. Halfway through the lab sessions, the facilitator spent one-on-one time with each participant, reviewing the results of his or her original 360-degree assessment, and putting it in context of his or her behavior in the simulator.

Negative Behavior - Self Beyond Service

		Pre	Post	Difference Score %	% Decrease
Superiority	Self	15.8	9.4	−6.4	−40.5%
	Superior	12.8	7.8	−5.0	−39.1%
	Peers	21.6	10.4	−11.2	−51.9%
	Subordinates	15.2	4.6	−8.6	−65.2%
Domination	Self	16.1	13.6	−2.5	−15.5%
	Superior	15.4	10.0	−5.4	−35.1%
	Peers	20.1	10.4	−9.7	−48.3%
	Subordinates	17.3	6.6	−10.7	−61.8%
Withdrawl	Self	22.1	15.9	−6.2	−28.1%
	Superior	18.7	12.5	−6.2	−33.2%
	Peers	19.6	15.5	−4.1	−20.9%
	Subordinates	16.7	7.6	−9.1	−54.5%
Average Decreases					−41.2%

The participants "graduated" five weeks after they began the program. Then, six months after the program began (five months after the last contact), the managers again were assessed both on business performance changes (something the organization rigorously tested), and a second 360-degree evaluation.

Positive Behavior - Self Beyond Service

		Pre	Post	Difference Score %	% Increases
Combination	Self	69.2	81.1	11.9	17.2%
	Superior	61.3	72.5	11.2	18.3%
	Peers	63.9	75.5	11.6	18.2%
	Subordinates	69.4	77.6	8.2	11.8%
Cooperation	Self	75.8	86.3	10.5	13.9%
	Superior	65.2	86.2	21.0	32.2%
	Peers	68.3	77.0	8.7	12.3%
	Subordinates	71.8	82.8	11.0	15.3%
Connection	Self	72.6	82.4	9.8	13.5%
	Superior	69.2	77.6	8.4	12.1%
	Peers	69.7	80.0	10.3	14.8%
	Subordinates	76.8	85.8	9.0	11.7%
	Average Increases				16.0%

Results

The participants who went through the coaching and simulation program improved their teams' relative performance rankings (a nonsubjective metric on volume of successful client jobs completed), on average, 22.0 percent.

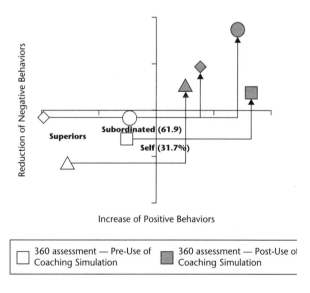

Just as relevant was the way that these managers got these accelerated results. Six months after the program, the increases in positive behaviors and the cessations of negative behavior across peers, subordinates, and superiors were unprecedented in the organization's fifteen-year history.

The simulation supported the increase of positive behaviors, but even more, reduced the occurrences of negative behavior. The students themselves, curiously, were least aware of their new capability, suggesting the value of external measurement rather than self-assessment.

Summary

The corporate managers who went through the assessment, coaching, and simulation program significantly improved their value to their organization, including their professional value, while strengthening their relationships with their peers, supervisors, and subordinates.

U.S. Military Academy—Self-Paced Practiceware Deployment Beats Traditional Approach

The U.S. Army has a highly developed doctrine on the process of leadership development. Recently the Army has put new emphasis on the self-development pillar to promote the development of self-awareness through the Leader Development Portfolio (LDP), which has elicited new approaches to training.

Process

Twenty-six cadets at the U.S. Military Academy were randomly assigned to either a case study (control condition) or a computer simulation (experimental condition) group.

The control condition consisted of a series of army leadership interactive case studies (of the branching story type) created by the Army Research Institute, and the experimental condition used a noncustomized version of SimuLearn's Virtual Leader practiceware program. Initial leadership tendencies were measured.

Participants worked through their respectively assigned methods in a completely self-paced process.

Participants then were measured on their preferences for leadership styles through a pre- and post-instruction survey for each of the styles, and the ability to apply the right leadership style to the right situation, with the "right" answer and approach determined by seasoned military officers.

Results

Military case study versus Virtual Leader in leadership comfort levels.

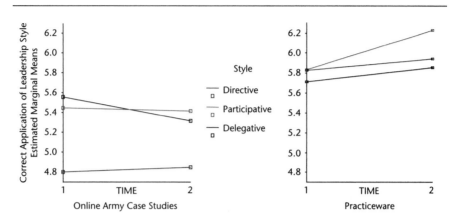

Increase in application of correct leadership approach.

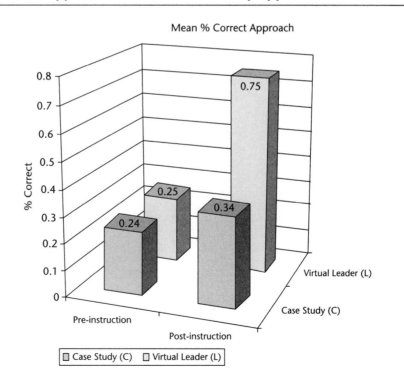

First, users of Virtual Leader showed an increase in the comfort levels with all three leadership styles.

The chart on the left of the figure shows the mean comfort level score for the case study group. The graph shows no overall change, but a significant decrease in the comfort level with the delegative style. The chart on the right shows the mean comfort level score within the Virtual Leader group. The graph shows an overall increase for each style, with the greatest increase in the participative style.

More important, the study found support for the hypothesis that the simulation method increases the ability to correctly apply theory taught within a program of instruction compared to case studies.

Summary

The Virtual Leader simulation increased the users' comfort with and use of alternative leadership styles over branching story case studies.

INDEX

A

AAR (after action review), 318, 324–326, 349

Abstraction: of actions, 57; design considerations for, 404; in geography-based maps, 110–111; of maps, 107; as pedagogical element, 288–289

Accelerometers, 406

Access, 393, 434, 449–450

Accidental success, 330

Accumulators, 142–143, 152–153

Achievements (awards), 260–261

Acrostics, 290

Action feedback, 479–480

Action gates, 322–323

Action learning simulations, xxxiv

Actions. *See also* Middle skills: abstraction of, 57; basic inputs for, 56–57; common to Sims, 62–63; contextual, 55; creating and implementing, 75; cyclical, 55–56; deception through, 76; defined, 55; desired results of, 52, 95–100;

doing nothing, 65–67; educational challenge of, 56; energy use by, 138–139; ergodic, 161; events in Sims, 165–170; examples, 59–61, 105–106; formation, 160; interfaces corresponding to, 57–61; layer between results and, 102; leadership, 57–58; list of, 64–65; mastering, 272; movement of units, 157–161; questions for researching, 64; results as, 95; teleportation, 160–161; understanding, 53

Actions-level leadership, 231, 233

Active links, 183

Activities, 207–208, 320

Activities-based training, xxxiv

Acton Foundation for Entrepreneurial Excellence, 61, 86–87, 209, 282, 342

Actualization, 431

Adaptation, 220–221

Adaptive problem solving, 176

Addictive behavior, 442–443

Advisers, 223, 228, 298–299

Aesthetics, 261–262, 346

Affiliation of units, 147–148

After action review (AAR), 318, 324–326, 349

Age of Empires (Microsoft), 37

Agents. *See* Artificial intelligence (AI) players and agents

Aggregation, 127–128, 194–195, 279

Aldrich, Clark, 519

Alerts, 293–294

Alignment, 70, 73, 225, 234

Allocation-based budget issues, 223

Allocation triangle, 371

All-or-nothing state, 191–192, 260, 339

Ally role, 383

Alpha Centauri (Sid Meier's), 185, 234

American Public Media's Budget Hero, 453

Amplification, 193

Analog information, 195

Analysis (middle skill), 70–71

Anecdotes, 244

Anecdotes, for evaluation, 496–497

Appearance for character, 263

ABOUT THE AUTHOR

As a designer, Clark Aldrich has created some of the most effective, celebrated, and innovative "soft skills" simulations of the past decade, including SimuLearn's Virtual Leader global product line (for which he was awarded a patent), which is the most popular leadership simulation in the world, and was the winner of the "best online training product of the year." SimuLearn's Virtual Leader (and the updated vLeader) is currently used in hundreds of corporations, universities, and military installations and has been translated into several foreign languages.

Most recently, he was the lead designer for a series of simulations for the Center for Army Leadership, which used a variety of short mini-game approaches to teach influencing skills.

Aldrich also advises many of the world's most influential organizations (private and government) and serves on over a dozen boards, including with magazines, and universities, and the National Security Agency, on educational and business analysis projects.

He is the author of four books, *Simulations and the Future of Learning* (Wiley, 2004), *Learning by Doing* (Wiley, 2005), *The Complete Guide to Simulations and Serious Games: How the Most Valuable Content Will Be Created in the Age Beyond Gutenberg to Google* (Wiley, 2009) and *Learning Online with Games, Simulations, and Virtual Worlds* (Wiley, 2009), as well as a columnist and analyst.

His work has been featured in hundreds of sources, including the *New York Times*, the *Wall Street Journal*, CNN, NPR, CNET, Business 2.0, *Business Week*, and *U.S. News & World Report*. Among other distinctions, he has been called an "industry guru" by *Fortune* magazine.

Aldrich is a founder and former director of research for Gartner's e-learning coverage. He graduated from Brown University with a degree in cognitive science, and earlier in his career worked on special projects for the Xerox executive team.

Pfeiffer Publications Guide

This guide is designed to familiarize you with the various types of Pfeiffer publications. The formats section describes the various types of products that we publish; the methodologies section describes the many different ways that content might be provided within a product. We also provide a list of the topic areas in which we publish.

FORMATS

In addition to its extensive book-publishing program, Pfeiffer offers content in an array of formats, from fieldbooks for the practitioner to complete, ready-to-use training packages that support group learning.

FIELDBOOK Designed to provide information and guidance to practitioners in the midst of action. Most fieldbooks are companions to another, sometimes earlier, work, from which its ideas are derived; the fieldbook makes practical what was theoretical in the original text. Fieldbooks can certainly be read from cover to cover. More likely, though, you'll find yourself bouncing around following a particular theme, or dipping in as the mood, and the situation, dictate.

HANDBOOK A contributed volume of work on a single topic, comprising an eclectic mix of ideas, case studies, and best practices sourced by practitioners and experts in the field.

An editor or team of editors usually is appointed to seek out contributors and to evaluate content for relevance to the topic. Think of a handbook not as a ready-to-eat meal, but as a cookbook of ingredients that enables you to create the most fitting experience for the occasion.

RESOURCE Materials designed to support group learning. They come in many forms: a complete, ready-to-use exercise (such as a game); a comprehensive resource on one topic (such as conflict management) containing a variety of methods and approaches; or a collection of like-minded activities (such as icebreakers) on multiple subjects and situations.

TRAINING PACKAGE An entire, ready-to-use learning program that focuses on a particular topic or skill. All packages comprise a guide for the facilitator/trainer and a workbook for the participants. Some packages are supported with additional media—such as video—or learning aids, instruments, or other devices to help participants understand concepts or practice and develop skills.

- *Facilitator/trainer's guide* Contains an introduction to the program, advice on how to organize and facilitate the learning event, and step-by-step instructor notes. The guide also contains copies of presentation materials—handouts, presentations, and overhead designs, for example—used in the program.

- *Participant's workbook* Contains exercises and reading materials that support the learning goal and serves as a valuable reference and support guide for participants in the weeks and months that follow the learning event. Typically, each participant will require his or her own workbook.

ELECTRONIC CD-ROMs and web-based products transform static Pfeiffer content into dynamic, interactive experiences. Designed to take advantage of the searchability, automation, and ease-of-use that technology provides, our e-products bring convenience and immediate accessibility to your workspace.

METHODOLOGIES

CASE STUDY A presentation, in narrative form, of an actual event that has occurred inside an organization. Case studies are not prescriptive, nor are they used to prove a point; they are designed to develop critical analysis and decision-making skills. A case study has a specific time frame, specifies a sequence of events, is narrative in structure, and contains a plot structure—an issue (what should be/have been done?). Use case studies when the goal is to enable participants to apply previously learned theories to the circumstances in the case, decide what is pertinent, identify the real issues, decide what should have been done, and develop a plan of action.

ENERGIZER A short activity that develops readiness for the next session or learning event. Energizers are most commonly used after a break or lunch to stimulate or refocus the group. Many involve some form of physical activity, so they are a useful way to counter post-lunch lethargy. Other uses include transitioning from one topic to another, where "mental" distancing is important.

EXPERIENTIAL LEARNING ACTIVITY (ELA) A facilitator-led intervention that moves participants through the learning cycle from experience to application (also known as a Structured Experience). ELAs are carefully thought-out designs in which there is a definite learning purpose and intended outcome. Each step—everything that participants do during the activity—facilitates the accomplishment of the stated goal. Each ELA includes complete instructions for facilitating the intervention and a clear statement of goals, suggested group size and timing, materials required, an explanation of the process, and, where appropriate, possible variations to the activity. (For more detail on Experiential Learning Activities, see the Introduction to the *Reference Guide to Handbooks and Annuals*, 1999 edition, Pfeiffer, San Francisco.)

GAME A group activity that has the purpose of fostering team spirit and togetherness in addition to the achievement of a pre-stated goal. Usually contrived—undertaking a desert expedition, for example—this type of learning method offers an engaging means for participants to demonstrate and practice business and interpersonal skills. Games are effective for team building and personal development mainly because the goal is subordinate to the process—the means through which participants reach decisions, collaborate, communicate, and generate trust and understanding. Games often engage teams in "friendly" competition.

ICEBREAKER A (usually) short activity designed to help participants overcome initial anxiety in a training session and/or to acquaint the participants with one another. An icebreaker can be a fun activity or can be tied to specific topics or training goals. While a useful tool in itself, the icebreaker comes into its own in situations where tension or resistance exists within a group.

INSTRUMENT A device used to assess, appraise, evaluate, describe, classify, and summarize various aspects of human behavior. The term used to describe an instrument depends primarily on its format and purpose. These terms include survey, questionnaire, inventory, diagnostic survey, and poll. Some uses of instruments include providing instrumental feedback to group members, studying here-and-now processes or functioning within a group, manipulating group composition, and evaluating outcomes of training and other interventions.

Instruments are popular in the training and HR field because, in general, more growth can occur if an individual is provided with a method for focusing specifically on his or her own behavior. Instruments also are used to obtain information that will serve as a basis for change and to assist in workforce planning efforts.

Paper-and-pencil tests still dominate the instrument landscape with a typical package comprising a facilitator's guide, which offers advice on administering the instrument and interpreting the collected data, and an initial set of instruments. Additional instruments are available separately. Pfeiffer, though, is investing heavily in e-instruments. Electronic instrumentation provides effortless distribution and, for larger groups particularly, offers advantages over paper-and-pencil tests in the time it takes to analyze data and provide feedback.

LECTURETTE A short talk that provides an explanation of a principle, model, or process that is pertinent to the participants' current learning needs. A lecturette is intended to establish a common language bond between the trainer and the participants by providing a mutual frame of reference. Use a lecturette as an introduction to a group activity or event, as an interjection during an event, or as a handout.

MODEL A graphic depiction of a system or process and the relationship among its elements. Models provide a frame of reference and something more tangible, and more easily remembered, than a verbal explanation. They also give participants something to "go on," enabling them to track their own progress as they experience the dynamics, processes, and relationships being depicted in the model.

ROLE PLAY A technique in which people assume a role in a situation/scenario: a customer service rep in an angry-customer exchange, for example. The way in which the role is approached is then discussed and feedback is offered. The role play is often repeated using a different approach and/or incorporating changes made based on feedback received. In other words, role playing is a spontaneous interaction involving realistic behavior under artificial (and safe) conditions.

SIMULATION A methodology for understanding the interrelationships among components of a system or process. Simulations differ from games in that they test or use a model that depicts or mirrors some aspect of reality in form, if not necessarily in content. Learning occurs by studying the effects of change on one or more factors of the model. Simulations are commonly used to test hypotheses about what happens in a system—often referred to as "what if?" analysis—or to examine best-case/worst-case scenarios.

THEORY A presentation of an idea from a conjectural perspective. Theories are useful because they encourage us to examine behavior and phenomena through a different lens.

TOPICS

The twin goals of providing effective and practical solutions for workforce training and organization development and meeting the educational needs of training and human resource professionals shape Pfeiffer's publishing program. Core topics include the following:

Leadership & Management

Communication & Presentation

Coaching & Mentoring

Training & Development

e-Learning

Teams & Collaboration

OD & Strategic Planning

Human Resources

Consulting

What will you find on pfeiffer.com?

- The best in workplace performance solutions for training and HR professionals

- Downloadable training tools, exercises, and content

- Web-exclusive offers

- Training tips, articles, and news

- Seamless on-line ordering

- Author guidelines, information on becoming a Pfeiffer Partner, and much more

Discover more at www.pfeiffer.com